6th Virginia Cavalry

2nd Edition

Michael P. Musick

Copyright 1990 H. E. Howard, Inc.

Manufactured in the United States by
H. E. Howard, Inc., Lynchburg, Virginia

Printed by H. E. Howard, Inc.

ISBN-1-56190-002-8

Acknowledgements

John E. Divine, of Leesburg, suggested the subject, provided all manner of help in the course of the research and writing, and cheered the project on to completion. His knowledge of Loudoun County and the cavalry of the Army of Northern Virginia is as boundless as the hospitality he and Mac extended. John's recollections of Chaplain Davis's daughters as they negotiated the streets of Leesburg in a Model "T" Ford are but one example of his ability to make the past live again (and of his sense of humor as well). If these pages find a modicum of favor in his eyes, the time expended on them will have been amply rewarded.

Robert K. Krick, of Fredericksburg, bids fair to have his visage carved on Stone Mountain, Georgia, for his contributions to Confederate history. He was the source of a veritable flood of documentation on the 6th Cavalry over the course of several years, particularly biographical data for the roster. Beyond that, he supplied valuable corrections in the manuscript. Bob embodies the ideals of scholarly commitment and generosity.

Harold E. Howard, the editor of the Virginia Regimental Series, displayed monumental tolerance for a string of missed deadlines, and gathered together and passed on much data from descendants of 6th Cavalrymen.

Prominent among my aiders and abettors are C. Bud Hall of Fairfax, who offered valuable criticism on Brandy Station, including the information that "Grimes" Davis was originally from Alabama, rather than Mississippi; Raymond W. Watkins, of Falls Church, an authority on Confederate burials; the inimitable Ben Ritter, of Winchester, who shared his trove of research material on members of the unit; F. Lawrence McFall, Jr., of Danville, who provided data on veterans from his area, and who allowed me to participate vicariously in the excitement of his discovery of the Flournoy family cemetery; and Robert L. Driver, of Brownsburg, who reviewed the roster, providing over 80 additions and corrections.

The flags of the regiment have been assiduously tracked down and documented by H. Michael Madaus, of Milwaukee, Wisconsin, the preeminent Civil War vexillologist. Photographs of flags were graciously obtained through the efforts of Dennis P. Kelly, Kenesaw Mountain Battlefield Park; R. Thomas Crew, The Mariners' Museum; and Arthur LaBonte, The War Memorial Museum of Virginia, Newport News.

Before I began this project, I already had three friends who were descended from 6th Cavalrymen, Lewis Leigh, Jr., of Fairfax; Mary Walton Livingston, of Alexandria; and Thomas Watson, of Brunswick, Md. In addition to the pleasure of their company, each made significant historical material available to me.

Other descendants who magnanimously shared information, beyond those who contributed to the U.D.C. genealogical data assembled by Harold E. Howard, are: James F. White, Savannah, Ga.; Marsha Burr, Raleigh, N.C.; Roger Keller, Hagerstown, Md.; Wynne C. Saffer, Leesburg; Gerald J. Bayer, Cockeysville, Md.; Thomas Katheder, Atlanta, Ga.; Kirby Vaden Nuckols, Lynchburg; Andrew A. Farley, Jr., Danville; William Mann, Fredericksburg; Mrs. Anne P. Scharf, Baltimore, Md.; Nancy C. Baird, Delaplane; Lauk Walton Ward, Herndon; Maddox G. Tapp, Front Royal; Jesse Russell, Berryville; and Mrs. Arthur Overby, Chatham.

Among the many unselfish spirits who rallied to the effort were: Lee A. Wallace, Jr., Arlington; Robert A. Hodge, Fredericksburg; Paul M. Shevchuk, Gettysburg, Pa.; James R. Mejdrich, Wheaton, Ill.; William A. Turner, Clinton, Md.; Dale S. Snair, Richmond; Michael A. Cavanaugh, Riverton, N.J.; Wendy Harlow, Baltimore, Md.; Greg Mertz, Fredericksburg; Richard L. Armstrong, Millboro; Walter Sanford, Alexandria; Ronald W. Blake, Waterford; Stuart Vogt, Springfield, Mass.; Lawrence E. Babits, Savannah, Ga.; John Graham, Alexandria; Henry Deeks, East Arlington, Mass.; Virginia G. Redd, Hampton-Sydney; Robert M. Kvashika, Springfield; Marie V. Melchiori, Falls Church; and Keith Bohannon, Smyrna, Ga.

Dennis Frye, of Harpers Ferry and Washington Co., Md., made a jaunt through Rappahannock County cemeteries an enjoyable experience, and his wife Susan employed her considerable skill on the maps in this volume. Ross M. Kimmel came through as always with splendid photography.

The convival gang from the after-meeting meeting of the Harpers Ferry Civl War Round Table, Denis Reen, Paul E. Barr, Jr., and Robert Dorrell, each lent help and encouragement.

Crucial institutional expertise came from Janet Schwarz, Sally Sartain, Linda Leazer, Sarah Bearss, and Waverly Winfree at the Virginia Historical Society; Robert Clay, Jane M. Pairo, and Louis Manarin at the Virginia State Library and Archives; Charlene S. Alling, Anne Burke, and Guy Swanson at The Museum of the Confederacy; Mrs. Lucille Boykin, at the Dallas, Tex., Public Library; Col. Beverly M. Reed at the V.M.I. alumni association and Diane B. Jacobs at the archives; Henry Mayer and Stuart Lee Butler at the National Archives; Richard Sommers at the U.S. Army Military History Institute Archives and his staff, Carlisle Barracks, Pa.; and the staffs of the D.A.R. Library, Washington, D.C., and the Virginia Room, Fairfax City Regional Library.

Earl J. and Norma J. Coates, of Columbia, Md., offered information and encouragement, and led me to Gwen L. Cohen, of Annapolis Junction, Md., who ably and painstakingly edited and retyped my manuscript (between attacks of the flu and issues of the Dwight Yoakum newsletter). Ruth Gardner transformed my handwriting into a typed roster.

Judith Z. Thorne, of Reston, helped me to explore the holdings of the Rappahannock County Historical Society, and the viands at The Inn at Little Washington.

I absolve all of these estimable folk from responsiblity for the undetected errors which inevitably appear in a work such as this, and ask the forgiveness of anyone whose assistance I have failed to note.

CHAPTER I

A Regular In Charge

"Change front forward on right company of first squadron!" The commands of cavalry officers rang out; soldiers made their dispositions. At the shout "Trot-MARCH!" the companies broke into motion. Charles William Field surveyed the movement with the critical eye of a connoisseur. Late captain, 2nd U.S. Cavalry, in this bright fall of 1861, he was a lieutenant colonel in the Provisional Army of the Confederate States.

Handsome and dashing, Kentucky-born Field at age 33 was a professional who knew how to mold horsemen into soldiers. After graduating from the Military Academy at West Point, he had toiled away the years since 1849 as an officer of the Regular Army. Part of that time he had served at the Cavalry School of Practice at Carlisle, Pennsylvania, and had worked as an assistant instructor in cavalry tactics at West Point. He had lived the curious, unique mixture of ennui and excitement at various Texas, New Mexico, and Missouri posts which was the stuff of frontier duty.

Beginning June 21, 1861, Field had commanded the Cavalry Camp of Instruction that the Old Dominion had set up after secession at Ashland, Virginia, 17 miles northwest of Richmond. Many companies of volunteers received the benefits of his instruction and that of his assistant adjutant general, Capt. Lunsford L. Lomax. Then, on September 11, Field was rewarded with an appointment as colonel. On the following day, by Special Orders Number 276, paragraph 16, of the Adjutant and Inspector General's Office, Headquarters, Virginia Forces, the 6th Regiment, Virginia Volunteer Cavalry was created. The new outfit was to be Field's own.

Colonel Field's first task was to find out just where at Ashland his new command was, and to bring them together for first drill. The order announcing formation of the regiment specified seven companies, with Williams C. Wickham as lieutenant colonel and J. Grattan Cabell as major. The companies were to be the Governor's Guard, the Henrico Light Dragoons, the Loudoun Cavalry, the Rappahannock Cavalry, the Wise Dragoons, the Fairfax Cavalry, and the Dulany Troop. However, at the date of organization only one of these units (the Dulany Troop, from Loudoun County, under Capt. Richard H. Dulany) was present at Ashland. Two other companies, added to the regiment almost immediately, were soon there - the Clarke Cavalry from Clarke County, under Capt. Hugh M.

Nelson, and the Rockingham Cavalry (also called the River Rangers) from Rockingham County, under Capt. Edward S. Yancey. These latter two companies, originally part of the 1st Cavalry, seem to have been substituted quickly for the Governor's Guard and the Henrico Light Dragoons, which never joined the 6th (and which became Company I, 4th Cavalry and Company I, 10th Cavalry, respectively). Wickham, like those phantom companies, was never mustered with Field's regiment, and exchanged places with Julien Harrison, of whom much will be heard later.

Companies were being sent off on various assignments for which mounted soldiers were suited, so it took some time for the regiment to take shape. By October 31, Company B, the Rappahannock Cavalry, had joined, as well as the first Company E, which was not even from the state. Because the elite Georgia Hussars of Savannah had placed themselves in the field at Richmond fully equipped, the authorities gave them the choice of joining one of two not yet fully organized Virginia Cavalry regiments — Beverly H. Robertson's 4th or Field's 6th. The Hussars' officers voted unanimously for Field's outfit, and on October 17 the Georgians set out from Richmond to join him at Camp Letcher at Manassas.

By November, the organization of the regiment appeared on returns as "perfected." The Dulany Troop became Company A; the Rockingham boys, Company C; the Clarke Cavalry, Company D; the Fairfax company, Company F; the Flournoy Troop from Halifax County (under Capt. Thomas Stanhope Flournoy), Company G; the Wise Dragoons, Company H; the Orange Rangers (from Orange County under Capt. Gustavus J. Browning), Company I; and the Loudoun Cavalry, Company K. These companies arrived at regimental headquarters at different times, originating as they did from the Potomac to the North Carolina border and beyond. Indeed, Company K does not appear to have come into Field's camp until December.

By the time the 6th Cavalry was fully formed, the war had been raging for more than half a year. Some of the companies had been in Confederate service for some time; a number had histories predating secession. Even after they joined the 6th Cavalry and were formed into five squadrons of two companies each, they were not often together. It will not always be practical to detail all of their assignments, but a few words about the experience of the companies before they came together under Field are in order.

Three companies were of recent origin; their annals are brief. The Dulany Troop, or Loudoun Dragoons (Company A) was organized in June 1861 and mustered into service July 1. It left Welbourne Hall, Loudoun County, on July 25, and spent four and a half days traveling the 125 miles to Ashland. The men were temporarily under 2d Lt. George E. Plaster during the march. They became lost, and for a while, "Dulany's lost company became quite a joke." The troop reported to Field on July 29.

The Flournoy Troop, or Halifax Cavalry (Company G) was raised after the Battle of Manassas and the first rush of volunteers by 49-year-old Thomas Stanhope Flournoy. Several of the men Flournoy enlisted, such as Thomas Fox, age 45, were almost as old as their captain, and one (Ephraim Crews) admitted to 65 years of age and may have been a War of 1812 veteran. This group left Cluster Springs on August 19, and arrived at Ashland on September 1. Field mustered it on September 10.

The Orange Rangers (Company I) were enlisted on May 4. Early in service, the Orange Rangers were at "Camp Henry," near Culpeper. On November 5 the company was ordered to join the regiment; they joined Field seven days later.

The remaining seven companies boasted an assortment of previous activity, some of it in combat. The Rockingham Cavalry (Company C), for example, served as the first Company K of the 1st Virginia Cavalry. It was present at the Battle of Manassas, but no detailed account of its operations has come to light. It reported to Ashland on September 1.

The Rappahannock Cavalry, or Old Guard (Company B), on the other hand, left a much fuller record. It traced its origins to the War of 1812, but its wartime service began on April 22, 1861, when it was enlisted at Washington, Virginia. It soon entered into hard service, scouting and doing outpost duty, first at Alexandria and then at Fairfax Court House. Near Fairfax on May 27, two of its members, Peyton Anderson and William Lillard, were surrounded by the 2d New York Cavalry while on picket. Anderson was wounded by a pistol shot and Lillard was captured. A small monument on the site was erected by the United Daughters of the Confederacy in 1927 and still marks the spot. Anderson's was the first blood shed by a soldier for the Southern Republic. The Rappahannock unit was present at a skirmish at Fairfax on June 1, but due to poor arms and lack of ammunition, took no active part. Its operations in this period were under Colonel, soon to be Brigadier General, Richard S. Ewell. It continued to serve with other units of his brigade at Blackburn's Ford and First Manassas. From August 13-27 the company was under J.E.B. ("Jeb") Stuart of the 1st Cavalry. On September 1 it was at Sangster's Crossroads in Fairfax County; 20 days later it was with Early's Brigade. By October 31 the Rappahannock Cavalry was reported to be with Field.

The Clarke Cavalry (Company D), like Company B, had its roots in a unit of the War of 1812. In the period 1845-1856, it was under Capt. Hugh M. Nelson, but at the time of the John Brown raid, command was exercised by Capt. E. P. C. Lewis. One source gives the company's date of organization as December 1859. Its first service in the war was as the first Company D of Stuart's 1st Cavalry. It was as part of that regiment that it performed at Harper's Ferry in April 1861. As one of six companies which formed the nucleus of Stuart's outfit, the Clarke Cavalry guarded the fords of the Shenandoah River and of the Potomac beyond Martinsburg. It served Gen. Joseph E. Johnston by keeping an eye on the movements of his opponent, Gen. Robert Patterson, and helped cloak Johnston's escape when his force slipped from Patterson and joined Beauregard for First Manassas. In the battle of July 21, the Clarke Cavalry was on the extreme left of the Confederate line, and was credited with routing a regiment of Federal zouaves. In this engagement Lt. David H. Allen received a wound from which he later died. Captain Joseph R. Hardesty resigned the morning of the fight.

When Stuart was later promoted to general there were two excess companies in the 1st that voted to join the 6th Cavalry. The Clarke men were assigned to their new command by an order dated October 9; by that time they were apparently already at Ashland.

The Georgia Hussars proudly claimed 1736 as the date of their origin. When the Confederate government was formed in February 1861 they offered their services, but were told no cavalry was needed. The need for horsemen became dramatically apparent at First Manassas, however, and their earlier offer to the Confederate government was accepted. The company had unfortunately accepted state arms, and when Georgia governor Joseph E. Brown learned that it proposed to take the arms out of the state, he demanded the return of his ordnance. The Hussars complied with the dictates of their chief executive, but rearming caused considerable delay in moving to Richmond. The Hussars' offer was a company for duty in Virginia without cost to the government. This meant that they had to expend nearly $25,000 of their own funds. On September 17 the unit finally left Savannah. On October 14 it was ordered to join Field's outfit, and left Richmond for Manassas on October 17.

The Fairfax Cavalry, also known as Washington's Home Guard, the Powell Troop, or sometimes General Johnston's Bodyguard (Company F), elected its officers at a meeting in Alexandria on April 20 and was mustered into state service there on April 27. The company covered the Confederate retreat from Alexandria, destroying railroad bridges as it withdrew. From the date of its organization to First Manassas, it did duty as a vidette force in the territory between Alexandria and the Little Falls of the Potomac. It supplied scouts and pickets for Gens. Maxcy Gregg and Millege L. Bonham of South Carolina, proving especially useful because of its intimate knowledge of the ground.

While guarding the approaches to Mitchell's Ford on July 18 and fighting at First Manassas on July 21, it was attached to Col. Richard C. W. Radford's regiment, known at that time as the 30th Cavalry, but later as the 2d Cavalry. During this battle, the company acted as the second company of the first squadron, and made an attack along the turnpike that contributed to the rout of the enemy. On the day after the engagement, the men served as pickets and scouts, capturing seven prisoners and some welcome supplies. Eleven of the Fairfax companys under Capt. Edward B. Powell charged a group of Federal pickets near Taylor's Hill on Middle Turnpike on July 25, inflicting several casualties and driving the pickets back to Bailey's Crossroads. From September 1-7, the company was at Colonel Radford's camp near Flint Hill, and from then into December it acted as couriers and guards at Johnston's headquarters. Lieutenants John A. Throckmorton and Samuel R. Johnston were aides to General Stuart at Dranesville on December 20, 1861.

The Wise Dragoons (Company H) from Fauquier was raised at the time of the John Brown raid in 1859, but was not ordered to Charles Town. It drilled for some time on foot, armed with Mississippi rifles. It was finally enrolled for actice service at Salem (now Marshall) on April 24, 1861. The Dragoons' early service was in scouting in the vicinity of Occoquan. This kind of duty wore down both men and mounts; sickness appeared in the company. It was under fire on July 18 while carrying dispatches for Gen. G. T. Beauregard. The company was transferred to Field in November from Col. Walter H. Jenifer at Leesburg.

The Loudoun Cavalry, or Leesburg Cavalry (Company K) was organized by Daniel T. Shreve in June 1858. Captain Shreve resigned in June 1861 and the command passed to Capt. William W. Mead. In July, five men of the company forded the Potomac River at Heator's Island and captured five Federals of the 1st New Hampshire Infantry. The Loudoun Cavalry was present at the Battle of First Manassas, and joined in the pursuit that followed. On August 5, 1861, some 60 men of the 1st New York Independent Battery (which became part of the 48th New York Infantry), reputedly led by Samuel Means, a Loudoun County Unionist, descended on the men of the company opposite Point of Rocks, killing George Orrison and capturing six others. Orrison is regarded as the first soldier killed in Loudoun County. The Loudoun Cavalry was present but not engaged at the Battle of Ball's Bluff on October 21. Within the next few days one of the company, William Grubb, was killed near Waterford. The Loudoun men took up their line of march from Leesburg on December 2 and arrived at Centreville to join Field on December 5.

A constant refrain in company reports before the regiment was brought together is the want of proper arms. This appears to have been especially the case with Companies B, F, H, and I. A report from Company B dated June 30 states that the unit had 62 sabres, but no pistols or firearms except a few double-barreled shotguns and pistols which were private property. On May 9 Company F reported that it had no arms or equipment of any kind except a few Colt revolvers. Company H reported on June 30 that it had only 60 sabres from the state, not nearly an adequate number, plus seven private shotguns and a few private pistols and

Bowie knives. These deficiencies are all the more remarkable in view of the fact that several of the companies had already been in battle.

Capt. John Shackleford Green wrote to the Secretary of War on September 21 and expressed chagrin that the much less seasoned Dulany Troop had now been issued revolvers and "improved" Hall's carbines, while his much more experienced men had to make due with sabres alone.

As Field's regiment assembled, it also experienced its first losses. Six men from Company F were dishonorably discharged by order of the Secretary of War on October 1, but the reason for this action was not recorded. The circumstances surrounding the loss of Sgt. William Gibson are known: he was the first man killed in action with the regiment. On October 15, Captain Nelson was on a foraging expedition inside Union lines with 17 men. They were ambushed; Sergeant Gibson was wounded, and died soon afterwar. As soon as he heard the shots, Captain Nelson charged, inflicting some loss. He carried off two prisoners as well as Gibson's body.

The best surviving evidence of what it was like to be in the 6th Cavalry in the first year of the war comes from the letters of Sgt. Daniel A. Grimsley of Company B, written to his beloved cousin Bettie Browning of Culpeper County. Grimsley, until then a school teacher, wrote on October 31 of his pleasure of now being in a regiment and of his awe at the spectacle presented by a grand review by Governor John Letcher of Jeb Stuart's Brigade. Stuart commanded the cavalry attached to Johnston's army at Centreville that day (which included the 1st, 4th, and 6th Virginia Cavalry Regiments, the 1st North Carolina Cavalry, and the Jeff Davis Legion from Mississippi). The stars and bars of the Georgia Hussars was the only Confederate flag available for the grand review.

Colonel Field impressed Grimsley as a commander: "I think him a perfect gentleman, very popular with his soldiers." By November 6, the sergeant's generally optimistic view of his soldier life was tempered by some unpleasant realities. Rainy weather made it almost impossible to keep tents up; sickness had caused some men to leave whom he hoped would return. Prospects for a fight were of keen interest to him and his comrades. On November 21 Grimsley pronounced the Confederate defenses around Manassas impregnable and noted that he had been able to witness some artillery practice. He was almost persuaded there would be no fight before winter set in. A degree of concern appeared when he remarked that the supply of forage for the horses was nearly exhausted.

Although the big battle that Grimsley and his comrades speculated about was not to come off that year, action against the enemy was not long in coming. On December 2 Field led detachments from Companies

A, B, H, and I on a scout some 14 miles from their base at Camp Letcher. This force of about 90 men attacked a party of Federals at the village of Annandale. The result was four or five of the enemy killed (or supposed killed) and 15 prisoners brought back into Confederate lines. Two men of Company H were taken prisoner, Alexander Maxwell and William A. Dennis.

Sergeant Grimsley rejoiced in the delightful weather on December 4, observing that it was particularly welcome after several wretched months. As he wrote, he could hear the enemy's guns; the chance to close with them excited the boys in camp. Captain J. Fred Waring decided to lead his Hussars against some of the 3rd New Jersey Infantry Regiment whom he knew to be nearby. His company had been detached to do picket duty on the line that stretched from Fairfax Court House via Fairfax Station, to Sangster's Crossroads, but such service he evidently deemed too tame. That night Waring and 23 of his men moved out in double file along the Braddock Road toward Accotink. They were armed with shotguns loaded with buckshot. Well into a boggy pine thicket, they discovered wires strung across the road to dismount unwary horsemen. Almost immediately they received a volley fired by 80 volunteers from among the Jerseymen.

Lieutenant Alex McC. Duncan of the Hussars, who was in the fight, remembered years later that Captain Waring's response to the volley was to order "Twos left about, Charge!" This command, Duncan recalled dryly, was interpreted by the men to mean "Get out of there!" They promptly high-tailed it back to Fairfax. The loss to the Hussars was four wounded, including Waring; one killed; and one wounded and left in the hands of the enemy. This affair was officially recorded as a skirmish near Burke's Station, but was known ever after by the Georgians as "The Bog Wallow Ambuscade."

On December 7 the Hussars were ordered to transfer from the 6th Virginia Cavalry to the Jeff Davis Legion, Mississippi Cavalry, of which they became Company F. Their subsequent career is a notable part of the history of the cavalry of the Army of Northern Virginia, and the names of their members appear with more than usual frequency on the Confederate War Department's official Roll of Honor.

Life for those left in the 6th Cavalry was less than idyllic in the remaining days of 1861. Company G took three prisoners on December 5 on a scout under Stuart, but activity for the most part was prosaic. Sergeant Grimsley wrote that the constant drill and picket duty required of the regiment had become exceedingly irksome. His fear was that his unit might not be allowed to settle into winter quarters, but rather kept on endless rounds of picket duty. His fear proved unfounded, for on December 27 it did finally settle into such protection at Camp G. W. Smith.

Even snug winter quarters could not keep the ravages of illness entirely at bay. A report of the sick and wounded for the regiment in December (consisting of Companies A, B, D, E, G, H, I, and K) showed a total mean strength of 519, of whom 107 had taken sick during the month. Surgeon George C. Carrington recorded three deaths, one discharge, fifteen remaining sick, and three convalescents. Forty-one men had been allowed to leave on furlough. Two of the deaths in the regiment were from typhoid fever; the other one was from a gunshot wound.

The rolls of the various companies for the reporting period of January-February 1862 generally show them stationed at Camp G. W. Smith near Centreville, although Company F is reported as on duty as couriers and otherwise at Army headquarters at the same place. A statement of the organization of the Potomac District under General Beauregard places the 6th Cavalry in Jeb Stuart's Brigade, along with the 1st North Carolina Cavalry, the 1st, 2d, and 4th Regiments of Virginia Cavalry, and the Jeff Davis Legion.

Although confinement to winter quarters kept the men away from ice-slick or mud-filled roads, it also deprived them of the occasional scout which, as Grimsley wrote, revived their spirits. The "Record of Events" section of the roll of Company K for this period shows that some spirits had fallen decidedly low. It records that the company left camp on January 11 for Leesburg, where it made several scouts looking for deserters from assorted regiments.

In fact, absenteeism had touched even the Clarke Cavalry, one of the best of the mounted companies in the army. On January 28 Capt. Hugh M. Nelson of that outfit composed a "Military Notice" for publication in the newspapers, which warned "Absent Members of the Clarke Cavalry, Look Out!" Captain Nelson announced that 11 of his men were then "lurking about their homes" in Clarke, Jefferson, and Frederick Counties, and threatened that if they did not return to the company within a week of that date, he would offer a reward of $30 apiece for their apprehension as deserters. He closed with the hope that the absentees would not cause him the "painful duty of placarding them by name."

Three days later the scholarly Nelson offered the press a considerably more light-hearted tidbit: "$30 REWARD - Deserted ... on the 6th October 1861, Private William P. Kramer." Nelson continued:

> Said KRAMER is about 5 feet 5 inches in height, has short frizzled hair, pop eyes, short arms, duck legs, squat body, big head and squeaky voice, fancies he can sing "Annie Laurie," and other sentimental songs....
>
> I should have advertised said KRAMER sooner, but have been deliberating whether he would be worth thirty dollars to

the Southern Confederacy, if recovered.

This notice was picked up by a number of newspapers, and led to several letters to the Secretary of War on Kramer's behalf, explaining that he had sought to aid the cause, but was unaware that he was formally enlisted into the company. Not long after this notice appeared, Nelson advertised rewards for five deserters, minus comic descriptions.

Lieutenant Colonel Julien Harrison of the 6th Cavalry found nothing comic in his own situation on February 5. He was selected as the bearer of dispatches between Gen. George B. McClellan, U.S.A., and Gen. Johnston regarding prisoners of war. Harrison found himself inside Union lines, cooling his heels at Arlington at Gen. James S. Wadsworth's headquarters, and he wanted an official receipt to take back, as well as an idea when he would receive a reply. Eventually Harrison got his receipt, and a statement from "The Young Napoleon's" adjutant that he need not linger further for a response.

Minor losses in Harrison's regiment continued. Some men were discharged for disability, and in February four troopers died of disease. In March, six more succumbed.

Then on March 27 a loss of another kind occurred, which highlighted a crucial need. Charles William Field was promoted to the rank of Brigadier General of Infantry, to date from March 9, 1862. For Field, it was another step forward in a distinguished career that earned him a well-deserved reputation as one of the best of the infantry commanders of the Army of Northern Virginia, and eventually the rank of Major General.

For the 6th Cavalry, however, it meant that the seasoned regular army discipline which could transform good citizen-soldiers into the best of full-time cavalrymen would not again be available. If, in the years of rigorous campaigning to come, the regiment had one preeminent need, it was to get and keep first-class officers like Field.

CHAPTER II
The Bloody Sixth

Colonel Field's departure set the stage for the reorganization in the regiment which was the main feature of the month of April 1862, and for the clash of arms that soon followed. The day before Field's appointment to a higher command, a special order directed that the size of the unit be augmented by the addition of another company.

The Pittsylvania Dragoons were from Pittsylvania County, and were led by Capt. Cabell E. Flournoy (son of Capt. Thomas Stanhope Flournoy of Company G). Both Flournoys were significant additions to the command structure of the regiment and both played prominent roles in the events of the spring and summer and beyond.

The Pittsylvania Dragoons were organized on January 7, 1861, but as early as December 6, 1860, Cabell Flournoy, their hot-blooded 19-year-old captain to be (described in the 1860 census as a law student) offered his services to the governor of South Carolina if Virginia failed to secede. The Dragoons and their leader were enlisted into the service of the Confederate States for one year on May 27, 1861. The company rode from Chatham eager to "punish the audacity of the Yankees," and so unaccustomed to military life that when it arrived at Richmond on the way to the camp of instruction at Ashland, then men took rooms in a hotel. In June, the men boarded railroad cars for the trip to Staunton to join Gen. Robert S. Garnett at Laurel Hill, in western Virginia. As an independent company, they protected Garnett in his retreat before Gen. George B. McClellan, and scouted in the campaign in which Garnett was killed at Corrick's Ford. Then they moved across the mountains to Monterey, in Highland County, where they joined Gen. Edward ("Allegheny") Johnson's command.

The Dragoons participated in several fights, including one at Camp Allegheny, after which they went into winter quarters in the mountains. After reenlisting for the war in February, and enjoying a well-earned furlough, the now-seasoned troops joined the 6th Cavalry at Gordonsville, where they became Company E. Flournoy's father was responsible for persuading the War Department to order the unit to Field.

The regiment covered the rear of Johnston's army when it abandoned the Centreville-Manassas line and moved toward Richmond. Lieutenant Daniel T. Richards, until then a Berryville merchant, was evidently displeased by this turn of events. He wrote to the War Department on April

6 on behalf of the Clarke Cavalry, asking to be transferred to a command that would serve in the Shenandoah Valley, home of most of his men, and to be placed under Gen. Thomas J. Jackson. Although his request for transfer was denied, the regiment was moved with Ewell to the vicinity of Culpeper when Johnston crossed the Rapidan River. In this period the outfit kept an eye on the Federals under Gen. Irvin McDowell at Fredericksburg.

Important organizational changes were in the works. On April 15, three field officers were appointed to the regiment: Julien Harrison, a wealthy farmer of Columbia (in Goochland County) and one with considerable slave property, as colonel; J. Grattan Cabell, a well-to-do Richmond doctor as lieutenant colonel; and Thomas Stanhope Flournoy, a planter and attorney in Halifax County as major. No sooner had this been done than the Confederate Congress passed a conscriptoin act which promoted reorganization through election of officers. Accordingly, company officers were chosen by vote on April 20. Twenty lieutenants and captains failed to win the favor of their men and lost their commissions. The new company officers proceeded to elect field officers ten days later. Harrison was retained as colonel, T. S. Flournoy was moved up to lieutenant colonel, and John Shac Green (who had just been voted out as a captain) was named major. This last elevation was one many would come to regret.

Colonel Harrison seems to have served only briefly as commander of the regiment, his hemorrhoids making field service difficult. His formal resignation bears the date of July 7.

Throughout the Shenandoah Valley campaign, the 6th Cavalry was referred to as "Flournoy's," and that officer merits particular notice. Thomas Stanhope Flournoy was a well-known personage in the Old Dominion. His personal popularity was such that he was elected to Congress in 1846 as a Whig in a heavily Democratic district. In that term he gained the friendship of Abraham Lincoln, but narrowly lost two bids to regain his seat. Strongly anti-Catholic and anti-immigrant, and with a reputation for opposition to slavery, Flournoy was chosen as the Know-Nothing candidate for governor in the contest against Henry A. Wise in 1855. Wise came out the victor, polling 83,424 votes to Flournoy's 73,244. Flournoy's recantation of anti-slavery sentiments proved futile, as did his refusal, in keeping with his party's policy, to debate or make a single speech. If he had appeared before the voters, he might have won the contest, as his powers of persuasion before juries were renowned.

At the time of the regimental reorganization, the 6th Cavalry and the 2d Cavalry formed the mounted force under Col. Thomas T. Munford that operated with Ewell's division. The 6th Cavalry went with Ewell to reinforce Gen. Thomas J. ("Stonewall") Jackson in the Valley. Ewell and his men (including the 6th Cavalry) crossed Swift Run Gap and joined Jackson near New Market on the evening of April 30. They then screened Jackson's movement as Stonewall headed west and fought the Battle of McDowell that defeated Gen. John C. Fremont. Thanks in part to the 6th Cavalry, Union General Nathaniel P. Banks remained mystified by the movements of his opponent.

After Jackson returned from McDowell, he ordered Flournoy's regiment across the Massanutten Mountain to join him at Luray, preparatory to a move on Front Royal. Private Jonathan Taylor Mann of Co. I wrote to his wife on May 20 that his regiment had been constantly scouting, and had engaged in two skirmishes. It crossed the Blue Ridge four times, passed through five counties, and marched nearly to Warrenton. Though Mann reported many horses broken down, spirits were high. With evident pleasure, he wrote that "we charged around in the rear of the enemy at one time[,] took two waggons[,] 10 fine horses[,] the mail riders with a bag full of letters and some gold[,] and 14 prisoners[.] killed one and shot another. . . they were running when shot."

The attention of Jackson and his army was now directed at the town of Front Royal. Stonewall's intention was either to destroy the garrison there and get in Banks's rear, or to force Banks to give up Strasburg, about nine miles to the west. The Confederates marched north and bivouacked ten miles below Front Royal. Company B, which had been picketing the roads north of Culpeper Court House, was ordered back to the main body of the regiment. With a presentiment of tragedy, old John Turner, a citizen, watched through tear-filled eyes as the boys of the Rappahannock company trotted west toward the mountains.

Old John Turner's premonition was borne out on May 23. That morning the 6th and 2d Cavalry, under Flournoy as senior officer present, crossed the South Fork of the Shenandoah River at McCoy's Ferry to destroy the Manassas Gap Railroad between Strasburg and Front Royal. This was accomplished by 2 p.m. Soon afterward, elements of the 6th Cavalry, who were serving as the vanguards of the attackers, drove in the Federal pickets at Front Royal. Infantry then made good the capture of the town. The retreating enemy set fire to the bridge over the North Fork of the Shenandoah, but not soon enough. Pursuing infantry partially extinguished the blaze; the 6th Cavalry was able to continue its advance in single file over the remnant of the smoldering span. Jackson was concerned by the time four companies had threaded their way across lest his prey escape. He rode up to Colonel Flournoy and commanded, "Colonel, they have two pieces of artillery, go and take them."

The horsemen galloped about three miles until they reached Cedarville (or Nineveh). Jackson was for a time unrecognized and rode part of the way with the column, urging it forward. When his identity was

ENGAGEMENT AT FRONT ROYAL MAY 23, 1862

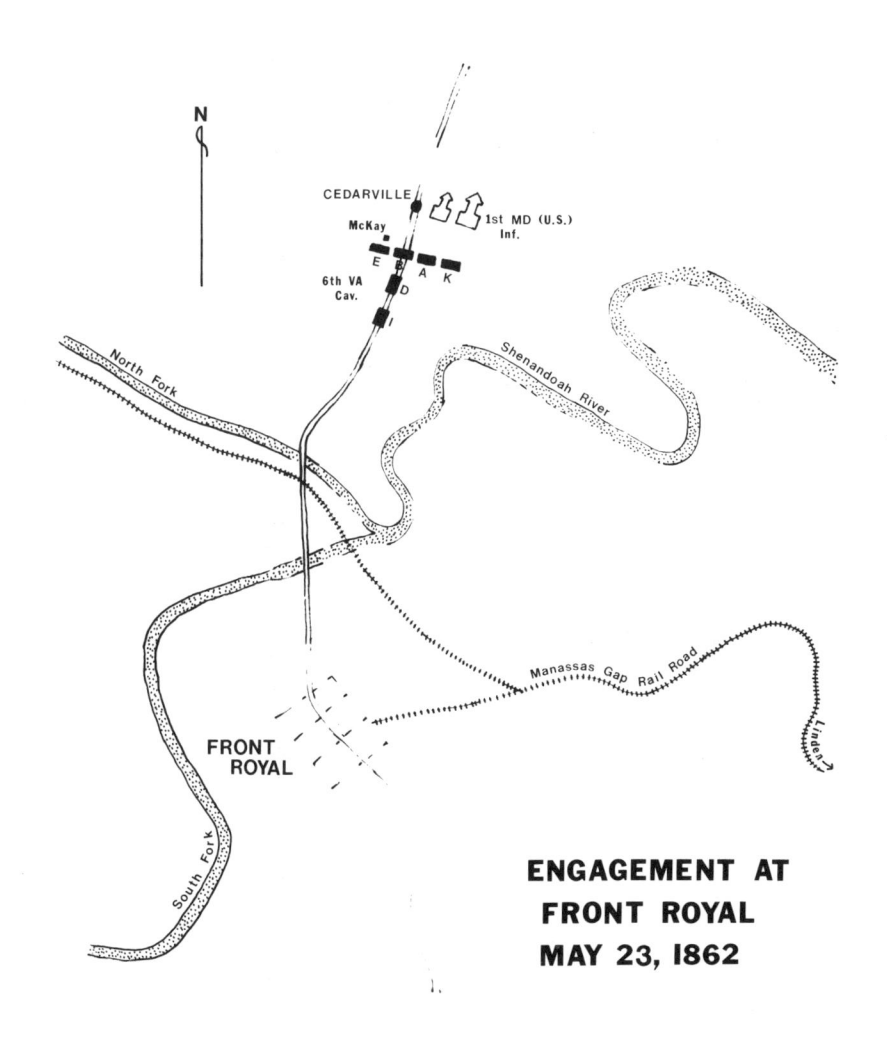

discovered, he was greeted with ringing cheers. The advance companies arrived before a resolute line of Federals; they spread out from the turnpike. Company E, under Cabell Flournoy, went to the left; Company K, under Capt. George A. Baxter, and Company A, under Capt. R. H. Dulany, went to the right; Company B, under Capt. (formerly sergeant) Daniel A. Grimsley, went straight ahead, up the pike.

Company B boldly dashed forward upon a sizeable body of infantry in the yard of the McKay house. The Rappahannock men bore aloft their distinctive blue and white flag, presented to them not long before by the ladies of Gordonsville. Of the 38 in the company, only three were without a scratch when the firing ceased. One of these, miraculously, was their leader, Grimsley. The colorbearer, 18-year-old Dallas Brown, was not so lucky. His body fell, riddled by some 20 balls. Eight other members of the company also died in the charge.

The momentum of the rush had been so great, however, that its object dissolved in disorder. Nine companies of the 1st Maryland (U.S.) Infantry were put to flight; their colonel, John R. Kenly, was captured. Two companies of the 29th Pennsylvania Infantry, part of the Pioneer Corps, and some of the 5th New York were also routed. Jackson had coveted the two guns of the Pennsylvania Light Artillery's Battery E; they were now his. A Federal survivor mistook the Gordonsville banner for the infamous "black flag" signifying no quarter and reported that "our whole force was cut to pieces."

Company B was not the only one involved. Three other advance companies of the 6th Cavalry charged with equal gallantry, but suffered less loss in their attack of the McKay orchard to the right of the pike. Company K's Captain Baxter was killed there. George F. Means, also of Company K, barely escaped when three infantrymen tried to bayonet him as he lay beneath his fallen horse. Fortunately, Sgt. John D. B. Fout arrived in time to drive off the attackers.

Companies D and I arrived to take up pursuit of the now panic-stricken Yankees. Company A suffered one killed and one wounded; Company K had lost their beloved Baxter. The following day, Pvt. John C. Donohoe of Baxter's company heard General Ewell lament these losses to Colonel Flournoy, but Ewell added, "You made a glorious charge." The road to Winchester now lay open.

Of the pursuit that followed the Cedarville success, Private Mann wrote home that he marveled at the sight of the bodies of dust-covered Federal soldiers and horses strewn among knapsacks, arms, blankets, and other impedimenta.

Courage and energy were the order of the day. General Ewell reported that an abandoned enemy Parrott gun "was brought off, within sight of the enemy's pickets, by Privates Fontaine and Moore (Company I, Sixth Cavalry) who, using two plow horses from a neighboring field, brought it back to Front Royal - a piece of cool daring hard to match."

On the morning of May 24, the 6th and 2d Cavalry, under the command of George H. ("Maryland") Steuart, rode on to Newtown (now Stephens City) on the turnpike between Strasburg and Winchester. There they continued to harass the enemy. Seeing evidence of a wagon train, the advance halted until all of the 6th Cavalry had caught up. The regiment was ordered to charge, which it did "as fast as the horses could go." Private Mann described the result: "the enemy took fright [,] threw of[f] their knapsacks and guns[,] and run for life[.]" Mann continued:

> I rode up to a stone fence[.] there was seven blue coats hid behind the fence[.] I presented my pistol to them and ordered them over the fence[.] to my great releaf they soon hopped over[.] I marched them back to head quarters.

He reported that he and his comrades captured about 225 men and "a great many waggons and horses."

At Winchester on May 25, Jackson's infantry scored another notable triumph, driving Banks's frightened troops out of the town. But when the Southern commander looked about for cavalry to reap the harvest of the day, none was to be found. He sent his aide, Lt. A. S. ("Sandie") Pendleton, in search of Steuart and his two regiments. He found them; the men were dismounted, the horses were grazing.

Steuart declared that he was under Ewell's command; orders to pursue would have to come through Ewell. Ewell was finally found and put his stamp of approval on the order to advance, but by that time Banks's main force was too far away for a successful chase. Stonewall was not pleased. The actors he had needed for a repeat performance of Cedarville were lounging in the wings.

Jackson's command moved north. The 6th Cavalry had a brush with the Federals at Charles Town on May 29; it took 12 prisoners. The advance reached the Potomac, across which Banks had fled, but danger loomed. With Fremont on the west and Gen. James Shields on the east, Jackson's route of retreat up the valley could be cut. A rapid movement south was in order.

Maryland Steuart's cavalry brought up the rear in the move south. Fremont's forward elements struck the 6th Cavalry in a surprise attack after dark on June 1 near Strasburg. Jackson reported that the regiment had been thrown into disorder by a ruse. The attackers supposedly identified themselves as "Ashby's Cavalry," thus confounding pickets who knew that a company of Confederate General Turner Ashby's men were in the vicinity. In the attack, Captain Dulany of Company A was severely wounded in the thigh. One private was killed and another was nowhere to be found afterward. Some confusion spread to the 2d Cavalry, but it soon rallied and saved the day.

The withdrawal south continued with the cavalry skirmishing almost every step of the way. After a stampede caused by Maryland Steuart's mismanagement on June 2, Ewell transferred the 6th and 2d cavalry from the command of Steuart to Ashby, and put the latter in charge of his rear guard, heeding Colonel Flournoy's entreaties.

Around 3 p.m. on June 6, while bringing up the rear along the Port Republic Road near Harrisonburg, the 6th Cavalry was surprised by enemy horsemen. Flournoy recovered his composure and ordered, "by fours right about wheel." His men charged, while the 2d Cavalry followed suit on the right. The Yankees fled more than a mile to the far side of a boggy creek, losing their dashing Colonel Sir Percy Wyndham to capture. Ashby found the enemy position inaccessible to mounted men and tried it with a nearby group of Confederate infantry. Ashby was shot by bluecoats on foot who were hidden beneath the crest of the hill he was climbing. His wound was mortal. Joseph Tarpley of Company E carried the general's body from the field. Major Green of the 6th Cavalry was also hit that day, but although his wound was severe, he recovered and later enlivened the record of his regiment.

The two climactic victories of the Valley campaign were fought at Cross Keys on June 8 and Port Republic the next day. The real honors of those cliff-hanging triumphs belonged to the infantry, but the 6th Cavalry contributed to the success by protecting the baggage train; following the routed enemy; and scooping up numerous prisoners, arms, and wagons.

The mounted arm, led tirelessly in these last battles by Col. Thomas T. Munford of the 2d Cavalry, finally camped on the summit of a nearby peak at midnight of June 9. In the next few days Munford garnered prisoners and plunder in the vicinity of Harrisonburg, New Market, and Mount Jackson, until he was reieved of command by the freshly promoted Gen. Beverly H. Robertson. By then Stonewall Jackson's Valley Campaign had passed from headlines into history.

Throughout that remarkable series of engagements and maneuvers, the 6th Cavalry had been almost constantly employed on grueling forced marches, bone-wearying scouts, and perilous outpost duty. Colonel Munford remarked in his report of Port Republic that "Our work had been eternal, day and night." Much the same could be said of the campaign as a whole. Private Mann's observation of May 27 aptly portrays the achievements of the period: "our regament has gained a considerable reputation[.] Gen[.] Ewell called it the bloody sixth . . .I Glory in the bloody sixth." The regard of Jackson himself was suggested when, following the army near Richmond, he took Company D along as an advance guard.

The month of July 1862 was one of further reorganization and maneuver in both Union and Confederate lines. The Federal forces in Northern Virginia were consolidated into three corps under Franz Sigel, Banks, and McDowell, to form the Army of Virginia. The whole was under John Pope, an import from the western theater from whom much was expected. Confederate General Robertson, an old regular army cavalryman whose ability to drill men would be proven to surpass his ability to fight them, was assigned to a brigade composed of the 2d, 6th, 7th, and 12th Regiments and the 17th Battalion of Virginia Cavalry. The brigade joined Jackson near Richmond on July 10, marched back to the vicinity of Gordonsville to counter Pope, and on July 27 was partly deployed as pickets on the upper fords of the Rapidan River. Meanwhile, on July 16, the field officers of the 6th Cavalry were reshuffled. Thomas Flournoy was named full colonel, and Cabell Flournoy major. Julian Harrison's resignation as colonel due to his painful hemorrhoids was finally accepted on July 28.

The 7th Cavalry mounted a Federal cavalry reconnaissance in force at Orange Court House on August 2, and, being joined by the 6th Cavalry, followed the retiring enemy to Rapidan Station. As Jackson moved to seize the opportunity to strike afforded by Pope's strung out command, Robertson's Brigade drove back the blue horsemen north of the Rapidan. On the evening of August 8 the 17th Battalion, under Maj. William Patrick, and part of the 6th Cavalry under Colonel Flournoy, trounced part of the 1st Maryland (U.S.) Cavalry at Madison Court House, chasing the Yankees some five miles and crushing their attempts to rally. Flournoy lost only one man to capture in this encounter.

At the Battle of Cedar Mountain on August 9, the 6th Cavalry led Ewell's division onto the field but played only a supporting role. Captain Charles H. Ball of Company K noted that "the cavalry was not in the fight." As Jackson was winning this hotly contested field, Company F picketed the road from Culpeper Court House toward Madison Court House. In the evening following the battle, Pvt. John C. Donohoe of Company K visited the scene of some heavy fighting and found himself tormented by the groans and shrieks of the wounded and dying Yanks. He dismounted and placed several in more comfortable positions, offering such succor as he could until he returned to his unit.

The next day the regiment scouted to within one mile of Culpeper, and on August 16 helped to run some enemy cavalry pickets into the Confederate infantry camp on the Rapidan, capturing several.

Jeb Stuart took command of Jackson's cavalry on August 17, thereby easing somewhat the concern that the hero of the Valley felt about

Robertson's ability to command. In fact, the performance of Stuart himself left something to be desired that night, when in a famous incident at Verdiersville, he allowed the Yankees to capture not only his plumed hat, but more importantly, Gen. R. E. Lee's plan of attack. Thus warned, Pope managed to elude, at least for a time, the trap being laid for him.

At around 4 p.m. on the morning of August 20, Stuart ordered Fitzhugh Lee's and Robertson's Brigades across the Rapidan in an effort to probe Pope's retreating forces. When the 6th Cavalry reached Culpeper, it was greeted with a huge tub of lemonade prepared in anticipation of the arrival of the Confederates, and by tales of the vile and licentious behavior of a party of Federals at the Albert Simms farm not far away. With thirst quenched and zeal renewed, the regiment and Robertson's other troops struck the enemy cavalry between Stevensburg and Brandy Station. The dust cloud raised by the Virginians prevented a surprise, but they pressed on undaunted. They continued skirmishing with the dismounted troopers of George D. Bayard. Robertson eventually flanked Bayard and forced him to withdraw, but the Federals took up another position on Fleetwood Hill.

Robertson ordered a charge on the heights. With a yell, the 12th Cavalry rushed the center of the enemy position as the 6th and 7th Cavalry drove in on the flank. A short, spirited hand-to-hand struggle led to Bayard's withdrawal across the Rappahannock, where he took shelter under the batteries of Pope's main army. Stuart was pleased enough with the events of the day to credit Robertson for the "superior discipline" he had given his brigade, which had performed with "the stability of veterans." The men, on the other hand, were inclined to feel that it was they who gave the luster to the brigade commander. As the 6th Cavalry again met the Simms family in Culpeper, someone shouted, "Ladies, your wrongs have been avenged!"

Still smarting from his humiliation at Verdiersville, Stuart received permission to conduct a raid on Pope's rear that would even the score. His primary objective was to cut the enemy's line of communications. He led the brigades of Robertson and Fitz Lee across the Rappahannock on August 22 without the 3d and 7th Cavalry, but including the 6th. Sweeping into Warrenton and then down to Catlett's Station on the Orange and Alexandria Railroad, Stuart's rush was a complete surprise to Pope. Pope's personal headquarters tent was captured, and one of his dress uniform coats was carried off, probably by W. Keith Armistead of Company A. One of the Clarke Cavalry appropriated a pair of Pope's own boots, and wore them with evident satisfaction for some time thereafter. Also among the trophies was a cache of official documents which enabled R. E. Lee to plan his next campaign at Manassas. Despite these rewards and an additional harvest of perhaps 300 prisoners, darkness and heavy rain prevented the destruction of the railroad bridge that had been the main goal of the expedition.

Stuart returned to Confederate lines via the Fauquier White Sulphur (or Warrenton) Springs. A Union force attempted to cut him off there on August 23. In a heavy cannonade several of the Rebel raiders were killed or wounded. Among the fatalities was Lt. Charles William Thrift of Company K, who was hit by a shell that struck him in the side, cutting off his left arm and nearly severing his body. The gruesome spectacle made a lasting impression on the young soldiers who witnessed it, but no other men from the 6th were lost that day.

On August 25 Stuart received his final instructions for his role in R. E. Lee's daring plan to demolish the army Pope had massed between Waterloo Bridge and Warrenton. When Lee split the commands of Jackson and Longstreet in the face of the enemy, Stuart and the 6th Cavalry followed Jackson. The horsemen marched early on the morning of the next day, moving by way of Amissville to cross the Rappahannock River at Henson's Mill. From there they rode to the vicinity of Salem (now Marshall) and over the Bull Run Mountains to Haymarket, taking care to avoid the Federals defending the vicinity of Thoroughfare Gap. Stuart reported to Jackson near Gainesville.

Stuart's cavalry guarded Jackson's flanks as he moved to capture Bristoe Station on the Orange and Alexandria Railroad. The horsemen fired into and captured three railroad trains at Bristoe, but one other train escaped northward to spread the alarm at Manassas. Frank Peake of Company A remembered seeing a large dust cloud approaching and he and his comrades prepared to fight Pope's main army. Much to their relief, the dust turned out to be from Jackson's men. Jackson ordered Stuart to continue on to Manassas and to capture the immense amount of stores there that were badly needed by his worn troops.

When he ordered the capture of Manassas Junction, Jackson wanted Stuart to cooperate with the infantry brigade of Gen. Isaac R. Trimble, the whole to be under Stuart. Stuart arrived at the site and determined that the defense was too strong to be carried by the cavalry, so it was Trimble's men who actually took the place, though an unseemly squabble over who most deserved the honor developed in the reports of the affair. Trimble and his subordinates stated that the first cavalry they saw was Flournoy's regiment at about 3 a.m. of August 27, approaching from the north of the railroad to ask if Manassas was taken. The remainder of August 27 was comparatively uneventful and was spent primarily in rounding up stragglers from Pope's army and chasing fugitives from his cavalry.

The next morning Robertson's Brigade rendezvoused near Sudley Church. The 6th Cavalry drew up in line of battle near Groveton, and Company K was detailed to lead the way west to Haymarket. At Haymarket the men could see Longstreet's command fighting its way through Thoroughfare Gap. Stuart sent a dispatch to Longstreet, but then learned that Jackson was himself facing the Federals, facing toward Manassas and Groveton from his position between the Warrenton Turnpike and Sudley Ford. Stuart hurried to put his horsemen on Jackson's right, but by the time he had done so, it was dark and the day's fighting was over.

On the morning of August 29 Stuart and his men set out to find Longstreet. While searching, they ran into a small force of Federals in Jackson's rear and drove it off. John C. Donohoe recorded that when he and his fellows reached Haymarket they were halted in a large field to watch a heavy column of infantry moving toward Gainesville. They had found Longstreet. Longstreet continued in the direction of Manassas and took up position on Jackson's right. Stuart's cavalry moved on Longstreet's right, with Robertson's Brigade in the lead. Robertson uncovered a threat to Longstreet's flank by at least a corps of the enemy moving from Bristoe Station toward Sudley.

A clever ruse by Stuart, in which his men gave the impression of a large force by dragging brush on the road, plus the arrival of three infantry brigades with artillery, persuaded the threatening Federals to withdraw. Jackson fought furiously against considerable odds that day, but the odds were decidedly better with the arrival of Longstreet.

Stuart seized a crucial point of observation on August 30 that enabled him to alert Lee to a large body of the enemy massing on Jackson. Sharpshooters of Company F, 6th Cavalry, under Capt. John A. Throckmorton, were posted behind a stone wall and held off some dismounted Yankee troopers who tried to take this invaluable spot. About 3 p.m. Robertson's Brigade advanced on the extreme Confederate right, accompanied by four batteries of artillery. The brigade and its supports raked the length of the enemy line and inflicted numerous casualties.

Around 5 p.m. the 2d Cavalry became involved in a fierce fight with Gen. John Buford's horsemen on the Lewis House Ridge above Bull Run. The 2nd Cavalry was eventually rescued by the timely arrival of the 7th and 12th Cavalry, with the 6th acting as a reserve. At length the Federals were repulsed and driven beyond the Stone Bridge, prompting Stuart to observe that "The Lord of Hosts was plainly fighting on our side." Longstreet struck Pope's left and forced him into a full retreat on Washington, D.C. Stuart, with Robertson's and Fitz Lee's Brigades, harassed the rear of the discomfited army.

Robertson's Brigade operated under Stuart in the vicinity of Chantilly (Ox Hill) following the Battle of Second Manassas, but the 6th Cavalry was not engaged with the enemy. One member of the regiment did note that several shells passed over his head. Some companies were detailed at this point on special duties. From September 1 until October 18, Company K was in Loudoun County arresting deserters and gathering conscripts. About this time some of Company I were ordered to Orange County to arrest citizens suspected of disloyalty. Company A served as headquarters guard for Gen. R. E. Lee until the army marched into Maryland.

Frank Peake thus found himself posted outside a small farmhouse near Chantilly which Lee was using as his command post. Peake was impressed with the seriousness of his duty. He halted two men who tried to enter the building without a pass from Lee. To his chagrin, it proved to be the commanding general himself and one of his aides. The company then had frequent opportunity to see the general first hand during this period, for most of which the general had his hands bandaged from a fall from his horse "Traveler."

The headquarters of the 6th Cavalry was at Centreville on September 3 and 4. Officers of the regiment were occupied with paroling the large number of wounded Federals in hospitals who had become prisoners of war. Lieutenant Colonel Edward P. Vollum, U.S.A., a medical officer with Pope, remembered that Colonel Flournoy was put in charge of the place. Vollum persuaded Flournoy to return the captured hospital supplies to him, which were then used to succor the wounded of both armies.

On September 5 the brigade lost General Robertson, but not to enemy action. He was relieved of command and ordered to North Carolina to organize cavalry in that state. The parting did not plunge the men of his old brigade into mourning, for while the men recognized his ability to instill discipline, it found his performance in action less than inspiring.

Robertson's replacement was Col. Thomas T. Munford of the 2d Cavalry, who was not promoted, however. September 5 was also the day that Stuart's horsemen forded the Potomac and rode into Maryland. It did so without the 6th Cavalry, which remained behind in Centreville to collect arms and guard property taken in the late campaign. Later the regiment forwarded stragglers from the main army to Winchester.

Some confusion followed in the wake of the move into Maryland. Private Donohoe (who was near enough to home for occasional visits) was twice separated from his command. His diary entries as he followed Dame Rumor in search of his regiment verge on the comic as he pursued its mirage-like image, finally rejoining at Haymarket at midnight of September 7. When he reported to Colonel Flournoy the following morning he found Flournoy "very worthy in consequence of so many having absented themselves without permission." His persistent search was rewarded by an order putting him on interior guard every night for the next month.

The day Donohoe returned, Companies E, I, and K were ordered to Warrenton and then to Salem to collect stragglers. Private Luther Hopkins of Company A found himself impressing wagons from the Quaker citizens of his native Loudoun County for use in taking wounded and injured stragglers to Winchester. The task led to some embarrassment when he found himself the dinner guest of one of those same citizens after the war.

Diarist Donohoe noted that from September 12 through 15 the regiment encamped at Antioch Church, in the vicinity of Thoroughfare Gap and surrounded by the mountains of northwestern Prince William County. The proximity of the "neat little stone church" and the dedication of the regimental chaplain, Episcopal clergyman Richard Terrell Davis, combined with visits from a Baptist preacher to produce considerable religious activity. Chaplain Davis reported to his wife, "We had services every day from Thursd. to Sunday & on Sunday twice." That religious joy was joined by the secular on September 15, when the regiment learned of the capture of the Federal garrison of Harpers Ferry by Stonewall Jackson. Luther Hopkins recalled that he and his comrades could hear the guns from that encounter.

On September 17, the regimental headquarters was near Salem, in Fauquier County. That was the day of the Battle of Sharpsburg (Antietam), Maryland. (Union General D. B. Birney reported, however, that his flag-of-truce party at the Manassas battlefield met one of the companies of the 6th there, rather than at Salem.)

Chaplain Davis reflected in a letter on his continued pleasant relations with the regimental staff, particularly Colonel Flournoy, but was saddened by the colonel's talk of resignation. Davis remarked that Lieutenant Colonel Green was well disposed to religion, but added that "he is said to be without tactical knowledge, or ability to keep up the discipline of the regt., and the prospect, if he succeeds to the command, is not pleasant, regarding either the mess, or the regt."

After the Battle of Sharpsburg the main body of Lee's Army of Northern Virginia withdrew across the Potomac to the vicinity of Martinsburg. The 6th Cavalry screened this movement and guarded Snicker's and Ashby's Gaps. On September 20, Col. R. Butler Price, 2d Pennsylvania Cavalry, led about 800 men of the cavalry brigade of the Union Army's Third Corps by way of Fairfax Court House and Aldie in the direction of Ashby's Gap. Their aim was to capture a supply train that was known to be near the gap and on its way to Lee. Price's substantial force included a section of the 3d U.S. Artillery. This expedition brought on an engagement that was not soon forgotten by the 6th Cavalry.

It happened near Paris on September 22. Company F met the 1st Vermont Cavalry, the enemy's advance, east of the village. The Alexandria boys put up a stubborn resistance as they fell back. At length, the Vermonters (under Lt. Col. Addison W. Preston) met the main body of the 6th Cavalry. They were arranged in platoons and filled the road between two stone walls, calmly awaiting attack. The Virginians, who numbered only about 130, were under Lt. Col. Green; two days before this, Colonel Flournoy had gone home sick.

While the Federals sent out flanking forces on either side and rushed boldly on, Green ordered his men, whose pistols were drawn and ready, to hold their fire. The charging enemy was momentarily bewildered by its motionless opponent, which remained absolutely silent. The Yankees halted in confusion, but under Preston's lead they regained their poise and pressed on.

When the Federals were within 50 feet, Green finally gave the order to fire; "A shower of pistol balls" struck the Vermont men. But Green had waited too long. Although Green's own shot killed Capt. Selah G. Perkins and other charging men were also hit, the impetus of the full-speed assault was too much to resist. The 6th Cavalry broke and fled toward the gap.

Private Donohoe said that Company E was the first to collapse, but the urge to escape soon spread to the other companies. Major Cabell E. Flournoy positioned himself behind his men to keep them closed up, but some interpreted his actions differently. Green's bravery, if not his judgement, was unquestioned, but when he turned around, his regiment had disappeared.

Green received three severe sabre wounds to the head (Jeb Stuart was said later to have called them well deserved), and was captured and taken to the rear, eventually to be paroled. Four men of the 6th Cavalry were killed, 13 wounded, and 14 captured. The enemy feared an ambush and slowed the pursuit, while the Confederates halted and rallied (minus a few), and fell back through the gap and across the river in the direction of Winchester. The Federals failed in their main objective, since the wagon train they had sought had moved across the ridge the day before; they got only three vehicles.

In spite of this disaster, and in spite of the hard service it had seen for some time, the 6th Cavalry got no extended period of recuperation. The 6th and its brigade went on a scout through Loudoun County beginning about September 28, and passed through Leesburg, Middleburg, and Upperville. The weary riders returned to Berryville the night of October 1. Reverend Davis wrote, "We had some 1000 cav. & 2 pieces of artillery. In Leesburg we arrived just at night & such a cheering as the ladies gave us."

The cheers of the fair were not enough to draw Colonel Flournoy back to his regiment. He wrote to Secretary of War George W. Randolph on October 6 from his home to tender his resignation. The colonel cited his *"imperative* duty," and referred to "domestic affliction." This was probably the death of his ten-year-old son not long before and the terminal illness of a four-year-old daughter. Flournoy observed that he would soon be 51 years-old, and that he had three sons in the army; he implied that he had done his share.

Evidently Randoph agreed, for on October 14, Flournoy's resignation was accepted. The date of commission of his successor, Julien Harrison, was recorded as September 23, but was apparently moved back, since the regimental rolls and returns continued to show Flournoy as colonel, absent sick, through December 1862.

Although he was not a professional soldier, Stanhope Flournoy's tenure as regimental commander was successful, if not spectacular. He was a man whom others gladly followed, and was aggressive enough to win for his men the appelation "The Bloody Sixth." In fact, aside from the actions at Cedarville and Paris, the regiment suffered few battle losses under him. Perhaps Flournoy's most notable legacy to his unit was his son, the major, who ultimately redeemed the honor tarnished near Paris on September 22.

CHAPTER III

Scouts, Raids, And Winter Quarters

With Col. Thomas S. Flournoy at home and Lt. Col. John Shac Green absent wounded and on parole, the command of the 6th Cavalry rested in October 1862 on the none-too-steady shoulders of 22-year-old Maj. Cabell E. Flournoy. The first engagement of the month was on October 9, but Flournoy was evidently not involved. At about midday, Lt. George F. Means of Company K and 21 of his men met a Federal reconnaissance force at Aldie. They were coming from the division of Fairfax Court House under Lt. S. B. Conger of the 3d (West) Virginia Cavalry.

Lieutenant Means bravely led seven of his poorly armed men in a charge; the rest were halted by an unnamed junior officer and did not participate. The Yankees stood long enough to deliver a fire that killed Means and Private Russell, and wounded Sgt. William Ball, Jr., before they retreated seven miles to the east of the town. The Federals reported no losses.

For about six weeks following the Battle of Sharpsburg, General Lee's army recuperated in the Lower Shenandoah Valley counties of Jefferson and Berkeley. Such idleness was not to the taste of Gen. Jeb Stuart, however. On the same day as Company K's skirmish at Aldie, Stuart gathered about 1,800 hand-picked cavalrymen at Darkesville, who were selected for the quality of their horses and for the reliability of the riders. Six hundred men came from each brigade. The contingent from Munford was under Col. William E. ("Grumble") Jones, and included Companies D and G of the 6th Cavalry. John W. Peake of Company A recounted his part in the raid years later, suggesting that his company may have also been chosen.

This splendid force, so carefully assembled, embarked on an adventure long celebrated by the horsemen of the Army of Northern Virginia — a raid into Pennsylvania that was to be Stuart's second ride around an army commanded by General McClellan. The object of this bold foray was the town of Chambersburg, in south-central Pennsylvania. After fording the Potomac at McCoy's Ferry, 10 miles above Williamsport, Maryland, early on October 10, the raiders reached Chambersburg by 8 o'clock the same night. When they crossed into the Keystone State, they sent out a number of parties to gather horses, a proceeding that proved remarkably successful. A dismal rain left his ability to recross the river into Virginia in doubt, but Stuart rode east, then south, and arrived at Emmitsburg,

Maryland, at dusk on October 11. The weary troopers, having ridden night and day, arrived at White's Ford on the Potomac the following day. They eluded all pursuers, bluffed their way past the defenders of the ford, and returned safely to the south bank of the river later on October 12. Not a single man of Flournoy's regiment was lost.

Active campaigning continued throughout October, as summer weather lingered. General Winfield S. Hancock, U.S.A., made a reconnaissance from Harpers Ferry to Charles Town with his own division and some 1,500 additional infantry of other divisions, four regiments of cavalry, and artillery support. For about four hours on October 16, Munford, with the 6th, 7th, and 12th, and part of the 2d Cavalry, and four guns, valiantly held Hancock's men at bay. Munford had the main body of the 6th Cavalry, but Bruce Gibson's Company A was off guarding first Snicker's then Ashby's Gap.

Gibson had a minor encounter on October 17 at Upperville with Federal cavalry under Gen. Julius Stahel, which was moving west from Gainesville. Captain Gibson tactfully ordered a retreat in the face of a superior force, in the course of which Pvt. Luther Hopkins found himself unhorsed and standing in the main street, clutching the handle of his pistol (all that remained of it after his tumble). When a Yankee demanded Hopkins's surrender, he passed on the handle to his puzzled captor.

Company F was likewise active, picketing near Charles Town, Halltown, and at two fords of the Shenandoah. They later guarded Chester Gap for two weeks.

Six of Flournoy's men were captured on October 29 near Petersburg, in Hardy (now Grant) County, when the enemy intercepted a cattle-gathering expedition. The month closed with the regimental headquarters near Charles Town, but Lee's army had already begun to forsake the Valley for the vicinity of Culpeper Court House in response to McClellan's long-awaited movement.

As the Army of Northern Virginia moved toward Culpeper, the brigade of which the 6th Cavalry was a part was left to bring up Jackson's rear. On November 6 the regiment was still at Middletown. Two days later Grumble Jones, who was a capable officer and a bitter foe of Stuart, was appointed brigadier general and brigade commander. He replaced Munford, who was transferred to Fitzhugh Lee's Brigade. At first viewed as a martinet, Jones soon won deep affection. Young John W. Peake of Company A recalled him as "a soldier, every inch of him." Soon after Jones's promotion, the composon of his command was announced. Known as the Second Brigade, it contained the 6th, 7th, and 12th Regiments, and the 17th and 35th Battalions of cavalry. The 17th Battalion was redesignated the 11th Regiment in January 1863.

On November 21, Companies C, E, I, and K were detached and reported to Gen. Stonewall Jackson at Winchester. Company K served as dispatch bearers for the general from December 1 to January 26, 1863, and was employed that way at the Battle of Fredericksburg on December 13. This detail came to an end when a pronouncement of Adjutant and Inspector General Samuel Cooper discontinued the practice of using cavalry as couriers. Company I visited Caroline County in this period, and at least one of its officers got as far as Orange County. The remaining six companies were ordered into winter quarters.

Winter quarters for the brigade in 1862-63 were a series of camps that moved as the availability of forage dictated. John N. Opie of Company D described a camp of Sibley tents late in the fall in the Luray Valley, where the horses, picketed behind each company, were watered in the Shenandoah River. Opie's recollections of this period are spiced with accounts of the capture of a barrel of oats from a nearby farmer (just before some of Company F were about to pounce on it), a personal trip into Jefferson County, and a bare-knuckles battle with a captain of the 12th Cavalry whom Opie took to have insulted his regiment by offering to buy his horse.

Luther Hopkins, back from captivity, remembered a harsh winter and a camp without tents that nonetheless proved cozy: "We sat on logs around the fire during the day and far into the night telling stories and entertaining ourselves in various ways. At night we crept under the roof of our shed, which was about a foot deep in leaves, and slept as comfortably as any farmer's hogs would do under similar circumstances."

When not participating in scouts or alarms, General Jones saw to it that the men were well drilled. From camp five miles south of Harrisonburg, newly commissioned Lt. Jonathan T. Mann of Company I wrote on December 24, "We are faring badly now[.] our horses get about half rations, I am getting verry tired of the war."

Reverend Davis contended with spiritual foes throughout the season, giving his regiment a reputation as "the citadel of religion of the brigade" due to the frequency of his prayer meetings. A member of Chew's Battery observed sardonically, however, "I do not know as the plane of practical ethics in general is any higher in this than in any other regiments of the brigade."

On December 13 the former Col. Julien Harrison wrote the Secretary of War from Goochland County and asked for reinstatment in the regiment as soon as a surgical operation enabled him to take the post. General Jones explained that for Harrison to return as colonel, Lieutenant Colonel Green agreed to step aside in his favor, and added his own blessing for the return by writing, "I know of no available man whom I would prefer as colonel of a regiment in my brigade."

The Secretary of War discovered a problem, however. The regiment had reorganized for the war, and that required promotion by grade and seniority only. Therefore, Harrison's reappointment could occur only if every officer in the regiment, in addition to Green, waived promotion. Such a total waiver seemed most unlikely.

Chaplain Davis wrote to his wife from Harrisonburg on December 7: "Things have been going on v[ery] badly in our regt. this week & of late. Our Maj. thinks of little else than drinking & horse-racing — & has actually ridden his own horse against one of his men at a quarter race. It is with joy I learn that they will not make him colonel. The Chaplain's work in a regt. under such commd. offr. is up hill. But, I hope my labors are not in vain."

As 1862 drew to a close, the regimental return for December furnished a succinct statement of the status of the regiment. It showed both the colonel (still identified as Thomas S. Flournoy) and lieutenant colonel (John Shac Green) absent, and the command exercised by Maj. Cabell E. Flournoy. Only Company K was reported still on detached service with Jackson. Present were 33 officers and 493 enlisted men. The absent numbered 12 officers and 216 enlisted men. Included among the absent were 4 officers and 93 enlisted men sick, and 1 officer and 12 enlisted men absent without leave. Sixty-five men were on detached service and 46 were on leave. The aggregate strength was put at 754, nine more than in November.

Not all information was available in the statistics, however. The return did not disclose that on December 29 Lee assigned Grumble Jones to command the Valley District in Jackson's absence, as well as such troops as were operating in the jurisdiction and not part of the Department of West Virginia. Likewise, it did not report Lee's order to Jones on the day of his assignment to drive the enemy out of the Valley of the South Branch of the Shenandoah.

Jones opened the year of 1863 with a descent on Moorefield, in Hardy County, which he reached on January 3. He held the place for two hours before the superior force of the enemy and the worthless artillery shells he had been issued forced him to withdraw. That evening the 6th and 7th Cavalry, under Capt. R. H. Dulany, captured 46 pickets at Petersburg. Jones declined to renew the attack when he took stock of the exhausted condition of the horses of Dulany's men, and of his meager commissariat, as well as of the approach of Yankee reinforcements. He fell back on January 5. His report claimed only a "partial success," but Lee expressed gratification nonetheless, and urged him to try to keep the enemy out of the Valley.

The regiment returned from this expedition to Camp Ashby (at least the second of its camps to bear that name), near Mount Crawford. The men returned to drilling when snow did not prevent it. Snow was not the only distraction. The quartermaster reported to Green that the 6th Cavalry had not been paid since June 30 and that clothing was in desperately short supply. The guard house burned to the ground during a storm on January 15.

In the face of these hardships, the prospect of peace was alluring, but Capt. Alfred B. Carter of Company F wrote on January 23 that "unless we can have our rights granted to us, I do not wish to see it. I would rather die than to surrender even the pearings of my finger nailes to the yankeys."

Lieutenant Mann related that he broke the monotony of camp life in January by a scout of some 60 or 70 miles in the direction of the Ohio River. He found out a good deal about the strength and dispositions of the enemy and concluded that they were oppressing the civilian population with threats of quartering soldiers on them and demands that they take the oath of allegiance to the Federal government not once, but twice.

Company A was detached for the first two months of the new year to Orkney Springs, about 12 miles northwest of Mount Jackson, to guard the road over the mountain. For a time the men were allowed to occupy the cottages of the Orkney Springs spa. Amanda Virginia Edmonds, sister of "Bud" Edmonds of Company A, recorded that "they were quartered in buildings with feather beds, looking glasses, wash stands, and working stoves, something the boys in Camp are not used to."

Chaplain Davis paid regular visits to Orkney Springs and found himself preaching in the ballroom of the establishment. The chaplain was able to luxuriate in a warm bath with plenty of soap. Such indulgence apparently did not agree with the men. Sickness appeared among them, and did not decline until they left the cottages for the woods nearby.

On January 27 the regiment left its main camp near Mount Crawford and marched north. It was halted for two days by a snowstorm, against which it pitched tents about five miles from New Market. On January 30 the troops erected their tents again about a mile from Mount Jackson, at what was named Camp Jackson. Life improved as stoves were installed, but the almost constant presence of snow dampened the men's spirits. Lieutenant Mann wrote that he spent much time reading his volume of tactics: "We have a class[.] I have to recite to our Coln [colonel, that is Lt. Col. Green] every day."

Capt. A. B. Carter reported numerous visits to the camp by ladies, but noted sorrowfully that they were "*Valley Dutch girls* . . . they are nothing like the people East of the ridge. They cook differently, they eat differently, and look differently, so that I think that they must be of a different race of beings."

As usual, campfire chats were enlivened by talk about officers and by rumors of all sorts. Captain Carter of Company F hoped that Julien Harrison would be appointed colonel, that Green would remain lieutenant colonel, and Cabell Flournoy major.

By January 8, Green was back with his unit, having served as a member of a court-martial since his wounding and capture at Paris. On February 9 both he and Col. Asher W. Harman of the 12th Cavalry had narrowly avoided capture by a large party of Yankees near Strasburg. Some feared that Jones's inactivity was giving his brigade a bad name, and rumor declared he would be transferred and replaced by Col. Andrew J. Grigsby. Rumor also had it that the brigade would be transferred to Kentucky, that Indiana and Illinois wanted to join the Confederacy, and that troops of those states had been tendered to the South. These tales gained little credence.

Picketing and scouting afforded some diversion, but they were not without trials. Captain Carter observed in a letter of February 15 that "these long scouts & Bivouacing at night, on the snow banks without shelter & with but little covering is enough to kill us all .... I had no idea of it before I came into the army. If a man had told me that I could ly out all night on a snow bank without freezing or without catching my death, I would have told him he was crazy but such is a fact."

Jones's spirits were renewed and his men were delighted by a clash on February 26 between the Federals and part of the brigade that did not include the 6th Cavalry. The enemy was driven for miles in the direction of Winchester. An exultant Jones declared to Chaplain Davis in his distinctive nasal drawl that he had no intention of allowing the Yankees to "poke their noses into his tent."

The arrival of March brought further activity. Company K finally rejoined the regiment on March 15 at its new camp a mile below Woodstock. Four days later the 6th Cavalry, along with the 7th and 12th and Chew's Battery, was ordered to move out for another camp at Front Royal. By month's end that camp was established and the men were sufficiently settled in by April 3 to wage a snowball fight which left Lt. John H. Matthews with a broken arm.

This was not, however, the sort of activity the regiment longed for. Captain Carter reflected that the unit had not been in a real fight since Paris, and that it had been laughed at for running there. The boys wished for a chance to "blot that stain out, as it has been much talked about." By April 18, Jones's Brigade was camped between Harrisonburg and Lacey's Spring; predictions flew of a campaign in the enemy's country.

Away from the regiment, events that had a significant bearing on its well being were unfolding. Julien Harrison continued to press the War

Department for reassignment to the colonelcy. Jones pointed out in a letter of April 1 to Lee's headquarters that the position was vacant. He added that Lt. Col. Green, Maj. C. E. Flournoy, and Capt. John A. Throckmorton were the officers in the case entitled to promotion by seniority. A week later, Jeb Stuart commented at length on the vacancy, revealing that an inspection showed the regiment to be in bad condition, notably more so than the rest of the brigade. Stuart opined that Green would not be a good choice for the spot ("though no doubt a gallant man") and desired that a good regular officer be appointed of the caliber of Charles W. Field. With such a leader, especially one *"whose habits are perfectly steady,"* he wrote, the regiment "would soon take high place in the Division." Of Flournoy and Throckmorton he found "nothing special to remark."

General R. E. Lee, writing on April 14, disagreed. He stated that the officers named by Jones were legally entitled, if competent, to the openings. Stuart's recommendation could only be complied with if Lt. Col. Green was brought before a board and disqualified. Secretary of War James A. Seddon agreed with Lee, and urged the appointment of a board to determine the competency and promotion in the regiment. There the matter rested for a while, as Thomas S. Flournoy entreated the Secretary to have Green brought before a board, to avoid putting "a stranger" over the regiment, and to remember the claims of his son Cabell.

Back in camp, rumor finally gave way to reality on April 21, 1863, as the troops moved out under Major Flournoy for a rendezvous with Jones's other units at Brock's Gap that initiated a raid none of the participants soon forgot.

General Jones, in conjunction with another column under Gen. John D. Imboden, had determined to poke his own nose into some Yankee tents in Western Virginia. The goal of this expedition was the disruption of the Baltimore and Ohio Railroad. On the second day out, Lieutenant Colonel Green assumed command of the 6th Cavalry.

Rainy weather soon forced a change of plans and a proposed crossing of the South Branch of the Potomac at Moorefield was frustrated by the raging torrent that watercourse had become. The small infantry and artillery support and the wagons traveling with the command were ordered to proceed no farther. Jones made a detour to nearby Petersburg, in the hope that the ford there would prove more feasible.

The swollen South Branch at Petersburg was almost as daunting as at Moorefield, and brought out a special brand of courage. The horsemen took great care to follow precisely the right path across. Several citizens of the area braved the waters to station themselves at intervals and to shepherd the Rebel band over.

The 6th Cavalry was the lead regiment, and it watched in horror as

Pvt. William Evans of Company F was swept to this death. At this juncture, Chaplain Davis rode boldly out into the middle of the rushing river and stationed himself there, earnestly praying for the safe passage of the troops until every man was over. The cleric's behavior inspired all who saw it, and won him admiring mention in the reports of the brigade commander.

On April 25, the day after the crossing, the raiders were unexpectedly delayed by a force of 83 stubborn Federals at Greenland Gap. Captain Martin Wallace of the 23d Illinois Infantry refused a series of requests to surrender, and did not give up until the Confederates set fire to the log church in which most of his men were sheltered. Jones suffered 42 casualties in the assaults on the defenders, but only one of these (surgeon James S. Lewis) was in the 6th Cavalry. Speed being essential to success, the raiders pressed on.

At 2 p.m. of the day following the Greenland Gap fight, Jones and his command (minus the 12th Cavalry, a squadron of the 11th, Brown's Maryland Battalion, and McNeill's company of Partisan Rangers) arrived at the Baltimore and Ohio Railroad bridge over the Cheat River near Rowlesburg. The detached troops had been sent to burn various bridges; Jones intended to inflict a similar fate on the Cheat River structure.

To his dismay, his plans were stymied by Lieutenant Colonel Green, who (in Jones's version) "allowed himself to be stopped by less than 20 men," and a similarly feeble performance by Capt. O. T. Weems of the 11th Cavalry. John N. Opie recalled the affair differently. According to Opie (who was present) Jones amended his original order to Green to capture Rowlesburg immediately after taking the bridge when a guide pointed out that the town was five miles from the bridge. Opie testified that Jones asserted that Green's horses were in no condition to make a charge of five miles. He then revised his instructions so that after surprising the bridge guard, Green would approach the town cautiously and would be supported by the brigade.

Whatever the truth of the matter, the Federals were not taken by surprise at Rowlesburg. They were dug in on the nearby heights, and put up a stiff resistance when charged by the dismounted men of the 6th Cavalry. Opie and some half dozen of his comrades were diverted by an abandoned meal in a house they entered, and when they emerged their brigade was gone. It was all they could do to reach the safety of the departing Rebel column. The Cheat River bridge stood unscathed, but the affair was not forgotten; Jones eventually filed charges of disobedience against Green. It was not until September 17 that a court-martial acquitted him.

Jones had more than Green's shortcomings to worry about. Food for man and beast was hard to come by. No word had been heard from General Imboden, and the countryside was alive with tales of superior forces gathering to crush him. Luckily, subsistence turned up at Evansville and word arrived of the success of Colonel Harman's sideforay at Oakland and Altamont.

At Morgantown on April 28 the 6th Cavalry had an exceedingly close call. It was leading the way onto the suspension bridge above the Monongahela River. When the head of the column reached the middle of the span, the center of the bridge slipped down, causing it to shift from its supports at either end, and leaving it precariously suspended by cables alone.

The horses staggered as if drunk, and for a time it looked like the whole concern would plunge 60 feet into the gorge below. A halt was called, the horsemen proceeded with great care, and disaster was averted. The bridge was not destroyed by the raiders, presumably because they regarded it as a greater hazard to the enemy if left as it was.

A night march brought the column to Fairmont on April 29. In the foggy morning the defenders were surrounded, charged by sharpshooters of the 6th and part of the 7th Cavalry, and compelled to raise the white flag. Two hundred sixty-eight prisoners were paroled. Just as the surrender was concluded, a train bearing enemy reinforcements and mounting cannon arrived. A sharp skirmish ensued, but the Confederates quickly seized some of the newly-captured arms and recovered the initiative. A surprise attack by the 12th Cavalry persuaded the Yankees to return to their train, which sped away as the 6th Cavalry poured volley after volley into it. Jones, without elaboration, reported to his superiors that "Colonel Green again failed to execute the part assigned him."

After several attempts the 6th Cavalry, under direction of Lt. W. G. Williamson of the C. S. Engineers, managed to destroy the iron and wood bridge over the Monongahela at Fairmont with gunpowder and flame. With satisfaction, Jones recorded that the bridge had taken a half million dollars and more than two years to construct. He reported the casualties of the 6th Cavalry at Fairmont as three wounded.

Bridgeport fell the following day, but 6th Cavalry participation was limited to some sharpshooting and throwing out pickets. Captain William T. Mitchell's Company E, again under the direction of Williamson, set fire to the trestling a half-mile above Bridgeport.

As the raiders penetrated farther and farther into the seemingly endless mountains, they became increasingly aware of vicious bushwhackers who sniped at them and lay in wait for stragglers. Known as "swamp dragons," the guerrillas actually provided the jaded column with amusement of a sort, as it watched the Confederate mountaineers of Witcher's Battalion ascend to nearby heights to chastise them. When a soldier asked Jones's permission to kill one of the irregulars, the general responded, "You should never have taken him alive, but since you have brought him to me, he shall be treated as a prisoner of war."

The Virginia cavalrymen were appalled by the conditions they found in the mountains. John C. Donohoe of Company K confided to his diary that "ignorance & poverty prevailed to a greater extent than it has ever been my pain to witness." Lieutenant Mann informed his wife that "I don't think I ever saw as many children before[.] nearly every woman I saw over fourteen had a child in her arms[.]" Donohoe was astonished that several of the people he met professed not to know what county they lived in, though not at all such lack of knowledge was genuine. When a Confederate officer questioned young Alf Greathouse, the lad pointed to his ears and mouth and shook his head to show that he was deaf and dumb. As the intruders left, one remarked, "Now there is a typical Goddamned Yankee for you. They can see a little, but they are all dumb as hell." Greathouse related the incident with obvious relish.

At Philippi, the 6th Cavalry was detached to watch over the horses and cattle as they proceeded to Beverly. Jones, with the main column, rested two days at Weston, during which the 6th Cavalry rejoined. Leaving Weston, the men marched all afternoon in a pouring rain, and Chaplain Davis averred that "the vision of home & wife & children, dressing gown & slippers, a couch and a warm fire, with a hot supper to boot, rose before me with a distinctness that was tantalizing." Davis carried with him some calico he had just bought for his wife; thoughts of home were natural for the chaplain.

The culmination of the expedition came on May 9 when the troops arrived at Burning Springs (known to the Confederates as Oil Town) in Wirt County. Lieutenant Mann stated that some of the men went to within eight miles of Ohio. Dozens of oil wells used to produce kerosene for lighting and for lubrication of machinery were located at Burning Springs. Jones declared that the property of Southern men in this boomtown had been expropriated by Northerners and the Federal government.

When a lack of funds foiled an effort to ransom the place, the oil wells and hundreds of barrels filled with the substance on nearby boats were set ablaze. As the oil from the boats spilled out over the Little Kanawha River, the river, too, caught fire. The spectacle illuminated the night and burned itself into the memories of all who saw it. Visions of the infernal regions were well-nigh universal.

Not only did the oil burn, but so did various nearby dwellings and the notorious Chicago House, the mainstay of local prostitution. The Chicago House was rebuilt in 1865, but charred underwater stumps bore evidence of the mighty conflagration well into the twentieth century. Around 150,000 barrels of oil were consumed, and the whiskey supply of nearby saloons suffered almost as greatly.

The return trip was described by Chaplain Davis as without interest. Northern newspapers obtained in Wirt County informed the men of the victory at Chancellorsville. The return journey also brought the depressing news of Stonewall Jackson's death. The West Virginia raid had been grueling, with continuous forced marches, and a commisariat so unreliable that Lt. Mann was forced at one time to eat raw bacon. Many horses had been secured, bridges and tunnels destroyed, and prisoners paroled, but by the time the regiment reached its old camp near Mt. Crawford on May 22 the trains of the Baltimore and Ohio had already resumed their former routes, and John Opie styled the whole enterprise a "fruitless and unimportant raid." The regiment's total losses were fewer than a dozen. Lieutenant Mann could truthfully inform his wife that "We whipped every time and drove them before us," but it would take more than this trek to redeem the regiment's reputation.

With the brigade safely back at Camp Ashby, the 6th enjoyed a brief reprieve from the rigors of campaigning. A "tabular statement" of the cavalry division at this time discloses that Green, Cabell Flournoy, and Throckmorton were acting as colonel, lieutenant colonel, and major, respectively, although not yet appointed. On May 24 General Jones finally issued an order for a board to convene to examine officers of the 6th Cavalry entitled to promotion as field officers. The board consisted of Col. A. W. Harman of the 12th Cavalry and Col. Lunsford L. Lomax and Lt. Col. O. R. Funsten of the 11th Cavalry. They began deliberations three days later. The record of the board's proceedings provides an unparalleled look at the circumstances of the regiment.

The May 27 meeting was uneventful, and was devoted to the examination of Lt. Col. Green, Major Flournoy, and senior Captain Throckmorton of Company F on proficiency in cavalry tactics and regulations. Green and Flournoy were found capable enough to command the regiment, while Throckmorton was pronounced "sufficiently conversant to perform the ordinary duties of an officer."

The heart of the business began at 4 p.m. the next day when four company officers of A, B, and D, plus acting quartermaster Robert Carter were asked a series of questions about Green's performance and the condition of the regiment in the presence of Green. There were usually nine questions, though Capt. D. T. Richards of Company D got 19. Some of them were, "What is your opinion as to the efficiency of the 6th Va. Cav. under Lt. Col. Green, cmdg.?; What is the feeling of the officers of the regt. as to the present cmdg. officer?; Is there a want of discipline...due to... Lt. Col. Green? Has [he] ... paid the proper attention to drills and the interior police of the regt.?; Does [he] show the proper energy in providing for the regt.?; and Has not a feeling arisen in your regiment resulting from the non-appointment of field officers subversive of discipline?"

The following day a lieutenant of Company H and one from Company I were interrogated about Green. The testimony suggested that the discipline, efficiency, and condition of the regiment had deteriorated under Green because he was long absent from the unit on account of wounds or prisoner-of-war status. Everyone liked him personally, but almost all were dissatisfied with him in his official capacity. Lieutenant C. G. Shumate of Company D stated that two-thirds of the regiment would prefer to have the secretary of war ignore seniority and appoint the officers, though he allowed that if the commander had to be from the regiment, they would favor Green. Green was found wanting in energy and firmness, though when asked if his courage was doubted, the usual response was "never." Some doubted Green's ability to handle the men well on the march and in action. Lieutenant Shumate remarked, "I do not think he can handle his men well anywhere, from want of confidence in himself."

The board concluded that the former colonel, Julien Harrison, should be appointed to command the regiment rather than Green, especially in view of the latter's formal request that this be done. If that proved impossible, the board believed that Green should be appointed. It then went on to consider the case of Major Flournoy, who was also allowed to be present, and in fact, allowed to cross-examine the witnesses.

Eight officers, beginning with Green, testified about the major. Green thought him efficient, but discerned a prejudice against him, and thought that the "murmurings of the men" showed a want of discipline when they were under him. Green admitted that he had heard Flournoy's courage doubted, but cross-examination and later testimony made clear that this was because the major had left the center of the regiment during the Paris fight, on Lt. John W. Woolfolk's advice, to stop stragglers. Flournoy had returned to rally the men and his bravery at Cedarville and Madison Court House was noted. He seems to have drilled the men well enough and kept up the unit's strength, but failed when it came to enforcing discipline and interior police, and in looking after the wants of the men.

Captain Carter felt there was not enough respect for Flournoy for him to be efficient. The board concluded that the major should be relieved from duty with the regiment "as soon as practicable" and that he be assigned to other duties. With that it adjourned, "to meet east of the Blue Ridge. . . the Brigade having marched and it being impossible to retain witnesses."

Jones and his men were ordered to join Stuart in Culpeper County, despite an effort by the latter to get his old adversary transferred to the infantry. The journal eastward was somewhat delayed in the vicinity of Brown's Gap by a hunt for deserters and others who were terrorizing the inhabitants of northwestern Albemarle County. The march resumed, however, and on June 3 the outfit encamped near Brandy Station in time to participate with the other units of the brigade in the grand review held there.

All the pomp and circumstance of "glorious war" were displayed in this massive ride-past. Stuart, himself, and a host of civilians, including many ladies, observed the mounted might of the army. Mock charges against artillery firing blanks enlivened the pageantry, but other concerns absorbed Major Flournoy, now commanding the 6th Cavalry.

The day after the review Flournoy wrote to Jones. The action of the board in regard to himself, he asserted, was patently illegal. It disregarded the evidence in his case and reached a conclusion based on views not openly presented. He had, he announced, received assurances from a majority of the regimental officers that he was in fact quite acceptable to them as their major, and to prove it he forwarded a petition signed by 28 of them testifying that it was so.

He did not remark that the names of Green and Throckmorton were conspicuous by their absence. The outfit under his command was as strong and efficient as any in the brigade. If he was to be relieved, he said, the board must give its reasons; otherwise he would resign. For all its obvious importance to Major Flournoy, however, the high command of the Army of Northern Virginia had other pressing matters to contend with just then. The report of the board was put aside for a season, as other guns were heard.

CHAPTER IV
Brandy Station And The Gettysburg Campaign

The grand cavalry review of June 5, 1863, so pleased Jeb Stuart that he repeated the performance three days later. This time General Robert E. Lee, who had missed the earlier event, was present, as were some of Lee's generals. The vast display was again enacted, although with somewhat less exuberance. The ladies were absent, and there was no artillery firing. General Lee hoped to spare the men and their mounts from any useless exertion, for he had serious work in mind for them.

Lee's plans for the cavalry called for them to move north across the nearby Rappahannock River. But fate and the designs of the Federals intervened. As at First Manassas, Union generals arranged to advance in the opposite direction, and again, they were the first to move. General Alfred Pleasonton divided his attacking force into two columns. One was made up of the First Cavalry Division, a reserve cavalry brigade, and infantry supports under the intrepid Gen. John Buford. They were to cross the river at Beverly Ford. The other column was composed of the Second and Third Cavalry Divisions, assisted by another brigade of infantry, and was led by Gen. David McM. Gregg, who was to cross six miles downriver at Kelly's Ford.

Beverly Ford was defended by the pickets of Company A, 6th Cavalry, under Capt. Bruce Gibson. Just before dawn on June 9 Buford's men broke upon the startled sentries, who put up such a resistance as they could to overwhelming numbers. Buford was briefly checked, after which Gibson and his men rode hard for the main body of the regiment, which was camped some distance away at the Gee house near St. James Church. There they sounded the alarm. The horses of the main body had been turned out unsaddled to graze, contrary to usual practice for a reserve picket. It was with some effort that Major Flournoy was able to mount about 150 men and rush to hold back the enemy. Flournoy's men charged up the Beverly Ford road and to its right, while Lt. Col. Thomas Marshall's 7th Cavalry charged to their left. They met the Yankees in the woods between the ford and the church, but could not hold them for long. After a fierce fight at close quarters, the Virginians fell back.

Then a show of singular valor occurred. Lieutenant R. O. Allen of Company D spotted Col. Benjamin F. ("Grimes") Davis urging on the 8th New York Cavalry, the lead element of his attacking brigade. Davis was a tough regular originally from Alabama who had gained distinction by saving the Federal cavalry from capture at Harpers Ferry the previous fall.

**OPENING PHASE
BATTLE OF BRANDY STATION
JUNE 9, 1863**

(Based on research by C. Bud Hall)

Allen could see that the Union officer was unaware that the Confederate was so close.

With only one load remaining in his pistol, the lieutenant rode up to Davis and fired, narrowly escaping a sabre stroke from Davis. It was a mortal shot; the colonel fell from his saddle. Two brave men had met in single combat; only one survived. Sergeant John B. Stone of Company H and Private LaRue of Company D rushed to Allen's assistance, as numerous Federals came up. Stone was killed, but Allen and LaRue were able to escape.

As Buford's advance continued, the Confederate artillery which was parked nearby barely avoided capture. The resistance of the men of the 6th Cavalry (and later of the 7th), together with a few well-timed shots from Capt. James F. Hart's Battery were all that allowed the guns and baggage to withdraw in safety. The two cavalry regiments then retired toward St. James Church. The 6th Cavalry moved to its left to unite with Gen. Wade Hampton's Brigade, and the 7th Cavalry went to its right to join Gen. W. H. F. ("Rooney") Lee's Brigade. The remainder of Jones's Brigade then went forward through the space formed by the parting units and attacked Buford.

Jones sustained a heavy fire but rallied and took part in a series of attacks and counterattacks that became a general melee. Eventually the Federals pulled back and a brief lull followed. Two officers of the 6th Cavalry were among the slain: Lt. C. B. Brown and Lt. Jonathan Taylor Mann of Company I (the writer whose letters portrayed the Valley Campaign).

Stuart received word that Gregg's column had gotten past the defenders of Kelly's Ford and threatened to take the commanding position of Fleetwood Hill, in the Confederate rear. With no time to spare, the 6th Cavalry followed the 35th Battalion, as the 12th Cavalry, Hampton's Brigade, and other troops were rushed back in succession from the St. James Church front to Fleetwood. Again, charge and countercharge were the order of the day.

Captain Grimsley could hear the voice of Stuart above the din, crying, "give them the sabre boys!" Major Flournoy led his men in the capture of a section of artillery, riding in among the tenacious gunners to struggle with them hand to hand. He was driven back, though (in the words of his report) "in confusion." Flournoy's followers soon rallied. To the great good fortune of the Confederates, Buford was menaced on his flank by Rooney Lee. Buford did not attempt to penetrate his part of the field after its defense was stripped to save Fleetwood. A charge at dusk was the regiment's final contribution to the battle.

It was the close of a day of fierce fighting, mainly conducted on the part of the Confederates with pistols and sabres, in actions both mounted and dismounted. When the smoke finally cleared, it became apparent that it had been the largest, most spectacular clash of cavalry yet seen on the continent (and as time was to show, of all the war).

Major Flournoy, who fought courageously and as though on probation, was generous in his praise of subordinates when it came time to write his report. He singled out Captains Gibson, Richards, Mitchell, and Throckmorton, and also credited Lts. Allen and C. G. Shumate. His own performance had come under the approving eye of Stuart.

The reported casualties of the 6th Cavalry in the Battle of Brandy Station were five killed, 25 wounded, and 25 taken prisoner (several of the wounded men later died). Lieutenant Allen, whose bravery was so conspicuous, was pierced through the shoulder by a canister shot late in the action that disabled him for the rest of the war.

The Federals, for their part, had not gotten off lightly, but they had done more than catch Stuart napping. Although they retired across the Rappahannock at the end of the fighting, their mounted arm proved itself a formidable opponent in a way it had not done before.

The horsemen of Jones's and Hampton's Brigades had a few too-brief days of rest, and were then thrown into line again guarding the line of the Rappahannock from prying Yankee eyes. Stuart's task was to screen the massive northward movement of all of Lee's army. The rank and file showed their usual curiosity about their new orders. Private Luther Hopkins and his friends began to catch on when they observed a line of wagons of unusual construction filled with odd objects covered in white canvas. Soon they realized what was afoot: the army was again going across the Potomac, this time, perhaps, on a pontoon bridge.

It was the business of Union cavalry commander Alfred Pleasonton to discover exactly what Lee was up to and to report it to Gen. Joseph Hooker. Toward that end he initiated a series of sharp, probing cavalry engagements, beginning at Aldie on June 17 and continuing at Middleburg and Upperville. The 6th Cavalry was not among the units in the first two of these encounters, although elements of it, including Company K, did exchange shots with the enemy at the "Pot House" (now Leithtown) between Middleburg and Union (now Unison) on June 19. The regiment took position at Upperville on June 21 behind a stone fence while covering the retreat of another body of cavalry. Although their pistols were useless against Yankee "long range guns," the men stood up well to a heavy fire. One of the regiment was killed and ten were wounded. Captain Owen and the "fifth squadron" (two companies) supported the artillery and aided it and the Confederate wagon train in making a safe withdrawal to Ashby's Gap. Private Opie attributed to General Jones the tactical error that brought the Virginians within range of the Federals without the chance to fire back.

General Pleasonton, for his part, was directing the blue horsemen with skill and abilty. The continuous four days of fighting halted Anderson's infantry division of Hill's corps in its march and diverted Gen. Lafayette McLaw's division by prompting its placement so as to defend Ashby's Gap. The reports that Pleasonton sent to Hooker on June 21 and 22 were accurate statements of Rebel movements. Had Hooker's generalship been of a higher order, the Union commander could have put the information to good use.

Major Flournoy of the 6th Cavalry discharged his obligations well also. Chaplain Davis wrote to his wife from camp at Berryville on June 28 that "Flournoy has conducted himself surprisingly well in the recent fights & altogether." Old Captain Throckmorton displayed his customary valor, but afforded the command much amusement by the manner in which he habitually scolded his servants and those who tried to look after his horses.

Before Davis sat down to describe the operations around Middleburg for his wife, Stuart had left the 6th Cavalry behind so that he could embark on another operation that was to lead to considerably more controversy. Indeed, it was perhaps the greatest controversy of the war. On June 25 Stuart set out to ride north around Hooker's army, to link up eventually with Ewell's infantry deep in Yankeeland. Much criticism was leveled at Stuart, particularly for his supposed failure to function as the "eyes and ears" of General Lee and for leaving his commanding officer to wander blindly at the mercy of an ever increasing foe. But Stuart left Lee with the largest cavalry brigade in his division, that of Jones, as well as with Gen. Beverly H. Robertson's two additional regiments. Had Lee managed to use Jones and Robertson effectively, he could have learned all that cavalry could tell him.

The troops that were left behind were commanded by Robertson as senior brigadier, although Robertson's initial units were numerically inferior. Robertson had previously commanded Jones's regiments in the Second Manassas campaign. Stuart assigned two reasons for leaving Jones behind, one being the size of his brigade, the other Jones's excellence as an outpost officer. A more telling factor was the bad feeling between the two men.

Robertson was ordered to keep an eye on Hooker, to harass him, and to guard the mountain gaps. Ultimately he was to move on the right and rear of Lee's army. An aggressive spirit might have made a success of such a mission, but Robertson was not such a spirit.

Finally, on June 29, Robertson followed Lee's orders to join him in

Pennsylvania. White's 35th Cavalry Battalion had been detached earlier and now the 12th Cavalry was also sent off to watch the Federals at Harpers Ferry. Nonetheless, the men were in high spirits at the prospect of carrying the war into the enemy's country. Chaplain Davis observed that "all seem to look upon Pennsylvania as a sort of El Dorado." Jones left Snickersville on June 29 and united with Robertson at Berryville. The line of march was by way of Martinsburg to the Potomac crossing at Williamsport on July 1. Maintaining its position on the right and rear of the enemy, Robertson's command passed through Chambersburg, Pennsylvania, and reached Cashtown on the fateful 3d of July.

The men of the 6th Cavalry felt somewhat uncomfortable in their new role as hostile invaders. Luther Hopkins watched with wry amusement as an irate farmer threatened his raspberry-picking comrades with an old shotgun. John Opie, assigned to gather up one of every four horses he found for use by the artillery, abandoned the quarry in one stable after receiving a severe tongue lashing from the matron of the place. Lieutenant and adjutant John Allan's uneasiness affected him to the point that on the evening of July 2 he wrote a note in his pocketbook, directing that anyone who found his body should deliver it to his father-in-law in Baltimore (he wrote down the address), where a reward of $500 would be waiting. We can only imagine the feelings of Pvt. Pius Topper of Company D when after dinner, the brigade was ordered at 1 p.m. on July 3 to proceed south in the direction of Fairfield, Pennsylvania. Fairfield was Topper's home town.

As the brigade approached Fairfield along the Fairfield-Orrtanna Road from the north, it could hear plainly the roar of the guns from Gen. George E. Pickett's struggle at Gettysburg, eight miles to the east. Eventually the riders encountered Confederate wagons "skedadling" toward them from the south. Unknown to them, Union cavalry Gen. Wesley Merritt, on the information supplied by a friendly citizen some hours before, had detached Maj. Samuel H. Starr and the main body of the 6th U.S. Regular Cavalry Regiment on an unsupported expedition to capture these supposedly undefended wagons that had been sent into the countryside to gather provender.

The order of march of Jones's column was so arranged that the 7th Cavalry led the way, followed at an interval by the 6th Cavalry, R. Preston Chew's Battery of horse artillery, and the 11th Cavalry. By the time the 6th Cavalry arrived, Jones had ordered the 7th Cavalry to charge the Federals, but it had been driven back in confusion by Major Starr's troopers. Starr deployed two of his dismounted companies on either side of the road as sharpshooters. Four of his still-mounted companies remained in the road. The regulars were aided by a post and rail fence and the slight elevation that they occupied near the B. A. Marshall house.

ENGAGEMENT AT FAIRFIELD
JULY 3, 1863

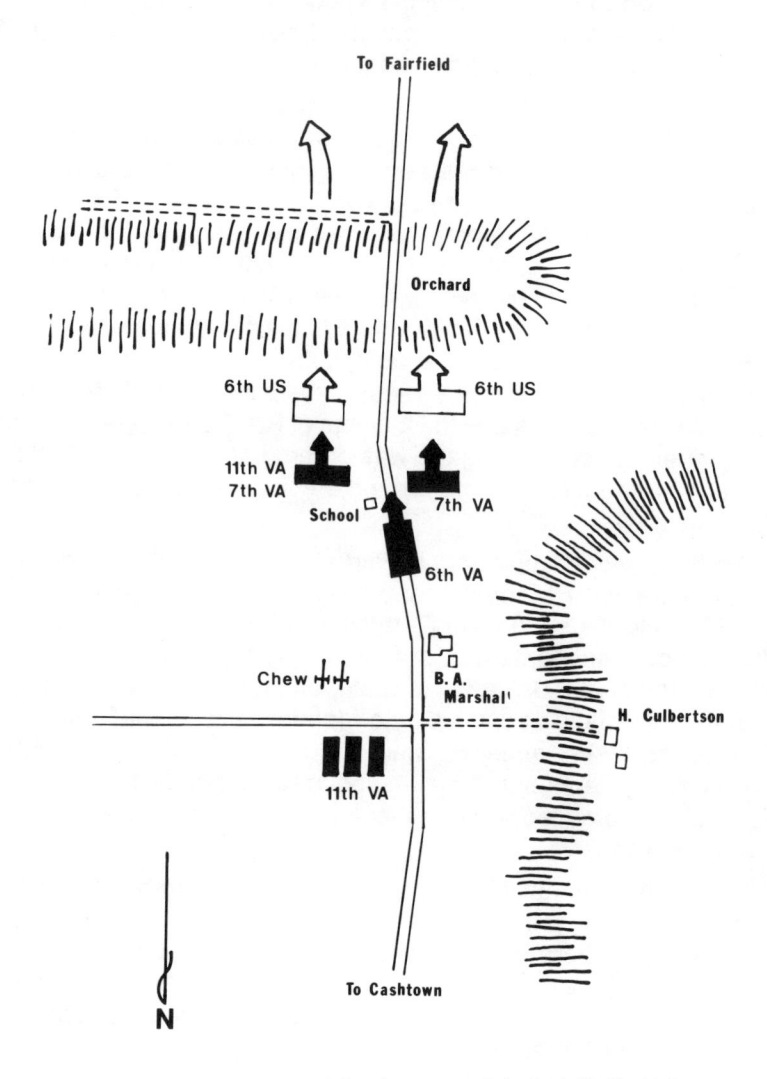

Confounded by the defeat of the 7th Cavalry, whose command he had inherited from Turner Ashby, Jones delivered a brief address to Major Flournoy's regiment as it arrived. "Shall one... regiment of Yankees whip my whole brigade?" he asked. The 6th Cavalry replied, "Let *us* try them!" And try them they did. The waiting Federals could hear the command "Draw sabre!" just before the assault hit them. At first the 6th Cavalry recoiled before the deadly fire of the dismounted men behind the fence, but it soon rallied and charged again. After a lively hand-to-hand fight, the Yankees were routed. Lieutenant Allan was cheering the men forward when he was struck dead by a well-aimed shot. The remnants of the 7th Cavalry took heart and joined in, as did Chew and the newly arrived 11th Cavalry.

The closely packed horses in the rear of the enemy added to its discomfiture. As pursuit went up and through the town, Ammi Moore saw that "there was hardly a fence corner along the line on either side... that was not occupied by a dead or wounded Yankee." Among the seriously wounded was the gallant Major Starr, whose leg was amputated as a result.

In his official report of this fight, Major Flournoy singled out Capt. D. T. Richards (whose Company D led the charge), as well as Captains Welch, Gibson, Grimsley, and Kemper for special commendation. He noted that Captain R. R. Duncan of Company B "sabred five Yankees, running his sabre entirely through one, and twisting him from his horse." The major put down his casualties as three men killed, 17 wounded, one officer killed and two wounded, and five men missing. He also stated that his men took some 150 prisoners. Pennsylvania may not have yielded the bounty the men hoped for, but it was an El Dorado for the reputation of the men within the brigade.

The Army of Northern Virginia was still on hostile ground. About 4 p.m. on July 4, as the regiment rested at Fairfield grazing its horses, one of Private Hopkins's friends spied a train of Lee's wagons moving toward Chambersburg and remarked, "That looks like a mice," meaning that such a movement did not follow a success. It was their first intimation of the calamity that had overtaken the main army at Gettysburg. That evening the brigade received orders to guard Ewell's train as it threaded its way through the narrow Fairfield and Monterey Passes at Jack Mountain in the nearby South Mountain chain. Along with darkness and a torrent of rain, a blanket of confusion descended on the withdrawal across the mountain. General Judson Kilpatrick's Federal cavalry, moving up from the south, managed to occupy part of the mountain.

Kilpatrick began to capture wagons as the cattle that were being brought along broke loose and clogged the narrow pass. Every few yards the wagons would stop. Some broke down. The Virginians were ordered to press on and retake the wagons (few of which, in fact, seem to have been taken). They advanced until the road joined the broad turnpike leading to Emmittsburg, Maryland. Jones, whose garb and demeanor made him easily mistakable for a citizen, became separated from his command, and he narrowly escaped capture. A Yankee battery opened up on the 6th Cavalry, which withdrew, firing as flashes of lightning revealed the enemy. Gunner George M. Neese of Chew's Battery met Captain Throckmorton coming down the mountain near dawn, with his men "in a stirred up condition." "A Yankee battery fired canister into the head of my command," proclaimed the captain, "and I am not going up there again until daylight."

Chew's Battery and the 6th Cavalry retired down the mountain. When daylight came, the enemy had disappeared, but the wreck of numerous wagons strewed the way. Some had fallen off the road onto the rocks below and others were cut down by citizens who turned out to show their sympathies.

Hooker's successor, Gen. George G. Meade, missed an important opportunity when he failed to send a more substantial force to occupy the passes near Fairfield, for the passes were on Lee's shortest route to Williamsport and safety. On July 6 the regiment moved by way of Ringgold and Leitersburg toward the river. The entire wagon train arrived at Williamsport and waited, halted by high water on the Potomac and a pontoon bridge that had been partly swept away. Kilpatrick attacked Gen. John D. Imboden's small force, but was driven away, as the 6th Cavalry posted a picket in the direction of Funkstown.

After uniting with Stuart's cavalry division at Hagerstown, the regiment marched to Boonsboro on July 8. It participated in a sharp fight there in defense of a battery, but was forced to withdraw behind Antietam Creek in the face of a Federal advance. At 7 a.m. the next morning, it was roused by the drums of approaching hostile infantry. The 6th Cavalry fell in behind a line of entrenched Confederate infantry on the left of the army and watched as Yankee sharpshooters and videttes moved forward. The anticipated attack never came. That night the regiment forded the Potomac. On the Virginia side it learned of the fall of Vicksburg.

Back in the Old Dominion, the outfit spent the next two weeks in the Shenandoah Valley, covering Lee's communications with Winchester. On July 15, below Charles Town, a small skirmish occurred, but a few shots from Chew's Battery dispersed the Union troops. As Lee's army strove to recuperate in Jefferson and Berkeley counties, Jones's Brigade picketed the swollen Shenandoah. In looking back on the campaign just concluded, the men of the regiment could take pride in the honorable, albeit remote, part they had played.

CHAPTER V
The Rappahannock, The Rapidan, And A Winter Respite

After the Gettysburg Campaign, Lee moved his army up the Valley to Front Royal, while Meade marched rapidly south on a parallel course east of the Blue Ridge. Meade then proceeded east from Manassas Gap along the line of the Manassas Gap Railroad through Thoroughfare Gap and then south to the Rappahannock. Lee managed to counter these moves by placing his army between his opponent and Richmond in the vicinity of Culpeper Court House. Lee's forces began to arrive around Culpeper on July 24.

Jones's Brigade was ordered to follow Lee's army. The 6th Cavalry rode to Front Royal and attempted to cross at Chester's Gap, but found the gap held by the Federals. It went south to Luray on July 26 and crossed at Thornton's Gap without opposition the next day. On July 28 the regiment camped near Culpeper Court House. A period of comparative calm followed, as the opposing armies watched each other along the Rappahannock line.

The main interruption in this lull occurred on August 1, when General Wade Hampton's cavalry brigade had a severe fight with a Union cavalry division. Hampton's men were driven almost to Culpeper, but were rescued in the afternoon by Jones's Brigade, two infantry brigades from Anderson's Division, and a battery. The reinforced Confederates pushed back their opponents across the plain which had been Stuart's reviewing ground and the 6th Cavalry came under a lively artillery fire until they were moved out of range.

Quiet returned, but the regiment was still kept in battle array, and Chaplain Davis saw an opportunity for some preaching. "The shade is pleasant," he observed, "& the men are unoccupied & not allowed to leave." As the days wore on, the opposing pickets began to fraternize, and a considerable exchange of goods and opinions took place. Confederate tobacco was bartered for Union coffee, sugar, and whiskey. A Yankee berated John Opie for the unfair tactics his side employed. "The right way," the man in blue suggested, "is to stand off and shoot, but" he complained, "you fellows run up on us."

When the guns were silent, there was time to attend to personal problems and a reorganization of the Confederate Cavalry. The record of the board for promotion of field officers in the 6th Cavalry was brought out. Despite Major Flournoy's good showing at Brandy Station on June 9,

Stuart was found to have endorsed the document on June 16 with a recommendation that Edward Dillon, "an officer who has served with great distinction as a cav. officer in the west," be appointed colonel. Dillon was a Virginia native and a former Regular Army infantry lieutenant.

On August 13 Gen. R. E. Lee inscribed his decision. Lee recommended that the board's conclusion on Green and Flournoy be approved. He opted for the reappointment of Julien Harrison as colonel, noting that a petition in Harrison's favor signed by all the officers except Flournoy had been received, and that Harrison gave "entire satisfaction" when he commanded the unit. The board had not authority to relieve Flournoy, but a special board to consider that step was to be named. "The speedy appointment of a Colonel of this regiment in respectfully urged as the evidence shows it needs one much." Lee believed the circumstances would allow the president to appoint a colonel from outside the regiment.

On September 1 Stuart placed Jones under close arrest and ordered his court-martial for using disrespectful language. Jones was sentenced to receive a private reprimand from Lee on September 17. On October 9 he was ordered to take command of the Department of Southwest Virginia and East Tennessee. Lunsford Lindsay Lomax, some ten years Jones's junior, was put in charge of his old brigade. Lomax was a West Pointer with Regular Army cavalry experience and had served in the western theater and as colonel of the 11th Virginia Cavalry before being appointed a brigadier on July 23, 1863. Stuarts' Cavalry Corps was reconstituted by a special order dated September 9, which placed Gen. Wade Hampton over one division and Gen. Fitzhugh Lee over the other. Jones' old brigade, (now under Lomax) was part of Hampton's command.

A week into September Lee shifted Longstreet's corps to the West to aid Gen. Braxton Bragg's Army of Tennessee. On September 11 Stuart reviewed the brigade now commanded by Lomax. No doubt it was the chance to strike Lee in a weakened condition, rather than a wish to punish another ostentatious display, that led the Federals to attack on both the Brandy and Rixeyville Roads on the morning of September 13.

The Confederates were forewarned by a local citizen. The front was first held by Major Flournoy and the 6th Cavalry, supported by a squadron of sharpshooters from the 9th Cavalry. The enemy was discovered to have crossed in force at both Stark's and Kelly's Fords. Beginning at 10 a.m. Flournoy began to fall back toward Culpeper. Moorman's Battery and the 13th and 15th Cavalry joined the fray. The strength of the attackers was overwhelming, however. Flournoy contested each rise of ground, but eventually he and his comrades were pushed two miles beyond the town. Cannon roared, women shrieked, and children burst into tears as the town was given over to the invaders. As the day closed, Stuart retired beyond the Rapidan River. He took such consolation as he could from the fact that the enemy's flanking column had failed to cut him off.

The next morning enemy cavalry appeared in strength before Rapidan Station. The 6th Cavalry watched as Confederate artillery blazed away at them until evening. Stuart assumed personal command of the field and Flournoy saw the chance he had been waiting for. He requested permission to take his regiment across the river and chastise the foe.

Permission granted, the major led his regiment in a splendid charge, squadron after squadron, against dismounted sharpshooters behind a post and rail fence. The advance was in full view of numerous infantry and cavalry not engaged, as well as Stuart himself. Though the end result was at most a few prisoners taken, the skill which which he handled his men won Flournoy the plaudits of every spectator. Losses in the regiment in the two days of fighting were moderate, perhaps two killed, four wounded, and 15 captured.

In the wake of Flournoy's spectacle, which someone immediately styled "the most brilliant charge of the war," no fighting occurred for several days. Lomax, who witnessed Flournoy's performance, was given a brigade in Fitz Lee's division on September 16 that included the 6th Cavalry, as well as the Maryland Battalion and the 5th and 15th Cavalry. That same day Julien Harrison at Goochland, unaware of Flournoy's triumph, wrote a caustic letter to Secretary of War James A. Seddon, reminding him of a recent interview and begging to be allowed to save a regiment that had been made "utterly worthless, reduced . . . to . . .chaos & wild confusion." He asserted that Flournoy was "universally conceded to be unfit for promotion." Harrison was also unaware that the court-martial of Lt. Col. Green was about to acquit him of all charges and specifications brought against him by Jones. Moreover, he could not know that on September 15 Stuart had written to recommend Flournoy's appointment as colonel for " *'extraordinary valor & skill'* under my eye at the battle of Fleetwood 9th June, Culpeper 13th, and at Rapidan the 14th (Sept. '63).''

Recent developments notwithstanding, Harrison was reappointed colonel of the regiment on September 23, 1863, to rank from September 19, and accepted the appointment the same day. A week later, Captain Throckmorton penned his resignation: "the Department having seen fit to promote an outsider to command of my Regt. thus stopping all other promotions in the same." This offer was not accepted until December 16. The captain explained that he was entitled to the majority and reminded the authorities of his sacrifices for the cause. On September 28 Lomax wrote a strong recommendation for Flournoy: "The officers of the Regt. are now much attached to Maj. Flournoy and have full confidence in him as a *leader. . . ."* Gen. R. E. Lee endorsed this letter with a statement that "I have been much gratified to hear of the good conduct of Major Flournoy, but it seems too late to rectify the proceedings in his case." From retirement in Halifax County, Thomas S. Flournoy wrote to a friend in Richmond, trying to get him to persuade Seddon to recall Harrison's appointment, although he must have known such an effort was destined to fail.

On September 22, in the midst of these paper battles, the war of lead and steel resumed. The regiment marched toward Barboursville, in the direction of a Yankee raid. Stuart was almost trapped between the Robinson River and the Rapidan in an action involving some losses in Jones's Brigade, but ultimately drove off the raiders. The next day the 6th Cavalry pursued this Federal force across the Rapidan and Robinson. Scenes of wanton destruction of farms evoked in diarist Donohoe a rebuke for "the brutality and baseness of the hated foe." After meeting only a rearguard, the regiment marched to Orange Court House. At the close of September, the Maryland Battalion was transferred out of Lomax's Brigade.

Now it was Gen. R. E. Lee's turn to maneuver. Two Union corps had been sent to the Western theater and Lee saw a chance to turn Meade's right flank and get between him and Washington. Fitz Lee's cavalry division was left to cover the main army as it bypassed Meade's encampment north of Culpeper. In a counter move on October 10, intended to discover the dispositions of the Confederates, Gen. Alfred Pleasonton ordered Buford's First Cavalry Division across the Rapidan at Germanna Ford. Buford crossed and headed west to uncover Morton's Ford on the same river. Before daylight on October 10, the 6th Cavalry, under the just-arrived Col. Julien Harrison, marched to drive Buford from the infantry trenches at Morton's Ford that he had just seized.

The regiment advanced against the Yankees to the sound of rapid firing nearby. The men dismounted and rushed with a yell on the Federals holding the breastworks on the south side of the river. The enemy was driven out of its position. When the men of the 6th Cavalry were reformed, they were instructed to lay down and hold their fire. For about an hour they endured a storm of shot and shell. Following this barrage, a squadron of Yankee cavalry charged them, but many were shot out of their saddles, and the rest withdrew in disorder. The Confederates now rushed to the attack and pushed the enemy over the river and into the fire of Wickham's Brigade. The men of the 6th Cavalry quickly mounted, forded the river, and joined in the pursuit.

The fleeing Federals tried to make a stand at Stevensburg, but were foiled by dismounted sharpshooters. The pursuit continued through Brandy Station. Kilpatrick's division appeared at the rear of the pursuers and they fell back to avoid being crushed between the Union divisions. Kilpatrick's men were soon driven off by a force led by Stuart which appeared in their rear. Kilpatrick was going at a rapid clip when he was hit by artillery fire on his flank which helped to increase his pace. Intervening ridge lines added a touch of surprise and confusion to the scene.

The arrival of Rosser and his 5th Cavalry inspired the Confederates to renewed efforts. They charged one of Kilpatrick's regiments in column of fours. Colonel Harrison received a severe wound through the thigh and was carried off. The enemy repelled this assault and six or eight more. The sounds of shells produced an unearthly din. To John C. Donohoe, "It seemed as though the fa[i]ries of the infernal regions had been simultaneously loosed to stir up carnage and confusion among men."

At length, the 6th Cavalry succeeded in holding the hill for which it had been contending and the appearance of Stuart, sabre in hand to urge them on, provided enough enthusiasm for the battered troopers to drive their opponents back across the Rappahannock. The struggle around the station lasted two or three hours. During one of the charges, Private Opie was hit by a carbine slug that passed through his wrist and came out below his elbow. The wound ended his service with the regiment. Lieutenant Colonel Green was now in command. He reported his loss as two mortally wounded, 15 wounded, and several horses killed.

The night after the battle the men of the regiment camped near Beverly Ford. The next morning a circular from Lomax was read to them, thanking them for their gallantry the day before. There was little chance to savor this recognition, however, for later the same day they were put into column and marched north across the Rappahannock in the direction of Warrenton Springs. The frightening nighttime sight of a vast bivouac disclosed to everyone's relief that they were on the heels of Ewell's corps.

The most notable event of this lackluster Bristoe Station campaign was A. P. Hill's disastrous and bloody assault near Bristoe Station on October 14. The 6th Cavalry skirmished and came under fire October 13, 15, and 18, but suffered no casualties. Sustained by a vision of bounteous captured stores like those taken in the summer of 1862, the regiment was ripe for disappointment. It found the Manassas area virtually abandoned and stripped of supplies. The return march to the Rappahannock line was only somewhat relieved by participation on October 19 in the "Buckland Races," in which Stuart trapped and nearly captured Kilpatrick's Third Cavalry Division and other troops. The 6th Cavalry was part of the force that struck the Yankees in the rear. Others under Stuart's command hit them in front, and were able to make a goodly number of captures during the pursuit. After the affair, Stuart's men camped near the scene. On October 20 the fatigued horsemen recrossed the Rappahannock and again went into camp.

Picketing and scouting along the old Rappahannock line occupied the next several weeks. On November 4 Lomax reviewed the brigade at

Brandy Station, and the next day Gen. R. E. Lee was the guest of honor at another grand review of the cavalry division. Once again, such activities seemed to call forth an advance of the enemy in force, but this time it resulted in no general engagement. The regiment fell back gradually, crossing between the forks of the Rapidan and Robinson Rivers on November 10.

In late November, Meade conceived a scheme for slipping past Stuart's cavalry screen by way of Germanna and Ely's Fords. Unanticipated delays and the vigilance of Confederate scouts prevented the surprise. The intrepid character of the Rebel videttes and exemplified by Lt. R. R. Duncan of Company B on November 24, when he ventured forth to capture several enemy pickets. Duncan ambushed the force sent out to account for the vanished pickets and bested an even larger party of the 3d West Virginia Cavalry sent out as supports. The lieutenant succeeded in returning to his lines without loss and with his prisoners safely in custody. In the process he inflicted a number of casualties on his opponents.

On November 27, sharpshooters from the 6th Cavalry drove back some Federals at Morton's Ford. This series of moves, part of what was known as the Mine Run Campaign, finally came to nothing.

The 6th Cavalry began to construct winter quarters in Orange County on December 14. The men did their best to make themselves comfortable and the familiar routines of picketing, scouting, and camp life again absorbed their attention. Chaplain Davis initiated construction of a log chapel under the watchful eye of architect Frank N. Wheat of Company D. The regiment produced both a singing class and a Christian Association.

Perhaps the situation was too cozy. Regimental pickets guarding the Robinson River were surprised on January 31 by a party of Yankees. Captain A. B. Carter felt that the pickets behaved badly, and came close to allowing the entire regiment to be captured. In fact, only six were taken. Chaplain Davis, on the other hand, more philosphically attributed the surprise to a fork in the road that caused the men of Company H who were responding to the emergency to ride past their quarry and into a trap. "On what slight things do the results of military operations depend?" he reflected. This was probably the picket affair remembered years later by Pvt. Luther Hopkins in which dense fog shrouded his narrow escape from capture.

In a letter of February 1, 1864, Captain Carter pondered the future. The men were in fine spirits, but expected the coming spring campaign to be the hardest yet. If they were successfull, Carter thought, it would be the last of the war. If not, only the Lord knew when it would end: "not during my lifetime, I am afraid. I am a soldier, in for the war, and if it lasts for 50 years, & I should live that long, I shall continue to fight until I am a free man, or until my children are free."

The enemy was still in the area. There was a demonstration at Barnett's Ford on the Rapidan, followed immediately by an engagement at Morton's Ford February 6-7. Stuart reviewed Lomax's Brigade on February 15, but before the Federals could make the kind of advance in force that such an occurrence usually seemed to elicit, the brigade was disbanded later that same day.

The order was to gather again in six weeks. The men who did not live behind enemy lines were to follow their captains to announced destinations in their home areas and to report to an officer regularly. Companies A, D, H, and K started homeward immediately. Some men were overjoyed. Others, like Captain Carter of Company F (the Alexandria company, well within Yankee lines) were not. "I feel like a fish out of water or a ship at sea without [a] rudder," he lamented. He wondered how, in a land denuded of supplies, he would feed himself and his horses, for no rations for either could now be drawn.

Perhaps he and his brother soldiers could take comfort in a resolution of the Confederate Congress passed February 15 that (like those for other units at this time) thanked Lomax's Brigade for its "lofty and determined spirit" in reenlisting for the war, and offered them "the lasting gratitude of their country." Others found solace elsewhere. Private Donohoe made his way to Leesburg and got married.

CHAPTER VI
The Wilderness To Ream's Station

The spring campaign of 1864 that so stirred the hopes and fears of Captain Carter began to take shape in March. Ulysses S. Grant arrived to oversee Meade's Army of the Potomac, and installed Philip H. Sheridan as his chief of cavalry. It was to be the 6th Cavalry's bloodiest season. It was also the occasion for its greatest achievements. Elements of the regiment began to reassemble at Staunton late in the month, girding for the death-struggle to come.

The rendezvous of the regiment was soon shifted to Ashland, north of Richmond, and there it assembled on April 1. Some of the men could remember that bright fall two and a half years before when the outfit gathered at this same place to first organize. Now rain and mud made Ashland a place of considerable discomfort. The regiment left it on April 19, but not before displaying its skill at a nearby tournament, in which its "knights" were reported generally victorious.

On April 21 the regiment arrived near Hamilton's Crossing, in the Fredericksburg area. The men established a camp that proved more pleasant. They busied themselves with church services and meetings of the Young Men's Christian Association. Some visited the renowned battlefield of Fredericksburg and toured the dilapidated town, although its stores were closed and many houses were in ruins.

General P. M. B. Young's Brigade put a seine in the Rappahannock River that supplied the men with fresh fish, the main staple of their diet. Young Samuel B. Rucker joined Company F while it was at this camp, and was taken to church his first night by Lt. William H. Thornton. Not everyone in the unit was of a religious disposition, for when Rucker returned he discovered that someone had rifled his haversack and made off with a peck of ginger cakes given him by his mother.

Another new recruit caught Jeb Stuart's eye at a review. Stuart urged Capt. W. T. Mitchell to get a better bridle for George Francis Miller of Company E, whereupon the boy piped up and pointed out that he was also without a gun. Before the day was over the needed equipment was issued, and not long afterward was put to good use.

Organizational changes were again in the air. The cavalry corps was now composed of three divisions under Wade Hampton, Fitz Lee, and Rooney Lee. Lomax's Brigade, together with that of Williams C. Wickham, formed Fitz Lee's division. Colonel Harrison's leg was still paralyzed from his wound and he was absent. Rumor said he was soon to be brought before a retiring board, but he was still officially the regimental commander. Lieutenant Colonel Green arrived at Ashland, but was withdrawn from the unit and went to Richmond on April 9. On April 23 he offered his resignation "for the good of the service," and R. E. Lee and Stuart recommended acceptance four days later. Stuart wrote an emphatic note that *"the service will be benefitted beyond a doubt."* Finally, on May 9, 1864, the resignation was accepted, and the lovable but inadequate figure of Green passed out of the history of the regiment. Maj. Cabell E. Flournoy was left to command in the strenuous days ahead.

The tactics of the regiment evolved gradually. The outfit was generally divided into five squadrons of two companies each. By the eve of the 1864 campaign, the men usually rode to battle, but dismounted to fight, with every fourth man detailed to hold the led horses. In the 6th Cavalry, one squadron (the "charging squadron") composed of Companies D and H, was ordinarily kept mounted and in reserve, so that it would be ready to ride into the enemy when the shock value of an attack by horsemen was called for. When it was time to retreat or withdraw, the men preferred to do so on horseback. The Yankees likewise developed a system that turned them into a species of mounted infantry, but with the added strengths of repeating carbines and a way to supply new mounts that did not require the men to return home and scare up whatever they could. The Confederate method, in which the men owned their own horses, and were allowed to leave the ranks on "horse leave" to get fresh ones, meant that the men were sometimes reluctant to hazard their best animals in battle. They occasionally succumbed to the temptation to remain at home once ordered there. Moreover, good horses were increasingly hard to find.

Riders prepared their steeds, good and otherwise, for a review of the division on May 4, but before it came off a horseman with well-lathered mount announced to Stuart that Grant's army had crossed the Rapidan in the night. It was time to sound "boots and saddles" and go to meet him.

The 6th Cavalry rode in column of twos until it reached a bivouac in the woods that evening. Private Hopkins took a few fish from his haversack, cooked them on his campfire, and ate them with a delight he would remember for many decades. Early on the morning of May 5 the regiment moved out to meet the enemy in the dense trees and undergrowth known as the Wilderness. Captain Mitchell instructed Pvt. George F. Miller in the use of his newly acquired firearm. "Wait until you see a bluecoat, then aim at the middle of him."

A target soon appeared, but Miller's first shot was a miss. Other shots followed. From then until June 11 the regiment was engaged in almost continuous fighting and marching. A series of dismounted withdrawals and advances in the heavy timber occupied most of two days.

The unit was about five miles to Longstreet's right and the men could hear the artillery and occasionally the infantry firing from the massive conflict to the left.

The mauling that Grant received in the Wilderness would have caused previous commanders of the Army of the Potomac to return north, but it failed to deter Grant. The 6th shared in the fierce cavalry fighting of May 7 near Todd's Tavern, in which Fitz Lee kept the Federal advance from reaching Spotsylvania Court House. The regiment drove the enemy for about two miles in the morning, but was forced back over the same ground later in the day. Major Flournoy reported that part of the attacking mass was infantry. General George A. Custer's cavalry division was also involved, and engaged the 6th Cavalry's charging squadron, which suffered considerable loss.

In fact, losses that day were particularly heavy. Joseph Donohoe of Company K, brother of diarist John C. Donohoe, was hit in the left side by a ball that passed through his lungs and eventually proved fatal. Another bullet hit Capt. Alfred B. Carter of Company F in the side, but he later recovered. Captains Charles H. Ball and Virgil Weaver were mortally wounded, as was Lt. William L. Fuller.

That night Grant tried to move his army beyond the right flank of the Army of Northern Virginia in an effort to get between Lee and Richmond. On the morning of May 8, only Fitz Lee and his men, including the 6th Cavalry, stood between Grant and his objective. Federal cavalry and infantry, supported by artillery, compelled the cavalry to fall back. But their stubborn resistance bought desperately needed time. When hope was nearly gone, Lomax decided that a suprise mounted attack by Company D against the massive array advancing against his brigade was called for.

The company was drawn up in line of battle in a slight depression in the ground, and prepared to sacrifice itself. The company historian, Ammi Moore, related that "at no period of the experience of this company in the war . . . was their courage and patriotism more severely tried."

Before the order to charge was given, the head of Gen. Richard H. Anderson's corps of infantry arrived. The infantry was placed laying down in a concealed position, but with open ranks to allow the cavalry to retire. Officers ordered the cavalrymen not to cheer as they moved through the lines of prone men. When the Federal infantry was within 100 yards, Anderson's troops rose and delivered a volley that stopped the Yankees in their tracks, securing the crucial position at Spotsylvania to the Confederates.

The field held by Fitz Lee's cavalry became the site of field works that were soon part of a long Confederate line that would include the famous Bloody Angle. That afternoon the regiment was grazing its horses a mile in the rear. They were in a position assumed to be safe, but a stray bullet killed Pvt. George Gilbert of Company E. After being relieved by Anderson's infantry, the regiment was moved a mile to the right, dismounted, and thrown at the enemy again. It was soon pulled back, however.

Sheridan failed to sweep away Fitz Lee's opposition at Spotsylvania and also failed to screen Grant's movements. He and Meade disputed the proper use of the cavalry. The result was that Grant gave the commander of his horsemen leave to cut loose from the Army of the Potomac, move around Lee's flank, and strike the Rebel cavalry. Sheridan began his large-scale raid early on May 9, but Stuart soon got word of it. He set out in pursuit with about 4,500 men. The force he was pursuing was well over twice his size and covered more than 13 miles of road from head to tail. Wickham's Brigade attacked the raiders at Jerrell's Mill and near Mitchell's Shop, thus notifying them that their incursion had not gone unheeded. At about 4 o'clock on the afternoon of May 9 the 6th Cavalry started after Sheridan, spending all that night in the saddle. The Federals moved southward along the Telegraph Road in the direction of Richmond.

At dawn on May 10 Wickham's Brigade crossed the North Anna under fire at Anderson's Ford, while Lomax's men forced a crossing at Davenport's Bridge. At Beaver Dam, the brigades of Wickham, Lomax, and James B. Gordon united and skirmished with Sheridan's rearguard.

Stuart stopped briefly at the home of Col. Edmund Fontaine to check on the well-being of his wife and children, who were visiting at the colonel's. He then left Gordon's Brigade to harass the enemy's rear. He himself took Fitz Lee's two depleted brigades under Lomax and Wickham and went to place them between the raiders and the capital. Stuart approved Fitz Lee's earnest entreaties for his men to rest for an hour and a half when they reached Hanover Junction. At 3 o'clock on the morning of May 11, the troops were roused for the march that would take them to the fateful rendezvous with Sheridan's troopers at Yellow Tavern.

When Stuart arrived in the vicinity of Ashland, he detached Wickham's Brigade with orders to move southward, and if the enemy were not found, to return immediately. Wickham's men encountered the Yankees at Ashland. They were consequently delayed while Stuart rode on at a gallop with only Lomax's Brigade to the junction of the Telegraph and Mountain Roads at Yellow Tavern. They reached the tavern, which was only about six miles from the Richmond defenses, before the Federals, at approximately 11 a.m. on May 12. The enemy soon approached, coming along the Mountain Road. Fitz Lee had managed to place Lomax's three decimated regiments in line directly across that road. Most of the Confederates were dismounted and placed along the sunken road and ditches in the fields. Colonel H. Clay Pate of the 5th Cavalry was in command of the men on foot. On the right, and somewhat to the rear, were a few artillery pieces under Maj. James Breathed, while concealed in a wood at a right angle to Lomax lay Wickham's men.

The first attack by dismounted Federals was repulsed, with Wickham striking them in the flank. Again they came on, laying prone for a time, only to get up and continue to advance. The tremendous superiority in numbers of the Federals was obvious to everyone. Troops to the left of the 6th Cavalry gave way, and Flournoy's men came under a deadly crossfire. Colonel Pate pleaded with the men to hold on another five minutes until reinforcements could arrive. No sooner had he spoken the words than a ball pierced his forehead and ended his brave stand. Each man looked out for himself as the mass of Federals overwhelmed the line. Some 30 of the 6th Cavalry were captured. Lomax appealed to the 20 or so men left in the charging squadron to rescue the imperiled guns of the Baltimore Light Artillery. Stuart waved his sword and cheered as the tiny band of horsemen under Capt. Daniel T. Richards struck the Federals "like an arrow from a cross bow." Two of the four guns (one with a broken axle) were lost and Richards was wounded, but the other two guns were able to withdraw safely. Lieutenant Charles Minnigerode of Fitz Lee's staff was freed from his recent captors.

General Stuart was mortally wounded by a stray dismounted Federal. The remnant of the 6th Cavalry sadly watched as he was borne to the rear. Chaplain Davis, whose brother Eugene was among the captured, described these events to his wife as "the darkest day I have seen since I have been in service." The same day Mrs. Stuart and Miss Fontaine did their best to give the consolation of religion to the dying S. Joseph Donohoe of Company K, unaware that those same offices would soon be performed for their beloved general.

The Confederates withdrew across the Chickahominy unmolested and took comfort in the valor that their two brigades had shown in the face of three divisions of the enemy. They also appreciated the value of the time that their resistance gave the defenders of the capital. Infantry from Chaffin's Bluff was filing into the northern defenses of Richmond while the fight near the tavern was raging.

The troops at Richmond deflected Sheridan and tried to trap him against the rain-swollen Chickahominy. He was able, however, to force aside Fitz Lee's cavalry at Meadow Bridge on May 12, ride eastward toward Bottom's Bridge, and escape. Later that day the Confederate cavalry struck the raiders at Pole Green Church, some four miles from Mechanicsville. A flank movement by Lomax's Brigade completely routed them. Here, Charles Cavendish, an English officer of the 18th Hussars, charged with the 6th Cavalry, killed a Yankee with his sabre, and had his horse shot out from under him, all within a few minutes of his reporting for duty.

Sheridan's column made its way southward to the James River, where it remained under the protection of gunboats until May 17. On that day it ventured north and succeeded in rejoining Grant on May 25.

It was clear that the 6th Cavalry suffered heavy losses in the series of engagements that began on May 4, but the original records are somewhat haphazard so that precise figures are difficult to compile. One reflection of the casualties was a nominal list that appeared in the Richmond *Sentinel* of May 27, 1864. This published list, while not entirely accurate for all individuals, gives a general picture. The newspaper stated that in the period May 4 through May 13, the 6th Cavalry had 14 killed, 58 wounded, and 35 missing, for a total of 107.

A letter from Chaplain Davis (dated on picket on the Darbytown Road, seven miles below Richmond, May 17) recounts the loss of officers that the constant combat was producing in the regiment: "Of our 10 captains only two are with their companies. One has been under arrest for some time & seven are killed, or wounded, or captured. Two are dead, three are captured & two are wounded ... Of 5 squadron commanders, we have only one left."

From May 23 to 26 Fitz Lee led an expedition to Kennon's Wharf with large contingents from each of his regiments to curb reported depredations by United States Colored Troops. If it was barren of success, it was also barren of further significant losses in the regiment. Major Flournoy's performance for most of the campaign appears not to have been recorded. He remained in camp during this foray.

On May 27 Fitz Lee was joined by the divisions of Wade Hampton and Rooney Lee. The following day these three divisions, soon to be officially under the command of Hampton, marched to the vicinity of Haw's Shop to discover the position of Grant's main army. At about this time Major Flournoy remarked to one of his officers while standing before his campfire, "I don't believe the bullet that is to kill me has yet been molded." His "extraordinary valor & skill" at Fleetwood Hill, Culpeper, and Rapidan that expunged the stain of Paris now sounded more like recklessness. Perhaps that trait had been there all along.

Fitz Lee received orders on May 29 to move to Altee's Station, and on the next day to Mechanicsville. He relieved Butler's Brigade of South Carolina Cavalry at Cold Harbor on May 31. That afternoon at 3:30 he was attacked by Torbert's Federal cavalry division. Torbert was repulsed, and Lee was reinforced by three infantry regiments of Clingman's Brigade from Hoke's division. The enemy force was reinforced too, and renewed its assault in an attempt to gain an advantageous position. An obstinate three-hour fight followed.

Major Flournoy reportedly mounted the breastworks behind which his men were firing and invited the Yankees to come out into the open. An enemy bullet went through his body, killing him as he bid his foes defiance. Fitz Lee epitomized him as a "dashing, zealous officer," and few would deny the characterization.

The Confederates were driven back a quarter of a mile. The remainder of Hoke's division came up, but by that time darkness had arrived and it was too late to take the offensive. The regiment lost about two killed, two missing, 10 wounded, and 11 prisoners of war at Cold Harbor. The command of Flournoy's regiment fell to Daniel T. Richards of Company D, a Berryville merchant. The date of the major's death was erroneously reported to Richmond as June 4, and when Captain Richards was promoted to lieutenant colonel some four months later, it dated from that incorrect day. For the period when a wound from Yellow Tavern incapacitated Richards, Capt. Daniel A. Grimsley of Company B exercised command. Flournoy's regiment remained in heavy skirmishing for two days after the major's death in the lines at Cold Harbor.

General J. C. Breckinridge's division relieved Fitz Lee's on the afternon of June 2. Lee was moved still farther to the right to keep Grant from crossing the Chickahominy downstream. Fitz Lee's men were near Bottom's Bridge from late on June 2 until the evening of June 8. Meanwhile, Grant made futile and costly frontal infantry assaults at Cold Harbor. The Federals also launched several diversions, including an advance by Gen. David Hunter in the Valley. Sheridan was sent to try to unite with Hunter in the vicinity of Charlottesville, and on June 8 Fitz Lee learned of the attempt.

Rooney Lee's division relieved Fitz Lee's. At midnight on June 8 the 6th Cavalry set off on a rapid, hot, and dusty march to join Hampton, who was already marching to intercept Sheridan. Fitz Lee reached Louisa Court House on the night of June 10. Hampton was already at Trevilian's Station on the Virginia Central Railroad a few miles beyond. The Confederate cavalry commanders were determined to strike the Federal force before it reached the Virginia Central at Trevillian's.

The Confederate battle plan for Trevillian's Station can be seen as a triangle. The apex was Clayton's Store, which Sheridan would be approaching from the east along the Fredericksburg and Louisa Road. The base was the Virginia Central Railroad, with Fitz Lee at Louisa Court House forming the right angle, and Hampton at Trevillian's as the left angle. Hampton's idea was to have Lee advance northward from Louisa, while Hampton moved north from Trevilian's, thus catching Sheridan at the apex. Hampton failed to reckon with the fact that the bluecoats already had possession of the apex, and he failed to reckon with Gen. George A. Custer.

BATTLE OF TREVILIAN STATION
JUNE 11-12, 1864
(LATTER PHASES)

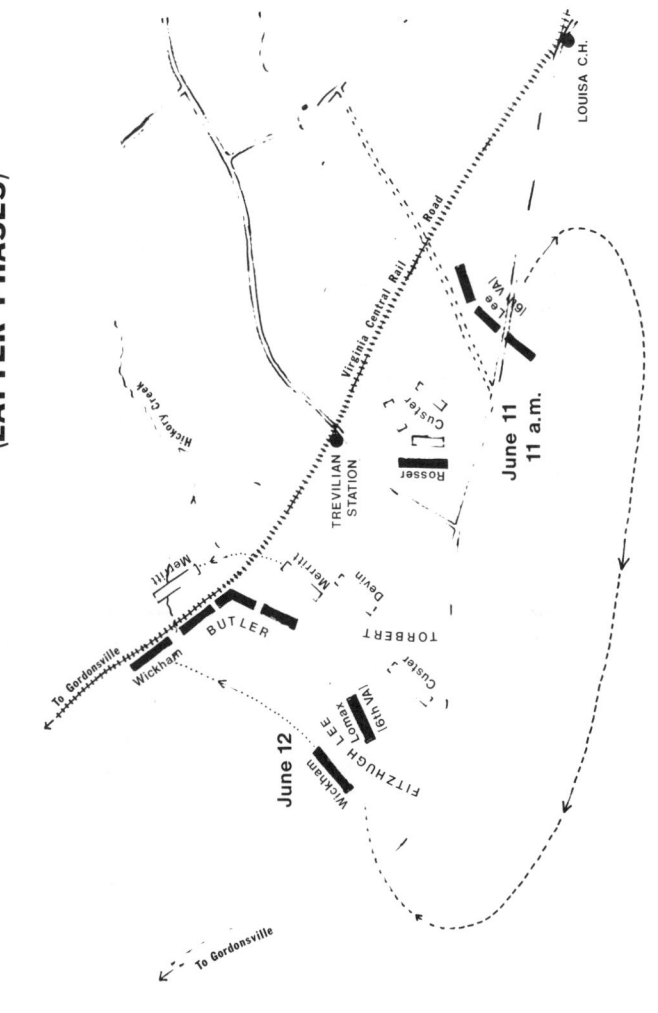

Hampton's men were in the saddle at dawn on June 11, and soon engaged with the enemy. Before Fitz Lee could strike his blow, however, word came that the enemy was in Hampton's rear. This was the Michigan brigade of Custer, which had slipped between the two Confederate wings by an unknown road. It was pillaging the wagons, ambulances, and led horses Hampton had left behind at the station. Gen. Thomas L. Rosser's Brigade appeared on the scene, charged Custer in front, and forced him back on Fitz Lee's approaching horsemen. Custer's recent booty was retaken, along with four caissons and Custer's headquarters wagon. Custer was reinforced by Gregg's division, which then pitched into Fitz Lee. The 15th Cavalry made a handsome though costly charge on Custer's rear, after which the 4th and 6th Cavalry, both dismounted, came forward and occupied some old hotel buildings commanding the road to the east. The 4th and 6th Cavalry stood their ground against repeated assaults, despite the galling fire of two Federal artillery pieces positioned nearby.

General Lomax ordered the battered but still responsive charging squadron of the 6th Cavalry to silence the annoying guns. The squadron, led by Capt. Joseph McK. Kennerly, moved out and formed at the edge of the field in which the battery was posted. The men threaded their way through a swamp in their path and galloped courageously toward the guns and toward a previously unseen dismounted regiment defending them. The Federals were temporarily overcome, but a nearby mounted regiment of Yankees appeared from nowhere and drove off the squadron, which had become disorganized during its charge. The enemy continued to occupy the vicinity of the station at nightfall and well into the next day.

Shortly before dark on June 12 Lomax's Brigade was taken from the Confederate right and moved in a wide arc to the extreme left. It formed at a right angle to the Confederate line on the railroad. In the darkness the brigade struck the enemy and doubled him up. This dismounted attack on the Yankee flank and rear seemed to John C. Donohoe "one of those sublime spectacles sometimes witnessed on the battlefield. Amid the surrounding gloom," he wrote, "could be seen a constant stream of fire from our lines as we advanced with victorious shouts upon the bewildered foe. Again the air was illuminated by the flash of opposing batteries as they belched forth their terrible thunders at each other while screaming shells traced fiercy arches through the air and bursting, scattered fire and death around."

The enemy was routed, but troops on the right failed to advance in coordination with the flank attack, and the men of the 6th Cavalry began to suffer more from the fire of Confederate guns than from those of the enemy. The confusion and darkness saved the raiders. In the morning the victorious Virginians found their opponents had retreated during the night into Orange County. Losses of the regiment were about five killed, 13 wounded, and seven captured.

In addition to a battlefield triumph, the Confederates garnered Custer's romantic correspondence, which they read, some with amusement, others with shock. Chaplain Davis declared that the letters painted "an odious picture of the state of morals in Dett. [Detroit]."

Fitz Lee's troopers followed Sheridan's retreating column through Spotsylvania, Caroline, King and Queen, and King William counties, but were unable to bring it to bay. The way was strewn with dead horses shot by the Federals when the horses gave out. The enemy had retired to the protection of his gunboats and earthworks at White House. The Confederates shelled the position on June 20, but found it too strong to assault. Sheridan declined to come out and fight the next day, so Lee retired to his old position at Bottom's Bridge, the same one he had left on June 8 when news of the beginning of "Little Phil's" raid was first received.

Lomax's Brigade monitored Sheridan's movement toward the James River, but did not participate in Hampton's brilliant victory at Samaria Church on June 24. The 6th Cavalry was assigned to watch one of the Federal divisions on the river road. It then erected and manned breastworks. On June 25 Sheridan crossed to the south side of the James; the next day Hampton followed suit. Fitz Lee crossed the river on June 28 and rode toward Petersburg.

Lee marched through Petersburg the next day and received orders to head south to Reams' Station on the Petersburg and Weldon (N.C.) Railroad. He watched for the Federal cavalry divisions of James H. Wilson and August V. Kautz. Wilson and Kautz had been busy destroying the South Side Railroad, a major communications link, but were turned back at Staunton River Bridge (an engagement in which former colonel Thomas S. Flournoy participated).

Hampton met and drove the Southside raiders at Sappony Church June 28, pushing them into two weak infantry brigades under William Mahone at Reams' Station the following day. Fitz Lee's riders arrived to assist Mahone about noon. Wilson was surprised by the arrival of the rebel horsemen. Discovering that he could not push through the now augmented force in his front, he decided to distribute extra ammunition, burn his wagons, and try to cross the railroad further down at Jarrett's Station. Before this could be done, Lomax dismounted his troops and maneuvered them into the Federal rear. The Unionists broke and fled to the right, hotly pursued by Lomax. Lomax called on some of the 6th Cavalry to save the burning Yankee wagons from the flames. The order was obeyed with considerable success, but the caissons had to be given up, as they were beginning to explode. Kautz split off from Wilson and his command broke up into small parties that made their way across country as best they could.

Lomax's Brigade mounted; the pursuit became a race. The road was covered with cast-off guns, swords, uniforms, and canteens. About 700 slaves were recovered, as were silver candlesticks, goblets, ladies' dresses, carriages, and buggies. The pursuers stopped to stare at a newborn black child, with no parents in evidence, among the wreckage. For years afterward Captain Grimsley wondered what had become of the child born under such circumstances.

At Stony Creek the enemy attempted to organize a stand. In fact, the pursuit was conducted with such haste that part of the Clarke Cavalry fell into an ambush. One color bearer after another fell, until Captain Kennerly, shouting, "Stand firm, men, rally to your colors!" eventually brought order back to the scene. The pursuit continued until after 10 o'clock that night. What remained of Wilson's command crossed the railroad at Jarratt's on June 30, but nothing on wheels escaped with it.

The month of July was comparatively uneventful. There was an alarm July 12, when the command turned out to repel a minor move on the Weldon Railroad. And there was a fruitless jaunt to the James River on July 28 through 31. The rest of the month was spent in camp near Reams' Station. The weather was hot and dry, and the horses seemed to be starving. There was enough corn for them to eat, but they could find no grass and few oats.

The tedium of camp life ended when on August 5 Fitz Lee received orders to report to Richmond with his division. At the capital, on the morning of the following day, Gen. R. E. Lee informed his nephew that he and his division were to report to Gen. Richard H. Anderson at Culpeper Court House.

The march began by way of Ashland, and continued on past Blunt's Bridge, Beaver Dam Station, Verdiersville, Somerville Ford on the Rapidan, and Mitchell's Station. The men arrived at Culpeper Court House on August 11, but hardly had they arrived when word came that the supposed destination of Alexandria was not longer practical.

General Jubal A. Early faced a vastly superior opponent in the Valley and desperately needed help. Early fell back to near Strasburg, and Fitz Lee's new line of march was to Front Royal, where "The Bloody Sixth" had been christened. The regiment headed out for the Shenandoah country on August 12, followed by Gen. Joseph B. Kershaw's infantry.

CHAPTER VII
The Valley Once More

The Shenandoah Valley in August 1864 still resembled the rich granary it had been in May 1862, despite the hardships endured by its people. Due to Philip H. Sheridan, the new Federal commander in the ara, that was about to change. And the campaign that General Early was about to fight, save for one short-lived moment, came as close to a reversal of Stonewall Jackson's fortunes as might be imagined. There was little gaiety when the weary men and horses of the 6th Cavalry rode into Front Royal via Chester Gap on August 14. The fighting and marching since May 4 had taken their toll.

Lomax had been elevated to major general on August 10 and his old brigade was temporarily commanded by Col. Reuben B. Boston of the 5th Cavalry. The 6th Cavalry was still commanded on paper by Col. Julien Harrison, and senior captains Daniel T. Richards and Daniel A. Grimsley functioned as lieutenant colonel and major, respectively. At the end of August Captain Richards was back from leave and he took over command of the regiment. Both captains were brave, true, and of long service, but neither had the ability of a Charles Field or the magnetism of a Thomas Stanhope Flournoy. Lomax requested the advancement of both on July 20, but the wheels of the War Department were slow in turning. Meanwhile, the wounded Colonel Harrison, in a letter to Secretary of War Seddon marked "Private," reminded the authorities that Lomax's promotion created a vacancy, and that while still unable to take the field, he hoped to do so in a few weeks. It was not a situation likely to produce optimum effectiveness.

The regiment participated in various of Early's feints and maneuvers in the Lower Valley, operations that gave Early the unfortunate impression that he faced a timid opponent. On August 21 the 6th Cavalry played a part in Early's advance, in which Torbert's stubborn Federal cavalry division was pushed out of its fortifications between Berryville and Winchester. Lieutenant John W. Woolfolk of Company I was involved, despite the fact that he had been discharged early in 1862 for heart disease because he was "unable to bear any excitement." The excitement near Berryville caused him a neck wound that put him out of service for some time. Captain C. M. Kemper sustained a severe throat wound. Three men were killed in action that day; two others were wounded. Another skirmish took place at Charles Town on August 27, but no casualties were reported by the regiment and more firing on the Charles Town Road on August 30 led to just two of Richards's men being captured.

Richards was formally appointed lieutenant colonel and Grimsley major on September 3, to date from June 4. September 3 was also the date when Col. William Henry Fitzhugh Payne of the 4th Cavalry was put in charge of Lomax's old brigade, displacing Colonel Boston. Payne was a Virginia Military Institute-trained lawyer and the son-in-law of an antebellum Alabama congressman. He had lost all of his property in Fauquier County to the Yankees. An inclination to find solace in a bottle made this bold former leader of the famed Black Horse Cavalry a less-than-ideal brigade commander.

For the first two weeks in September, the brigade under Payne marched back and forth in the vicinity of Winchester, often picketing. On September 15 Kershaw's division of infantry left Early and headed east toward Culpeper. Early filled Kershaw's position at Winchester with Ramseur's division, and established his headquarters at Bunker Hill to the north.

The 6th Cavalry picketed east of Winchester, in the direction of Millwood. The regiment held an inspection on September 17 at its camp near Milltown, just south of Winchester. The next day another scout toward Millwood proved fruitless.

At dawn on September 19, Sheridan, having learned of Early's weakness due to the loss of Kershaw, attacked Ramseur's left, in company with Wickham's Brigade. Rodes' and Gordon's infantry divisions arrived to stave off the Federal corps that were assaulting Ramseur from the direction of Berryville. Before long Payne was shifted to the right to guard against a possible move by Wilson's cavalry against the army's line of communications on the turnpike to the south.

With attention centered on the Berryville Pike, little thought was given to the ill-disciplined, poorly-armed, and shrunken cavalry brigades of Imboden and McCausland. They were acting under the direction of Lomax, and were left to defend the approach from the direction of Martinsburg. Both units were driven into headlong flight by the powerful Federal cavalry of Torbert and Averill. Payne was brought over to deal with this disaster to the Confederate left. His men charged in with a will and drove the enemy three-quarters of a mile, but were pushed back by a countercharge. Despite assistance from Col. George W. Patton's infantry brigade, Early's left disintegrated. Fitz Lee was overseeing the cavalry; he was wounded in the thigh. Chaplain Davis admitted the next day that he himself ran, but "in company with our whole brigade, general, Colonels & all, no further & no faster than they."

For a while it seemed as though the Yankee cavalry would sweep all before it, but the Federals failed to press forward immediately with their entire line. Early suffered much less than he might have. John C. Donohoe and some of his comrades halted near Newtown (now Stephens City), south of Winchester, about 11 p.m. The regiment's loss in this, the Third Battle of Winchester, was some two killed, 10 wounded, eight captured, and one missing. Captain Alfred B. Carter, who had been ready to fight for 50 years, was so severely injured that part of his arm was amputated, thus ending his active military life.

The day after the battle the regiment was at Fleming's Mill. Then on September 21 it was ordered to Browntown, in the Page Valley near Front Royal. After picketing there that night, they retired to Milford Creek early the next morning. Payne's and Munford's Brigades, under Wickham, proceeded to throw up entrenchments at Milford (now Overall), and then held back an advance by Torbert in a small action. During this fight Pvt. Daniel B. Harrison was hit in the middle of the forehead by a musket ball, which then passed out at the back of his right eye. Part of his brain exuded from the wound, but he managed to live another 39 years. Pius F. Topper, the member of Company D from Fairfield, Pennsylvania, gave his life for Southern independence here. Fortunately for the 6th Cavalry, it missed Early's debacle at Fisher's Hill, which occurred near Strasburg the same day, but its own humiliation was not long in coming.

After the successful defense at Millford that prevented Torbert from pressing Early after Fisher's Hill, the Federals pulled back to Front Royal, while Payne moved off to Luray. On September 24, Payne was told to head back to Milford, but before he got there he ran into two brigades of Wesley Merritt's cavalry, under Custer and Col. Charles R. Lowell, Jr. Payne decided to fight it out. He dismounted part of his force and placed it behind fence rails. Only three squadrons of the 6th Cavalry were present; these were arranged so as to support the sharpshooters. The Yankees opened with artillery and charged. A mounted squadron of the 6th Cavalry was ordered to countercharge. No sooner had it begun to obey than it was told to "right about" and attack a force on its left and rear. The force was overtaken, but soon another appeared on the right and rear. The officers told their men to save themselves.

Two lieutenants of the regiment and some half dozen privates, including John Donohoe, were taken prisoner. Among the wounded was Lt. Col. Richards, who vacated command of the regiment. Because of this wound and a subsequent bout with bronchitis, he was thereafter little heard from. Perhaps most stinging of all, a regimental flag was lost to the 2d Massachusetts Cavalry.

While Sheridan pursued his heartless and systematic burning of Valley farms, the regiment fought three small actions: Port Republic on September 27, Bridgewater on October 4, and Back Road about October 7. It sustained virtually no casualties.

Thomas L. Rosser was appointed to command Early's cavalry. He was stimulated by both the cruelties of the enemy toward the civilians of the area and by his successes in such skirmishes, so he recklessly led his own command (including Payne) and Lomax's into Torbert's deadly snare at Tom's Brook on October 9. At first he was successful, but Rosser was then forced to enact a Confederate version of the "Buckland Races" of the previous year. This became known as the "Woodstock Races": the regiment lost three killed and 10 wounded, with five captured. Rosser lost Custer's headquarters wagon that had been captured at Trevillian's Station. The cavalry of the army had become an embarrassment.

The Battle of Tom's Brook occurred as Sheridan was falling back down the Valley toward Winchester. Sheridan's evident intention of withdrawing and forwarding reinforcements to Grant's army inspired Early with a daring and vigor reminiscent of Stonewall at his best. He formed a bold plan to strike the unwary Federal encampment at Cedar Creek, near Middletown and north of Strasburg, at 5 p.m. on October 19. Payne's Brigade was assigned to accompany Gordon's infantry division in its carefully plotted path along the base of the Massanutten Mountain to the rear of Crook's corps. It was also assigned to capture Sheridan himself.

When the Confederate divisions charged among the sleeping Federals the surprise was complete. Almost all the startled invaders fled, with the exception of Wright's Sixth Corps. A generation after the war, Pvt. N. C. Fontaine of Company G related how most of a New York heavy artillery battalion surrendered to him in the pre-dawn fog before the attack was launched. Sheridan himself was not taken, since (unknown to Early) he was in Winchester. A squadron of the 6th Cavalry claimed to be the first troops into the Union camp. Many of the attackers fell to looting the tents of their well-supplied enemies. Private John W. Furr of Company A picked up a straight razor that became an heirloom in his family. Another member of the regiment declared that Payne sent a man from Company I to fetch him a canteen of whiskey and later in the day a bottle of brandy. This may have influenced Payne's subsequent direction of his men as they operated on the Confederate right. When they charged a wagon park near Belle Grove Plantation, the 5th and 6th Virginia Cavalry Regiments accidentally fired into each other.

Sheridan returned from Winchester in a dramatic ride and the Confederates faltered in their advance. The Unionists rallied to the standard of their returned leader. In an astonishing reversal of fortune, Early's troops were driven from the field. An intelligent and respectable member of the 6th Cavalry explained it by saying, "After we stopped, the officers took to drinking and frolicking & left the privates to take care of themselves; and they went to pillaging, and the glory of the day was over."

Early's infantry retreated to New Market. Rosser with the cavalry formed a line on Stony Creek, from Columbia Furnace to Edinburg, about seven miles from Mount Jackson.

The losses of the 6th Cavalry at Cedar Creek were five killed and about the same number wounded. Steps were taken to tighten the discipline of Rosser's horsemen. As evidence of this, on the last day of October a court-martial found a private of Company E guilty of desertion an sentenced him to four years at hard labor. Payne's questionable behavior on the field did not tarnish his luster with Army officialdom. On November 4 he received an appointment as brigadier general; he was 34 years old at the time. Chaplain Davis commented succinctly, "My pleasure in his promotion would be greater, if he did not drink so much."

Food for men and horses was scarce around New Market, so Early was compelled to take his men still farther south to Staunton, where they could be supplied by the Virginia Central Railroad. This produced a situation in which the officers neither could nor would restrain their men. The move to Staunton exposed still more of the countryside to Yankee depredations. Bands of the enemy energetically set about firing homes, barns, mills, and stacks of grain. They drove off or shot family milch cows. When Rosser's men apprehended these parties in the act of destroying the shelter and sustenance of women and children (which happened often) they could not be held back. Ammi Moore testified, "no prisoners were taken."

Payne's Brigade began a more conventional encounter with the Federals on the afternoon of November 11 near Newtown. The next day Rosser's Brigade was driven back in that vicinity by a superior force; Col. Thomas Marshall of the 7th Cavalry was mortally wounded. Payne's Brigade was called up, and together with the 4th Cavalry of Wickham, hit the pursuers in the flank and drove them, taking scores of prisoners. It was charge and countercharge "with an abundance of firing, bugling & yelling," but not even the seven-shot Spencer repeating carbines of the Yankees were enough for them to prevail.

Payne directed his men with bravery and skill, and was surprised to find out after the fight that Early was withdrawing. Perhaps the fallback demoralized him, for Chaplain Davis reported shortly thereafter that at that point the general was "palpably and notoriously drunk, behaving in a foolish and ridiculous manner to his bugler & couriers, and giving his Colonels wild and random orders, which would have destroyed his brigade, if they had tried to carry them out." The 6th Cavalry suffered Pvt. Edward M. ("Mike") Slaughter of Company B killed that day, and two other men wounded.

That night the regiment halted at Strasburg and built fires to drive off the cold. As Major Grimsley stood warming himself, young Thomas

Slaughter of Company B approached him and asked, "Major, was any body hurt tonight?" Grimsley's reluctance to answer was apparent. Then he finally replied, "Yes, Thomas, Mike was killed." Chaplain Davis did his best to comfort the stricken youth and recalled that Mike Slaughter had sought him out only the night before to make a religious profession.

The brigade marched from Strasburg to its old encampment near Timberville, in Rockingham County. On November 17 it moved up the Valley to Augusta County. The men were disconsolate; rumors were rife. Some said the brigade would be disbanded for the winter. Others talked of a possible march to Richmond.

Supplies were desperately short; something had to be done. The counties west of the Valley were known to be relatively untouched and to contain numerous cattle and horses. Thus it was to West Virginia (now set up as a separate Yankee state) that hungry Confederate eyes again turned.

On November 26 Rosser led his command, including the 6th Cavalry, westward through Brock's Gap. The next day they penetrated to Moorefield, in Hardy County. Captain Jesse C. McNeill's company of rangers skirmished with some bluecoats, taking care not to reveal the size and identity of the expedition. Rosser moved on to near Burlington, where he considered his chances for capturing New Creek Station (now Keyser). New Creek was on the Baltimore and Ohio Railroad, almost in Maryland. It was a tempting target, for it bulged with supplies used by Federal troops on their forays into Hardy and Hampshire counties, but it was hardly undefended. In fact, it was the size of the imposing Fort Kelley that had baffled McCausland and other Rebel chieftains who had thought to take it before. It had earned a reputation as "the Gibraltar of West Virginia."

The Unionists were so convinced of the impregnability of this depot that it worked against them. Payne was always eager for a fight and urged Rosser to make the effort. Thanks to a ruse, it succeeded. Twenty handpicked Confederates clad in the issue light-blue overcoats of the U.S. uniform led the raiders into the heart of the defences in broad daylight at noon on November 28. Miraculously, no one challenged them. The 6th Cavalry took one fort, riding behind Captain Fitzhugh of the 5th Cavalry. Before the Yankees knew what hit them, and with hardly a shot fired, the whole post was in Rebel hands. Those hands quickly turned to grasping whatever goods were in sight. Reverend Davis, who was there, described the scene:

> Many had bolts of calico, or flannel, or linsey strapped on behind their saddles, whilst others had hand trunks or carpet bags attached to theirs. Many had stacks of hats on their heads, and pairs of boots slung about their horses. Some had

pockets filled with maple sugar and nuts & cheese and sweet crackers &c &c. One fellow had a violin case attached to his saddle, & whilst one was playing on the violin, another was performing on the accordian, & very sweetly, too.

Rosser was alarmed at the disorder such antics produced and was fearful of a counterattack. He ordered the supply buildings torched immediately to put a stop to the carnival.

When the expedition rode back toward the Upper Valley, the men took stock of what they had accomplished. Some two or three hundred prisoners were brought back, as well as cattle and horses. The colors of the 5th and 6th West Virginia Cavalry, the garrison flag, and five guidons were trophies, redeeming the flag lost near Luray on September 24. The 6th Cavalry suffered no casualties whatever. "There has not been such a surprise in this war," the usually reserved Chaplain Davis concluded. Nevertheless, New Creek did not solve the now-chronic supply problems. The specter of starvation returned to hover over the cavalry of the Valley District.

The headquarters of Payne's Brigade on December 1, 1864, was on the South Fork of the South Branch of the Potomac River, 14 miles southwest of Moorefield. A table of organization of Early's Army of the Valley District for the day before puts the brigade in Rosser's division. It was composed of the 6th Cavalry and its associates of long standing, the 5th and 15th Cavalry. The 8th Cavalry and 36th Cavalry appear as part of the brigade roster for the first time.

By December 6 the brigade appears to have established itself in the vicinity of Centerville and Mount Solon, in northern Augusta County. At that time many of Rosser's men (although not the 6th Cavalry) were furloughed to go home and look after their famished mounts and prepare themselves for the spring campaign.

Alexander Maxwell of Company H had already given himself a permanent furlough sometime after recovering from a wound he received in the Wilderness-Spotsylvania Campaign. He was renewing his spirits as best he could in Maryland. He took the oath of allegiance to the U.S. in Berlin (now Brunswick) toward the end of November. Then he was arrested December 12 at Queenstown (on the Maryland Eastern Shore), splendidly attired in the uniform dress coat of a Federal officer. The Federal authorities concluded that he was harmless and allowed him to take the oath again at the Baltimore City jail. They banished him to the regions north of Philadelphia, which were undoubtedly more refreshing than anywhere in the Upper Valley that winter.

Early was doing his best to see to it that the dubious officers in Rosser's Cavalry were weeded out. The general directed that a board examine all officers of and below the rank of lieutenant colonel to eliminate those who were unfit, careless, or inattentive to their duties. Richards and Grimsley were scrutinized. General Payne was president of the board, assisted by Col. Thomas Thomas J. Berry of the 7th Cavalry and Lt. Col. W. A. Morgan of the 1st. These officers, in a regrettably brief report of their proceedings, expressed themselves "not perfectly satisfied" with Major Grimsley's efficiency, but concluded that he was "rapidly improving," and passed him at the rank he then held.

The next day they examined Lieutenant Colonel Richards. They put him down as "capable of making a fine officer," but lacking "the energy, decision, and as thorough knowledge of his duties [as are] indispensible to the commander of a Regt." He, as well, passed at the rank he held, but with a recommendation that he not be promoted to fill the vacancy "occasioned by Col. Harrison's being retired." A nameless War Department official endorsed this document with an observation that the matter of Colonel Harrison's status had not in fact been settled, and that the records as submitted were not full enough to comply with general orders. In truth, both Richards and Grimsley continued to chafe under a situation that denied them the possibility of promotion until Harrison was finally retired on March 6, 1865. Neither ever did advance any further in rank.

On December 9 it snowed. On December 10 the regimental headquarters was moved from near Mount Solon to the banks of the South River, in Augusta County, about midway between Port Republic and Waynesboro. Tents were pitched, fires lit, and the best made of what little there was. A roofless enclosure of evergreens served as a chapel. The supply of forage improved somewhat, but was still not enough. The horses posted down on the picket line near New Market were rumored to be "literally starving." Chaplain Davis opined that the cavalry would surely be disbanded, but noted Major Grimsley was joyful enough, having been granted a 20-day furlough that he intended to use for ccurting. Well before the major returned, the 6th Cavalry moved its camp again, this time to near Buffalo Gap, at Swoope's Depot on the Virginia Central Railroad (about eight miles west of Staunton). Company D's historian recalled that his comrades believed that despite their tattered and sore condition, they would at long last get a rest from campaigning. The Yankees, he ruefully added, had other ideas.

Custer's division marched south in conjunction with a Federal effort to move on Gordonsville and destroy the railroad there. The Federal column marched from Kernstown on December 19 and eventually reached Lacey Spring on the Valley Pike in Rockingham County. Rosser moved off from his camp at Swoope's early on December 20, determined to strike Custer. The division commander explained to his lieutenants that the size of his force precluded a daylight attack. He announced he would make a night descent on the foe.

After a miserable march in freezing rain, the Virginians did their best to surprise Custer before dawn on December 21. When the order to advance was given, Payne (described as "somewhat under the influence") strove to encourage a few slow starters with the flat of his sword. One of those he hit was the Reverend Davis, whose cry of "Chaplain!" went unheard in the turmoil.

Some of the Federals were caught asleep, but others were already stirring and mounting up. The chance to catch them all off guard was lost. Confusion was indescribable, as Federal and Confederate troopers, both clad in light-blue U.S. overcoats, slashed and shot at one another. In the end it could only be called a partial victory; both sides withdrew in the direction from which they had come. The 6th Cavalry had two good men killed and three captured, one of whom was wounded. The men got back to camp at Swoope's the night of December 22, only to be ordered out again at 2 a.m. the next morning.

This alarm was for the arrival of a force of Federals at Charlottesville that threatened the large park of unsupported Confederate artillery there. Payne's Brigade marched by way of Staunton and Waynesboro, through Swift Run Gap, to within 12 or 15 miles of Charlottesville. At that point it learned that the artillery, long accustomed to fighting without the benefit of the normal infantry or cavalry protection, had repulsed the Yankee raiders alone. They no longer needed help. The cavalry retraced its steps to Swoope's.

The brigade camp was soon shifted again; the remainder of the year was spent near Waynesboro. On December 26 Chaplain Davis expressed a fear that although most of Rosser's cavalry had been disbanded, Payne's Brigade would not be. He was correct. The horses were dying. Corn had to be hauled in from Amherst, eight days away. But the men were not sent home. By December 30 the 5th Cavalry had been sent to Rockbridge County. Rosser talked of taking what remained of his command to Highland County for forage. Only part of Payne's lonely brigade remained near Waynesboro.

The start of 1865 brought wretched weather to the camps. The streams overflowed and water covered everything. The arrival of extreme cold froze the countryside solid. The regiment marched to the village of McDowell, in Highland County. There were few tents available, but there was an abundance of straw. For a day or two the men enjoyed relative comfort in quarters fashioned from the straw and piles of rails.

Rosser, however, was not thinking of comfort. He learned that the Federal garrison at Beverly, in Randolph County, West Virginia, had accumulated substantial stores. Despite wind, snow, and ice, he was deter-

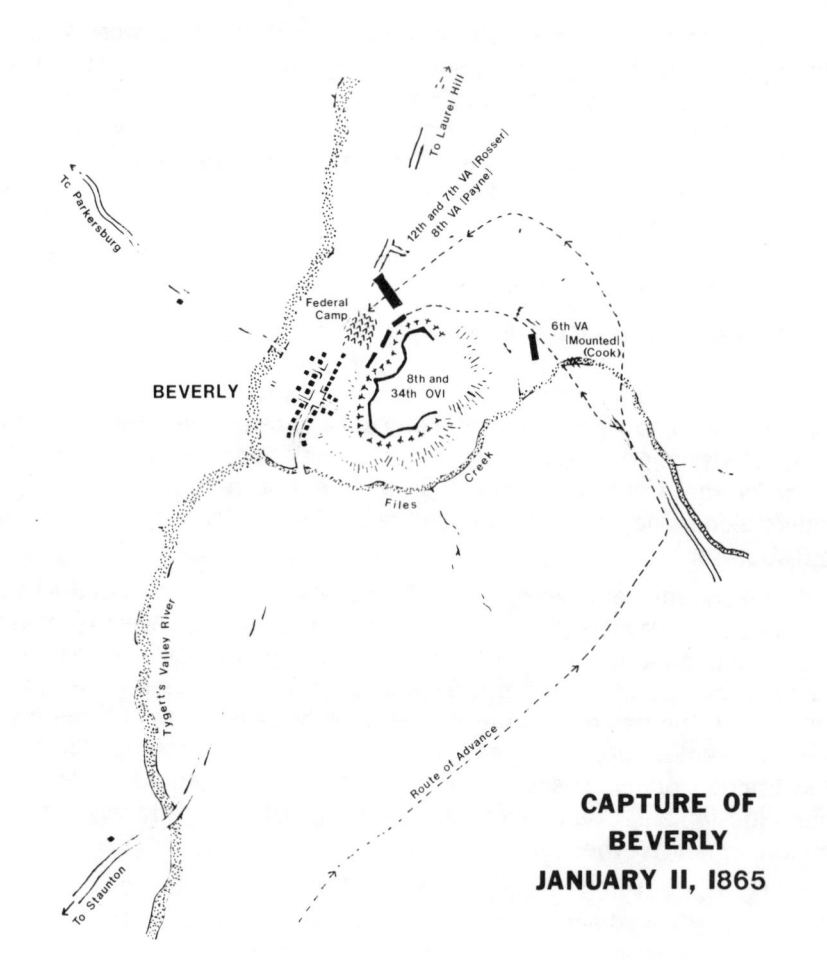

mined to get them. He rode out from Swoope's on January 7 and joined Payne (minus the 5th Cavalry) at McDowell the following day. Three hundred intrepid volunteers, under the immediate direction of Colonels William A. Morgan of the 1st Cavalry and Alphonso F. Cook of the 8th Cavalry, threaded their way over narrow mountain roads until they reached their target early on January 11.

The men swooped down on the unsuspecting Yankees. But that day, Ammi Moore recorded, many were "so stiff with cold that they had to be taken from their horses, their pistols removed from the holster and placed with the cock drawn in their hands." The Rebels burst in the doors of the huts of the garrison and received the surrender of whole companies of the 8th Ohio Cavalry and 34th Ohio Infantry.

Thornton Fontaine Hite of Company D had accompanied the raiders on foot in hope of getting a mount from the enemy. He was mortally wounded by a Federal who produced a pistol when roused. Colonel Cook received a wound that required the amputation of a leg. They were among the few casualties during the capture.

Payne's men took 580 prisoners. Their captors struggled to take them back into Confederate lines. When the men finally got back as far as Warm Springs on January 18, it was difficult to determine who had endured the most intense distress, the captives or their guards. Many were grievously frostbitten. The horses were so worn out as to make them useless for some time to come.

George W. E. Row of Company I wrote to his sister from his camp at Natural Bridge on January 29 that "Rosser has ruined our Brigade[;] we have not over a hundred men in my Regt." Years later, when Major Grimsley reviewed his experience during the Beverly Raid, he wrote, "I witnessed suffering during the war in all of its forms, but never any that was so acute, so intense, and so universal, as that which was endured by the Confederate soldiers, and Federal prisoners, on that occasion." It was his regiment's last trek to West Virginia. Those who were on it considered it one too many.

As Payne's Brigade was recuperating at its camps in Rockbridge County (southeast of Lexington) John C. Donohoe was told that there were only seven or eight men with Company K and that those were expected to return to Loudoun County soon. What was left of the regiment remained in Rockbridge County until February 7, when it was summoned toward Richmond for what would be the final campaign.

CHAPTER VIII
The Final Campaign

Payne marched his brigade eastward from the Valley along the James River. It took up its station a few miles east of Richmond at the Nine Mile Road. By February 24 its reports were dated "near Richmond." Although boasting on paper a strength of 2,730, Payne actually brought to the defenders of the capital only a few men to swell their ranks. He had only 497 officers and men "effective for the field." An inspection of this little band among the pines at New Bridge Church on February 28 was revealing.

When acting Assistant Inspector General Charles W. Digges reviewed Payne's command on that date, what he found was not particularly heartening. The 15th Cavalry was no longer part of the command and the 36th Cavalry Battalion had been detached by Early's orders since December 15, 1864. Since April, the troops had been almost continually in motion: the hard service had left its mark. There was no opportunity for drill, the desertion rate was high, and discipline was (as Payne himself wrote) "not near as good as it ought to be." Five hundred eighty-three men of the brigade were absent as prisoners of war. The horses still suffered for lack of forage.

When Digges focused on the 6th Cavalry, he found only nine of its 10 companies represented. He mentioned specifically only one company in the brigade, Company K of the 6th. That company, he explained, had been detached to collect wheat in Bedford County in October 1864 and no official word had been heard of it since. When it left, it had two officers and 20 men present for duty, four on detached service, one absent with leave and 11 without. Fifteen men were sick. When the commanding captain had returned with just four men ("the rest having left & gone home") the five were ordered out to find the absentees and bring them back; nothing had been heard from them since.

The situation in the remaining companies was better, but still bleak. Both Richards and Grimsley were with the regiment. In numbers, however, only eight officers and 96 enlisted men were present for duty, for a total of 104. Seven officers and 245 men were away on detached service; seven officers and 149 men were sick; 21 men were absent by authority and 139 without leave. Ten officers and 117 men were reported in the hands of the enemy. If everyone had been present, there would have been 684 (23 officers and 661 men). There was a bright spot in the numbers; no one was in arrest or confinement.

There were other high points in the regiment's turnout. Digges felt that the men showed a good military appearance and soldierly bearing. Their arms, though dirty, were Sharps and Burnside carbines. They had their sabres and pistols (though there were deficiencies in the number). Their clothing was in good condition. The sanitary condition was good, and it was the only outfit in the brigade to hold regular religious exercises. The officers were graded "generally efficient."

The number of men in the Yankee cavalry brigades was considerably greater, and they had a few efficient officers of their own. Sheridan crushed what remained of Early's army at Waynesboro on March 2. By March 4 he was at Charlottesville with yet another powerful contingent of raiders. He bypassed well-defended Lynchburg, and sent out the divisions of Custer and Devin north of the James on eastward-ranging errands of destruction. Sheridan intended to unite Custer and Devin, cross the river by bridge, and continue his devastation in Southside. The 6th Cavalry's job was to prevent that.

As the regiment moved to head off Sheridan, one of its officers received a remarkable communication. Addressed to "Lieut. J. D. B. Fout, Commanding Co. B, Sixth Virginia Cavalry," and dated from the War Department at Richmond on March 7, it read, "Move toward Columbia carefully, as a force of the enemy is reported moving down Rivanna River." This bit of tactical advice to a company grade officer was signed by Secretary of War John C. Breckinridge.

Confederate officials moved Fout's regiment to the vicinity of Farmville to guard the high bridge of the South Side Railroad, Sheridan's presumed goal. But on March 10, Sheridan arrived at Columbia, in Goochland County (home of Julien Harrison) only to find that citizens had destroyed all the bridges across the rain-swollen James. He gave up his intention of crossing. He decided instead to rejoin Grant by way of the White House, and directed his column north on March 12. The 6th Cavalry skirmished with the raiders at Ashland March 15, losing one man killed. Realizing that substantial numbers of cavalry and infantry had been sent after him, Sheridan detoured north to reach his objective. After halting several days at the White House, he marched to join his superior at Petersburg.

Company K had finally returned to the regiment by March 22, but counted only nine men besides officers. John C. Donohoe rejoined after being paroled from Point Lookout Prison. Donohoe wrote his aunts from camp near Hampton's Brigade, excoriating absentees who, "lost to every sense of honor, patriotism and self respect, are skulking from their duty at their homes and elsewhere at a time when their country needs the services of every man capable of bearing arms." It was a problem not only for

Company K, but for the army as a whole. The young trooper refused to despair, however. He took cheer from reports of successes by Hampton, Braxton Bragg, and Joseph E. Johnston. He reflected that "If we fail we will yet command the respect of mankind."

By March 28 Sheridan was encamped south of Petersburg. On that day Fitz Lee moved his cavalry, including the 6th, from its position on the far left of the Richmond defensive line toward Petersburg. Fitz Lee reached Sutherland's Station on March 29. The next day he met part of Sheridan's massing cavalry near Five Forks and drove it off. In the fight, Payne was wounded; Col. Reuben B. Boston of the 5th Cavalry took charge of his brigade. That evening Fitz Lee took command of all the cavalry, now consisting of the divisions of Rosser and Rooney Lee, and his own, now commanded by Munford.

All three divisions made a fierce, sudden attack on March 31. They pushed back the Yankees until dark. But these successes ended dramatically at 4 p.m. on April 1, when Warren's Fifth Federal Corps overwhelmed Munford's two tiny brigades positioned to the left of Pickett's infantry. A Confederate retreat turned into a rout. The Union troops had seized the key to the position of the Army of Northern Virginia at Petersburg and forced the evacuation of that city and the capital of the Confederacy as well. The operations around Five Forks on March 31-April 3 were the last important actions in which the 6th Cavalry participated. In their course, it lost one killed, three mortally wounded, 13 wounded, and about 25 prisoners.

Paradoxically, the regiment could claim victory in three actions during the westward flight of the army. Major Grimsley, who had charge of the outfit since Richards was hospitalized with acute bronchitis on March 10, remembered with pride his part in the encounter in front of Namozine Church at Scott's Corner, on the night of April 3. Grimsley believed Fitz Lee's report erred in calling the fight Deep Creek and in dating it April 2. Lee's report did note the "valor and discipline" of the troops that took part. Again on April 6, as the better known Battle of Sayler's Creek was being fought, the 6th Cavalry scored a success at High Bridge. Grimsley's dismounted regiment played a significant role in neutralizing a threat to the army's main line of retreat past Farmville. Finally, near Appomattox on April 9, the regiment helped to clear the Lynchburg Road and opened the way for Fitz Lee's men to avoid the surrender at Appomattox Court House the same day.

Thirty-one men of the 6th Cavalry are reported as paroled at Appomattox on April 9. Almost all of them were detached from their unit as teamsters, blacksmiths, forage masters, and the like. The best organized and most effective of the Confederate infantry to surrender on that day was the division of Maj. Gen. Charles William Field. As he learned that

Rosser's and Munford's cavalry were not included in the capitulation but had instead broken out to the west, perhaps he thought for a moment of the eager troopers to whom he had taught the mounted drill at Ashland nearly four years before.

Fitz Lee's thoughts were certainly of the present and future. Well aware that his men owned their own horses, and mistakenly believing that the terms of the surrender would not allow them to be kept, he expected to continue the struggle. A few days later he reconsidered, and entered the Yankee lines to accept the terms offered at Appomattox.

Most of the 6th Cavalry, too, abandoned the hope of joining Johnston's still-active forces in North Carolina. When word of Johnston's armistice of April 18 reached the Old Dominion, they came in to be paroled also. In the course of the conflict the regiment lost some 10 officers killed in action or mortally wounded, and lost in excess of 65 enlisted men. Seventy-seven men had died of disease, and two drowned. Thirty-one died in Union prisons. Not surprisingly, many were reluctant to acknowledge defeat, but gradually, acknowledge it they did. Most, regardless of hometown, were paroled at Winchester. On April 21 there were 17 who signed at that town. The next day Lt. Col. Richards and 35 others did likewise.

On Saturday, April 22, 1865, 26 year old Amanda Virginia ("Tee") Edmonds, of Paris in Fauquier County, traced three reluctant capitulations in her diary. They were her brothers' and a friend's, veterans of Company A: "Syd [Edmonds], Bud [Edmonds] and Douglas [Gibson] this morning went to Winchester, concluding it was the best plan since living within the lines. Oh! How they did hate to go; returning late, they were treated with great respect and kindness. That is something strange. Why treat Southerners so different from what we expected?" Then she added, "I hope it may be lasting."

Daniel A. Grimsley, a year younger than Amanda Edmonds, did not come into Winchester for parole until May 9. His six foot, two inch frame remained unwounded, although he had led the way in countless charges. The next year he married Bettie Browning, to whom he had been writing since he first entered the service.

On June 23 Julien Harrison, whose property had been assessed at more than $20,000 (and who was therefore in a special category) sought an amnesty from Attorney General James Speed. "I renounce and disclaim all right, title, claim, and interest whatsoever to any and all slaves now or heretofore possessed by me," he wrote. He was pardoned July 3, 1865.

A veteran of the 6th Cavalry who attended the 1888 Gettysburg reunion visited Fairfield and was regarded as a celebrity by his erstwhile enemies, but no other member of the regiment was there. Seven years later, about 100 former 6th Cavalrymen gathered at Fauquier White Sulphur Springs to commemorate old times. The men continued to turn out until old age and decrepitude felled them one by one in the new century.

Richard T. Davis was active in the Clinton Hatcher Camp of the United Confederate Veterans in Leesburg. From 1868 until his death in 1892, he served as rector of St. James Church in that pleasant town, in an area he had come to love during the war. Washington and Lee University awarded him an honorary Doctor of Divinity degree in 1877. One of his congregation marked his passing by writing, "His delight was where his duty led, or fixed him, and his faithfulness in all was grand. We thank God for the gift of such a pastor."

George F. Miller of Company E, whose bridle drew the attention of Jeb Stuart, who followed orders to "aim at the middle" of the Yankees, and who followed Cabell Flournoy into the Wilderness, lived long enough to attend a showing of *Gone With the Wind* in Hollywood. "It wasn't like that at all!" he declared excitedly. Despite the assertions of someone who claimed to be James Walton of Company K, and who died August 30, 1947, Miller was probably the last survivor of the 6th Cavalry when he died at the Confederate Home in Ardmore, Oklahoma, on July 29, 1947.

The history of the 6th Virginia Cavalry, like the histories of the other Confederate mounted regiments, encompassed success and defeat, exhilaration and despair. The men began as determined recruits, ready to give their lives for the cause. Many did; the rest did what they could in the face of superior force. They fought bravely. They sweated, froze, and suffered the hardships of war. There was illness, desertion, and at times leadership unequal to their mettle, but there was also steadfastness and humor. Above all, there was always hope. In the end, however, resignation to the victory of the Union was the only recourse.

For many, one lasting legacy of their service was a religious faith nurtured and strengthened in the crucible of conflict. That faith sustained them after the paroles were signed, allowing them to wrest from public calamity a personal victory.

Flag of the 6th Virginia Cavalry reportedly issued in March 1865, and preserved at Appomattox by colorbearer Samuel W. Young of Company A. Battle honors, not visible in the photograph, are inscribed inside each star. Courtesy of Arthur LaBonte, The War Memorial Museum of Virginia, Newport News; flag on loan from the Museum of the Confederacy.

John Saunders Row, Elkanon W. Rowe, and James Roach, all of Company I. This reversed image shows the letters "O.R." on the forage caps, for Orange Rangers.

George W. Chappelear, Co. A

William Taylor Hammond, Co. D.

Maj. Daniel A. Grimsley in a postwar photograph.

Henry L. D. Lewis of Company D.

Lt. Robert O. Allen, Co. D, hero of Brandy Station, in his United Confederate Veterans uniform many years after the war.

Capt. John A. Adams of Company H

Lt. William Taylor of Company D

Chaplain Richard Terrell Davis. A postwar photograph.

Lt. Col. Daniel T. Richards

William Daniel Sowers, Co. A

Postwar photograph of Col. Julien Harrison.

Capt. William Worsly Mead of Company K

Lt. Jonathan T. Mann of Company I

Cornelius B. Hite of Company D

Middleton M. Johnson of Company B

William E. Grubb of Company K

The flag of Company B presented by the ladies of Gordonsville, and carried at Cedarville on May 23, 1862. The odd design caused Federals to refer to it as a "black flag."

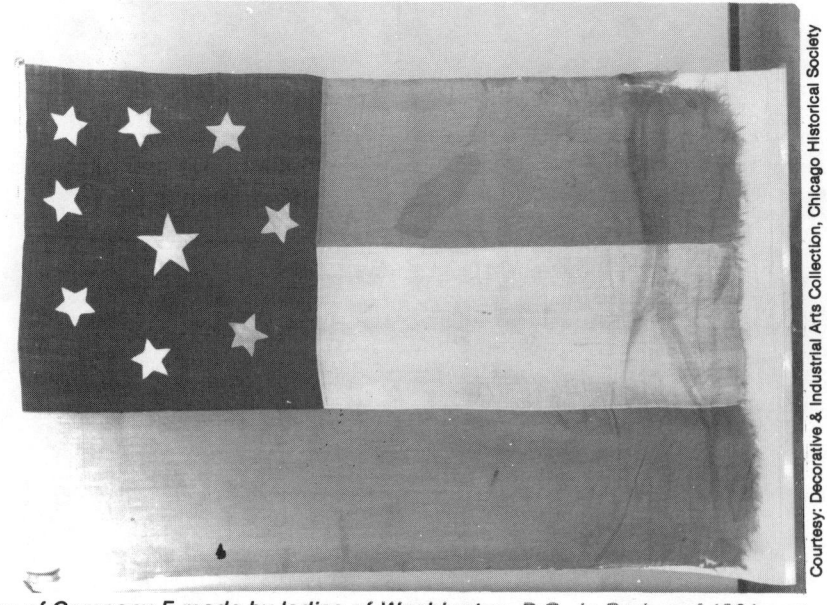

Flag of Company F made by ladies of Washington, D.C., in Spring of 1861 and presented April 18, 1861.

David Holmes McGuire, Co. D. Clarke Co. Courthouse

Dilwin S. Carter, Co. A. Copyright 1972 by Ben Ritter.

William T. Marr of (2d) Company E. Charcoal enlargement from a tintype taken in Charles Town, (W.) Va., in May 1862. "Sabre shown presented in person by Col. T. S. Flournoy."

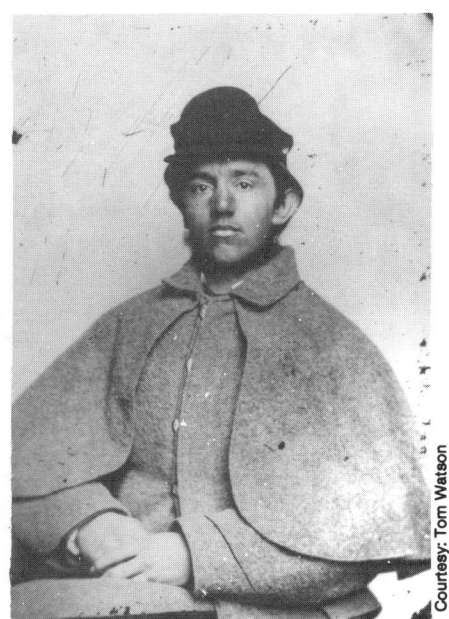

Thomas Sylvester Watson, Co. D

Lt. Col. John Shackleford Green

Courtesy: Library of Congress

George H. Forrest Macrae of Company F. The Yankee-like coat bears Virginia buttons.

Courtesy: Henry Deeks

Fielding L. Marshall of Company H (right), and his son Richard C. Marshall, who may also have served in that company.

From Marshall, Recollections and Reflections

Stephen Clinton Adams of Company K (right) and unknown associate.

Courtesy: Library of Congress

INTRODUCTION TO THE ROSTER

The basic source for this roster is the Compiled Military Service Records for the 6th Virginia Cavalry available on microfilm from the National Archives in Washington, D.C. These service records consist of full and accurate transcriptions of bi-monthly muster rolls transmitted to the Confederate Adjutant and Inspector General's Office in Richmond. They also include transcriptions from Union prisoner of war records and hospital records, and sometimes contain original documents such as discharges for disabilty, vouchers, and correspondence.

The service records are supplemented by postwar rosters, generally those at the Virginia State Library and Archives, and pension applications in that repository. In addition, published biographical sketches, compilations of tombstone inscriptions, data supply by descendants, and other sources have been relied upon. The compiler hopes that the usefulness of these unofficial sources will more than offset such errors as they may contain.

There is an unavoidable element of subjectivity in determining which names appear in the roster. The main criterion for inclusion was representation in the Compiled Service Records, which for this regiment are comparatively complete. A partial exception is records for Company C, which are less full than those for the other companies. Men in the first Company E, from Savannah, Ga., are included only if they served during the period when it was part of the 6th Virginia Cavalry. Names with variant spellings are under those that appear most consistently in the records, with other versions included where possible.

Not all men shown in the official records as "absent without leave" or "deserted" were actually in those categories. Some were legitimately detached or unable to rejoin their units. The collapse of the Confederate government meant that formal applications for correction of records never received the official stamp of approval available to those who served the Federal authorities. Such injustices were but one of the irreversible results of defeat. The state did, on occasion, make allowances, as in the case of John H. Burruss of Company I.

Anyone who regards identification of Confederate soldiers as a simple matter, should consider the case of "Henry E. West" of Company G. If "West" had not applied for a pension based on his Federal service, even the most assiduous search would have failed to uncover his story. "West" is one of a host of fascinating characters whose careers are only hinted at in these pages. Among these lively folk are Thomas Kinloch Fauntleroy of

Company D, who rejoiced in the title of "ugliest man in the Confederate Army," and Eugene B. Van Camp of Company F, the son of a *bona fide* Rebel spy, who may have been a spy himself — we are never likely to learn how he came to be employed as a civilian in Ft. Pillow, Tenn., before that place was taken by Nathan Bedford Forrest. The well-documented heroism of Virgil Weaver of Company H and the pitiable effort of John W. Lawrence of Company A to take the Federal oath of allegiance and gain release from confinement at Elmira deserve more notice than such a roster can provide.

The state identification of prison camps has generally been omitted in the roster. These are Point Lookout, Maryland; Fort Delaware, Delaware; Johnson's Island, Ohio; Camp Chase, Ohio; and Elmira, New York. Virginia place names are not usually idenitified by state.

6th Virginia Cavalry

AARON, WILLIAM THOMAS: enl. 5/27/61 in (2d) Co. E. Discharged 2/19/62. On a roll of 3d Regt. Local Defense Troops, ca. 1/65. Mechanic postwar. Applied for pension at Danville 5/14/1900, age 64, giving his unit as Capt. V. V. Vaughn's Co. Local Guards, Richmond. Discharged from Lee Camp Soldiers' Home, Richmond, 9/2/1908. d. 4/9/1921.

ABBOTT, JOSEPH: b. 10/3/34. enl. 4/22/61 in Co. K. Bugler. Detailed as courier for Gen. N. G. Evans 7/15/61. Sick furlough 2/28/62. AWOL from 5/1/62. d. 12/19/98, bur. Union Cem., Leesburg.

ADAMS, DABNEY: b. 8/4/45 in Rockingham Co., enl. 4/15/64 in Co. I. wded. 5/26/64. AWOL on 3/20/65 final roll. Stock dealer postwar. d. 7/24/30 at Lee Camp Soldiers' Home, Richmond, bur. St. Johns Lutheran Church Cem., near Singers Glen.

ADAMS, EDWIN TURNER: b. 2/20/33. enl. 4/24/61 in Co. H. Farmer. Cpl. on April-June roll. Went home sick 2/10/62. Absent sick, Pvt., 5-6/62, then present until shot in mouth at Brandy Station, 6/9/63. Absent wded. through final roll 3/22/65. m. 1/12/61. d. at Morrisville 6/13/1914, bur. Cedar Grove Cem., Bealton.

ADAMS, JOHN A.: b. 8/5/19 at "Oak Hill," Fauquier Co. grad. U.Va. and U. of Pa. enl. 4/24/61 in Co. H as Capt. Physician. Absent on sick leave for most of his service because of dropsy. Col. Flournoy wrote "I have never known him to drill his co. at all... Capt. Adams is physically incapable of discharging the duties of an officer." Resigned 9/19/62. d. 1/19/82. bur. Cool Spring Methodist Church Cem., Delaplane.

ADAMS, JOHN HENRY: b. in Halifax Co. enl. 8/19/61 in Co. G. Farmer. Absent at home on sick furlough from 11/23/61 to 5-6/62 roll, when present. Discharged on 7/21/62 for fistula in ano with chronic rheumatism, age 45. Went to Lamar Co., Texas, in 1870, and d. at Bardwell, Ky., 6/08.

ADAMS, JOHN Q.: enl. 3/15/62 in Co. I. Absent wded. on 11-12/62 roll. Returned 2/15/63, then furloughed 30 days. Occasional absences until present on 3/20/65 final roll. Postwar roster says wded. at Five Forks.

ADAMS, STEPHEN CLINTON: b. 1/16/36 in Frederick Co., Md. enl. 5/22/61 in Co. K. POW 9/13/62, held at Old Capitol Prison; exchanged 11/10/62. To Sgt. 11/1/62. AWOL on final 1-2/65 roll. POW at Frederick Hall 3/13/65. Took the oath at Pt. Lookout 6/22/65. m. Elizabeth Nichols. d. 1877, bur. Leesburg Union Cem.

ADAMS, THOMAS F.: b. 12/29/34 in Loudoun Co. enl. 6/1/61 in Co. K. POW at Waynesboro 9/24/64. Took the oath at Pt. Lookout 6/22/65. Resid. Clifton Station, Fairfax Co., as a farmer postwar. d. at Lee Camp Soldiers' Home, Richmond, 5/19/20, bur. Hollywood Cem.

ADKINS, JOHN M.: enl. 4/1/62 in (2d) Co. E. d. at Charlottesville General Hosp. 4/29/62 of pneumonia.

ALDER, FLAVIUS J.: enl. 9/9/62 in Co. A. Wded. at Brandy Station 6/9/63, and reported as deserting from Charlottesville General Hosp. 8/28/63, "supposed to have been taken off by his father at night, as he was not in a condition to travel." d. of wounds, 9/17/63.

ALLAN, JOHN: b. 8/23/31 in Richmond. Att. U.Va. Commissioned adjutant with rank of Lt. 10/29/61. Previously Pvt., Co. I, 4th Va. Cav. Absent on special duty by order of Gen. W. E. Jones, 11/62. KIA at Fairfield, Pa., 7/3/63.

ALLDER, GEORGE F.: b. 9/12/29 in Loudoun Co. enl. 10/1/62 in Co. A. POW at Brandy Station 6/9/63, and horse KIA there. Held at Old Capitol Prison. Next record is final roll, ca. 3/65, which shows him AWOL since 1/23/65. Paroled at Charles Town, (W.) Va., 5/19/65. 1913 pension application states "Farmer until I got too old," resid. Loudoun Co. d. 7/2/18 at Lee Camp Soldiers' Home, bur. Ebenezer Cem., Bloomfield. Apparently identical to Frank Alder, wded. at Spotsylvania and POW at Brandy, shown on a postwar roster.

ALLDER, JOSEPH: enl. 10/12/62 in Co. K. Deserted near Warrenton 10/20/63. Arrested by Cole's Union cavalry 11/28/63 at Snickersville, age 22, resid. there. Transferred 9/30/64 from Ft. Delaware to Aiken's Ldg. for exchange. AWOL on final 1-2/65 roll.

ALLDER, NATHAN N.: b. 3/3/40 in Loudoun Co. enl. 7/24/61 in Co. A. Wded. 5/23/62 at Front Royal in leg, and thereafter on rolls as absent sick through final 3/27/65 roll. Paroled at Charles Town, (W.) Va., 5/19/65. Farmer postwar, resid. Hillsboro. "Did not return on account of my wound, being on crutches until after the surrender." d. 11/3/1917, bur. Ebenezer Cem., Bloomfield.

ALLEN, GEORGE J.: Co. G. clothing books show joined co. 8/21/63 and present thru ca. 1/23/64.

ALLEN, GEORGE TAVENNER: b. 1840. enl. 4/24/61 in Co. H. Lawyer. Present on 4-5/61 roll. Lt. in Co. B, 8th Va. Inf. d. 10/9/62, bur. Marshall Cem.

ALLEN, JOHN L.: enl. 3/10/62 in Co. G. POW 5/11/64 at Yellow Tavern. d. 9/27/64 of chronic diarrhea at Elmira, bur. there.

ALLEN, ROBERT OWEN: b. 11/33. enl. 7/2/61 in Co. D. Appointed 2d Lt. 4/20/62. Wded. 6/9/63 at Brandy Station, and absent wded. until retired to Invalid Corps 11/15/64, and stationed at Richmond. Paroled 4/15/65 at Winchester. d. 8/18, bur. Green Hill Cem., Berryville. Famous as the man who killed Union Col. Benjamin F. ("Grimes") Davis at Brandy Station.

ALLEN, WILLIAM PERKINS: enl. 5/21/61 in Co. E. Absent on sick leave and not re-enlisted on 2/16/62 roll, but present on 5-6/62 roll. Acting QM Sgt. 12/62. Teamster 8/24-9/21/63. POW 5/7/64 near Spotsyvlania C.H. Transferred for exchange from Pt. Lookout 11/1/64 ("some prisoner unknown assumed this name and was transferred to Elmira, N.Y.," 8/8/64). Paroled at Appomattox 4/9/65. m. 1853, resid. Weal postwar. d. 2/26/03, wid. Giddy Ann.

ALLISON, BAILEY A.: enl. 11/1/62 in Co. H. AWOL since 11/25 on 11-12/62 roll and marked as a deserter. Present on 2/28/63 roll. Shown as permanently disabled from date of Brandy Station 6/9/63, and thereafter absent sick until final 3/22/65 roll, where he is shown as having deserted in 1/64. On ca. 1898 Fauquier Co. veterans census as a member of Co. C, age 67. d. before 8/2/1910.

ALLISON, BASIL: enl. 9/14/62 in Co. H. Absent from company as wagoner in the regiment, 11/62. POW in Fauquier Co. 6/20/63. d. 8/22/64 at Pt. Lookout.

ALLISON, JOHN: b. 6/6/36. enl. 9/14/62 in Co. H. Present until shown absent sick on 7-8/63 roll, then as AWOL since 8/28/63. 9-10/64 roll has him deserting on 3/24/64. d. 2/2/1919, bur. Marshall Cem. Confederate records give his middle initial as "A".

ALLISON, WILLIAM: enl. 9/14/62 in Co. H. POW near Salem 8/20/63, and held at Pt. Lookout, but no release recorded. Signs parole by mark at Winchester 3/3/65, age 23.

ALLMAN, C. C.: Shown as enl. 1/5/65 in Co. F on a roll supposed to cover 9-10/64, but which is dated 2/24/65. This roll, his only record, has him absent on horse detail.

ALMOND, BAKER: enl. 4/1/64 in Co. I. Present on rolls for 7-10/64. A notice of desertion issued in Richmond on 3/1/65 says he can be sought in Spotsylvania Co. Apparently identical to Bonnie Almond, shown on a postwar roster.

ALMOND, ETHELWIN A.: b. 4/24/45 in Spotsylvania Co. enl. 4/1/64 in Co. I. Laborer. Absent sick since 3/20/65 on final 3/20/65 roll. Living 6/14/09 at Granite Springs. d. 11/6/33, bur. Spotsylvania Confederate Cem.

ALMOND, LISTON V.: enl. 5/4/61 in Co. I, age 18. Present, except for occasional illnesses, until final 3/20/65 roll, on which he is AWOL. d. 4/1/1907, bur. Turner-Almond Cem. on Rt. 608, west of Orange.

ALMOND, THOMAS J.: b. 3/26/42. enl. 4/1/62 in Co. I. Absent sick on 11-12/63 and 11-2/63 rolls, otherwise present until wded. 8/21/64. Marked as returned on 7-8/64 roll, but thereafter wded. and absent thru final 3/20/65 roll. d. 12/9/09, bur. Zoar Baptist Church Cem. m. 1868, wid. Lucy (who subsequently married another Confederate veteran named Johnson.)

ALMOND, WILLIAM L.: Shown as a member of Co. I on a postwar roster. No official record.

AMBLER, RICHARD JAQUELIN: b. 4/13/31. enl. 12/6/64 in Co. D. POW 4/1/65 at Dinwiddie C.H. Took the oath at Pt. Lookout 6/13/65. Resid. Fauquier Co. d. 2/17/76, bur. Leeds Episcopal Church Cem. Hume.

AMIS, W. H.: Only record is a return for 12/62 which shows a man of this name as a deserter from Co. H.

AMISS, EDWARD L.: enl. 7/19/61 in Co. B. AWOL since 4/28/62 on 5-6/62 roll, thereafter absent sick thru 1-2/63 roll. Admitted 4/14/63 to general hosp. at Staunton with secondary syphilis. Transferred to Co. E, 49th Va. Inf. 9/9/63. Paroled at Winchester 5/18/65. Reportedly alive in 5/07. Resid. Montgomery Co., Md., postwar.

AMISS, THOMAS BENJAMIN: b. 7/4/39 in Rappahannock Co. grad. VMI and U. of Pa. enl. as Cpl. 4/1/62 in Co. B. Absent on detached service in Medical Department in Richmond on 5-6/62 roll, his only official record with the regiment. Subsequently surgeon at Salisbury and Weldon, N.C., and with 31st Ga. Inf. m. Mary E. Miller 1861. Physician in Rappahannock and Page Cos. postwar. d. 11/9/13, bur. Luray Cem.

ANDERSON, ELIJAH C.: b. 7/8/36. enl. 10/30/62 in Co. F. Generally present to 2/24/65 final roll, when absent on horse detail. Reported by Richmond as deserter on 3/1/65. Paroled at Winchester 4/24/65. Resid. near Orlean, Fauquier Co., postwar. m. 1861, wid. Adaline L. d. 3/16/90, bur. Creel Cem., Marshall.

ANDERSON, GEORGE R.: enl. 9/17/61 in (1st) Co. E, age 21. Present on 11/1/61 roll. Resid. Liberty Co., Ga. Wded. 10/63. Drowned after close of war in Ogeechee River while returning home.

ANDERSON, JAMES: On a 1913 roster of (2d) Co. E, enl. 5/61. d. after the war. No official record.

ANDERSON, JOHN HENRY: b. 7/24/29. enl. 10/7/62 in Co. D. Present except for 8/3/63 roll, when absent at "horse hospital," and final 3/22/65 roll, when absent as regimental blacksmith. Paroled at Appomattox 4/9/65. d. 9/6/01 at Berryville, bur. Green Hill Cem., Berryville. m. 1851, wid. Ann N.

ANDERSON, JOSEPH A.: enl. 10/1/62 in Co. A. Present on 9-10/62 roll, dated 12/5/62. No further record. May be the man of this name who d. 8/13/98, and is bur. Union Cem., Leesburg. There is some confusion with Nimrod F. Anderson, under whose name this record is filed in the CSRs.

ANDERSON, JOSEPH E.: b. Pittsylvania Co. enl. 8/19/61 in Co. G, age 24. Clerk. Present until granted sick furlough on 3/25/62. d. in Pittsylvania Co. 5/13/62.

ANDERSON, MILTON BOLIS: b. Berryville 8/24/34. enl. 10/7/62 in Co. D. Lost his carbine, sabre, and pistol in action 9/13/63. In hosp. at Charlottesville 11/28-12/10/63. Otherwise always present until 3/22/65 final roll, when AWOL. Paroled 5/5/65 at Winchester. Farmer in Rappahannock Co. postwar, wife Francis Mildred.

ANDERSON, NATH C.: enl. 4/1/62 in (2d) Co. E. Absent on detached service on 5-6/62 roll. Otherwise always present through 3/4/65 final roll.

ANDERSON, NIMROD F.: enl. 10/1/62 in Co. A. On detached service guarding a bridge at Mt. Jackson on 11-12/62 roll, from which duty he was relieved on 1/10/62. Absent sick in hospital from 10/28/63, and still sick on 7-8/64 roll, the last on which he appears. Apparently the "Anderson" shown on a postwar roster of the company as discharged.

ANDERSON, PEYTON L., JR.: b. 7/4/37 at Amissville, Rappahannock Co. enl. 4/22/61 in Co. B. Farmer. Wded. 5/27/61 by a pistol shot through his right arm near Fairfax C.H. while on picket. Thereafter absent unfit for service until discharged for disability 1/18/62. Later served in Co. C of Mosby's 43rd Bn. Va. Cav. m. 1876 Louemma Miller. Noted as the first Confederate soldier to shed his blood, an event commemorated by a small monument at the site. d. 1/12/14, bur. Anderson family cem. near Amissville.

ANDERSON, STEPHEN THOMAS: b. Monroe Co., Mo. Carpenter. enl. 8/19/61 in Co. G, age 18. Discharged 1/16/62 due to a pistol shot through the foot. Resid. Pittsylvania Co.

ANDERSON, T.: On a 1913 roster of (2d) Co. E as enl. 4/61. d. in Pittsylvania Co. No official record.

ANDREWS, WILLIAM SAMUEL: enl. 5/4/61 in Co. I as Sgt., age 23. Lt. on 7-8/63 roll. In hospital with dislocated ankle 11-12/63, and absent sick on 9-10/64 roll. Present as Lt. commanding the company on 3/20/65 final roll. Paroled at Bowling Green 5/10/65. A comrade recalled in 1907 that Andrews "lived in Spotsylvania. . . since the war lived for a long time in Caroline Co. but I understand he is now dead."

ANGLE, M. J.: This name appears as a member of Co. A only in a Danville hosp. register, suffering from a gunshot wound 11/1/63 to 12/8/63. Angle's company commander is given as a "Capt. Wilson," and the entry is probably erroneous.

ANKERS, JAMES E.: b. 11/21/37 in Loudoun Co. Resided Alexandria. enl. 10/1/62 in Co. K. Wded. slightly at Upperville 6/21/63. POW at Cold Harbor 5/31/64. Apparently used an assumed name for the purpose of being exchanged from Pt. Lookout about 6/8/64. POW in Loudoun Co. 1/6/65. Took the oath at Elmira 7/11/65. Signs by mark. Laborer at Colvin Run, Fairfax Co., postwar. d. 4/16/09, bur. (old) Sterling Cem.

APPERSON, GEORGE F.: b. 2/27/25. enl. 2/12/64 in Co. F. Later records have him in Co. E, but throughout his service he was detailed as a teamster, wagonmaster, or similar job (except for one reference to detail as a scout for Gen. R. E. Lee). Paroled at Appomattox 4/9/65. Resid. Culpeper Co. d. 11/9/19, bur. Apperson Cem., Culpeper.

APPERSON, WILLIAM CUMBERLAND: b. 10/19/35. enl. 2/2/64 in Co. F. Later records show him in Co. E. All his service was on detail on extra duty as teamster, forage master, etc. (one roll mentions his detail as a scout for Gen. R. E. Lee). Paroled at Appomattox 4/9/65. d. 3/13/30, bur. Apperson Cem., Culpeper.

ARENDALL, FRANCIS M.: enl. 8/19/61 in Co. G, age 39. Absent on sick furlough early in 1862, and absent "sick at home but never sent any certificate from surgeon" on 9-10/64 roll. Otherwise present thru 3/22/65 final roll.

ARMISTEAD, BOWLES EDWARD: b. 4/26/38. enl. 7/24/61 in Co. A as Cpl. To Lt. 4/20/62. Wded. 10/19/64. Absent on 2/28/65 to bring in absentees. Present on 3/27/65 final roll. Postwar roster says wded. at Cold Harbor, Fishersville, and Five Forks. Paroled at Winchester 5/17/65. m. 1) Susan Lewis Marshall 1867, dau. of Fielding L. Marshall, 2) Elizabeth Lewis Marshall 1871. d. 10/16/16. bur. Ivy Hill Cem., Upperville. Son of Gen. Walker Keith Armistead, USA, and brother of Gen. Lewis A. Armistead, CSA.

ARMISTEAD, WALKER KEITH JR.: b. 1835 at Ft. Monroe. Att. Georgetown Univ. Resid. Fauquier Co. and California. enl. 9/15/61 in Co. A. Sgt. on 11-12/61 roll thru 8/31/63 roll, and on 10/8/63 clothing roll, otherwise Pvt. Sick on 5-6/62 roll and 6-9/63 with paraplegia. Absent detailed in brigade ordnance dept. 11/1/63 thru 3/27/65 final roll. Paroled at Winchester 5/17/65. Resid. Abingdon postwar. d. at Lee Camp Soldiers' Home, Richmond, 9/1 (9 or 3)/04. Known as Walker K., he was brother of Gen. Lewis A. Armistead.

ARMISTEAD, WALKER KEITH: b. 12/11/44 at St. Davids, Alabama. enl. 5/1/62 in Co. A. Student. To Lt. and aide de camp to his father Gen. L. A. Armistead 4/6/63, but lost the appointment automatically when his father was KIA at Gettysburg. Because he was also on detached service as courier with Gen. Jeb Stuart from 8/18/62, detailed to division HQ 10/20/63, and to division HQ ordnance dept. 1/1/65, he seems rarely to have been with the company. Wded. 6/29/64. Paroled at Appomattox 4/9/65. Wded. at Stoney Creek on postwar roster. m. Julia Francis Appleton 1871. d. 3/28/96 at Newport, R.I. Known as W. Keith.

ARMSTRONG, JOHN W.: enl. 5/8/61 in Co. B, age 18. Wded. 6/29/64 and furloughed. Otherwise almost always present thru 3/2/65 final roll. His name is on a Pt. Lookout roll of POWs captured at Five Forks 4/1/65 and "arrived at this station under assumed name, or who assumed one for the purpose of being transferred, exchanged, or released." Postwar roster says wded. at Spotsylvania and Reams Station. d. 8/17/11. bur. Confederate section of City Cem., San Antonio, Tex.

ARMSTRONG, WILLIAM CLEMINSON: Federal records show him as POW 4/19/64 in Rappahannock Co., and a member of Co. B (or D, which seems less likely), held at Old Capitol Prison, and paroled at Pt. Lookout 1/17/65. Not in Confederate records or postwar rosters. m. Sarah Catherine Slaughter. Resid. Woodville, Rappahannock Co., a wagonmaker and farmer.

ARNALL, WILLIAM M., JR.: b. at Sperryville. enl. 4/22/61 in Co. B. Farmer. Cpl. on 5-6/62 roll. Absent on furlough or sick much of 1862. Deserted to Federals 7/23/63 at New Creek, (W.) Va. Took the oath at Camp Chase, Ohio, 12/1/64 and released. U.S. records give his occupation as printer. d. 12/1/21 at Towson, Md., age 79.

ARNETTE, WILLIAM: enl. 9/17/62 in Co. A. AWOL since 7/3/63 on 8/3/63 roll, otherwise present until transferred 8/1/64 to Co. E, 1st Bn. Va. Inf. Probably the man of this name who d. 3/4/11 and is bur. at Ebenezer Cem. (Bloomfield), Loudoun Co.

ARNN, ISAAC CLAY: b. 12/3/44 in Pittsylvania Co. enl. 12/25/62 in (2d) Co. E. Farmer. Present on every roll thru 3/4/65 final roll. In hospital ca. 6/24-7/26/64 with scabies. Served previously in Co. B, 38th Va. Inf., where he was described as a clerk. m. 1867, wid. Mary A. d. 4/13/24, bur. Arnn Cem., Callands. A purported signature on a pension application of J. E. Gatewood in 1923 is "I. Clay Aaron."

ARRINGTON, DAVID T.: enl. 8/19/61 in Co. G, age 29. Absent at home sick, awaiting discharge from 11/5/61 until discharged 12/25/61.

ARRINGTON, JOHN R.: enl. 8/19/62 in Co. G, age 36. d. 3/11/62 in a Richmond hosp. while on his way home on sick furlough. Left a mother, Martha Arrington, of Red Bank, Halifax Co., but no father, widow, or child.

ARRINGTON, J. W.: on postwar "original list" of Co. F.

ARTHUR, JOSEPH LINDSEY: b. 1822. enl. 4/1/62 in (2d) Co. E. Absent sick at Danville hosp. on 11-12/62 roll. POW at Beverly Ford 6/9/63 and paroled at Old Capitol Prison 6/25/63. In Chimborazo Hosp. No. 4 5/20/64 with lumbago, transferred 7/8/64 to Lynchburg. Thereafter absent sick thru 3/4/65 final roll.

ASHBY, BERTRAND STUART: b. 3/13/39 in Fauquier Co. Att. Dickinson College. Enl. 9/1/62 in Co. H. Always present except for furlough on 11-12/63 roll until marked absent sick at hosp. since 2/1/65 on 3/22/65 final roll. Paroled at Winchester 4/27/65. Civil service clerk. d. 1/26/90 at Washington, D.C., bur. St. Paul's Episcopal Cem., Alexandria.

ASHBY, BUCKNER G.: enl. 4/18/61 in Co. D as Sgt. Present thru 11-12/61 roll, then no official record until paroled at Winchester 4/27/65. A reliable postwar roster states he transferred to Co. I, 12th Va. Cav. Another states he was discharged under the 20 Negro law. May be the man of this name (12/3/34-2/5/01) bur. Graham Cem., Route 20 West on outskirts of Orange.

ASHBY, EDWIN T.: enl. 7/24/61 in Co. A as Sgt. Absent recruiting since 2/21/62 on 1-2/62 roll. Reduced to ranks 12/15/62. Shown as Sgt. again, AWOL since 6/1/63, on roll dated 8/31/63, and AWOL on all rolls thru 9-10/64 (except 7-8/64 roll, which has him a deserter since 7/12/64).

ASHBY, GEORGE H.: b. Clarke Co. enl. 3/19/62 in Co. D. Blacksmith. AWOL since 6/1/62 on 5-6/62 roll, then absent on sick furlough prior to 10/22/62 discharge for scrofula, age 17.

ASHBY, JAMES LEWIS: b. 11/6/31 in Clarke Co., grad. VMI. enl. 7/18/62 in Co. D. Engineer in Missouri, in Kansas troubles prewar. Milling business in Va. Absent on detached service in Signal Corps. from 9-10 thru 11-12/62 rolls, otherwise present until KIA at Trevillian's Station 6/11/64. Never married.

ASHBY, NIMROD THOMSON: enl. 3/16/62 in Co. H. Absent sick since 4/1/62 on 5-6/62 roll, and since 11/1 on 11/62 return. Otherwise present on all rolls thru 3/22/65 final roll. Paroled 4/25/65 at Winchester. Farmer postwar. Resid. Conde, age 79, on 1/19/23. d. 1/23/24.

ASHBY, SHIRLEY C.: enl. 9/22/62 in Co. D. Horse KIA near Strasburg 6/1/63. Absent sick at hosp. on 11-12/63 roll, and AWOL on 9-10/64 roll. Present on all others thru 3/22/65 final roll. Paroled 4/20/65 at Millwood, age 23.

ATKINS, DEWITT CLINTON: enl. 11/1/61 in Co. B, age 24. Harness maker. AWOL from 6/10/62 and POW 7/14/62 while visiting Rappahannock Co. At Old Capitol Prison and released about 8/1/62. Under sentence of court-martial on 1-2/63 roll. Deserted to Federals, who made him POW 7/23/63 at New Creek, (W.) Va. d. 4/12/64 of pneumonia at Camp Chase, Ohio, bur. there. Postwar roster says "deserted, accidentally wounded."

ATKINS, GEORGE PEYTON: b. 10/13/44 in Sperryville. enl. 2/20/63 in Co. B. Absent sick since 8/1/63 on 11-12/63 roll. Reported by Richmond as a deserter on 2/28/65. Present otherwise thru 3/21/65 final roll. d. 1/8/20, bur. family cem. near Sperryville. m. 1868, wid. Mary Washington Atkins.

ATKINS, SILAS M.: enl. 4/22/61 in Co. B, age 19. Saddler. Injured shoulder 6/1/61 and sent home. Absent sick since 2/27 on 1-2/62 roll. Severely injured by fall from horse in engagement at Cedarville 5/23/62. Wded. in finger at Fairmont 4/29/63. POW at Sperryville 11/14/63. Paroled at Pt. Lookout 5/3/64. Absent wded. since 1/16/65 on 3/21/65 final roll. Paroled at Winchester 5/9/65. Resid. Rappahannock Co.

ATKINS, THOMAS V.: b. Rappahannock Co. enl. 4/22/61 in Co. B, age 20. Farmer. Discharged 5/23/61 as unfit for service, "having had a wound in his leg unknown . . . at the time of enlistment." enl. again 2/1/63. Absent sick since 9/1/63 on 11-12/63 and 7-8/64 rolls. AWOL since 1/15/65 on final 3/21/65 roll. On pension application claimed he was shot in the hand, and came home wded. in 1864. Resid. near Sperryville, a miller, age 65, on 6/11/06. Still drawing pension in 1923.

ATWELL, RICHARD M. JOHNSON: b. 1838 in Belmont Co., Ohio. enl. 7/24/61 in Co. A. Schoolteacher. Absent scouting by order of Gen. W. E. Jones on 11/62 return. Otherwise almost always present until detailed as scout with Lt. Stringfellow on 12/12/63, which service continued until final 3/27/65 roll, when absent as scout with Gen. Lomax. Postwar roster says wded. at Snickersville. Farmer and real estate broker in Loudoun and D.C. m. Carrie V. Young 1869. d. 4/29/02 in Washington, D.C., bur. Middletown, Md.

ATWELL, THOMAS HENRY: b. 11/24/29. enl. 4/22/61 in Co. K. Teamster at various times in 1862. Wded. 8/19/62 at Brandy Station. AWOL in Loudoun Co. on 12/27/64 roll. AWOL on final 1-2/65 roll. Paroled at Harpers Ferry 4/21/65, signs by mark. d. 3/7/02, bur. Union Cem., Leesburg.

AUDAS, JOHN D.: enl. 9/17/61 in (1st) Co. E, age 24. Resid. Savannah, Ga. Paroled at Greensboro, N.C., 5/1/65.

BADENHOP, CONRAD: b. 2/1/43 in Hamburg, Germany. enl. 4/5/62 in Co. G as "Henry E. West," a substitute. Clerk. Previously Sgt., Co. D, 1st S.C. Art., which he deserted on furlough. POW at Snickers Gap 7/17/63 as bugler. Enl. 1/24/64 in Co. E, 1st U.S. Vol. Inf. at Pt. Lookout. Mustered out as drum major 11/27/65 at Ft. Leavenworth, Kansas. m. Catherine Mueller 1869. d. Manhattan, N.Y. City, 2/21/76, bur. Lutheran cem. there.

BAGBY, SAMUEL P.: b. 8/30/42 in Halifax Co. enl. 8/19/61 in Co. G, age 19. To Cpl. 11/1/62. Except for furlough on 5-6/62 roll, present at all musters thru 3/22/65 final roll. Living in Halifax Co. in 2/04 when he stated he was paroled at Appomattox 4/9/65. m. 1870 Mary Annie Crowder. d. 11/26/26, bur. Shady Grove Methodist Church, Hyco Road.

BAGGARLY, MARTIN LAFAYETTE: b. 1834 in Va. Farmhand. Resid. near Flint Hill, Rappahannock Co., when paroled from Co. B at Winchester 4/29/65, age 30. This is his only official record. Also on postwar roster. d. 1917, bur. Flint Hill Methodist Church Cem.

BAILEY, JOHN: enl. 10/20/62 in Co. C. Sgt. on 7-8/63 roll. Absent wded. 9/64 on 9-10/64 roll, and absent in Richmond hosp. on final ca. 3/25/65 roll. POW in Libby Prison, Richmond 4/10/65, "deserter." Transportation ordered to "Millersonville" (probably Millersville), Md., by provost marshal at Washington, D.C., 4/18/65. May be the man of this name who d. 11/18/92, age 59, bur. Early Cem., Rockingham Co.

BAILEY, WILLIAM E.: enl. 10/26/61 in Co. A. Detailed as brigade teamster 7/21/63 thru 3/27/65 final roll. Paroled at Staunton, 5/14/65, age 24. Resid. Fairfax Co. Postwar roster says "captured."

BAKER, E.: Only mention is in a register of General Hosp., Farmville, which has this man in Co. D, transferred to Richmond as nurse 5/17/64. Not on reliable postwar rosters, and probably an error.

BAKER, JOHN RUDOLPH: b. 1846 in Shenandoah Co. enl. 11/1/61 in Co. F, transferred from Co. A, 39th Bn. Va. Cav. Paroled 4/20/65 at New Market as in Co. I. Signs by mark. d. 1/28/01 in Frederick Co. Wid. Susan A., m. 1870.

BAKER, JOSEPH H.: enl. 5/4/61 in Co. I, age 19. Resid. Rockingham Co. MWIA in thigh 6/9/63 at Brandy Station, d. at General Hosp., Charlottesville, 8/29/63. bur. Confederate Soldiers' Cem., Charlottesville.

BAKER, WILLIAM H.: enl. 3/27/64 in Co. F, transferred from Co. A, 39th Bn. Va. Cav. Farmer, resid. Louisa Co. Absent sick since 9/8/64 on roll ostensibly dated 8/31/64. POW at Woodstock 3/20/65. Took the oath 6/9/65 at Ft. McHenry, Md.

BALL, CHARLES H.: b. 4/15/35. enl. 4/22/61 in Co. K as QM. Sgt. on 1-2/62 roll. Farmer. To Lt. 4/20/62. Capt. on 6/30/62 roll. General Hosp. No. 4, Richmond, 10/23-11/3/63 with contusion of leg from fall from horse, furloughed 30 days. MWIA 5/7/64, near Spotsylvania C.H. in thigh, amputation 5/9/64. d. 5/14/64, bur. Union Cem., Leesburg.

BALL, CHARLES H.: b. Indiana. enl. 5/26/61 in Co. K. Assistant messenger in U.S. Treasury Dept., resigned 4/23/61, denounced as "an out and out secessionist." enl. 5/26/61 in Co. K. Discharged on order from Secretary of War 11/16/61, probably for poor health. Still shown as present on 6/30/62 roll. Appointed messenger in Comptroller's Bureau, C.S. Treasury Dept. 4/1/62.

BALL, HENRY E.: b. Beaufort Dist., S.C. enl. 9/17/61 in (1st) Co. E, age 31. Merchant. Resid. Tattnall Co., Ga. Discharged for disability 3/4/62.

BALL, JAMES: enl. 12/21/61 in Co. A. Present until KIA 10/16 (or 17)/62 at Upperville. A member of the regiment identified only as "Ball" is bur. in the Upperville Cem. cf. John Ball, Co. K. Substitute for Eli J. Hamilton.

BALL, JOHN: enl. 9/1/61 in Co. K. Present thru 6/30/62 roll. No further record. A postwar roster of Co. A has John Ball killed at Upperville, with no date.

BALL, MOTTROM McCABE: enl. 9/1/61 in Co. K. Admitted 3/14/62 to Chimborazo Hosp. No. 2, Richmond, with typhoid fever. Absent on sick furlough 6/30/62. No further record.

BALL, WILLIAM, JR.: b. 9/12/37 in Loudoun Co. enl. 4/22/61 in Co. K as Sgt. Furloughed 30 days on 2/11/62. Wded. slightly at Aldie 10/9/62. Horse KIA 10/11/63 at Brandy Station. In Charlottesville General Hosp. 1/7/64, morbi cutis. POW in Loudoun Co. 10/1/64. Paroled for exchange 2/2/65 at Elmira. Paroled 4/17/65 at Harpers Ferry. m. Musadora Harris 1867, farmer postwar. d. 3/17/07 at Leesburg. Brother of Capt. Charles H.

BALL, WILLIAM HENRY: b. Loudoun Co. enl. 5/28/62 in Co. K. Clerk. Wded. slightly 6/21/63 at Upperville. POW 3/4/64 at Hamilton while disbanded, age 22. Took the oath at Ft. Delaware 5/30/65.

BALLENGER, ROBERT WASHINGTON: b. 7/1/37 in Alexandria. enl. 4/20/61 in Co. F. Farmer. Horse KIA 6/26/63 at Fairfax C.H. Present on every roll until POW 2/19/64 at Upperville. Took the oath 5/31/65 at Ft. Delaware. d. 11/17/19 or 29 in Fairfax Co., bur. St. Paul's Cem., Alexandria.

BALTHIS, CHARLES: b. Loudoun Co. enl. 9/13/62 in Co. A. Deserter since 4/1/64 on 7-8/64 roll, and AWOL on 9-10/64 roll. d. 1/26/09 at Charles Town, W.Va., supposedly bur. Harpers Ferry.

BALTHROPE, JEREMIAH A.: enl. 4/24/61 in Co. H. Farmer. Furlough 2/10-3/14/62. Detailed as blacksmith 9-10/62 roll thru 11-12/63 roll. POW at Beverly Ford 6/9/63, paroled at Old Capitol Prison 6/25/63. Present with Co. H on 12/30/64 and 9-10/64 rolls. POW at Rectortown 1/14/65. Took the oath at Elmira 7/7/65. Resid. Point of Rocks, Md.

BANEY, THADDEUS: enl. 6/7/61 in Co. D. AWOL from 9/27/61, "sick," no further record. Postwar roster says d. of disease contracted in service. Maybe identical to Thaddeus Baney, Jr., b. 7/20/42-KIA '63, aged 21 years, 2 months, and 29 days, who served in Co. B, 12th Va. Cav., and is bur. in Edge Hill Cem., Charles Town, W.Va.

BANKS, WILLIAM G.: enl. 8/19/61 in Co. G as Lt., age 43. Absent on sick furlough from 11/7/61, resigned 1/15/62. Dropped 4/20/62. Resid. Pittsylvania Co. Postwar roster says "resigned age limit."

BARBEE, GEORGE T.: enl. 3/16/62 in Co. H. Absent as courier to Gen. Jeb Stuart on 9-10/62 roll and 11/62 return. Cpl. on 11-12/63 roll. Horse KIA 6/11/64 near Louisa C.H. Absent, wded. 10/9/64 on final 3/22/65 roll. Paroled at Winchester 4/22/65, resid. near Piedmont Station, Fauquier Co. d. 7/27/92, age 49, bur. Cool Spring Methodist Church Cem., Delaplane.

BARBEE, JOHN: enl. 5/25/63 in Co. D. KIA 6/9/63 at Brandy Station, erroneously carried on rolls as POW.

BARBEE, ROBERT S.: enl. 3/14/62 in Co. H. Cpl. on 2/28/63 and Sgt. on 11-12/63 rolls. Present on every roll until 3/22/65 final roll, when absent sick since 3/1/65. Paroled 4/22/65 at Winchester. Resid. Langley, Fairfax Co., a carpenter, on 12/20/97, when he applied for pension, age 58. Claims wds. in picket skirmish 6/5/62 near Big Spring, Shenandoah Co. and at Winchester 9/19/64, in shoulder. d. 1/4/18, bur. Arlington National Cem. Wid. Susan C., m. '67.

BARBEE, SAMUEL A.: enl. 4/24/61 in Co. H. Merchant. Sent home sick with typhoid fever 9/21/61 and never returned.

BARBER, A. JONES: Detailed to Co. A by order dated 4/6/63. Apparently served as wagonmaster at various times thru 12/31/64, as wagonmaster for the 4th N.C. Inf., and as Pvt. in Co. D, 12th Va. Inf.

BARBER, THOMAS: On postwar roster of Co. A, "discharged."

BARBOUR, WILLIAM NEWTON: enl. 8/19/61 in Co. G, age 29. To Sgt. 12/26/61. In Chimborazo Hosp. No. 3, Richmond, with typhoid fever 3/20-3/27/62, furloughed 30 days 4/17/62 and absent on sick furlough on 5-6/62 roll. KIA at Paris 9/23/62. Resid. Pittsylvania Co. Wid. Amanda V., m. '55. Chaplain Davis described him on 9/23/62 as "a consistent Xn & excellent soldier. I had noticed him as one of our best singers & very fond of singing hymns."

BARKSDALE, M. S.: On 1913 roster of (2d) Co. E as enl. 4/61 and d. at home. No official record.

BARNHOUSE, JONAS P.: b. 2/22/38. enl. 4/22/61 in Co. K. Deserted 9/1/62. d. 10/12/10, bur. Mt. Pleasant Methodist Episcopal Cem., Loudoun Co. Postwar roster says "went home and stayed."

BARRETT, CAMPBELL BOYD: b. 5/23/38 in Loudoun Co. enl. 4/22/61 in Co. K as Sgt. Absent since 2/21/62 on sick furlough on 1-2/62 roll. Transferred to Co, A, 35th Bn. Va. Cav. 5/1/62 as Pvt. Lived postwar in Alexandria and Washington, D.C. Moved to South Dakota in '83 and ran the Aberdeen *Republican* 1884-1893; also receiver of U.S. Land Office. Alive in Aberdeen 7/27/1910. m. Mollie D. Fadeley.

BARRETT, JOHN WADE: enl. 4/22/61 in Co. K as Lt. Absent on sick furlough since 1/24/62 on 1-2/62 roll, "still forwarding certificates of inability to date." Dropped 4/20/62.

BARRON, H. K.: On muster-in roll of (1st) Co. E, dated 10/16/61, "detained in Burke Co., Ga., by illness in family," name cancelled.

BARTLEY, HENRY A. M.: b. in Va. enl. 8/24/64 in Co. I. Store keeper. Present on 7-8/64 roll. "Absent with leave as constable of Orange Co." on 3/20/65 final roll. U.S. mail contractor in Orange Co., age 53, on 10/6/71, when he swore "I never did a day's duty... told my neighbors that if I should fight at all, it should be for the stars and stripes." Radical Republican postwar. Alive in 1901. Three brothers in C.S. service.

BARTLEY, WALKER OLIVER: b. 12/31/32 in Louisa Co. enl. 4/1/62 in Co. I. AWOL on 8/31/63 roll. In Chimborazo Hosp. No. 2, Richmond, 4/7-5/7/64. Present until final 3/20/65 roll, when AWOL. Farmer in Orange postwar. d. 6/28/13, bur. family cem. near Louisa C.H.

BATEMAN, ELIJAH: enl. 9/1/63 in Co. C. Absent under arrest on 9-11/63 roll, the only one he is on. Resid. Port Republic. d. at General Hosp. No. 13, Richmond, of typhoid pneumonia 12/26/63, bur. Oakwood Cem., Richmond.

BATEMAN, JAMES: enl. 11/20/63 in Co. C. Present on 11-12/63 roll, and on 1/64 clothing roll. No further record.

BATEMAN, JONATHAN: enl. 5/28/61 in Co. C. Teamster in QM Dept. at various times. AWOL since 8/23/63 on 7-8/63 roll. Otherwise always present thru ca. 3/30/65 final roll. Paroled at Harrisonburg 5/2/65, age 26. Resid. 4/27/03 at Port Republic. First name also shown as John.

BATEMAN, WILLIAM HENRY: Conscript assigned 4/4/64 to Co. C. In Chimborazo Hosp. No. 1, Richmond, 3/30/65. Otherwise present thru ca. 3/30/65 final roll. Paroled at Harrisonburg 5/2/65, age 19.

BATES, EDWARD: Reported on Union records as a deserter, no Co., who came in 6/24/64 near Ft. Powhatan. Resid. Petersburg. Took the oath at Ft. Monroe 7/2/64. Released and sent to Philadelphia, Pa. Probably not 6th Va. Cav.

BATTAILE, WILLIAM D.: enl. 11/1/62 in Co. I. d. 2/22/63 of typhoid fever in hospital at Mt. Jackson, bur. Our Soldiers' Cem., Mt. Jackson. Survived by his mother, Mary Battaile.

BAXTER, GEORGE A.: b. "1830-33" in Richmond. Att. Washington College. enl. 5/21/61 in Co. K as Lt. Lawyer and editor in St. Joseph, Mo. Provost marshal in Leesburg on 7-8/61 roll. Hunting deserters 1/13-1/19/62. To Capt. 4/20/62. KIA 5/23/62 at Cedarville.

BAYLY, JAMES P.: enl. 1/10/62 in Co. H. Substitute for Sampson P. Bayly. Presence or absence not stated on 1-2/62 roll, the only one with his name.

BAYLY, SAMPSON P.: enl. 4/24/61 in Co. H. Farmer. "On business at home for the company" on 6/30/61 roll; present on detail on 9-10/61 roll. Absent to procure clothing for company in Fauquier Co. on 11/61 return. Got James P. Bayly as substitute. Age 45 on 8/8/65 amnesty petition.

BEACH, ALFRED: b. near Alexandria. enl. 5/1/61 in Co. F. Laborer. In arrest for drunkenness and insubordination 8/19. Dishonorably discharged by order of Secretary of War 10/1/61. Age 24 on 10/31/61 when he went to Federals and was put in Old Capitol Prison. Took the oath at Washington, D.C., ca. 11/2/61.

BEACH, WILLIAM H.: enl. 5/1/61 in Co. F. Farmer. Resid. one mile south of Burke Station. Sick to 7/31/61, when given 30 days furlough and never returned. In Old Capitol Prison 3/17/63 when he said "I was in the first battle at Bull Run but never shot off my gun, never made a charge, or wounded a man in my life."

BEANS, AARON HUMPHREY: b. 5/31/42. enl. 10/1/62 in Co. K. POW 9/14/63 near Rapidan Station. Paroled 3/10/65 at Elmira and sent to James River for exchange. Paroled at Edwards Ferry 4/22/65. d. 11/28/16. Bur. Harmony Methodist Church Cem., Hamilton. m. 1885, wid. Louisa.

BEARD, LAWSON G.: enl. 10/1/62 in Co. K. POW 4/28/63 in Loudoun Co., paroled 5/10/63. Wded. slightly by shell fragments at Upperville 6/21/63. Cpl. on 12/27/64 roll. POW 4/1/65 at Five Forks. Took the oath at Pt. Lookout 6/7/65.

BEAVERS, BENJAMIN E.: b. 8/9/39. enl. 9/26/62 in Co. A. Detailed as ordnance teamster on 11-12/63 roll. Absent sick since 9/24 on 9-10/64 roll. AWOL on final 3/27/65 roll. Paroled 4/21/65 at Winchester. Resid. Clarke Co. d. 9/1/21, bur. Edge Hill Cem., Charles Town, W.Va.

BEAZLEY, FERDINAND: enl. 5/1/63 in Co. I. POW at Summit Pt., (W.) Va., 8/30/64. Release ordered by Lincoln 2/2/65. Took the oath at Camp Chase 5/10/65, age 38.

BECKETT, WILLIAM M.: b. Prince George's Co., Md. enl. 9/10/61 in Co. G, age 21. Farmer. In Richmond hospitals with typhoid fever 3/7-5/17/62. Discharged 10/21/62 after expiration of enlistment. Captured by Union steamer *Freeborn* ca. 11/12/62 crossing Potomac into Maryland with five others.

BECKON, W.: Only record is a list of POWs at Old Capitol Prison dated 7/28/62, which has him in Co. F, captured 5/30/62 at Front Royal. Probably a garbled record meaning someone else.

BELL, GEORGE H.: On postwar "original list" of Co. F.

BELL, JAMES D.: enl. 4/25/61 in Co. D. AWOL since 12/20 on 11-12/61 roll. POW 6/9/63 near Millwood, age 26. Paroled at Old Capitol Prison 6/10/63. Otherwise present until KIA 8/21/64 at Berryville.

BELL, JOHN WILLIAM: b. 6/13/38 in Loudoun Co. enl. 4/27/61 in Co. D. Wded. 9/13/63 at Culpeper C.H. Furlough for 30 days to 10/15/63, then absent wded. thru final 3/22/65 roll. POW "for about fifteen minutes." m. Mary E. Minnich, 5/65. Postwar miler, resid. Rockingham and Alleghany Cos. d. 9/5/24 at Covington, bur. Cedar Hill Cem., Covington.

BELL, JONAH: enl. 6/1/62 in Co. D. Present thru 11-12/62 roll. Postwar roster says KIA 6/11/64 at Trevillian's Station.

BELL, R. W.: On a postwar roster of Co. C, enl. 1861.

BELT, ALFRED CAMPBELL: enl. 4/22/61 in Co. K. Present on 7-8/61 roll, "has been AWOL." Absent sick since 9/20 on 12/61 return. AWOL since 12/3/61 on 1-2/62 roll. Paid for service thru 3/9/62. Arrested 3/26/62 for horse stealing, treason, and saying "If the Yankees were agoing to trespass on Southern soil, he was agoing to stain his blood with it." Discharged from Ft. Delaware 12/26/63. Resid. near Leesburg. d. 1883 in Missouri.

BENNETT, GEORGE RICHARD: b. 3/13/26 in Pittsylvania Co. enl. 9/10/64 in Co. E. Present thru 3/4/65 final roll. On a postwar roster of Co. E, 57th Va. Inf., as serving 18 months. m. Mary Catherine Owen 3/7/61. d. 9/29/18 in Pittsylvania Co.

BENNETT, JOHN H.: enl. 4/1/62 in (2d) Co. E. Present until POW 5/11/64 at Yellow Tavern. Paroled 3/14/65 at Pt. Lookout for exchange. Resid. Franklin Co.

BENNETT, JOHN KELLY: enl. 4/1/62 in (2d) Co. E. POW 6/9/63 at Beverly Ford, paroled 6/25/63 at Old Capitol Prison. Otherwise always present, except for details, until 3/4/65 final roll, when absent sick in Pittsylvania Co. on surgeon's certificate.

BENNEZETTE, CLINTON L.: enl. 5/22/61 in Co. F. Resid. Alexandria. Present until POW 9/13/63 at Culpeper. Paroled 3/10/65 at Elmira, and transferred to James River for exchange. Took oath of amnesty at Alexandria 6/17/65.

BENSON, JOHN: (2d) Co. E. Only record is of death 2/23/65 from chronic diarrhea at Camp Chase, which is probably an error.

BENT, J. J.: Shown as in Co. C in Rockingham *Register* of 5/31/61. No other record.

BENTON, JAMES MONROE: b. 9/18/19 at "Oak Hill," in Loudoun Co. enl. 4/20/61 in Co. F. Absent, detailed for special service in QM Dept. from 7/1/61 through 5-6/62 roll, the last on which he appears. Justice of peace in Fairfax and Loudoun Cos. postwar. d. 7/13/95, bur. Sharon Cem., Middleburg.

BERKELEY, CARTER N.: b. 10/9/37 in Staunton. enl. 7/10/62 in Co. A, transferred to Co. D on 9-10/62 roll. Previously in Capt. Garber's Co., Va. Lt. Art. (Staunton Artillery). Absent as hospital steward in Staunton thru 1-2/63 roll. Afterward Lt. in Capt. McClanahan's Co., Va. Horse Art. Physician and insurance agent postwar. d. 3/7/05, bur. Thornrose Cem., Staunton.

BERNARD, JOHN: enl. 8/7/61 in Co. K. Present thru 6/30/62 roll. No further record.

BERRY, JOHN HENRY: enl. 5/28/61 as Sgt. in Co. K. Present on 9-10/61 roll. Got Augustus Eckhart as substitute. Age 29 in 10/63.

BEST, ELIAS: enl. 3/14/62 in Co. H. AWOL from 5/25/62 and marked as a deserter.

BIBB, WILLIAM C.: Conscript assigned to Co. F on 3/14/64. Absent sick since 5/6/64 on 9-10/64 roll, and still so absent on 2/24/65 final roll.

BICKERS, JOHN M.: enl. 5/4/61 in Co. I. Various absences and illnesses before and after wound in left thigh 5/26/64. Present on final 3/20/65 roll. Age 65 on 5/23/00, resid. Nason's, Orange Co., signs by mark. d. 3/15/08, bur. Bickers Cem. on Rt. 600 southwest of Orange.

BIGGS, JED W.: enl. 10/7/61 in (1st) Co. E. Bugler. POW 2/26/65 at Tiller's Bridge, S.C. Took the oath at Hart's Island, N.Y. Harbor, 6/23/65, resid. Augusta, Ga.

BILLINGSLEY, JOHN DABNEY: b. 10/8/33 in Spotsylvania Co. (one source says Kentucky). Conscript assigned 3/1/64 to Co. F. Present thru final 2/24/65 roll. Age 81, a farmer, resid. Lignum, on 4/11/14 pension application. d. 3/19/24.

BIRCH, WILLIAM JOSEPH ROWAN: b. 11/2/39 (one source has 1842) in Arlington area of Alexandria Co. enl. 5/25/61 in Co. F. Farmer. Typhoid fever from 7/8/61 thru 9-10/61 roll. POW 7/14/62 at Sperryville, exchanged 8/5/62. Present until POW again 2/20/64 at Upperville. d. at Ft. Delaware 7/20/64 of "influenza of tonsils." Bur. Oakland Cem., Falls Church.

BIRD, FRANKLIN: enl. 9/17/61 in (1st) Co. E, age 24. Resid. Effingham Co., Ga., d. 4/15/62 at General Hosp. Orange C.H., from accidental wd. Announced 12/10/64 on Roll of Honor for Accotink River.

BISHOP, ELIJAH E.: enl. 9/13/62 in Co. H. Left in charge of sick man near Harrisonburg since 12/19/62 on 11-12/62 roll. Ordered to report to 8th Va. Inf. on 1/30/63.

BISHOP, HAMILTON S.: enl. 4/24/61 in Co. H. Carpenter (U.S. POW records show farmer). AWOL 9/1-10/1/61. AWOL since 10/13/62, marked as a deserter on 11-12/62 roll. Absent sick at hosp. on 11-12/63 roll. POW 10/17/64 at Salem. Tried as a spy in Washington, D.C., 11/29-11/30/64, and found not guilty. Took oath at Ft. Warren, Mass., 6/13/65.

BISHOP, HARVEY B.: enl. 4/24/61 in Co. H. Farmer. Re-enlistment furlough 2/9-3/13/62. Absent sick on 9-10/62 roll. POW. 10/19/62, exchanged 11/2/62. Court martial for "conduct to the prejudice of good order" announced 3/7/64. Served 6 months at hard labor, back on duty with co. on 12/30/64 roll. Reported as deserter by Richmond on 2/28/65. Present on 3/22/65 final roll. Paroled 4/9/65 at Appomattox. Living at LaBelle, Lewis Co., Mo., age 72, in 1913. Applied to Missouri Confederate Home in 1925.

BISHOP, HEZEKIAH: b. 3/9/43 in Fauquier Co. enl. 9/13/62 in Co. H. Wded. at Paris 9/22/62 and not recovered until 7-8/64 roll. Absent sick since 3/1/65 on final 3/22/65 roll. Paroled 4/22/65 at Winchester. Farmer postwar, claimed two wounds. d. 1/18/28, bur. Warrenton Cem.

BISHOP, ROBERT A.: enl. 9/13/62 in Co. H. Present until ordered to report to 8th Va. Inf. on 1/30/63.

BITZER, GEORGE W.: b. 5/4/35. enl. 7/24/61 in Co. A. On extra duty in QM Dept. as teamster since 10/21/61 on 9-10/61 roll. AWOL since 12/18/61 on 11-12/61 roll. Otherwise present thru 5-6/62 roll. Transferred to Co. A, 8th Va. Inf. 8/31/62. d. 2/6/11 near New London, Md., bur. Mt. Olivet Cem., Frederick, Md. Wid. Annie E.

BLACKBURN, JOHN SINCLAIR: b. 10/9/38. enl. 4/18/61 in Co. D. Present thru 5-6/62 roll. Later acting Lt. of artillery for Thomas' Brigade. Ordnance officer for Gen. L. L. Lomax's Brigade 2/7/63. Paroled at Summit Pt., (W.) Va., 5/1/65. d. 12/1/11, bur. St. Paul's Cem., Alexandria.

BLADEN, THOMAS: b. 1841. enl. 10/20/61 in Co. F. Absent on sick furlough near Mt. Crawford on 5-6/62 roll. Absent, sent back with horses on 7-8/63 roll. Detailed as teamster on 9-10/64 roll thru final 2/24/65 roll. POW 4/5/65 at Amelia C.H. Took the oath 6/23/65 at Pt. Lookout, signs by mark. Postwar roster says "captured by some of Gen. Pope's men, but returned to the armies were under flag of truce." d. 12/27/08, bur. Ashburn City Cem.

BLANKENSHIP, GEORGE W.: enl. 1/15/63 in (2d) Co. E. Horse KIA near Fairfield, Pa., 7/4/63. Presence or absence on final 3/4/65 roll not stated. Postwar roster says resid. Franklin and/or Henry Cos.

BLEDSOE, JESSE N.: enl. 10/1/62 in Co. I. AWOL on 11-12/62 roll, for which offense he was tried, "sentence not read." Wded. in head at Fairfield, Pa., 7/4/63. Absent sick at hosp. since 12/1/63 on 11-12/63 roll. Admitted to Chimborazo Hosp. No. 2 with fever 6/1/64, d. 6/6/64, bur. Oakwood Cem., Richmond.

BLEDSOE, MOSES GARNETT: b. 3/26/34. enl. 4/1/62 in Co. I. Absent on sick leave on 5-6/62 roll. Wded. in back at Paris 9/22/62. Wded. 6/11/64 at Trevilian's Station and absent wded. thru 9-10/64 roll. Present on 3/20/65 final roll. d. 3/20/15, bur. Bledsoe family cem. on Rt. 611.

BLONDEAU, GASTON: b. Paris, France. enl. 3/1/62 in Co. A. Engraver. Resid. Washington, D.C. Previously in 7th Va. Inf. Absent sick on 5-6/62 roll. Discharged 10/5/62 for wds. of both arms and foot, age 25. Returned to Co., POW and wded. 7/14/63 at Williamsport, Md. Paroled at Elmira 10/11/64. In Richmond hospitals for debility, old wd. of foot 1/10-1/17/65 (one record says he deserted on the latter date, another that he was discharged). Paroled at Charlotte, N.C., 5/24/65.

BOGGESS, JOHN W.: enl. 7/24/61 in Co. A. AWOL since 10/28/61 on 9-10/61 roll. AWOL since 12/23/61 on 11-12/61 roll. In confinement since 1/24/62 on 1-2/62 roll. Deserted 10/15/62 at Paris. Paroled 11/9/62 near Warrenton, name cancelled on later list of parolees. Name also appears as Boggs, Boggiss, and Bigges.

BOCOCK, JESSE LOUIS: b. 6/7/37. enl. 5/28/61 in Co. C. Farmer. Sgt. on 9-10/62 roll. Discharged, age 27, on 1/19/63 after furnishing James Martin as substitute. Shown as enlisted by conscript officer and AWOL on final 3/30/65 roll. d. 1/31/12 in Rockingham Co. bur. McGaheysville Cem.

BOND, JOSEPH H.: enl. 4/1/62 in Co. I. AWOL on 5-6/62 roll. Detailed as teamster in QM Dept. from 1/25/63 thru final 3/20/65 roll. Absent sick at home since 8/12/63 on 7-8/63 roll. Paroled at Appomattox 4/9/65.

BOND, THOMAS P.: enl. 9/17/61 in (1st) Co. E. Slightly wded. at Hanover Junction. Resid. Savannah, Ga.

BONHAM, GEORGE S.: enl. 7/24/61 in Co. D. AWOL since 8/30/61 on 9-10/61 roll. "Discharged, dropped from rolls having never been regularly enlisted & never received any pay" on 11-12/61 roll.

BONHAM, ISAAC: enl. 10/1/62 in Co. D. On horse furlough on 11-12/62 roll. On duty in brigade commissary dept. on 11-12/63 roll. POW in Clarke Co. 3/20/64. Paroled at Camp Chase, Ohio, and transferred for exchange 2/25/65. In Richmond hospital with debilitas on 3/8/65. Paroled at Winchester 4/20/65, age 18, resid. near Berryville.

BONHAM, WILLIAM: enl. 4/18/61 in Co. D. Absent sick from 6/20/62 thru 8/31/63. Horse KIA 10/11/63 at Brandy Station. AWOL since 11/12/63 on 11-12/63 roll. Otherwise present to 3/22/65 final roll, when on scout for Gen. Lee. Paroled at Winchester 4/19/65, age 25, resid. near Berryville.

BONNER, WILLIS: enl. 5/21/61 in Co. K. Present to 7-8/63 roll, when absent sick in hosp. at Lynchburg since 8/11/63. Courier for Gen. L. L. Lomax on 11-12/63 roll. KIA 5/7/64 near Spotsylvania C.H. 1917 roster says "of Alabama."

BOOTH, JAMES THOMAS: enl. 8/19/61 as Cpl. in Co. G, age 22. To Sgt. 12/26/61, and Lt. 4/20/62. On sick furlough on 9-10/62 roll. Wded. 10/19/64 at Cedar Creek. Absent sick, ordered before medical board at Danville on final 3/22/65 roll. In hosp. at Danville with wd. 3/22/65, returned to duty 3/25. Alive at Oxford, N.C., in 1913.

BOOTH, PATRICK A.: enl. 9/4/63 in Co. G. Transferred from Co. K, 23d Va. Inf. In Richmond hosps. with camp itch 6/17-7/5/64. KIA 10/19/64 at Cedar Creek.

BOOTH, SAMUEL D.: enl. 11/16/63 in Co. G. Transferred from Co. A, 53d Va. Inf. Also in Montague's Bn. Inf. POW 5/7/64 near Spotsylvania C.H. Took the oath at Ft. Delaware 6/19/65. Resid. Charlotte Co. Physician and superintendent of health of Granville Co., N.C., postwar. d. 6/28/16, bur. Elmwood Cem., Oxford, N.C.

BOTTS, ANDREW TUTT: b. at Woodville, Rappahannock Co. enl. 4/22/61 in Co. B as Cpl., age 20. Farmer. Absences for illness, furlough, and detailed service as shoemaker before being wded. 5/11/64 at Yellow Tavern through right arm. Absent wded. to final 3/21/65 roll, when detailed grazing cattle. d. 12/12/28 at Woodville. Wid. Cora Miller Botts, m. 1870.

BOURNE, WILLIAM T.: enl. 5/4/61 in Co. I, age 22. Re-enlistment furlough of 34 days from 2/9/62. d. before 7/21/63.

BOWEN, HENRY: enl. 5/8/61 in Co. B, age 28. Farmer. Absent sick at home 7/1-9/1/61. Absent sick since 12/20/62 on 11-12/62 roll. Absent driving ambulance from 7/1/64 thru 9-10/64 roll. Reported as deserter by Richmond on 2/28/65. Present on final 3/21/65 roll. Paroled at Winchester 5/11/65. Reportedly alive in 5/07.

BOWEN, WILLIAM F.: b. 7/30/24. enl. 5/8/61 in Co. B. Farmer. Overage and declined to re-enlist on 5-6/62 roll, but horse KIA 6/11/63 at Upperville and Bowen wded. 6/21/63 at same place. Absent on horse detail on 9-10/64 roll. Thereafter present thru 3/21/65 final roll. Paroled 5/11/65 at Winchester. d. 1/23/12, bur. Bowen Cem. in Shenandoah National Park.

BOWIE, WILLIAM JACKSON: b. 12/29/22. enl. 5/24/62 in Co. H. Detailed as wagoner thru 3/22/65 final roll, except 12/30/64 and 9-10/64 rolls. d. 2/1/95, bur. Aylor Cem., Franklin Co.

BOWLES, JOHN R.: enl. 1/15/63 in Co. F. Absent, detailed to attend horses on 7-8 and 11-12/63 rolls. Present as Cpl. on 7-8/64 roll thru final 2/24/65 roll. Took the oath as Sgt. at Lynchburg 5/31/65, resid. Baltimore, Md., and destined to go there.

BRABHAM, CHARLES H.: b. 1/29/36. On postwar roster of Co. D as enl. 4/61 and discharged on surgeon's certificate. d. 4/9/01. bur. Green Hill Cem., Berryville.

BRACKETT, JOHN W.: enl. 3/1/62 in Co. A. AWOL on 5-6/62 roll, the only one he is on.

BRADEN, GABRIEL V.: b. 9/2/41. enl. 6/1/61 in Co. K. Sgt. on 6/30/62 roll. Pvt. again on 11-12/62 roll and thereafter. Present on 11-12/63, then no further record. Resid. Washington, D.C., postwar. d. 3/1/21, bur. Union Cem., Leesburg. Postwar roster says wded. in Loudoun in 3/64.

BRADEN, J. HECTOR: With Co. K when MWIA in Loudoun at home of Washington Vandevanter 3/4/64, in ambush by Loudoun Rangers. d. 3/9/64, age 18, bur. Catoctin Free Church Cem. No official record.

BRADEN, OSCAR S.: b. 1818 in Loudoun Co. enl. 4/18/62 as Lt. in Co. K. Wded. slightly at Fairfield, Pa., 7/3/63. In charge of disabled horses from 8/25/63 on 7-8/63 roll. To Capt. 5/13/64. Resignation for health dated 8/12/64, but shown present on 7-8/64 roll, dated 12/27/64. No further record until paroled 4/27/65 at Edwards Ferry, Md. President Loudoun Mutual Fire Insurance Co. postwar. d. 1/4/95.

BRADFORD, HILL C.: b. 1838. enl. 3/1/63 in Co. B, age 24. Previously in Capt. Cayce's Co., Va. Lt. Art. POW 9/25/63 at Griffinsburg, exchanged from Pt. Lookout 2/24/65. Absent with leave on final 3/21/65 roll. Paroled 6/5/65 at Charlottesville. Resid. Fayette Co., Ky., and Culpeper Co. d. 1908, bur. Old City Cem., Jacksonville, Fla.

BRADY, ALBERT: enl. 4/26/61 in Co. B, age 27. Sick in camp on 1-2/62 roll. Severely wded. 5/23/62 at Cedarville. Absent wded. to 1-2/63 roll. Wded. 6/29/64 at Reams Station through left arm, and absent wded. thru 3/21/65 final roll. d. between 4/17/99 and 5/07. Resid. Rockingham Co. postwar.

BRADY, JOSEPH M.: enl. 12/1/61 in Co. B, age 23. Cpl. on 11-12/63 roll. Present to final 3/21/65 roll, when AWOL. d. before 5/07.

BRADY, SIDNEY G.: enl. 10/15/62 in Co. F. On horse furlough on 7-8 and 11-12/63 rolls. POW 5/19/64 in Fauquier Co. d. of pneumonia ca. 4/20/65 at Ft. Delaware, bur. Finn's Pt. Cem., N.J. Resid. Fairfax.

BRADY, WILLIAM BARNET: b. in Rappahannock Co. Farmer. Transferred from Co. G, 49th Va. Inf. to Co. B. Only records are Federal, showing POW about 1/6/64 at Front Royal (or Fauquier Co.). Paroled 2/24/64 at Pt. Lookout, and transferred for exchange. Age 21 on 12/1/61.

BRAGG, PHILIP EVANS: b. 1/18/41. enl. 4/22/61 in Co. B. Farmer. Absent sick since 10/5/61 on 1-2/62 roll. Apparently declared unfit because of sickness ca. 9/25/62, but re-enlisted and present on 7-8/64 roll. AWOL on 9-10/64 roll and AWOL since 12/16/64 on final 3/21/65 roll. Reported by Richmond as deserter on 3/1/65. Paroled 5/9/65 at Winchester. d. 10/16/19, bur. Culpeper Cem., Rt. 522. Postwar roster says "put in substitute and discharged."

BRANCH, WILLIAM ROSCOE: b. Prince Edward Co. enl. 8/19/61 in Co. G as Sgt., age 44. Farmer. Discharged 9/10/61 for incipient phthisis and rheumatic disorders. Elected Capt. of Co. E, 1st (Farinholt's) Va. Reserves. Served at Staunton River Bridge.

BREADY, DANIEL CALVIN: b. 11/4/42 in Md. enl. 6/16/61 in Co. K. Farmer. Cpl. on 6/30/62 roll. Sgt. on 7-8/63 roll. Wded. slightly at Fairfield, Pa., 7/3/63, and 5/5/64. Wded. in arm near Cedar Creek 10/9/64. Present on final 1-2/65 roll. POW 4/1/65 at Five Forks. Took the oath at Pt. Lookout 6/16/65. d. 7/19/29, bur. Mount Olivet Cem., Frederick, Md.

BREEDLOVE, DAVID R.: enl. 5/27/61 in (2d) Co. E. Present on 7-8/61 roll. No further record.

BRENT, A. MONT: enl. 3/1/62 in Co. A. Present until 1-2/63 roll, when in arrest, forfeiting a month's pay by sentence of regimental court-martial. Cpl. when KIA 6/9/63 at Brandy Station.

BRENT, COURTENAY B.: b. in Alexandria. enl. 5/25/61 in Co. F. Student. Previously served in U.S. Navy. Under arrest 8/19/61 for disobedience and insubordination. Dishonorably discharged 10/1/61. Lt. of artillery under Turner Ashby, Capt. 5th Va. Cav., then commanded a Bn. of rangers. Bearer of dispatches to England for Secretary of War. Took the oath at Johnson's Island 7/6/65 as Lt. Col., 4th (Special) Bn. Ky. Cav. (acting), age 24. Wife Kate E. Brent.

BRENT, WILLIAM A.: b. 4/3/42. enl. 4/24/61 in Co. H as Cpl. Clerk. Sgt. on 11-12/61 roll. Present up to furlough of 2/11-3/15/62. Transferred to Co. A, 7th Va. Cav. d. 10/4/04 in Baltimore, Md., bur. Sharon Cem., Middleburg. Never married.

BREWARD, JOHN H.: enl. 4/22/61 in Co. K. POW and paroled 9/22/62 at Paris, thereafter absent until marked AWOL since 3/1/63 on 7-8/63 roll. Later shown as deserting 12/15/63. Postwar roster says he never returned after parole.

BRIGHTWELL, JOHN DABNEY, JR.: enl. 7/19/61 in Co. I, age 31. Admitted 2/24/62 to Orange General Hosp. with rheumatism. Otherwise always absent, on furlough or without leave. AWOL on 8/31/63 roll, the last one he is on. Also in Co. E, 9th Va. Cav.

BROCKMAN, ROBERT: enl. 10/15/64 in Co. I. Present on 9-10/64 roll, the only record for him.

BROCKMAN, W. ALFRED: enl. 10/1/64 in Co. I. Present on final 3/20/65 roll as W. A. Brockman. Doubtless the same as Ally Brockman, reported as a deserter by Richmond on 3/7/65, to be found in Orange Co. Postwar roster shows Alfred Brockman.

BRODEN, JOHN WILLIAM: b. 5/16/30 in Fauquier Co. enl. 5/25/63 in Co. C. Miller. POW 7/3/63 at Fairfield, Pa. Took the oath and enl. 1/24/64 in Co. B, 1st U.S. Vol. Inf. Discharged 1/27/65 at Ft. Leavenworth, Kansas. Signs by mark. m. 1) Fannie Deeds 1854, 2) Rebecca Frances Fultz 1873. d. 11/28/14, bur. Mabel Memorial Chapel, Route 6, Harrisonburg.

BROOKE, JOHN M.: enl. 4/24/61 in Co. H. Drover. Present up to furlough from 2/9 to 3/13/62. Marked as a deserter from latter date. Resid. with S.C. Young at Edwards Ferry, Md., sent after a horse of Young's taken by Federal cavalry. Arrested as a spy, and held at Ft. McHenry, Md., 7/6/63. Released on taking the oath 7/24/63.

BROOKE, ROBERT DAVID: b. in Rappahannock Co. enl. 4/22/61 in Co. B, age 36. Farmer. d. suddenly of disease while on picket duty 5/6/62.

BROOKE, WILLIAM P.: enl. 5/8/61 in Co. B, age 33. Farmer. On extra duty as teamster in QM Dept. from 10/16/61 thru 5-6/62 roll. Present from 11-12/63 thru 9-10/64 rolls. On extra duty as teamster on 3/21/65 final roll. Paroled 4/9/65 at Appomattox. Postwar roster says "prisoner at Yellow Tavern, captured his captors, escaped to our line." Reportedly d. before 5/07.

BROWN, AMBROSE: Told Federals he was conscripted in 3/63 (in Co. B), and deserted 8/1/63 at New Market. They reported him POW 8/19/63 at Waterloo. Took the oath 3/22/64 at Washington, D.C., and sent to New York. Resid. Rappahannock Co. Signs by mark. Age 18 on 3/1/64, "says he is opposed to secession." Not on Confederate records or postwar roster.

BROWN, ANDREW J.: b. in Rockingham Co. enl. 3/5/62 in Co. C. AWOL since 12/25 on 12/62 return. On detached service 7/63. Otherwise always present thru ca. 3/30/65 final roll. Paroled 4/24/65 at Winchester, age 20, resid. Martinsburg. Signs by mark. Resid. North River 3/2/05, ditcher, wded. in leg at Wilderness. May be Andy J. Brown, 1843-1926, bur. Mill Creek Church of the Brethren, Rockingham Co.

BROWN, CHARLES BARBOUR: enl. 4/1/62 in Co. I. To Lt. from Sgt. 12/4/62. KIA 6/9/63 at Brandy Station.

BROWN, CHARLES THOMPSON: b. 1821. enl. 3/18/62 in Co. H. POW 5/7/62. Sent from Ft. Delaware to Aiken's Ldg. and exchanged 8/5/62. Absent sick on 9-10/64 roll and AWOL since 1/20/65 on final 3/22/65 roll. Reported as deserter by Richmond 2/28/65. Paroled 4/22/65 at Winchester, resid. Fauquier Co. d. 1885, bur. Marshall Cem.

BROWN, DALLAS: A reliable postwar roster, etc., show him as enl. 3/62 in Co. B, age 18. KIA 5/23/62 at Cedarville, where he carried the flag, and was hit by 21 balls. No official record, but may be the same as James H. Brown, who is on the company roll.

BROWN, FRANKLIN: Appears in Union records as a member of Co. H, POW 2/6/64 in Fauquier Co., received at Ft. Delaware 6/17/64. No further record, and does not appear in Confederate records or postwar roster.

BROWN, G. M.: On a list of POWs committed to Old Capitol Prison, Washington, D.C., 8/19/63, no company shown. No other record.

BROWN, GIDEON THOMPSON: b. in Culpeper Co. enl. 3/10/62 in Co. B. Merchant. Discharged for disease of the heart 8/5/62. Previously served at Lexington, Mo. Paroled at Harpers Ferry 4/22/65, age 27. Postwar roster says wded. at Slaughter Mountain in August 1862 and unfit for duty afterward, d. before 5/07. Another such roster has a John Thompson Brown, wded. and assigned to commissary detail.

BROWN, HENRY CLAY: b. 1841 in Rappahannock Co. enl. 3/1/62 in Co. B. Horse KIA 5/23/62 at Cedarville. On sick leave 12/62. Otherwise present thru 3/21/65 final roll. Reported as deserter by Richmond 2/28/65. Resid. Midland, Fauquier Co., on 5/21/15, farmer, claiming two wounds. d. 1923, bur. Cedar Grove Cem., Bealeton.

BROWN, JAMES H.: enl. 3/1/61 in Co. B. KIA 5/23/62 at Cedarville on the single roll with his name. May be the same as Dallas Brown, who appears on poswar rosters.

BROWN, JAMES HARVEY: b. in Warren Co. enl. 3/1/63 in Co. B. Absent sick in Richmond hosps. with intermittent fever to final 2/16/65 roll, when AWOL. Carpenter postwar..d. 4/15/24 at Winston. Wid. Lucy C., m. 1866.

BROWN, JAMES R.: enl. 8/24/64 in Co. I. Absent sick on 9-10/64 roll, and absent sick since 1/1/65 on final 3/20/65 roll.

BROWN, JAMES WILLIAM: enl. 5/4/61 in Co. I, age 18. Detailed as teamster, apparently in the regiment, on 6/27/62, a position he seems to have had for most if not all of his remaining service thru 3/20/65 final roll. Paroled 4/9/65 at Appomattox. Pension records show d. 12/21/87 at Nason's, wid. Mary E., m. 1866. Another source gives his dates as 7/1/16 — 3/18/81.

BROWN, JOHN D.: enl. 8/24/64 in Co. I. POW 9/19/64 at Winchester. Paroled at Pt. Lookout and transferred for exchange 2/15/65. Present with a detachment of paroled prisoners at Camp Lee, near Richmond, 2/17/65.

BROWN, JOHN RICHARD: b. 1845 in Pittsylvania Co. enl. 12/1/63 in Co. G. Present to final 3/22/65 roll, when absent sick. Resid. Chatham. Deputy sheriff for 20 years after the war. d. 10/31/27, bur. Chatham Cem. Widow Hattie A.

BROWN, JOHN S.: b. 3/18/31, near Sperryville. enl. 4/18/62 in Co. H. Carpenter. Detailed as wagoner in brigade for much of his service, and thru 3/22/65 final roll. Resid. Rectortown, Fauquier Co., on 6/17/02, and claimed typhoid fever during war. d. 7/31/04, bur. Ivy Hill Cem., Upperville. m. 1861.

BROWN, ROBERT WILLIAM: enl. 9/1/63 in Co. B. Present thru 3/21/65 final roll. In Chimborazo Hosp. No. 1, Richmond, on 3/28/65. m. Elizabeth Thornhill. Farmer in Rappahannock Co. postwar. Postwar roster gives his middle initial as "C", and says he was 40 when he enlisted.

BROWN, THOMAS EDWARD: enl. 5/28/61 in Co. C. AWOL on 11-12/62 roll, but also in column of names present. A month's wages stopped by order of court-martial on 1-2/63 roll. AWOL from 3/17/63 on 7-8/63 roll, and "deserter" on 11-12/63 roll.

BROWN, WILLIAM H.: enl. 4/18/61 in Co. D. AWOL since 7/2/61 on 11-12/61 roll. Announced as deserter 1/31/62. Teamster in regiment 10/12/62 thru 1-2/63 rolls. Absent sick in hosp., and one month's pay deducted by court-martial on 11-12/63 roll. Absent with leave on 9-10/64 roll.

BROWN, WILLIAM TRAVIS: b. 1833. enl. 4/22/61 in Co. B. Farmer. AWOL from 6/10/62 until POW 7/14/62 at Sperryville. In Old Capitol Prison and exchanged 8/5/62. Generally present until dropped from the rolls for desertion on 3/21/65 final roll. d. 1908, bur. Sperryville Cem. His widow Elizabeth's pension claim (m. 1885) was disallowed in 1927, leading to much correspondence.

BROWNELL, WILLIAM H.: b. 1837 in Newport, Rhode Island. enl. 4/22/61 in Co. B. Tanner. To Cpl. 7/26/61. AWOL since 10/15/61 on 9-10/61 roll. Discharged 2/23/62 for chronic inflammation of the bowels and stomach, dependent on a scrofulous condition. enl. 3/31/62 in Co. G, 12th Va. Cav. as Sgt. To Lt. 1/10/63. Resid. Sperryville postwar. d. 6/8/09 at Lee Camp Soldiers' Home, Richmond, bur. Hollywood Cem.

BROWNING, GUSTAVUS JUDSON: b. 5/16/30 in Rappahannock Co. enl. 5/4/61 in Co. I as Capt. Ankle broken by fall of horse 10/5/61 at Culpeper C.H., and at home recovering thru 11-12/61 roll. Dropped 4/20/62. Farmer in Orange postwar. m. Sarah Thomas. House of Delegates 1866-67. d. 4/9/85, bur. Graham Cem. on Rt. 20 west of Orange.

BROWNING, HENRY R.: enl. 5/1/63 in Co, B, age 25. AWOL since 12/15/63 on 11-12/63 roll. Present on 7-8/64 roll. AWOL on 9-10/61 roll, and so marked on final 3/21/65 roll, since 2/1/65. Reported by Richmond as deserter 2/28/65. Postwar roster says "accidently wounded, unfit for duty for rest of war." Reportedly d. before 5/07.

BROWNING, WILLIAM S.: b. in Rappahannock Co. enl. 4/22/61 in Co. B as Cpl., age 27. Farmer. Absent sick in Rappahannock Co. from 8/28/61 thru 9-10/61 roll. To Lt. 4/20/62. Present except for occasional leaves until KIA 10/19/64 at Middletown.

BROY, ISAAC N.: enl. 10/26/61 in Co. A. Farmer. Substitute for Henry C. Gibson. Resid. Warren Co. AWOL twice in 1861-2. Absent sick since 2/15/62, recommended for discharge for "white swelling" on 1-2/63 roll. Deserter since 2/15/62 on 8/31/63 roll. POW 2/13/62 at Front Royal. Age 17 on 3/9/63. Transferred 3/28/63 at Camp Chase for exchange. In Chimborazo Hosp. No. 1 4/5/63 for debility, returned to duty 4/6/63. No further record. d. 7/10/11, bur. Prospect Hill Cem., Front Royal.

BRUCE, WILLIAM P.: enl. 4/22/61 in Co. B, age 23. Mechanic. On furlough on 1-2/62 roll. Courier for Gen. W. E. Jones on 11/62 return. Otherwise always present thru 3/21/65 final roll. Postwar roster says wded. at Five Forks. Reportedly d. before 5/07.

BRUCE, WINFIELD SCOTT: b. 4/3/24 in Fauquier Co. enl. 5/8/61 in Co. B as Cpl. Mechanic. To Sgt. 7/26/61. In arrest, then Pvt. on 5-6/62 roll. With Gen. Trimble on 10/8/62. Hip dislocated in fall from horse 11/20/62. Wded. 10/1/63. Reported by Richmond as deserter 2/28/65, but present on 3/21/65 final roll. In 1st Va. Vols., Mexican War. m. Martha F. Bruce, 1852. d. 3/11/12 at Sperryville.

BRUDDLER, JAMES: Only record is a Union roll dated Harpers Ferry, (W.) Va., 8/3/64, which has him in Co. C, POW 7/21/64 at Upperville, and sent to Washington, D.C., 8/24/64. Doubtless an error, referring to someone else in garbled form.

BURCH, EDGAR FRANCIS: b. 2/12/45 in Loudoun Co. enl. 3/1/64 in Co. K. Wded. near Trevillian's Station 6/6/64 and at Louisa C.H. 6/11/64. Present on final 1-2/65 roll. Paroled 4/24/65 at Conrad's Ferry (signing "Edgar F. Birch"). m. Mary Groome Thompson. Farmer postwar. d. 2/27/00, bur. Union Cem., Leesburg.

BURCH, JAMES: b. in Fairfax Co. enl. 6/16/61 in Co. K. Present until sick in camp on 1-2/62 roll. d. 3/25/62 in Loudoun Co.

BURCH, THOMAS, SR.: enl. 4/22/61 in Co. K. Detailed as wagonmaster for 7th Brigade 8/29/61. 11-12/62 roll says he did not reenlist, and thus his term of service expired 4/22/62, he being over 40 years old. He continues to appear on rolls as absent, detached as above, thru 7-8/63.

BURCH, THOMAS F., JR.: b. 4/30/39 in Loudoun Co. enl. 6/16/61 in Co. K. Absent on sick leave since 11/17/61 on 1-2/62 roll, after which he was carried as AWOL until dropped by order of Gen. L. L. Lomax 12/26/63 (dates of illness vary). m. Helen Hammerley 1872. Present at 1st Manassas. Farmer in Broad Run Dist. of Loudoun Co. in 1883 (Name appears as Birch also).

BURGESS, HORACE PEYTON: b. 1/17/36 in Fauquier Co. enl. 10/1/62 in Co. H. Absent sick since 11/25/62 on 11-12/62 roll. POW 7/21/63 at Chester Gap, wded. Exchanged 2/10/65 from Pt. Lookout. Paroled 4/22/65 at Winchester. Farmer resid. near The Plains postwar. m. Elizabeth Cockrill before 1861. d. 12/4/22, bur. Marshall Cem.

BURKE, CORNELIUS W.: enl. 4/22/61 in Co. B, age 22. Sgt. on 9-10/62 roll. Sick since 12/24/63 on 11-12/63 roll. Reported by Richmond as deserter 2/28/65, but otherwise present on all rolls thru 3/21/65 final roll. Reportedly alive in 5/07.

BURKE, GEORGE FESTUS: enl. 10/1/62 in Co. B, age 20. Present until absent wded. 7/3/63 at Fairfield, Pa. Signs clothing rolls on 5/2 and 5/19/64. Confederate records and a postwar roster report him POW at Cold Harbor and d. of disease in prison 7/5/64, but there are no Federal records on him. Resid. Culpeper Co.

BURKE, JAMES EDWARD: enl. 2/1/63 in Co. B, age 20. Present until final 3/21/65 roll, when marked AWOL since 1/21/65. Reportedly d. before 5/07. Resid. Culpeper Co.

BURKE, JAMES M.: enl. 9/1/62 in Co. B. Present until POW 5/31/64 at Cold Harbor. d. 6/28/64 at Pt. Lookout of acute dysentery and bur. there. May be the same as Mike Burke, shown below.

BURKE, JOSEPH: enl. 2/15/63 in Co. B, age 18. Absent sick on 7-8/64 and AWOL on 9-10/64 rolls. Admitted to Charlottesville General Hosp. 12/30/64 with pneumonia, returned to duty 2/14/65. AWOL since 2/21/65 on 3/21/65 final roll. Reportedly d. before 5/07.

BURKE, MIKE: Shown on a postwar roster as enl. 3/63 in Co. B, age 20. KIA at Spotsylvania C.H. May be identical to James M. Burke, shown above.

BURKE, M. N.: b. Madison Co. enl. 1862 in Co. B. Farmer, resid. Boston, Culpeper Co., age 63 when he applied for pension on 5/30/08. No official record. On postwar roster.

BURKE, NAPOLEON: enl. 2/1/65 in Co. B. AWOL since 2/7/65 on 3/21/65 final roll. Probably identical to men of this name who served in Co. H, 2d Va. Art., Co. H, 22d Bn. Va. Inf., and as detective in Dept. of Richmond (the latter reported 5/27/64 as age 46, b. in Va., citizen of Richmond, appointed 11/22/62 and employed thru 10/31/64).

BURKE, ROBERT A.: b. in Rappahannock Co. enl. 3/1/62 in Co. B. Absent sick since 1/25/63 on 1-2/63 roll. Provost guard since 10/6/63 on 11-12/63 roll. Absent sick on rolls for 7-10/64. Reported as deserter by Richmond 2/28/65. AWOL since 1/21/65 on final 3/21/65 roll. Wheelwright, age 70, resid. Boston, Culpeper Co., 5/3/06. d. 9/10/08, at Staunton. Wid. Roberta, m. 11/64.

BURKE, ROBERT E.: enl. 3/1/62 in Co. B, age 20. He and horse KIA 5/23/62 at Cedarville. Left no wife or child. Known as "Tony."

BURKE, THOMAS G.: b. in Loudoun Co. enl. 3/9/62 in Co. F. Cpl. on 7-8/62 roll. Sgt. on 7-8/64 roll. Present on final 2/24/65 roll. Paroled 4/9/65 at Appomattox. Resid. Tucker Co., W.Va., postwar. Age 81 on 6/14/22. d. 3/1/28 at Lee Camp Soldiers' Home, Richmond.

BURKETT, JAMES E.: b. 1844 in Rockingham Co. enl. 3/5/62 in Co. C. Present on all rolls thru ca. 3/30/65 final roll. Paroled 5/2/65 at Harrisonburg. Farmer postwar, resid. in Kentucky since 1882. d. 3/29/30 at Moreland, Lincoln Co., Ky., bur. Kentucky. The surname of 4 men in Co. C appears as Burkhead, Burgett, Burkit, etc. All have been standardized as above in this roster.

BURKETT, JOHN WILLIAM: b. 8/16/37 in Albemarle Co. enl. 5/28/61 in Co. C. Teamster in QM Dept. on 10/30/63. Otherwise present on all rolls thru ca. 3/30/65 final roll. Paroled 5/31/65 at Harrisonburg, signs by mark. Farmer postwar, resid. near Elkton. d. 1/7/16, bur. East Point Cem. Wid. Emmaline, m. 1864.

BURKETT, THOMAS: b. in Albemarle Co. enl. 3/5/62 in Co. C. Laborer. 11/62 return says deserted at Rippon, since dead. d. 8/17/62, without wife or child.

BURKETT, WILLIAM: enl. 3/5/62 in Co. C. At home sick since 1/30/63 on 1-2/63 roll. On returns for 11 and 12/62 as teamster. Otherwise present thru 1/1/64 clothing roll. No further record. d. 8/1/01, wid. Mary A. Mrs. Burkett's pension application declares she was *married* in 1820 or 1821.

BURNER, ALBERT A.: b. 9/3/38. enl. 7/5/62 in Co. F. Farmer. Previously in Co. F, 2d Va. Inf. Wded. 5/6/64, in Chimborazo Hosp. No. 2, 5/9/64. Present thru ca. 3/30/65 final roll. To hosp. at Farmville 4/15/64, released 5/6/65. d. 10/21/05, bur. Mt. Olivet Cem., Route 33 East, McGaheysville.

BURNER, JACOB B.: b. 9/3/33. enl. 5/28/61 in Co. F. Farmer. In charge of baggage at Manassas 10/61. Horse KIA 9/22/62 near Paris. Wded. 5/5/64 in groin and penis. Wded. 9/19/64. Present on final ca. 3/30/65 roll. POW at Jackson Hospital, Richmond, 4/3/65. Paroled at Richmond, 4/24/65. "Deserted" Jackson Hospital 4/27. d. 4/13/27 at McGaheysville, bur. Mt. Olivet Cem. Wid. Barbara A.

BURNER, LAYTON W.: b. 1842 in Rockingham Co. enl. 7/2/62 in Co. F. Previously in Co. F, 2d Va. Inf. Horse KIA at Paris 9/22/62. POW 5/31/64 at Cold Harbor. d. of exhaustion from gunshot wds. 10/4/64 at Lincoln General Hosp., Washington, D.C. Resid. McGaheysville, single. Previously in Co. F, 2d Va. Inf.

BURROUGHS, R. F. WILLIAMS: enl. 9/17/61 in (1st) Co. E, age 23. On extra duty in QM Dept. on 10/61 return, and a teamster since 11/1 on 11/61 return. Admitted 12/29/61 to General Hosp. No. 1, Danville, with pneumonia, sent to hosp. at Front Royal. Resid. Savannah, Ga.

BURRUSS, JOHN HERSCHEL: b. 9/9/47 in Orange Co. Att. VMI. Enl. 2/1/64 in Co. I. Absent wded. on 9-10/64 roll and AWOL on final 3/20/65 roll. Farmer at Monrovia on 2/12/19 when he applied for pension. W. W. Scott, state law librarian, vouched for him, explaining he was youngest of 4 brothers in army (3 KIA 6/26/62). Burruss had no recollection of being absent, said he was wded. 10/9/64 near Strasburg, and got his pension. d. 11/30. Wid. Alena H., m. 1887.

BURRUSS, THOMAS F.: enl. 3/1/63 in Co. I. Horse KIA 7/3/63 at Fairfield, Pa. Detailed at horse pasture 7/9/63. Sgt. on 11-12/63 roll. Absent sick at hosp. on 9-10/64 roll, and AWOL on final 3/20/65 roll.

BURRUSS, WILLIAM TERRILL: b. in Orange Co. enl. 5/4/61 in Co. I, age 30. In hosp. at Orange 3/21-3/26/62 with orchitis. AWOL since 2/17/63 on 1-2/63 roll, and since 8/31/63 on 7-8/63 roll. AWOL on final 3/20/65 roll. Farmer postwar. d. 11/14/15 at Gordonsville. Wid. Nannie A., m. 2/65.

BURTON, JAMES D.: Conscript assigned to Co. F 5/25/64. Absent on detail on 9-10/64 roll, and sick at hosp. on final 3/24/65 roll. Postwar roster says POW at Trevillian's Station, but escaped.

BUTLER, JOHN: On a generally reliable postwar roster of Co. B as enl. 3/62, age 27, and serving rest of war, d. before 5/07. Got William C. Wilson as substitute 6/30/62 on 5-6/62 roll.

BYRD, BARRY: enl. 9/17/61 in (1st) Co. E, age 22. Resid. Tattnall Co., Ga. d. 12/21/61 at Georgia Hosp., Richmond, of typhoid fever.

BYRNE, JAMES N.: enl. 10/1/62 in Co. K. Present until POW 10/17/64 near Middleburg. Sent from Elmira to James River for exchange 3/14/65. Present at Camp Lee near Richmond 3/19/65. Paroled at Winchester 4/25/65, age 21, resid. Fauquier Co. Alive at Browningsville, Md., 8/26/11. d. 1/2/21, aged 77 years, 9 months, and 24 days. bur. Bethesda Methodist Episcopal Church Cem., Browningsville, Md.

BYWATERS, JAMES EDWARD: enl. 4/1/62 in Co. B, age 31. d. 8/7/62 of typhoid fever at General Hosp. No. 2, Lynchburg. bur. Old Town Cem., Lynchburg. Wid. Sallie Hill, m. 1851.

BYWATERS, ROBERT H.: enl. 2/15/63 in Co. B, age 33. Present on 1-2/63 roll, on 11-12/63 roll (joined from desertion 12/10/63), and on 5/2/64 clothing roll. d. 12/23/81. Wid. Adelia P., m. 1851.

CABANISS, WILLIAM M.: enl. 10/19/61 in Co. G. Sick furlough since 12/31 on 11-12/61 roll. Sgt. on 5-6/62 roll. Sick since 7/21 on Nov. return. Discharged on surgeon's certificate of disability 11/7/62. Previously served in Co. D, 4th Texas Inf., age 21 on enl. 7/27/61.

CABELL, JOHN GRATTAN: b. 6/17/17. Att. Washington College and U. Va., grad. U. Md. as M.D. Capt. Co. I, 4th Va. Cav. Physician in Nelson Co. and Richmond. Appointed Major 6th Va. Cav. 9/11/61. To Lt. Col. 4/15/62. Appointed surgeon 9/19/63, superintendent Jackson Hosp. Richmond. d. 3/26/96 in Richmond.

CALMES, FIELDING HELMS: b. 6/17/32 in Clarke Co. enl. 4/61 in Co. D as Cpl. Farmer. Hunting deserters since 10/23 on 9-10/61 roll. Present thru 1-2/63 roll. To what became the 23d Va. Cav. 9/7/63, where he rose to Major. m. 1) Margaret Moore, 2) Mildred Meetze. d. 12/12/01 at "Helmsley," Clarke Co., and bur. there.

CALMES, MARQUIS: enl. 6/1/62 in Co. D. POW 6/9/63 at Beverly Ford, exchanged 6/25/63 at City Point. Absent on scout for Gen. T. L. Rosser on 9-10/64 roll. KIA while on scout, 11/4/64.

CAMPBELL, ANDREW J.: b. near McRae in Telfair Co., Ga. enl. 9/17/61 in (1st) Co. E, age 31. Resid. Telfair Co., Ga. d. 9/9 (or 10/14)/63 of disease at Huguenot Springs. Brother of Robert.

CAMPBELL, JOSEPH: enl. 4/22/61 in Co. K. Sick in camp on 1-2/62 roll. d. 3/15/62 in Loudoun Co.

CAMPBELL, ROBERT: b. near McRae in Telfair Co., Ga. enl. 9/17/61 in (1st) Co. E, age 33. Resid. Telfair Co., Ga. Wded. 8/1/63 at Brandy Station. d. of wound at home in Telfair Co., 10/63. Brother of Andrew J.

CANADA, DAVID: enl. 7/21/64 in Co. G. Absent on horse detail on 9-10/64 roll. Present on final 3/22/65 roll. Paroled at HQ 2d Division, 6th Corps 5/9/65.

CANADA, JOHN W.: Conscript assigned 10/8/63 to Co. G. Consistently AWOL or in Richmond or Farmville hosps. with rheumatism and lumbago. AWOL on final 3/22/65 roll.

CANADAY, ADOLPHUS ANTHONY: b. in Orange Co. enl. 3/15/64 in Co. I. Present until absent sick in hosp. on 9-10/64 roll. Reported as deserter by Richmond on 2/28/65, but present on 3/20/65 final roll. Living in Spotsylvania Co., age 66 on 7/15/12. d. 4/22/22 at Fredericksburg. Wid. Virginia H., m. 1869.

CANADAY, JAMES DANIEL: enl. 5/4/61 in Co. I, age 22. Absent on sick furlough on 11-12/61 and 1-2/62 rolls. Wded. 7/7/63 at Funkstown, Md. Wded. 5/26/64 and absent wded. thru 3/20/65 final roll.

CANADAY, THOMAS G.: enl. 4/1/62 in Co. I. AWOL on 5-6/62 roll. 30 day furlough 12/28/62 and still absent on 1-2/63 roll. Thereafter present to 3/20/65 final roll, when AWOL.

CANARD, GEORGE: enl. 10/30/62 in Co. F. Deserted 11/1/62. Doubtless identical to George Kennard, q.v.

CANNON, ELIJAH: enl. 4/22/61 in Co. B, age 25. Farmer. Sick since 9/18/61 on 9-10/61 roll. Found not guilty of AWOL 1/23/62. Wded. through hand 5/23/62, then absent wded. or sick thru 1-2/63 roll. Absent wded. since 10/11/63 on 11-12/63 rolls. AWOL on 7-8 and deserted on 9-10/64 rolls. Paroled 4/27/65 at Winchester, age 28. d. 3/8/85, wid. Lucy M., m. 1865. Postwar roster says discharged for ill health.

CANNON, GEORGE WASHINGTON: b. in Rappahannock Co. enl. 4/22/61 in Co. B, age 21. Farmer. Discharged 8/25/61, for ill health according to postwar roster. Later in Mosby's 43d Bn. Va. Cav., Co. B. d. 2/14/16 in Rappahannock Co., resid. near Castleton.

CANNON, JOHN ROBERT: b. 9/23/30. enl. 4/1/63 in Co. B. Present on all rolls thru 3/21/65 final roll. d. 4/11/06, bur. Culpeper City Cem. Wid. Virginia A., m. 1867.

CAPP, PHILLIP: Conscript assigned to regiment 4/20/64, no company shown. POW 5/2/64 in Frederick Co., age 29, farmer. Resid. Shenandoah Co. Took the oath and released at Wheeling 5/10/64.

CARBERY, JAMES LOUIS: b. 1831 in Georgetown, D.C., att. Georgetown Univ. enl. 5/22/61 in Co. K. Clerk. Present on 7-8/61 roll, then absent sick from 1/1/62 until discharged 9/5/63 as a resident of D.C. Resid. Rappahannock Co., unmarried, on 3/5/64 when in Old Capitol Prison. "Refuses oath, wants to be sent South." d. 11/23/91. bur. Oak Hill Cem., Georgetown. Wid. Eliza.

CAREN, CHARLES M.: Shown as a member of Co. I on a postwar roster. No official record.

CARICKHOFF, JOHN CHRISTOPHER: b. 4/22/43. enl. 5/5/62 in Co. C. Present until deserted 1/15/63. d. 12/31/06 at Philadelphia, Pa., and bur. there.

CARNER, HENRY A.: enl. 11/1/64 in Co. I. Present on final 3/20/65 roll. d. before 10/13/30, bur. Zion Methodist Church Cem., Spotsylvania C.H.

CARNER, JOHN WILLIAM: b. 7/28/46 in Bedford Co. (another source says Spotsylvania Co.), enl. 1/1/64 in Co. I. Present thru final 3/20/65 roll. Pension claims wded. at Winchester. Farmer and railroad contractor postwar. m. Annie E. Jones 1867. d. 3/17/15 in Richmond. Resid. Spotsylvania Co.

CARPENTER, JAMES E.: enl. 3/1/62 in Co. B, age 21. Absent sick from 5/20/62 thru 12/62 return. Detailed to get clothing 12/30/62. POW 1/12/64 in Rappahannock Co. d. 7/6/64 at Pt. Lookout.

CARPENTER, MATTHEW C.: enl. 4/22/61 in Co. B, age 24. Farmer. Sgt. on 5-6/62, Pvt. on 11-12/63 rolls. POW 1/12/64 in Rappahannock Co. Exchanged from Pt. Lookout 2/13/65. d. 3/1/65 of pneumonia at Camp Lee, near Richmond. Wld. Lucy M., m. 1860.

CARPENTER, WILIAM JOHNSTON: enl. 3/1/62 in Co. B, age 28. Present until final 3/21/65 roll, when shown AWOL since 1/21/65. Reported by Richmond as deserter 2/28/65. d. 10/16, near Woodville. Wld. Elizabeth, m. 1872.

CARPENTER, WILLIAM T.: Shown on enrollment book for Rockingham Co. in Va. Hist. Soc. as in Co. C, age 27, farmer, getting Samuel Sandy as substitute.

CARPER, JOHN B.: enl. 7/25/63 in Co. D. Present thru 3/22/65 final roll. Resid. Fauquier Co. in 1898, age 68.

CARPER, JOHN HENRY: b. 1/16/41 in Frederick Co. enl. 10/30/62 in Co. F. Present until 9-10/64 roll, when AWOL. William H. Barr, Co. K, 23d Va. Cav., swore on 10/12/32 that Carper was serving as recruiter for the 6th Va. Cav. when erroneously marked AWOL. m. Elizabeth M. Gibbons, 3/7/65. d. 2/18/18 at Grandview, Johnson Co., Texas.

CARR, JAMES WILLIAM: b. 6/22/41 (or 1842) at Alexandria. enl. 4/22/61 in Co. K as Cpl. Pvt. on 6/30/62 roll. POW 6/25/63 near Leesburg while scouting. Enteritis at Pt. Lookout. Took the oath at Ft. Delaware 1/27/64 and released. Commission merchant and wholesale grocer postwar. Brother of Peter H. d. 5/4/08, bur. Carr-Gaines Cem., Prince William Co.

CARR, JOHN O.: enl. 6/1/63 in Co. B, age 18. Absent sick at hosp. 12/20/63 on 11-12/63 roll. KIA 5/64 at Spotsylvania C.H., bur. Confederate Cem., Spotsylvania C.H.

CARR, PETER HENRY: b. 1/29/43 in Loudoun Co. enl. 7/1/61 in Co. K. Farmer. Sick in camp on 1-2/62 roll. Otherwise always present thru final 1-2/65 roll. Paroled 4/22/65, at Edwards Ferry, Md. d. 3/11/22 at Waterford, bur. Leesburg Union Cem. m. Roberta Elgin. Brother of James W.

CARR, THOMAS E.: b. 5/8/35. enl. 9/8/62 in Co. A. Horse furlough 12/16/63, leave 12/16/63. POW 5/12/64 in Hanover Co. Exchanged 2/18/65 from Pt. Lookout. Absent with leave on 3/27/65 final roll, "exchanged but not yet notified." Paroled 4/20/65 at Winchester. d. 10/21/02, bur. Leesburg Union Cem.

CARRINGTON, CHARLES SCOTT: b. 1820 at "Mildendo" in Halifax Co. Grad. Hampden-Sydney College. enl. 8/19/61 in Co. B. Age 41 on 9/10/61 roll. Discharged as "Quartermaster at Yorktown" 10/28/61. Appointed Capt. in QM Dept. 6/6/62. Paroled 4/26/65 at Greensboro, N.C., as Major. Resid. Halifax Co. and Richmond. President James River and Kanawha Canal Co. m. Susan Smith Preston McDowell. d. 1892.

CARRINGTON, GEORGE CABELL: b. 10/13/19. Appointed acting surgeon 12/8/61. Joined regiment 12/13/61. Resigned 7/28/62 with chronic diarrhoea. Physician postwar. m. Sarah Winston Henry. d. 9/23/80, bur. St. John's Episcopal Church, Halifax.

CARRINGTON, JOHN RAGLAND: b. 1840. enl. in Co. G. Previously in Co. A, 53d Va. Inf. In General Hosp., Petersburg, 7/28-8/4/64, injured in fall from horse. Present on final 3/22/65 roll. Paroled 5/25/65 in Richmond. d. 1908, bur. St. John's Episcopal Church, Halifax.

CARROLL, JAMES F.: enl. 9/25/62 in Co. A. Present until AWOL since 8/26/63 on 8/31/63 roll. Absent in arrest, Richmond, on 11-12/63 roll. d. 8/64.

CARROLL, LEWIS: enl. 3/1/62 in Co. A. Horse KIA 6/9/63 at Brandy Station. Absent sick since July on 8/31/63 roll. Present on 11-12/63 roll. Postwar roster says discharged, over age. Resid. Clarke Co.

CARROLL, THOMAS: enl. 9/25/62 in Co. A. Always present until final 3/27/65 roll, when AWOL since 1/23/65. Paroled 4/22/65 at Winchester, age 30, resid. Clarke Co. near Snickersville. d. 4/27/98, wld. Serah E., m. 1867.

CARSON, J.: Only record is a return for 11/62, which has him enl. 11/25/62 in Co. F.

CARSON, JOHN R.: enl. 7/21/61 in Co. D. To Sgt. Maj. 12/1/61. Absent on sick furlough since 1/16/62 on 1-2/62 roll. Signs receipt 11/17/63 as Pvt. No further record. Clerk of Winchester city court postwar. d. 5/24/86, bur. Mt. Hebron Cem., Winchester.

CARSON, THOMAS G.: enl. 5/4/61 in Co. I, age 20. To Cpl. on 1-2 and Sgt. on 5-6/62 rolls. Horse captured 7/18/62. Carson paroled 8/9/62 at Ft. Monroe. Reduced to ranks 12/15/63 for being dismounted. In Richmond hosps. with camp itch 11/27/63-2/7/64. POW 10/9/64 at Strasburg. Paroled 2/18/65 at Pt. Lookout. Present 2/27/65 at Camp Lee near Richmond with detachment of paroled POWs.

CARTER, ALFRED BALL: b. 12/5/23 in Prince William Co. Appointed Lt. in Co. F 4/20/62. To Capt. on 11-12/63 roll. Wded. in left side 5/7/64. Wded. 9/19/64 and arm amputated. Retired to Invalid Corps 3/8/65, assigned to Va. Reserves 3/15/65. Discharged from hosp. 4/17/65. m. Elizabeth Hill 1851. d. 3/11/01 at Memphis, Tenn.

CARTER, DILWIN S.: enl. 1/1/63 in Co. A. Transferred from Co. H, 1st Va. Cav. Absent sick since 6/12 on 8/31/63 roll. Present on 11-12/63 roll. Postwar roster says KIA at Trevillian's Station.

CARTER, EDWARD J.: b. Pittsylvania Co. enl. 8/19/61 in Co. G, age 43. Farmer. Present until discharged 8/19/62. Resid. Pittsylvania Co.

CARTER, FRANKLIN R.: b. 1843 at Upperville. enl. 3/16/62 in Co. H. In Chimborazo Hosp. No. 1, Richmond, with morbi cutis 4/9-5/4/64. Otherwise usually present thru 3/22/65 final roll. Paroled 5/8/65 at Winchester. Prospector postwar. d. 1927, bur. Sharon Cem., Middleburg.

CARTER, GEORGE F.: enl. 8/1/62 in Co. F. To Sgt. on 9-10/62 roll. Absent sick since 1/1/64 on 7-8 roll, Pvt., and absent sick on 9-10/64 roll, dated 2/24/65. Alive in Fairfax Co., 1898, age 76.

CARTER, HENRY S.: enl. 4/24/61 in Co. H. Clerk. Accidentally shot thru hand 6/3/61, and unfit for duty thru 9-10/61 roll. Present as company commissary on 11-12/61 and 1-2/62 rolls. Name cancelled on 5-6/62 roll. No further record.

CARTER, JAMES FRANKLIN: b. 1842 in Fauquier Co. enl. 3/1/62 in Co. A. Present until POW 10/11/63 near Brandy Station. Paroled from Pt. Lookout 2/13/65. With detachment paroled POWs at Camp Lee, near Richmond, 2/18/65. Absent with leave, exchanged but not yet notified on 3/27/65 final roll. Paroled 4/22/65 at Winchester. m. Mary Frances Seaton 1867. Ran sawmill postwar. d. 1909, bur. Marshall Cem.

CARTER, JOSEPH H.: enl. 5/27/61 in (2d) Co. E. Age 36 on 2/16/62 roll. Detached guarding bridge on 11-12/62 roll. Horse WIA 10/11/63. Present thru 3/4/65 final roll. In Chimborazo Hosp. No. 5, Richmond, with primary syphilis 3/28/65. 1913 roster says d. in California after war.

CARTER, LANDON E.: enl. 5/1/62 in Co. F. Transferred 10/6/62 to 8th Va. Inf. Postwar roster says wded., disabled for life.

CARTER, ROBERT: enl. 7/24/61 in Co. A as Lt. Acting Regimental QM and Commissary 10/2 (or 21)/61. To Capt. and QM 11/16/61. Absent sick without leave on 11-12/61 roll, then generally present thru 4/9/65 parole at Appomattox.

CARTER, ROBERT CHAMP: b. 1840. enl. 7/24/61 in Co. A. 30 day re-enlistment furlough on 2/9/62, otherwise always present until wded. 10/9/64. Absent sick on surgeon's certificate since 3/20 on 3/27/65 final roll. Paroled 4/29/65 at Winchester, resid. Loudoun Co. near Upperville. d. 1873, bur. Sharon Cem., Middleburg.

CARTER, THOMAS ARTHUR: b. 1/29/40, enl. 7/24/61 in Co. A. Absent 10/21/61 for accidental wound in foot thru 1-2/62 roll. Some illnesses before POW and horse KIA 6/9/63 at Brandy Station. Exchanged 6/30/63 from Old Capitol Prison. AWOL since 7/23 on 8/31/63 roll. Clothing detail 12/31/63. Present on final 3/27/65 roll. Paroled 4/26/65 at Winchester. d. 5/21/07, bur. Leesburg Union Cem.

CARTER, THOMAS T.: enl. 7/24/61 in Co. A as Cpl. On extra duty as wagonmaster from 10/25/61 thru 4/30/62. To Sgt. on 5-6/62 roll. Absent sick since 11/5/62, reduced to ranks from Sgt. on 11-12/62 roll. Absent at corps horse hosp., apparently as veterinary surgeon, 8/63 thru 3/27/65 final roll. Sgt. on 2/17/65 report of detached men employed by QM at Lynchburg, "indispensable to identify the horses." Resid. Burke Station, Fairfax Co., on 5/22/88, age 70, suffering from opthalmia. Probably identical to Thomas Goody Carter shown on postwar roster, "Goody" evidently being a nickname. d. 10/6/01.

CARTIN, P. G.: Only record is of parole as a member of Co. A at Appomattox 4/9/65, resid. Loudoun Co.

CARTLEY, _____: Shown on a postwar roster of Co. I as discharged in 1862. No official record.

CASTLEMAN, EDWARD PREBBLE: b. 9/20/42 in Clarke Co. enl. 5/20/62 in Co. D (but actually a deserter from Co. A, 5th Va. Inf.). Farmer. Discharged 10/10/62 at Richmond for heart disease and hemorrhage from lungs. Authorized on 5/30/63 to raise a co. for Mosby, but authority revoked because of depredations and horse stealing. Family declared he was "drafted" into U.S. Army, and d. in 1863 in fall from horse.

CASTLEMAN, JAMES ROBERT: b. 8/7/45 at Berryville. Att. VMI. enl. 8/1/63 in Co. D. Clerk. POW 7/2/64 at Snickers Ferry. Transferred for exchange from Elmira 2/13/65. In detachment of paroled prisoners at Camp Lee near Richmond 2/21/65. Paroled 4/25/65 at Winchester. Clerk in stores and hotels postwar. d. 11/23/85 at Toledo, Ohio. bur. Green Hill Cem., Berryville.

CASTLEMAN, MANN R. PAGE: b. 5/12/38. enl. 4/2/62 in Co. D. Color Sgt. from 11-12/62 roll to discharge on 3/30/65 because of election to House of Delegates. Horse KIA 6/11/64 at Trevillian's Station. Paroled 4/24/65 at Summit Pt.,(W.) Va. d. 10/28/99, bur. Green Hill Cem., Berryville. Postwar roster says "brought out the original colors with not less than 50 bullet holes in them."

CASTLEMAN, ROBERT H.: b. 1827. enl. 4/21/61 in Co. D. Absent as brigade Commissary Sgt. until transferred 10/23/63 to Co. B, 12th Va. Cav. Paroled 4/26/65 at Charles Town, (W.) Va. d. 7/30/04 at Castleman's Ferry, bur. Mt. Hebron Cem., Winchester.

CATLETT, HENRY C.: enl. 4/18/61 in Co. D. Announced as deserter 1/31/62. Otherwise present until detailed as clerk of general court martial for Hampton's Div. 8/23/65-1/25/64. Present with co. on 7-8 and 9-10/64 rolls. AWOL on final 3/22/65 roll. Paroled 4/19/65 at Winchester, age 27, resid. Clarke Co. near White Post.

CATLETT, HENRY C.: enl. 11/10/61 in Co. K. AWOL on 6/30/62 roll. Present on 12/12/62 roll. Transferred 12/12/62 to (2d) Co. F, 5th Va. Cav., which became Co. I, 11th Va. Cav. Took the oath at Alexandria 5/10/65, resid. St. Joseph, Mo.

CHANCELLOR, JAMES MONROE: b. 1841. enl. 4/22/61 in Co. B. Farmer. Sick with measles on 6/30/61 roll. Present, but two months AWOL noted on 6/30/61 roll. Sick since 2/3/62 on 1-2/62 roll, and absent sick at hospital on 11-12/62 roll. AWOL since 6/4/63 on 1-2/63 roll (sic), but appointed AQM, 9th Va. Bn. 1/2/63. Lt. Col. G. W. Hansbrough described him as "a brave, patriotic, steady & intelligent young man. . . distinguishing himself at Front Royal." d. 1919.

CHADWELL, C. W.: On postwar "original list" of Co. F.

CHAPPELEAR, GEORGE WARREN: b. 9/8/42. enl. 7/24/61 in Co. A. Present until detached as courier for Gens. Walker and Jackson, 10/15/62-1/1/63. In Charlottesville General Hosp. with scabies 12/29/64-1/29/65. Present on final 3/27/65 roll. Paroled 5/17/65 at Winchester. Postwar roster says wded. at Five Forks, promoted for gallantry. d. 11/3/22 at Delaplane, bur. Ivy Hill Cem., Upperville.

CHAPPELEAR, JAMES PENDLETON: enl. 7/24/61 in Co. A. POW ca. 9/7/62, exchanged 9/21/62. Otherwise always present thru 12/5/62 roll. Transferred to Mosby. KIA 2/22/64 at Dranesville, aged 31 years, 2 months, and 11 days, bur. Fletcher Cem. at "Oak Spring" near Upperville.

CHAPPELEAR, JOHN ARMISTEAD: b. 12/1/35. enl. 11/12/63 in Co. A. On detail after horse 11/14-29/63. Absent with leave on 9-10/64 roll and AWOL since 3/7/65 on 3/27/65 final roll. m. Amanda Virginia Edmonds 1870. d. 6/1/16 at "Belle Grove," Fauquier Co., bur. Edmonds Cem. near Paris.

CHELF, JAMES MADISON: enl. 10/1/64 in Co. B. Present on all rolls until 3/21/65 final roll, when AWOL. Reported by Richmond as deserter on 2/28/65. Paroled 5/9/65 at Winchester, age 27. d. 2/31.

CHEWNING, GEORGE WASHINGTON: enl. 10/1/64 in Co. I. On horse detail on 9-10/64 roll. AWOL on final 3/20/65 roll. d. 10/18/27 at his home in Belmont section of Spotsylvania Co., age 80. Wid. Sarah Alice, m. 1873.

CHEWNING, ROBERT E.: enl. 3/1/62 in Co. B, age 30. Absent sick since 6/9/63 on 11-12/63 roll. POW 11/17/63 in Rappahannock Co. Paroled at Pt. Lookout and transferred for exchange 2/24/65. In General Hosp., Howard's Grove, Richmond, 2/26/65, 30 days furlough. Absent with leave on final 3/21/65 roll. Reportedly alive in 5/07.

CHILDRESS, HENRY PATTON: b. 11/25/37 in Alexandria. enl. Co. I as bugler. Courier for Gen. Jeb Stuart since 12/24/62 on 11-12/62 roll. Courier for Gen. Jones on 1-2/63 roll. Detailed as bugler 8/15/63. Chief bugler from 7-8 thru 9-10/64 roll. No further record. Postwar roster says wded. at Tom's Brook. Resid. Maryville, Mo., for many years. m. Virginia Elvira Tinder, 1862. d. 12/14/29 at Los Angeles, Cal., bur. Maryville, Mo.

CHILDRESS, WILLIAM ELLIOTT: b. 1842 in Orange Co. enl. 5/4/62 in Co. I. 10 day furlough from 2/20/63. Detailed on provost duty from 7-8/64 thru final 3/20/65 rolls. d. 11/28/09, bur. Antioch Baptist Church Cem., Orange Co.

CHINN, BENTON: b. 7/17/44 in Fauquier Co. enl. 9/29/62 in Co. H. AWOL since 8/25 on 7-8/63 roll. Otherwise present on all rolls thru 3/22/65 final roll. Found not guilty of AWOL by courtmartial 3/7/64. Reported by Richmond as deserter 2/28/65. Paroled 4/25/65 at Winchester. Bookkeeper postwar. d. 4/16/26, bur. Ivy Hill Cem., Alexandria. Wid. Elizabeth McKay, m. 1877.

CHISHOLM, TIMOTHY B.: enl. 9/17/61 in (1st) Co. E, age 21. Resid. Savannah, Ga. Wded. in the neck at Pony Mountain, Va., 10/63.

CHITTUM, JAMES ALEXANDER: enl. 6/25/61 in Co. C. b. 11/26/40 at Lexington. Shoemaker. POW 9/13/63 at Culpeper. Paroled for exchange 10/11/64 at Elmira. Present with his co. on ca. 3/30/65 final roll. Paroled at HQ Army of the Shenandoah 4/30/65, age 24, resid. Rockbridge Co. Farmhand postwar. d. 4/02, bur. House Mountain Cem.

CHURCH, HENRY S.: b. Alexandria. enl. 4/20/61 in Co. F. Painter. Sick leave 8/1/61. Discharged 11/1/61 because of a dropped hand resulting from lead poisoning, age 22. Postwar roster says "carried his arm in a sling until it became useless, discharged."

CLARK, JOHN S.: b. in Charlotte Co. enl. 5/27/61 in (2d) Co. E. Discharged 2/4/62, age 21, on surgeon's certificate. His service record contains a receipt for rations while on furlough 8/24-9/8/63, but no explanation of this post-discharge service.

CLARK, NOBLE B.: enl. 10/15/62 in Co. F. Present with Co. F until re-enlisted 1/1/64 in Co. H. In Chimborazo Hosp. No. 5 for disability 7/30-8/22/64. Gave himself up to Federals 9/28/64 at Harpers Ferry, resid. Fauquier Co., age 30. Took the oath at Washington, D.C., 9/30/64, and transported to Cleveland, Ohio. "Clarke" on postwar roster.

CLARK, RO.: Conscript assigned to Co. F 2/25/64. AWOL on 9-10/64 roll, the only one with his name.

CLARK, STOKELY T.: enl. 5/4/61 in Co. I, age 44. d. 10/25/61 at his home in Orange Co. His wid. Susan stated that he died from a fall from a horse during drill, after which a fever proved fatal.

CLARK, THOMAS W.: enl. 10/15/62 in Co. F. Re-enlisted 1/1/64 in Co. H. Usually present to 4/29/64, after which he was in Richmond hosps. with dysentery or gastroenteritis until furloughed 7/27/64. Gave himself up to Federals 9/28/64 at Harpers Ferry, resid. Fauquier Co., age 28. Took the oath at Washington, D.C., 9/30/64 and transported to Cleveland, Ohio. "Clarke" on postwar roster.

CLARK, WILLIAM: enl. 10/1/62 in Co. G, substitute for Matthew H. Pate. Deserted 11/1/62.

CLARK, WILLIAM E.: b. in Rappahannock Co. enl. 4/22/61 in Co. B, age 23. Farmer. 9/1/61 roll says discharged 6/8/61 for hernia unknown on enlistment, but 11/22/61 discharge paper says hernia came from fall from horse in action on 7/1/61, and that he was a laborer. Re-enl. 6/1/62. Various illnesses. Deserted and present in confinement on 11-12/62 roll. Present on 5/2/64 clothing roll, but no further record. Postwar roster gives "Clarke," d. before 5/07.

CLARK, WILLIAM T.: enl. 5/27/61 in (2d) Co. E. Present thru 2/16/62 roll, when age shown as 24, but AWOL on 5-6/62 roll. 1913 roster says d. at his home in Wilson, N.C., "a few years ago."

CLARKE, ARCHIBALD MEANS: enl. 6/1/61 in Co. K. POW 6/9/63 at Beverly Ford, paroled 6/25/63 at Old Capitol Prison. POW 2/21 (or 3/15)/64 near Leesburg while disbanded. Took the oath at Ft. Delaware 6/4/65, resid. Loudoun Co. Living at Lynchburg in 1917.

CLARKE, ISAAC VANDEVANTER: b. 3/30/45 in Loudoun Co. enl.5/22/63 in Co. K. Farmer. POW 3/4 (or 15)/64 at Hamilton while disbanded. d. 4/21/65 at Ft. Delaware of acute diarrhea, bur. Presbyterian Church Cem., Leesburg.

CLARKE, J. WILLIAMS C.: enl. 9/17/61 in (1st) Co. E, age 19. Resid. Darien, Ga. Paroled 5/1/65 at Greensboro, N.C. Might also be I. Williams C. Clark.

CLARKE, MICHAEL: enl. 9/17/62 in (1st) Co. E, age 22. Resid. Savannah, Ga. Discharged at Richmond 1/7/62 for disability.

CLARVOE, NAPOLEON BONAPARTE: b. Washington, D.C. enl. 5/1/61 in Co. F. Bricklayer. Transferred 11/1/61 to Co. E, 1st Va. Vol. Inf. Took the oath at Ft. Monroe and again later in Washington, D.C., 1864. One record indicates he was discharged 5/9/62 from Co. H, 7th Va. Inf., as a non-resident of the Confederacy.

CLEARWATER, JAMES: b. Orange, N.Y. Federal records show him as in Co. C, POW 6/5/54 at Cold Harbor. Baker. Enl. 6/17/64 in Co. K, 1st U.S. Vol. Inf. at Pt. Lookout. Deserted U.S. service 8/18/64 at New York City. No Confederate records.

CLEMENS, LAUCHLAN H.: enl. 9/17/61 in (1st) Co. E, age 22. Resid. Telfair Co., Ga. Teamster on 11/61 return. Wded. 12/4/61 at Bog Wallow ambuscade, then in hosps. at Danville and Charlottesville. POW 11/7/63. On Roll of Honor 12/10/64 for Rappahannock River. Sgt. when war ended. A postwar source has him as Locke Clements, b. near Horse Creek, Telfair Co., Ga., a farmer postwar.

CLEMENT, HENRY CLAY: b. 1/22/40 in Franklin Co. enl. 5/27/61 in (2d) Co. E. Present until POW 5/11/64 at Yellow Tavern. Took the oath at Elmira 6/23/65, resid. Danville. Farmer near Callands postwar. m. Harriet Morrison 1866. d. 11/19/19 in Pittsylvania Co., wid. Callie M., m. 1886.

CLEMENT, JAMES T. W., SR.: enl. 4/1/62 in (2d) Co. E. AWOL, exchanged POW on 12/62 return, but no record of capture. Absent wded. in Pittsylvania Co. on 11-12/62 roll. POW 5/11/64 at Yellow Tavern. Exchanged 10/29/64 from Pt. Lookout. AWOL on final 3/4/65 roll. Bur. Hunter's Chapel Cem., Rt. 773, west of Ararat, in Patrick Co.

CLEMENTS, LAFAYETTE W.: enl. 8/19/61 in Co. G, as Sgt., age 38. To Lt. on 1-2/62 roll. Resigned 2/15/62 on account of "scrofulous enlargement of the glands of the neck." Postwar roster says QM Sgt., resid. Pittsylvania Co.

CLOWE, ROBERT G.: b. 1831. Enl. 1/31/62 in Co. K. POW 3/16/63 near Leesburg, exchanged 3/29/63 from Old Capitol Prison. POW 6/25/63 near Leesburg. Paroled 1/17/65 from Pt. Lookout. Present with detachment of paroled prisoners on 1/26/65 roll of Camp Lee, near Richmond. Paroled 4/17/65 at Darnestown, Md. d. 7/24/96, bur. Leesburg Union Cem.

CLOWE, WILLIAM H.: b. 2/15/22. enl. 4/22/61 in Co. K. Sick in camp on 1-2/62 roll. Otherwise present on every roll until final 1-2/65 roll, when AWOL. Paroled 4/24/65 at Conrad's Ferry, Md. d. 3/26/90, bur. Leesburg Union Cem.

CLUTE, JOHN W.: On postwar "original list" of Co. F.

COATES, JOHN T.: enl. 8/19/61 in Co. G, age 26. d. 11/21/61 at his home on sick furlough in Halifax Co.

COATES, R. S.: Conscript assigned 2/25/64 to Co. F. Absent on detail on final 2/24/65 roll. One *Henry* S. Coates, Co. F, witnessed a pension application on 4/7/09. This is probably the same man.

COATS, JOHN: Shown on a postwar roster of Co. F. No other record.

COBBS, WILLIAM W.: b. 12/7/35. enl. 5/27/61 in (2d) Co. E as Cpl. Elected Sgt. 7/23/61. Absent on sick leave and not re-enlisted on 2/16/62 roll. m. Louisa Banks Flournoy, daughter of Col. T. S. Flournoy, 3/25/63. d. 5/30/00, bur. Cobbs Cem., Pittsylvania Co. 1913 roster says d. at Colon, Panama.

COCKE, GOURLY W.: enl. 3/16/62 in Co. H. Wded. and horse KIA at Paris 9/22/62. POW 12/21/64 at Lacey Springs. Paroled 2/10/65 from Pt. Lookout 4/25/65 at Winchester, age 20, resid. Fauquier Co. On ca. 1898 Fauquier Co. veterans census.

COCKRELL, JOHN: b. 3/26/37. enl. 6/16/61 in Co. H. Carpenter. Sent home with rheumatism 10/15/61 thru 11-12/61 roll. Deserted 3/4/62. d. 9/20/12, bur. Cool Spring Methodist Church Cem., Delaplane.

COCKRELL, JOSEPH: enl. 7/25/61 in Co. H. Furlough 2/10-3/14/62. Otherwise present on all rolls until final 3/22/65 roll, when shown absent sick since 3/1. Reported as deserter by Richmond on 3/1/65. To Cpl. on 5-6/62 roll, then Pvt., then back to Cpl. on 11-12/63 roll. Paroled at Winchester 4/28/65, age 23, resid. Fauquier Co., as Pvt.

COCKRELL, WILLIAM: b. in Fauquier Co. enl. 4/23/61 in Co. H. Carpenter. Shot accidentally in the left hand while drawing a load from a double-barreled gun on 8/4/61 at Manassas, which led to his discharge on 1/4/62. Alive in Fauquier Co. in 1898.

COCKERILLE, SETH: enl. 6/16/61 in Co. K. In guardhouse since 2/28/62 on 1-2/62 roll. Transferred 11/11/62 to Co. I, 11th Va. Cav. Farmer living at Philomont, Loudoun Co., on 9/6/06, age 74.

COGBILL, DAVID JORDAN: enl. 5/27/61 in (2d) Co. E. Absent on detached service on 4-5/62 roll. Absent wded. or sick from 9/22/62 thru 7-8/63 roll. Thereafter generally absent on detached service as brigade postmaster or clerk thru 3/4/65 final roll. Paroled 5/17/65 at Staunton, age 30.

COLE, JOHN: Shown as in Co. G, enl. 1862, on postwar roster.

COLE, ROBERT: Transferred 10/12/63 to Co. G from 1st Va. Lt. Art. Previously enl. 4/24/61 in 14th Va. Inf., age 20, farmer. Arrested as deserter 11/6/63. Otherwise usually present thru 3/22/65 final roll. Claimed slightly wded. at Cold Harbor and Yellow Tavern. Carpenter postwar. Dismissed from Lee Camp Soldiers' Home, Richmond, 8/29/02. Alive at Vernon Hill 11/19/04.

COLE, WILLIAM: enl. 10/13/63 in Co. G, transferred from 1st Va. Lt. Art. Previously enl. 4/24/61 in 14th Va. Inf., age 23, farmer. In Richmond hosps. 6/20-7/7/64 with scabies. Present on 11-12/63 roll. Transferred 7/26/64 to 1st Bn. Va. Inf. and (apparently abortively) to 14th Va. Inf. 7/28/64. Signs by mark.

COLEMAN, FRAZIER: b. in Orange Co. No official record, but pension application says enl. 10/1/64 in Co. I at Orange C.H. and left service 5/9/65 at close of war. Farmer and clerk in store, resid. Verdiersville postwar. d. 7/12/33, bur. Antioch Baptist Church Cem., Orange Co. Wid. Carrie B., m. 1882.

COLEMAN, GEORGE W.: enl. 10/1/62 in Co. I. Present until 3/20/65 final roll, when AWOL. d. 3/29/07, bur. at Antioch Church, age 63, resid. St. Just.

COLEMAN, JOHNSTON CLEVELAND: b. 1837. enl. 7/1/61 in Co. K. Farmer. Absent on sick furlough from 2/21/62, then AWOL to 9/1/62. POW 6/9/63 at Beverly Ford, paroled 6/25/63 at Old Capitol Prison. Discharged 8/1/63 on receipt of subsitute James Strother, but again present on 11-12/63 roll. Wded. 5/6/64 at Spotsylvania. Wded. 10/9/64 at Cedar Creek. POW 4/1/65, took the oath at Pt. Lookout 5/28/65. d. 9/29/95 at his home near Guilford, Loudoun Co. Reinterred in Chestnut Grove Cem., Herndon.

COLEMAN, PHILIP J.: b. in Loudoun Co. enl. 5/22/61 in Co. K. Farmer. Previously in Co. C, 17th Va. Inf. Sick in camp on 1-2/63 roll. MWIA 6/9/63 at Brandy Station. d. 7/23/63, age 25. Reinterred in Chestnut Grove Cem., Herndon.

COLES, ISAAC: b. in Pittsylvania Co. enl. 5/27/61 in (2d) Co. E as Cpl. Age 27 on 2/16/62 roll. Lt. on 11-12/62 roll. POW 6/9/63 at Brandy Station. Held at Hilton Head, S.C., in retaliation ("Immortal 600"). Took the oath at Ft. Delaware 6/12/65. Reportedly alive on his farm at Java, Pittsylvania Co., in 1913.

COLES, ISAAC: b. 1816. enl. 8/19/61 in Co. G. Farmer and physician. Detailed 12/19/61 as steward at hospital on 11-12/61 roll and 2/1-3/31/62. AWOL on 5-6/62 roll. Discharged 9/6/62 as over 35 years of age. d. 1883, bur. St. John's Episcopal Church Cem., Halifax.

COLES, JACOB THOMPSON, JR.: b. 7/15/44 at "Elkhorn," near Peytonsburg, Pittsylvania Co. In postwar records as in (2d) Co. E. Att. VMI. Brother of James D. Coles. No official record.

COLES, JAMES DODDRIDGE: b. 9/10/37 at "Elkhorn," near Peytonsburg, Pittsylvania Co. enl. 5/27/61 in (2d) Co. E as Lt. Resigned 8/61. Later Capt. 53d Va. Inf. m. Sallie Munford. Judge of Pittsylvania Co. court for several years postwar. d. 7/5/96 at Chatham, bur. Chatham Cem.

COLES, JOHN: On postwar rosters as enl. 4/61 in (2d) Co. E, transferred to infantry. No official record.

COLES, THOMAS J.: enl. 3/21/64 in (2d) Co. E. Present thru 3/4/65 final roll.

COLLIN, M. V.: Conscript assigned 1/5/64 to regiment, no company shown. No further record.

COLLINS, WILLIAM: enl. 1/23/63 in Co. G. Substitute for Thomas Hodnett. Deserted 3/27/63.

COLLINS, WILLIAM S.: b. in Culpeper Co. enl. 5/4/61 in Co. I, age 35. At home on sick furlough since 2/13/62 on 1-2/62 roll. Sick in hospital at Harrisonburg on 5-6/62 roll. AWOL on rolls for 11/62-2/63. Thereafter present until 3/20/65 final roll, when absence or presence not stated. d. 2/8/02 at Lee Camp Soldiers' Home, Richmond, age 76, bur. Hollywood Cem., Richmond.

COMER, JAMES M.: b. in Halifax Co. enl. 3/1/62 in Co. G. Farmer. Discharged 5/4/62, age 30, for chronic cystitis and enlarged prostate gland. Probably identical to James Marion Comer, 1832-97, bur. Comer and Harvey Cem., Pittsylvania Co., and probably the man of this name who served later in Co. C, 38th Va. Inf. and Co. D, 39th Va. Cav. Bn.

COMER, THOMAS JEFFERSON: Teamster, no company shown. d. 4/1 (or 4)/62 of typhoid fever and pnuemonia at General Hosp., Charlottesville. bur. Confederate Soldiers' Cem., U.Va., Charlottesville.

COMER, WILLIAM D.: Claimed to be a member of Co. G, later in 25th Va. Inf. Bn., in a 2/09 horse claim, age 74, living in Halifax Co.

COMPTON, ERASTUS E.: b. in Warren Co. Only record is of parole 4/29/65 at Winchester as in Co. B. Farmer, resid. Browntown, Warren Co., age 81, on 10/21/26. d. 12/13/36, wid. Willie Ann, m. 1881.

CONCEDINE, JOHN: enl. 12/17/62 in Co. G, substitute for O. R. Wootton. Deserted 1/23/63 at Front Royal.

CONCHA, J. D.: Shown as member of Co. G, in Richmond hosps., 6/1 and 6/2/64. Incredible as it seems, these are probably garbled names referring to John D. Glenn, Co. G. Also shown as Cenchi.

CONER, R.: Shown as member of Co. K on a regimental return for 11/61, absent with leave on 12/3/61. No other record.

CONNER, E.: Shown as member of Co. B, paroled 4/27/65 at Winchester.

CONNER, WILLIAM: Paroled 5/31/65 at Winchester as member of Co. B, age 16, resid. Rappahannock Co.

COOK, ENOCH: b. in Fairfax Co. enl. 5/1/61 in Co. F. Farmer. Dishonorably discharged 10/1/61 by order of Secretary of War. Later served with Mosby. Said he was caretaker of R. E. Lee's Arlington estate before the war. Resid. Alexandria postwar. d. 11 (or 12)/14/10, age 74, bur. Arlington National Cem.

COOK, HARMON: b. 9/5/25 near Chatham, Pittsylvania Co. enl. 1/10/63 in (2d) Co. E. In hospitals at Petersburg and Danville 7/13-8/15/64 with acute bronchitis and debility, then furloughed. Present on 3/4/65 final roll. Living in Keller, Texas, in 1910. d. 10/17/15, bur. Bourland Cem., Keller, Tex.

COOK, MORTIMER: enl. 5/22/61 in Co. F. Under arrest for drunkenness, disobedience of orders, and insubordination 8/19/61. Dishonorably discharged by order of Secretary of War 10/1/61.

COOKE, NATHANIEL BURWELL: b. 4/24/45 in Clarke Co. enl. 10/20/62 in Co. D. Transferred from Co. C, 2d Va. Inf. Student. Absent as courier for Gen. Jeb Stuart on all rolls thru 1-2/63. No further record. Brother of novelist John Esten Cooke. d. 4/30/18 in Hanover Co.

COOKSEY, JAMES W.: enl. 9/20/64 in Co. B. Present on final 3/21/65 roll. Paroled 4/29/65 at Winchester, age 44, resid. Flint Hill. Postwar roster says enl. 4/62, served to close of war, wded. at Five Forks, and alive in 5/07.

COOPER, ALEXANDER HUMPHREY: enl. 5/4/61 in Co. I, age 25. AWOL on 5-6/62 roll. Absent sick on 7-10/64 rolls. Otherwise always present thru 3/20/65 final roll. Paroled 6/1/65 near Verdiersville. d. 1/25/99 at Richardsville, Culpeper Co. Wid. Margaret J., m. 12/65.

COOPER, ALFRED: enl. 5/4/61 in Co. I, age 18. Except for short sicknesses and for horse-details, present on all rolls thru 3/20/65 final roll.

COOPER, BENJAMIN: enl. 4/28/61 in Co. H. Sent home sick 9/1/61 and never mustered.

COOPER, JOHN J.: b. 10/23/32 in Orange Co. enl. 5/4/61 in Co. I as Cpl. Sick on 12/1/61. Thirty-four day re-enlistment furlough 2/9/62. To Pvt. on 5-6/62 roll. Returned from desertion on 12/62 roll. Court-martial for AWOL, "sentence not read," on 1-2/63 roll. Sick on 8/25/63. Otherwise present thru 3/20/65 final roll. Paroled 4/9/65 at Appomattox. Farmer, resid. Danton postwar. d. 3/19/12 at Orange Springs in Orange Co.

COOPER, WILLIAM J.: enl. 12/20/62 in Co. I. Absent sick on 12/1/63. Otherwise present until 3/20/65 final roll, when AWOL. Reported as a deserter by Richmond 2/28/65.

CORBELL, SAMUEL VAUGHAN: enl. 5/4/61 in Co. I, age 20. Sick in Richmond 2/2/62. AWOL or deserter on 5/62-2/63 rolls. In hosps. in Charlottesville 11/23-12/15/63 with remittent fever, Richmond 7/18/64 with chronic diarrhoea. POW 8/30/64 at Summit Pt., (W.) Va. Took the oath 6/11/65 at Camp Chase, age 25, resid. Nansemond Co. Postwar resid. Gloucester Co., clerk. d. 5/9/13 at Lee Camp Soldiers' Home, Richmond.

CORBIN, HENRY MILTON: enl. 4/22/61 in Co. B, age 23. Farmer. Accidentally killed his horse 6/24/61. To Cpl. and on furlough on 1-2/62 roll. To Sgt. on 5-6/62 roll. Sick on 12/62 return. Thereafter present thru 3/21/65 final roll. Paroled 5/18/65 at Winchester as Lt. d. 6/10/19 near Amissville. Wid. Ella M., m. 1881.

CORBIN, JAMES W.: enl. 3/1/62 in Co. B. Wded. 6/6/62. In hospital at Charlottesville from 6/10/62 until he deserted 7/11/62. POW 8/16/62, paroled 9/27/62 at Aiken's Ldg. Wded. 5/5/64 at Spotsylvania, tongue severed. Thereafter furloughed and absent wded. thru 3/22/65 final roll. Paroled 5/16/65 at Winchester, age 21. d. 9/6/99, bur. Southern Cem., Barnesville, Ohio.

CORBIN, ROBERT L.: enl. 3/1/62 in Co. B, age 30. Absent as teamster on extra duty with QM Dept. from 6/10/62 until final 3/21/65 roll, when absent with leave. Postwar roster says d. before 5/07, and gives middle initial as "D."

CORSMOVER, J. L.: On postwar "original list" of Co. F.

COUSINS, CHASTAIN R.: b. in Pittsylvania Co. enl. 4/1/62 in (2d) Co. E. Mechanic. Discharged 5/6/62 for chronic bronchitis of several years duration and general debility, age 26. d. 9/20/97 (or 1898) at Swansonville. Wid. Sallie B., m. 1859, gave his first name as Chastine on her pension application. Shown as Teen Cousins on postwar rosters. May be identical to C. R. Cousins, Co. I, 21st Va. Inf.

COUSINS, F. ROY: enl. 9/10/64 in (2d) Co. E. POW 9/23/64 at Strasburg. Paroled 3/17/65 at Pt. Lookout. Present on 3/20/65 roll of Camp Lee, near Richmond, as paroled prisoner. Resid. 4/30/00 at Callands, age 70. Still alive in 3/22/07. Identical to "F. R. Cozzens" in Co. I, 50th Va. Inf.

COUSINS, JOHN C.: b. 1/12/34 at Callands in Pittsylvania Co. Transferred 11/10/63 to (2d) Co. E from Co. I, 6th Miss. Inf. Farmer. Absent on scout 12 days in 10/64. Present on 3/4/65 final roll. Alive 2/29/08 at Callands, age 74, formerly tobacco dealer. 3 brothers in the regiment. d. 9/27/10 at Columbia, S.C., bur. Leemont Cem., Danville.

COUSINS, WILLIAM: b. 3/18/40. enl. 5/27/61 in (2d) Co. E. Absent on sick furlough beginning 8/6/64. On horse detail 22 days from 10/27/64. Otherwise present thru 3/4/65 final roll. Horse MWIA 10/19/64 near Middletown. d. 1/17/03 at Callands. Wid. Fannie James, m. 1870.

COWHERD, FRANK: b. 9/25/29 in Orange Co. Att. Columbian College, D.C. enl. 9/1/64 in Co. I. Previously in Wise Artillery. Farmer. Absent on horse detail on 9-10/64 roll. Present on final 3/20/65 roll. Paroled 4/9/65 at Appomattox. On county board of supervisors postwar. d. 6/17/95 in Orange.

COX, JOHN H.: enl. 9/10/64 in (2d) Co. E. POW 9/23/64 at Strasburg (or Fisher's Hill). Paroled 3/17/65 at Pt. Lookout. Present on roll of paroled prisoners at Camp Lee, near Richmond 3/20/65.

CRAIG, JOHN H.: enl. 10/15/62 in Co. F. Present thru 11-12/62 roll. No further record.

CRAVEN, CHARLES M.: enl. 5/4/61 in Co. I, age 21. Placed in arrest 6/28/62 by Col. Harrison. Otherwise present on all rolls thru 3/20/65 final roll. Reported as deserter by Richmond 2/28/65, to be found in Orange Co.

CRAWFORD, JAMES: enl. 9/1/62 in Co. B, age about 25. Deserted from hosp. 2/15/63. Transferred 11/1/63 to Co. I. In Charlottesville hosp. 1/12/64 with scabies, but deserted ca. 1/22/64. POW 6/4/64 at White Oak Swamp. Escaped from Elmira by tunneling 10/7/64 and walked back to Va. Furloughed 11/24/64. Reported as deserter by Richmond 2/28/65, but present on 3/21/65 final roll. Alive in Cincinnati, Ohio, in 1912.

CRAWFORD, MAGNUS S.: b. in Augusta Co. enl. 11/9/61 in Co. I, age 14. POW at Winchester, then paroled there 6/62. Later joined Mosby's command. Farmer, resid. Staunton postwar. d. 11/20/95 at Lee Camp Soldiers' Home, Richmond, age 47, bur. Hollywood Cem., Richmond.

CRAWLEY, ADAM G.: enl. 5/4/61 in Co. I, age 33. Absent at home on sick furlough 12/19/61 to 5-6/62 roll, when AWOL. No further official record, but postwar rosters for Co. I show an A. G. Crowley, discharged in 1862, and an Adam J. Crowley.

CREEL, ADDISON F.: enl. 9/19/62 in Co. H. Present until wded. 6/17/63. Another official record has him severely wded. 6/21 at Upperville. Returned by 12/30/64 and present thru 3/22/65 final roll. Paroled 4/25/65 at Winchester, age 20, resid. Fauquier Co. Postwar roster says d. before 1910.

CREWS, EPHRAIM: enl. 8/19/61 in Co. G, age 65. Absent at home on sick furlough since 11/5/61 on 1-2/62 roll. Postwar roster says "discharged age limit." May be identical to Ephraim Crews, Pvt. in William Bailey's Co., 4th Regiment (Greenhill's) Va. Militia in War of 1812, resid. 3/17/55 in Halifax Co., age 65.

CROPLEY, ARTHUR: enl. 10/15/64 in Co. K. Present on final 1-2/65 roll. Paroled 4/24/65 at Edwards Ferry, Md. Took the oath 5/10/65 and transport furnished to D.C. Resid. Georgetown, D.C.

CROUCH, FRANKLIN: enl. 9/14/62 in Co. H. AWOL since 2/9/63 on 2/28/63 roll and since 12/28/63 on 11-12/63 roll. KIA 6/11/64 at Trevillian's Station. Wid. Ann Virginia, m. 1858, resid. Middleburg postwar.

CROW, HENRY CLAY: b. 4/16/46. enl. 3/22/62 in Co. D. Absent sick on 9-10/64 roll. Wded. 10/19/64 at Middletown. AWOL on final 3/22/65 roll. Paroled 4/24/65 at Winchester, age 19, resid. Berryville. d. 8/17/65, bur. Grace Episcopal Church Cem., Berryville.

CROW, JOHN THOMAS: b. 1848 at Berryville, att. VMI. Student enl. 6/25/63 in Co. D. Present until 6/20/64, when in Richmond hosp. Absent as scout for Gen. T. L. Rosser on 9-10/64 roll. Absent on horse detail on final 3/22/65 roll. Paroled 4/15/65 at Winchester. Postwar source says wded. near Luray in 1864. m. Isabella Settle 1866. Sheriff of Clarke Co. 1873-87. Magistrate of Battletown District. d. 12/9/29, bur. Green Hill Cem., Berryville.

CRUMP, DANIEL O.: On postwar "original list" of Co. F.

CUNNINGHAM, ROBERT: On a postwar roster of Co. G as enl. 1862, discharged age limit.

CURTIS, H. A.: On a postwar roster of Co. I.

CURTIS, J. B.: enl. 8/20/64 in Co. I. On horse detail on 9-10/64 roll. Present on 3/20/65 final roll. Paroled at Farmville between 4/11 and 4/21/65. May be identical to J. U. Curtis, shown on a postwar roster of Co. I as wded. in the Valley.

CURTIS, JOHN C.: enl. 4/1/63 in Co. B. Civilian teamster with the regiment on 9/30/62. Absent on all rolls thru 3/21/65 final roll as teamster on detached service at brigade HQ. Reportedly d. before 5/07.

CURTIS, T. C.: On a postwar roster of Co. I.

CURTIS, W. H.: On postwar "original list" of Co. F.

CUTHBERT, ALFRED: b. 1826. enl. 9/17/61 in (1st) Co. E, age 35. Assigned to laboratory duty at Richmond 2/28/63. Paroled 5/20/65 at Augusta, Ga., resid. there. d. 12/5/80 in Morristown, N.J. bur. Evergreen Cem. m. Anne Mary Davis 1856.

DABNEY, CHARLES EDWARD: b. 2/15/35. Att. U.Va. Lawyer. enl. 5/27/61 in (2d) Co. E as Lt. Absent on sick leave and not re-enlisted because of ill health on 2/16/62 roll. 1913 roster says discharged on account of rheumatism. Lawyer at Chatham postwar. m. Berth Durrett. d. 1885.

DAILEY, JOHN: enl. 2/15/63 in Co. C. Deserted 3/31/63.

DALTON, THOMAS M.: enl. 8/19/61 in Co. G, age 23. In hosp. at Petersburg 3/31-5/7/62 with diarrhea and bronchitis. Horse KIA 6/9/63 at Brandy Station. In Richmond hosps. with gunshot wound of right thigh 5/13-5/23/64, then 60 day furlough. Present on all rolls thru 3/22/65 final roll. Resid. Ray, Pittsylvania Co., on 11/18/89. Carpenter on 7/9/90, when application to Lee Camp Soldiers' Home, Richmond, was revoked. Wartime signature appears to be Daulton.

DANIEL, ALPHEUS R.: enl. 4/22/61 in Co. B as Sgt., age 22. Teacher. Absent sick since 6/28 on 9/1/61 roll. Discharged on certificate of disability 9/23/61. Reportedly alive in 5/07.

DANIEL, BYRD TYLER: enl. 4/22/61 in Co. B, age 26. Farmer. Absent on leave, sick, etc. 10/61-2/62 on rolls and returns. Absent on parole since 7/15 on 9-10/62 roll. On leave to get horse on 11-12/62 roll. POW 8/17/63 at Waterloo. Took the oath 9/23/63 at Washington, D.C., resid. Rappahannock Co. Released from Old Capitol Prison and sent to Philadelphia, Pa., 9/24/63. Postwar roster says served one year and deserted.

DANIEL, JAMES: enl. 7/15/61 in Co. K. POW 8/5/61 near Point of Rocks, Md., then paroled and exchanged. AWOL from 12/1/62. No further record.

DANIEL, WILLIAM U.: b. in Rappahannock Co. enl. 4/22/61 in Co. B, age 25. Farmer. Absent sick since 6/25 on 9-10/61 roll. Discharged 11/24/61 for phthisis, dysentery, or general disability and predisposition to consumption. d. 10/13/03 near Delaplane, wid. Annie T., m. 1886, who gave his middle initial as "A." Postwar roster says wded.

DAVENPORT, FRANCIS M.: enl. 11/8/61 in Co. G. To Cpl. 11/7/62. Reduced to ranks 6/25/63. Usually present until 7-8/63 roll, when AWOL. Found not guilty of AWOL 3/7/64. In Richmond hosps. 6/9-6/27/64 with diarrhea. AWOL on final 3/22/65 roll. Farmer and teacher in Negro school in Pittsylvania Co. postwar. Dropped from Lee Camp Soldiers' Home, Richmond, 12/12/93. Age 68 in 1900, claiming wound in left ankle. Alive 5/29/02 in Halifax Co.

DAVENPORT, JOHN S.: enl. 3/15/62 in Co. G (another official record says 11/7/61). Absent sick on 9-10/62 roll and AWOL sick on 11-12/62 roll. Absent sick on surgeon's certificate on 1-2/63 roll. Deserted 6/25/63 near Berryville. d. 2/5/86 at Gretna. Wid. Hattie R., m. 1879.

DAVIDSON, JAMES GEORGE: b. in D.C. enl. 7/26/61 in Co. K. Butcher, resid. D.C. POW 8/5/61 at Point of Rocks, Md. Detailed as regimental butcher on 6/30/62 roll. Discharged 11/22/62 as citizen of Maryland, age 20.

DAVIDSON, R.: Shown in a hosp. register as a paroled prisoner of (2d) Co. E in Chimborazo Hosp. No. 9, Richmond, on 3/28/65. Probably an error referring to someone else.

DAVIS, ALBERT F.: enl. 10/12/63 in Co. C. One month's pay deducted by court-martial on 11-12/63 roll. In General Hosp., Charlottesville, 1/24-2/5/64 with scabies. Absent with leave on 9-10/64 roll. Otherwise present until POW 1/13/65 at Kabletown, (W.) Va. Took the oath at Elmira 6/27/65, resid. Charles Town, (W.) Va.

DAVIS, A. STROTHER: enl. 5/31/61 in Co. D. AWOL sick since 10/3/61 on 11-12/61 roll. POW 10/16/62 at Charles Town, (W.) Va., paroled 10/22/62 at Harpers Ferry. POW 1/16/63 near Berryville on horse leave, paroled 2/15/63 at Ft. McHenry. In General Hosp., Petersburg, 2/18-2/24/63 with debilitas. Otherwise present until absent with leave on 9-10/64 roll. AWOL on final 3/22/65 roll. Resid. Jefferson Co., (W.) Va.

DAVIS, CHARLES E.: enl. 6/20/61 in Co. H. Cooper. "Used as wagoner, has no horse" on 6/30/61 roll. Absent sick since 6/28/61; another record says sent home sick 10/9/61. Never mustered.

DAVIS, CHRISTOPHER T.: enl. 4/1/62 in (2d) Co. E. Absent sick on 5-6/62 roll, and on 20 days leave to get a horse from 12/17/62. On detached service as courier for Gen. W. E. Jones on 1-2/63 roll. Sick in General Hosp., Lynchburg, on 7-8/64 roll. Otherwise present thru 3/4/65 final roll. 1913 roster says d. in Missouri.

DAVIS, EUGENE: b. 3/26/22 in Middlesex Co. grad. U.Va., M.A. there before he was 18. Enl. 8/15/63 in Co. D. Lawyer. Previously Capt., 2d Va. Cav. Detailed in QM Dept. 12/21/63. In General Hosp., Charlottesville, with scabies 11/5-11/24/63 and 12/19/63-1/30/64. POW 5/11/64 at Yellow Tavern. To Sgt. Maj. on 7-8/64 roll while still POW. Paroled 2/25/65 at Elmira. Farmer postwar near Charlottesville. d. 5/20/94. Brother of Richard T.

DAVIS, GEORGE WILLIAM: b. in Pittsylvania Co. enl. 4/1/62 in (2d) Co. E. On detail to get clothing for co. 12/16/63. Otherwise present on all rolls until KIA 5/7/64 at Spotsylvania C.H., "seen struck by a ball & never heard from."

DAVIS, GEORGE W.: b. in Alexandria. enl. 4/24/61 in Co. H. Farmer. To Cpl. on 11-12/61 roll. To Lt. 4/20/62. POW, wded., and horse KIA 6/2/62 at Woodstock, leg amputated 6/29/62. Davis wrote that he was paroled after capture and exchanged in 11/62, then captured again and held as a civilian at Old Capitol until paroled ca. 1/16/64. His 4/5/64 resignation was accepted with unflattering endorsements. Merchant and watermill operator postwar, m. Sallie Ann Lucy Smith. d. 11/09.

DAVIS, GEORGE W.: enl. 5/28/61 in Co. C. Sick in hosp. since 10/1/61 on 9-10/61 roll. Teamster for co. on 10/61 return. No further record. Alive at Elkton, age 75, on 5/8/00, when he claimed a wound at 1st Manassas in the leg below the knee.

DAVIS, HOMER L.: b. 1824 (or 1829) in Pittsylvania Co. enl. 4/1/62 in (2d) Co. E. Detached service on 5-6/62 roll. Kicked by horse ca. 10/22/62 and put in hospital at Staunton. Sick in Staunton hosp. on 7-8/64 roll. Twenty-day horse detail from 10/27/64. Absent sick in Pittsylvania Co. on final 3/4/65 roll. Claimed hernia from tearing up railroad near Front Royal during war on 5/1/00 pension claim ("age 67"). d. 1909, bur. Davis Cem., Pittsylvania Co. Farmer postwar, m. Catherine Robertson.

DAVIS, JAMES COLEMAN: enl. 4/24/61 in Co. H as Lt. Blacksmith. Resigned 6/9/61. Farmer, resid. Orange Co. postwar. d. near True Blue 5/17/09, age 64, bur. family cem. nearby.

DAVIS, JAMES M.: enl. 4/1/62 in (2d) Co. E. Present, except for detail as teamster on 11-12/62 roll, until 8/29/63 transfer to Co. I, 53d Va. Inf. Resid. Pittsylvania Co.

DAVIS, JOHN G.: b. in Halifax Co. enl. 8/19/61 in Co. G as Sgt., age 34. Farmer. Absent on sick furlough from 1/22/62 thru 5-6/62 roll, when Pvt. Discharged 7/20/62 for phtisis pulmonalis with hemorrhage from lungs. Conscripted 2/9/63. Horse detail on 7-8/64 roll. In Richmond hosps. with diarrhea 11/29-12/7/63. Sick in Staunton hosp. since 10/1/64 on 9-10/64 roll. Transferred 9/24/64 to Co. D, 38th Va. Inf. Paroled 4/9/65 at Appomattox.

DAVIS, LITTLETON MORGAN: b. in Alexandria. enl. 5/17/62 in Co. H. Carpenter. Previously in Co. F, Kemper's Battery (18th Bn. Va. Heavy Art.). Discharged 7/14/62 for deafness and rupture. Later in Co. E, Mosby's 43d Bn. Va. Cav. Reportedly alive in Alexandria in 1909, still a carpenter.

DAVIS, RICHARD TERRELL: b. 1/30 in Charlottesville, grad. M.A. U.Va., Va. Theological Sem. Episcopal minister. Appointed chaplain 8/20/62. Absent on 12/62 return. Thirty days leave on surgeon's certificate from 11/3/63. Leave until 11/2 on 9-10/64 roll. Paroled 4/9/65 at Appomattox. Rector St. James Church, Leesburg, 1868-92. D.D., from W. & L. 1877. d. 5/3/92, bur. Union Cem., Leesburg. Brother of Eugene. "He charged at the head of the regiment in every battle" (John N. Opie).

DAVIS, SIMEON BENTON: b. 8/5/42 in Pittsylvania Co. enl. 5/27/61 in (2d) Co. E. Absent on detached service on 5-6/62 roll. Shown as AWOL 11/1/62 and exchanged POW on 12/62 return. AWOL on 11-12/62 roll. On 25 day horse detail from 8/23/64. Otherwise present thru 3/4/65 final roll. Resid. near Chatham postwar, claiming 4 wounds. d. 5/27/16, wid. Celestia R., m. 1887, bur. Davis Cem., Pittsylvania Co.

DAVIS, THOMAS PHILIP: enl. 7/1/61 in (2d) Co. E. Wded. 9/22/62 and thereafter absent sick until 11/11/63 when detailed to QM Dept. on surgeon's certificate. On extra duty as courier 1-3/64. In Chimborazo Hosp. No. 5 with diarrhea 5/24-30/64. Later absent in QM Dept., Cavalry Corps, as forage master until present on 3/4/65 final roll. d. 2/19/05, bur. private cem., Woodsdale, N.C.

DAVIS, WILLIAM G.: enl. 7/1/61 in (2d) Co. E. Present until POW 5/30/64 at Cold Harbor. Took the oath 6/27/65 at Elmira, N.Y. "Desires to go to his friend at Niagara Falls, N.Y." Resid. Niagara Falls.

DAWSON, ARTHUR: b. 1843. enl. 7/15/61 in Co. K. POW 8/5/61 in Loudoun opposite Point of Rocks, Md. Edward S. Joynes wrote on 12/16/61 "The tender years and estimable character of this young man induced many persons at the time to interest themselves to procure his exchange." See Official Records, series II. Apparently paroled 3/24/62 from Ft. Warren, Mass. AWOL from 11/1/62. No further record. Justice of Peace in Loudoun Co. postwar. d. 1908.

DAWSON, BENJAMIN F.: enl. 10/18/62 in Co. H. Horse KIA 7/3/63 at Fairfield, Pa. Detailed as scout on 7-8/63 roll. In Chimborazo Hosp. No. 1, Richmond, with gunshot wound 10/17-11/1/64. On detached service with Gen. Stuart since 12/27 on 11-12/63 roll. AWOL since 12/1/64 on 3/22/65 final roll. Postwar roster says d. before 8/2/10.

DEACON, WILLIAM: Shown as a member of Co. A, captured at Shepherdstown, on a postwar roster. Possibly an error, meaning J. R. H. Deakins.

DEAHL, HORACE PEAKE: b. 3/26/36 at Berryville. enl. 10/7/62 in Co. D. Previously Lt., Co. I, 2nd Va. Inf. Always present until absent as scout for Gen. T. L. Rosser on 9-10/64 roll. POW 2/14/65 in Clarke Co. Held as "guerilla, not to be exchanged," until he took the oath 5/1/65 at Ft. McHenry, Md. Merchant at Berryville postwar. Claimed two wounds at Brandy Station, and one at Trevillian's Station. d. 1912, bur. Green Hill Cem., Berryville.

DEAKINS, JAMES ROBERT H.: b. 7/26/40. enl. 11/16/61 in Co. A. Present until AWOL from 7/6/63 on 8/31/63 roll. POW 7/14/63 at Falling Waters, Md., but escaped 9/4/63 from Pt. Lookout. Horse KIA 9/13/63 near Culpeper. With Co. on 11-12/63 roll. In hosp. at Charlottesville 1/21-5/3/64 with pneumonia. Transferred 4/29/64 to Co. B, 1st Md. Cav. Bn. d. 6/16/23, bur. Pinckney Memorial Episcopal Church Cem., Hyattsville, Md.

DEAL, GEORGE W.: enl. 4/1/62 in Co. B. Generally present until AWOL on 11-12/63 roll. Told Federals he deserted in September. Sent in as rebel deserter 1/9/64 at Rapidan River. "Says he never was a rebel." Resid. Culpeper, age 37 when he deserted. Took the oath and sent North 3/8/64. A 11-12/63 roll of Co. B shows two George Deals (George and George W.), but compare George Washington Deal below.

DEAL, GEORGE WASHINGTON: b. in Page Co. enl. 9/1/63 in Co. B. Absent on duty with provost guards from 10/10/63 on 11-12/63 roll. POW 4/22/64 at Culpeper. Took the oath at Ft. Delaware and released 6/19/65, resid. Culpeper. Resid. Viewtown, age 64, on 9/15/05. Claimed wound on shoulder by shell. d. 1/9/19 near Laurel Mills. Wid. Victoria, m. 1867.

DEARMONT, JAMES THOMAS: b. 1844. enl. 8/5/63 [sic] in Co. D, but POW 6/9/63 near Millwood. Paroled ca. 6/26/63 at Ft. McHenry. Carbine lost in action 9/12/63. In General Hosp., Charlottesville, 12/24/63-1/27/64, with morbi cutis. Absent sick on 9-10/64 roll thru 3/22/65 final roll. Paroled 4/15 and 4/22/65 at Winchester. Postmaster of Mound City, Mo., postwar, and alive there ca. 1924. m. 1) Matilda Bell 1865, 2) Helen Pipher 1879, 3) ?

DEARMONT, JOHN: b. 1841. enl. 4/19/61 in Co. D. AWOL since 12/3 on 11-12/61 roll. Fifteen days leave from 12/21/63. To Cpl. on 7-8/64 roll. Absent with leave on 9-10/64 roll. Otherwise present until KIA 12/20/64 at Lacey Springs.

DEARMONT, PETER: b. 4/17/35. enl. 6/1/62 in Co. D. Farmer. Previously in Co. C, 2d Va. Inf. Absent with leave on 11-12/62 roll. POW 2/7/63 in Clarke Co. Exchanged 3/28/63 from Camp Chase. Carbine lost in action 9/12/63. Paroled 4/15/65 at Winchester. Moved to Holt Co., Mo. 1871. d. 1/17/15 near Mound City, Mo.

DEATHERAGE, ROBERT: enl. 10/1/62 in Co. B, age 30. Absent on detached service with Gen. I. R. Trimble since 10/8/62 on 9-10/62 roll. Present thru 5/2/64 clothing roll. No further record. Postwar roster gives middle initial as "R." Reportedly d. before 5/07.

DEATHERAGE, WILLIAM R.: enl. 3/15/63 in Co. B. AWOL 8/16/63 on 11-12/63 roll. On 5/2/64 clothing roll, then absent sick thru 9-10/64 roll. AWOL on 3/21/65 final roll. Paroled 4/29/65 at Winchester, age 28, resid. Washington, Rappahannock Co. Apparently identical to Robert Deatherage, enl. 4/63 at age 32, served until close of war and d. by 5/07, as shown on a postwar roster.

DEBUTTS, RICHARD EARL: b. 1823 in Prince George's Co., Md. Shown as a member of Co. H, a farmer, on a 6/30/61 roll, absent due to rupture unfitting him for duty. Also on a regimental return for 11/61, "absent with leave on account of disease which disqualifies him." Presumably never mustered. Later in Mosby's 43d Bn. Va. Cav. d. 7/6/92 at "Mount Welby," near Linden, and bur. there.

DEMENT, THOMAS JEFFERSON: b. 7/4/38 in Washington, D.C. enl. 1/23/63 in Co. D. Previously in "Beauregard Rifles" for 90 days. Absent sick in hosp., one month's pay deducted by court-martial on 11-12/63 roll. Absent as scout for Gen. Fitzhugh Lee on 3/22/65 final roll. Paroled 4/15/65 at Winchester, resid. Maryland. Moved to Tennessee 1866. m. Zoe Louise Ickes 1870. d. at his home in Chattanooga, Tenn., 9/19/15.

DEMERE, RAYMOND M.: enl. 9/17/61 in (1st) Co. E, age 18. Transferred 10/6/62 to Hardwick Mounted Rifles (Ga.) in exchange for A. R. Waller. Later transferred to 7th Ga. Cav., in which he was Lt. Took the oath at Ft. Delaware 6/4/65, resid. Bryan Co., Ga.

DENEALE, GEORGE E.: enl. 3/16/62 in Co. H. Absent with leave 11/26/62. Present, detailed as wagoner on 2/28/63 roll. Absent with disabled horse on 7-8/63 roll. Absent sick since 3/7 on 3/22/65 final roll. Paroled 5/8/65 at Winchester, age 35, resid. Rappahannock Co. On ca. 1898 Fauquier Co. veterans census, age 68.

DENNIS, JOSEPH A.: enl. 7/24/61 in Co. A. Absent with leave to get clothing on 11/62 return. AWOL since 12/23 on 11-12/61 roll. Forfeited $24 pay by sentence of court-martial on 1-2/62 roll. POW 6/1/64 at Louisa C.H. d. 3/29/65 of pneumonia at Elmira, bur. there.

DENNIS, NEWTON T.: enl. 5/8/61 in Co. B, age 40. AWOL on 6/26/62. "Declined to re-enlist, over 35 years" on 5-6/62 roll. Reportedly d. before 5/07.

DENNIS, P.: Only record is of parole as member of Co. H on 5/10/65 at Winchester, age 18, resid. Fauquier Co., signs by mark.

DENNIS, WILLIAM: enl. 4/1/61 in Co. B. "Discharged 1862" on 5-6/62 roll, the only one on which he appears.

DENNIS, WILLIAM A.: enl. 4/24/61 in Co. H. Planter. Exceeded his leave 6/27 and not yet returned on 6/30/61 roll. AWOL 9/1-9/24/61. POW 12/2/61 at Annandale. Exchanged ca. 2/14/62. Thirty days furlough from 2/21/62. Present on 5-6/62 roll. No further record. Compare with William H. Dennis.

DENNIS, WILLIAM H.: enl. 4/24/61 in Co. H. Transferred to infantry by Gen. T. J. Jackson 11/14/62, but this was evidently not done. Deserted 11/25/62 near Salem, but returned 12/6/62 and put under arrest. Present on 2/28/63 roll. AWOL since 7/1/63 on 7-8/63 roll. Transferred 11/24/63 to 8th Va. Inf., but no record of him in that unit. Compare with William A. Dennis.

DENNISON, JOHN E.: b. 1842. enl. 4/20/61 in Co. F as bugler. Present until POW 6/9/63 at Beverly Ford, paroled 6/25/63 at Old Capitol Prison. Horse KIA 10/11/63 at Brandy Station. To chief bugler on 11-12/63 roll. Transferred 4/19/64 to 1st Md. Cav.

DEVEREIUX, WILLIAM: enl. 5/1/63 in (2d) Co. E. Present until d. 12/2/64 at General Hosp., Harrisonburg, of acute rheumatism.

DICK, HENRY: b. 1838. enl. 10/1/62 in Co. F. Absent, sent back with horses on 7-12/63 rolls. AWOL on 7-8/64 roll. m. Mary Louisa Carper. d. 1/29/09 (but stone says 1906), bur. Old Chapel Cem., Millwood.

DICK, JOHN: enl. 9/16/64 in Co. F. AWOL on 8/31/64 roll. May be John M. Dick, 5/29/44 - 2/29/24, m. Sarah J., bur. Old Chapel Cem., Millwood, next to Henry Dick.

DICK, WILLIAM B.: enl. 10/1/62 in Co. F. Absent with leave on 1-2/63 roll. Reported as POW in 3/63 in Clarke Co., but no Federal records. "Not heard from since." Postwar roster says AWOL; another source says he may have d. in Missouri.

DICKINS, FRANCIS A.: enl. 2/11/62 in Co. A. Sick in quarters on 1-2/62 roll. In arrest since 2/3/63 on 1-2/62 roll. Orderly at regimental HQ on 8/31/63. Admitted 11/25/64 to Charlottesville General Hosp. with gunshot wound of left leg, then in Richmond and Amelia hosps. until present on final 3/27/65 company roll. His uniform jacket is in the Museum of the Confederacy.

DICKINSON, CHARLES WILLIAM: b. 9/15/46. enl. 3/10/65 in Co. I. Present on 3/20/65 final roll. Postwar sources say enl. 5/64, in 9 engagements. Schoolteacher, drugstore owner, and superintendent of schools in Cumberland and Goochland Cos. postwar. d. 5/3/32 at Richmond.

DICKINSON, R. Q.: enl. 10/15/64 in Co. I. Present thru 3/20/65 final roll.

DICKINSON, ROBERT: Only record is of parole as member of Co. A on 4/27/65 at Winchester, age 26, resid. Albemarle Co.

DILLARD, PETER F.: enl. 3/28/62 in Co. G. Deserted 6/1/62.

DILLARD, W. V.: enl. 12/1/62 in Co. B. Only record is 12/62 return. No further record, and not on postwar rosters. May refer to William J. Lillard.

DILLON, GEORGE W.: enl. 9/17/61 in (1st) Co. E, age 27. Resid. Savannah, Ga. To Cpl. on 11/1/61 roll.

DODD, CHARLES H.: enl. 10/15/62 in Co. K. Always present until 9/19/64, when AWOL sick in Loudoun Co. No further service record. Paroled 4/27/65 at Edwards Ferry, Md.

DODD, WILLIAM H.: enl. 3/8/62 in Co. K. Detailed as regimental blacksmith 8/12/62 on 12/12/62 roll, then present until again detailed as regimental blacksmith. Present on 7-8/63 roll thru 1-2/65 final roll.

DODSON, ELISON C.: enl. 5/27/61 in (2d) Co. E. Age 26 on 2/18/62 roll. To Cpl. on 5-6/62 roll. AWOL on 11-12/63 roll. POW 1/31/64 at Robinson River, Madison Co. Paroled 9/28/64 at Ft. Delaware. Present with co. on 3/4/65 final roll. Paroled 4/9/65 at Appomattox, resid. Pittsylvania Co.

DOLANE, WILLIAM C.: Only record is a Federal list of POWs at Atheneum Prison, Wheeling, dated 12/5/63, which has him as a member of Co. C, age 18, a shoemaker, resid. Luray, who gave himself up to the Federals on 12/2/63 at Paw Paw, (W.) Va., and was sent to Camp Chase 12/7/63.

DONALDSON, ARMISTEAD M.: b. 12/14/39 near Bailey's Crossroads. enl. 5/25/61 in Co. F. Horse KIA 6/9/63 at Brandy Station. Detailed and sent back with horses on 7-12/63 rolls. POW 6/10/64 at Louisa C.H. Took the oath 6/19/65 at Elmira, resid. Washington, D.C m. Mildred M. Birch (wid. of W. J. R. Birch) 1870. d. 1/7/06, bur. Oakwood Cem., Falls Church.

DONALDSON, MARTIN FLETCHER: b. 1840. enl. 10/1/61 in Co. F. Shown as discharged 7/30/62, but present again on 11-12/62 roll and so borne until 11-12/63, when absent on furlough to get a horse. Later present until absent on horse detail on 2/24/64 final roll. Paroled 4/21/65. Took the oath 6/17/65 at Alexandria, resid. Alexandria. Postwar roster says "captured at Fairfax C.H. by Scott's Nine Hundred, retaken by Fitz Lee's brigade." d. 1/2/04, bur. Oakwood Cem., Falls Church. Wid. Martha A.

DONOHOE, JOHN CARROLL: enl. 4/22/61 in Co. K. Thirty days furlough from 2/11/62. Thereafter present until POW 9/24/64 near Luray. Paroled 3/17/65 at Pt. Lookout. Present on final 1-2/65 roll. Bookkeeper postwar. d. 2/28/21 in Baltimore, Md., age 82. m. Delia N. Saunders.

DONOHOE, SAMUEL C.: b. 4/1/39. enl. 4/22/61 in Co. K. Present on all rolls but final 1-2/65 roll, when AWOL. Paroled 4/9/65 at Edwards Ferry, Md. d. 5/24/01, bur. Leesburg Union Cem.

DONOHOE, STEPHEN JOSEPH: enl. 6/26/61 in Co. K. Thirty days furlough from 2/11/62. To Cpl. 11/1/62. In hosps. on 5/21, 9/8, and 12/17/63. In General Hosp., Charlottesville, 1/7/64 with morbi cutis, transferred 1/8/64 to Lynchburg. MWIA 5/7/64 near Spotsylvania C.H. d. 5/14/64 at Beaver Dam Station.

DONOHOE, WILLIAM F.: enl. 4/22/61 in Co. K. His only record is the 7-8/61 roll, where he is marked "absent six weeks from sickness." Not on the postwar roster compiled by John C. Donohoe.

DOUGLASS, JOHN W.: enl. 8/19/61 in Co. G. Age 32 on 9/10/61. Absent on sick furlough from 2/25/62 until 1-2/63 roll, when present. To Cpl. 6/1/64. Present thru 3/22/65 final roll. Resid. Riceville postwar. d. 5/00. m. Nancy V., 1855.

DOVE, JOHN: enl. 3/19/62 in Co. D. Only record is 5-6/62 roll, which has him AWOL, "recruit, but has never been in the company except for a few days." d. 9/4/04 in Loudoun Co., age 65.

DOVE, THOMAS: enl. 4/1/62 in (2d) Co. E. Reported by General Hosp. No. 2, Lynchburg, as d. in quarters on 5/1 (or 2 or 5)/62, from effects of measles. Wid. Mary T., m. 1835. 1913 roster says d. in camp at Gordonsville.

DOVEL, JOHN: enl. 3/5/62 in Co. C. Deserted 5/6/62 at Elk River. enl. 4/3/64 in Co. A, 3d Bn. Valley Reserves.

DOWDELL, JOHN THOMAS: b. in Loudoun co. enl. 7/24/61 in Co. A. Clerk. Ten days sick furlough from 1/2/62. Discharged 5/1/62 for heart disease (hypertrophy), age 23. POW 10/8/63 at Point of Rocks, Md. ("gave himself up"). Exchanged 2/10/65 from Point Lookout. Resid. near Leesburg. d. 3/3/03 in Texas.

DOWDELL, WILLIAM FLAVIUS: b. 1835. enl. 7/24/61 in Co. A. Twelve days sick furlough from 2/25/62. To Sgt. on 9-10/62 roll. Present thru 12/5/62 roll. To Capt., 35th Bn. Va. Cav. d. 3/30/88, bur. Lakeview (City) Cem., Hamilton.

DOWN, WILLIAM S.: Federal records show a man of this name in (2d) Co. E as POW 9/28/64 at Port Republic and paroled 1/17/65 at Pt. Lookout, resid. Rockingham Co. One W. P. Downs, supposed to be this man, d. 2/2/26 at Hickory Grove, age 83, and bur. Antioch Cem., a resident of Prince William Co.

DOWNER, WILLIAM WALKER: b. 10/7/32. enl. 1/1/64 in Co. I. POW 8/30/64 at Summit Pt., (W.) Va. Took the oath 6/11/65 at Camp Chase, resid. Orange Co. d. 1/9/21, bur. Maplewood Cem., Orange Co.

DRANE, ROBERT: enl. 4/22/61 in Co. K. POW 8/4/61 at Point of Rocks. Confined at Ft. Lafayette, N.Y. Paroled 3/24/62. Resid. Fairfax Co. "A widower with ten little children, who 'cry for their Pa.' "

DRISCOL, RICHARD A.: enl. 10/8/62 in Co. A. POW and horse KIA 6/9/63 at Brandy Station. Paroled 6/5/63 at Old Capitol Prison. Absent with led horses on 8/31/63 roll, POW 5/11/64 at Yellow Tavern. d. 7/24/64 at Pt. Lookout.

DRISCOLL, PATRICK H.: enl. 10/1/62 in Co. A. Admitted to General Hosp., Charlottesville, 6/13/63, with gunshot wound, returned to duty 7/2/63. Wded. 10/19/64 near Cedar Creek, and absent wded. on 1-2/65 final roll. Paroled 4/25/65 at Winchester, age 25, resid. Fauquier Co. Resid. Bennings, D.C., 1910. Witnessed James N. Byrne's 8/11 application to Marr Camp 72, U.C.V., Fairfax Co.

DRUMMOND, J. M.: No company shown. Assigned 10/25/64 as forage agent in Pittsylvania Co. under Walter Coles, AQM, on a report dated 2/17/65.

DRUMMOND, ROBERT F.: enl. 7/1/61 in (2d) Co. E. Discharged 7/20/61 by Gen. T. J. Jackson on account of disease. enl. 3/5/62 in Capt. Patterson's Co., Va. Heavy Art.

DULANY, BLADEN T.: enl. 7/24/61 in Co. A. AWOL since 8/22/61 on 7-8/61 roll, and since 10/3/61 on 9-10/61 roll. Shown as discharged and substitute William Nightingale furnished on 11-12/61 roll.

DULANY, CASSIUS C.: enl. 7/24/61 in Co. A. Absent sick since 10/7/61 on 9-10/61 roll. Shown as discharged, and substitute J. R. H. Deakins furnished, on 11-12/61 roll. Farmer, between 35 and 40 years old, resid. Prince William Co., worth over $20,000 on 8/31/65 amnesty petition: "Since [1861] I have remained quietly upon my farms & have had no participation either directly or indirectly in the rebellion." Apparently d. ca. 1/69.

DULANY, HENRY GRAFTON: b. 5/24/34. enl. 7/24/61 in Co. A. Elected Lt. 8/1/61. Seven days leave from 8/29/61. Tendered resignation 7/6/62 "because having lost an eye, I find the other so much impaired by exposure as seriously to endanger the sight." Resignation accepted as of 7/21/62. Paroled 4/24/65 at Winchester, resid. Upperville. d. 10/10/88, bur. Sharon Cem., Middleburg.

DULANY, RICHARD HENRY: b. 8/10/20 in Loudoun Co. enl. 7/24/61 in Co. A. Elected Capt. 8/1/61. On sick leave since 12/24 on 11-12/61 roll. Absent recruiting since 2/15 on 1-2/62 roll. Absent, wded. at Strasburg, on 5-6/61 roll. To Lt. Col., 7th Va. Cav. 6/20/62, Col. 3/23/65. d. 10/31/06 in Loudoun Co.

DUNCAN, ALEX McC.: enl. 9/17/61 in (1st) Co. E as Lt., age 24. Resid. Savannah, Ga.

DUNCAN, BENJAMIN FRANKLIN: enl. 4/22/61 in Co. B, age 23. Farmer. To Cpl. 7/26/61. To Sgt. 1/1/62. Re-enlistment furlough from 2/12/62. KIA 5/23/62 at Cedarville. "Submissive and obedient to orders himself, he exacted obedience of others." Brother of Robert R.

DUNCAN, ROBERT RUSSELL: b. 4/23/33 (or 1832) in Rappahannock Co. enl. 8/26/61 in Co. B. Previously in the Kansas troubles and at Battle of Carthage, Mo., in 1861. On re-enlistment furlough on 1-2/62 roll. To Lt. 4/20/62. Wded. and POW 10/9/64 at Strasburg. Left arm amputated 10/10/64. Paroled 2/27/65 at Ft. Delaware. Admitted to Howard's Grove Hosp., Richmond, 3/3/65. To Capt. 3/18/65. Absent since wded. 10/9/64 on 3/21/65 final roll. Farmer postwar in Culpeper Co. m. Lucy C. Browning 1868. d. 9/22/13, bur. Culpeper Masonic Cem.

DUNHAM, THOMAS H.: b. in Liberty Co., Ga. enl. 9/17/61 in (1st) Co. E, age 26, as Sgt. Wded. and POW 12/4/61 in Bog Wallow ambuscade. Back with co. by 2/7/62. Discharged 5/13/62 for "epilepsy, resulting from injuries of the head, received in a skirmish in 12/61."

DUNKLEY, JOHN H.: b. in Halifax Co. enl. 3/6/62 in Co. G. Laborer. Present until 7-8/63 roll, when absent on 20 day detail to get horse. Transferred 10/13/63 to Co. C, 1st Va. Lt. Art., in exchange for William Cole. Paroled 5/9/65 from Young's Co., Va. Art., at HQ, 2d Division, 6th Army Corps, U.S.A. Resid. Scottsburg, wheelmaker, age 69, on 8/11/05. d. 3/26/23, bur. Shady Grove United Methodist Church, Hyco Road, Halifax Co.

DUNN, JOHN W.: enl. 9/2/61 in Co. I. Absent at home sick in Orange Co. on rolls and returns for 11/61-2/62, then no further record until enl. again 1/20/63 in Co. I. He and his horse KIA 6/9/63 at Brandy Station.

DUNNIVAN, JOHN: enl. 5/25/62 in Co. C. Wded. 5/31/64 in right thigh. Admitted to Chimborazo Hosp. No. 5, Richmond, on 6/3/64, and furloughed for 60 days 7/2/64. Present on 3/30/65 final roll. Previously in Co. C, 11th Va. Cav.

DURRER, JOHN CHRISTOPHER: enl. 6/23/61 in Co. I, age 26. Detailed as teamster 11/21/61. Detailed as butcher in commisary dept. 12/11/61, and so borne until sent to hosp. in Culpeper C.H. 8/18/62. Thereafter present until 3/20/65 final roll, when again absent, detailed in commissary dept. Appointed Commissary Sgt. 3/31/65. Paroled 5/25/65 at Gordonsville, resid. Greene Co. Alive in Greene Co. in 1908.

DURRER, WILLIAM W.: b. in Greene Co. enl. 3/15/64 in Co. I. Absent on horse detail on 9-10/64 roll. Present on final 3/20/65 roll. Paroled 5/25/65 at Gordonsville, resid. Greene Co., signs by mark. Farmhand, resid. Keezletown, age 64, on 11/27/08. d. 8/2/14 in Rockingham Co. Also spelled "Derrer" on pension application.

DURRETT, RICHARD: Appears only on a postwar roster of Co. I.

DURRETT, WILLIAM: Appears only on a postwar roster of Co. I.

DWYER, ALFRED HARRISON: b. 1831. enl. 9/1/6? in Co. B AWOL since 10/1/62 on 9-10/62 roll. Found not guilty of desertion by court-martial on 11/24/63, but guilty of AWOL 7/1 to 10/18/63. Sentenced to wear a barrel shirt marked "Absence Without Leave," to guardhouse 15 days, and to carry a log in a circle 4 hours a day. Present until AWOL on 9-10/64 roll. d. 3/25/19, bur. Dwyer Cem. in Shenandoah National Park, Rappahannock Co. Wid. Mary Ellen, m. 1861.

DYER, FRANCIS E.: b. 9/1/43. enl. 5/25/61 in Co. F. To Sgt. on 9-10/62 roll. With exception of absence on horse furlough on 7-8/63 roll, present consistently until POW 6/10/64 at Louisa C.H. Reported exchanged from Elmira 2/13/65, but apparently not released until 6/14/65. Took the oath 6/14/65 at Elmira, resid. Washington, D.C. d. 12/4/81, bur. Ballston Central M.E. Church South, Fairfax Co.

DYER, JAMES: enl. 2/16/62 in (2d) Co. E, age 24. Absent guarding bridge at Mt. Crawford on 11-12/62 roll. POW 6/9/63 at Beverly Ford, paroled at Old Capitol Prison 6/25/63. In General Hosp., Petersburg, 6/30-7/7/63 with remittent fever. Absent sick at General Hosp., Lynchburg, on 11-12/63 roll. POW 5/11/64 at Yellow Tavern. d. 1/16/65 at Elmira of chronic diarrhea and bur. there.

EANES, POPE DRYDEN: b. in Pittsylvania Co. enl. 1/15/63 in (2d) Co. E. Previously Capt. Co. I, 57th Va. Inf. Detailed 4/25/64 as armorer at C.S. arsenal at Danville because of physical disability and so shown on final 3/4/65 roll. Age 40 on 1/27/65 report of arsenal employees. Moved to Bowie, Texas, postwar and d. in Texas. m. Martha Jane Cooper.

EASLEY, JOHN PYRANT: b. in Pittsylvania Co. enl. 5/27/61 in (2d) Co. E. Detailed 15 days to get a horse from 8/31/64. Otherwise present on all rolls thru 3/4/65 final roll. Resid. Dry Ford RFD, Pittsylvania Co., on 6/4/19, age 83. d. 8/13/19.

EASTHAM, FRANKLIN DABNEY: b. 3/3/43. enl. 7/19/61 in Co. B. Sick in Rappahannock Co. on 9/1/61 roll. Absent sick since 12/15/61 on 1-2/62 roll. Severely wded. 5/23/62 at Cedarville. Postwar roster says unfit for service afterwards. d. 2/9/15 in Rappahannock Co.

EASTHAM, GEORGE LAWSON: b. 12/2/42. Att. VMI. Enl. 10/20/62 in Co. B, age 18. To Cpl. on 11-12/63 roll. Present on all rolls until KIA 10/9/64 at Tom's Brook, when he was shot through the head.

EASTHAM, ROBERT WOODFORD: b. 2/28/42 near Flint Hill, Rappahannock Co. enl. 4/22/61 in Co. B, age 19. Farmer. Deserter since 12/26/62 on 11-12/62 roll, then present on 1-2/63 roll. AWOL from 10/12/63. Later in Co. D, Mosby's 43d Bn. Va. Cav., where he was famous as "Bob Ridley." m. Mary C. Reid 1869. Moved to Tucker Co., W.Va., postwar, then returned to Rappahannock Co., where he d. 4/7/24, bur. Eastham Cem., Rappahannock Co.

ECHOLS, WILLIAM E.: enl. 3/10/62 in Co. G. To Cpl. 6/25/63. In Chimborazo Hosp. No. 5 with gonorrhea 11/63-2/18/64. POW 5/11/64 at Yellow Tavern. Recorded as d. 3/23/65 at Elmira from pneumonia and bur. there, but he appears inexplicably on the final 3/22/65 roll as "absent with leave, just returned from prison." Postwar roster has John Echolds, presumably meaning this man.

ECKHART, AUGUSTUS: enl. 5/28/62 in Co. C. Substitute for J. H. Berry. AWOL since July on 9-10/62 roll, and shown as deserting at Richmond on 11/62 return.

EDMONDS, BENJAMIN J. SYDNOR: b. 1843. enl. 7/24/61 in Co. A. To Cpl. 2/1/62. Absent sick with broken arm since 2/1/63 on 1-2/63 roll. To Sgt. on 11-12/63 roll. Otherwise present on all rolls thru 3/27/65 final roll. Paroled 4/24/65 at Winchester. Postwar roster says wded. at Five Forks. Resid. Fauquier Co. "Moved to Missouri, where he became a prominent businessman and a member of the state legislature."

EDMONDS, EDWARD GILBERT: b. 10/4/21 in Fauquier Co. enl. 9/20/62 in Co. A. After horses in Fauquier on 12/62 return. Absent sick since 2/21/63 on 1-2/63 roll and sick from 8/2 on 8/31/63 roll. Wded. 5/12/64 near Yellow Tavern, lost an eye, and thereafter wded. in hosps. at Richmond and Scottsville thru 3/27/65 final roll. Paroled 4/24/65 at Winchester. Known as "Bud." Treasurer of Fauquier Co. postwar. m. Adeline Edmonds. d. 12/23/97, bur. Warrenton Cem.

EDMONDS, LANDON CARTER: b. in Fauquier Co. enl. 4/24/61 in Co. H. AWOL 9/1-9/25/61. Furlough 2/9-3/13/62. Absent, "detailed to wait on his brother who is sick near Harrisonburg since 14th inst. (marked as a deserter)" on 11-12/62 roll. Present from 2/28/63 roll to 12/30/64 roll, when shown sick at hosp. since 8/1/64. Thereafter sick until 3/22/65 final roll, on which he is shown as deserting 3/6/65. Paroled 4/24/65 at Winchester. d. 1/29/00 at Lee Camp Soldiers' Home, Richmond, age 71, bur. Hollywood Cem., Richmond, wid. Martha J., m. 1873.

EDMONDS, PHILLIP M.: enl. 3/16/62 in Co. H. Absent as courier to Gen. Jeb Stuart on 9-10/62 roll. Absent sick at Keezletown since 12/14 and marked as deserter on 11-12/62 roll and 12/62 return. 2/28/63 roll says marked as deserter from 1/1/63.

EDWARDS, BENJAMIN: enl. 9/15/61 in Co. A. Detailed as teamster in commissary department 12/12/62. AWOL since 6/23 on 8/31/63 roll. 11-12/63 roll says deserted 7/23/63 at Snickersville.

EDWARDS, CHARLES A.: enl. 4/1/62 in (2d) Co. E. Present until POW 5/11/64 at Yellow Tavern. Paroled 1/17/65 at Pt. Lookout. In detachment of paroled and exchanged POWs at Camp Lee, near Richmond, on 1/26/65 roll. Absent on furlough on 3/4/65 final roll.

EDWARDS, DANIEL C.: enl. 4/1/62 in (2d) Co. E. Absent sick on 5-6/62 roll. Wded. 5/11/64 at Yellow Tavern in left thigh. In Chimborazo Hosp. No. 4 5/14-5/20/64 and recovering at home in Pittsylvania Co. on 7-8/64 roll. Present on 9-10/64 roll. Absent sick in Pittsylvania Co. on final 3/4/65 roll.

EDWARDS, DANIEL C.: enl. 9/20/64 in (2d) Co. E. Present thru final 3/4/65 roll.

EDWARDS, GEORGE H.: b. in Pittsylvania Co. enl. 4/1/62 in (2d) Co. E. Farmer. Discharged 5/2/62 for pulmonitis with frequent hemorrhages from lungs, had been unfit for duty for 60 days, age 39. Alive 5/1/00 at Sandy Level, age given as 81.

EDWARDS, JOSEPH: enl. 9/15/62 in Co. A. Present on extra duty as co. teamster on 1-2/63 roll. Absent as co. teamster since 7/23/63 on 8/31/63 roll. 11-12/63 roll has him deserting at Snickersville on 7/23/63. No further record.

EDWARDS, JOSEPH: enl. 6/20/61 in Co. K. Absent sick with leave since 2/20/62 on 1-2/62 roll. AWOL from 5/1 to 9/1/62. Present on 12/12/62 roll and thru 7-8/63 roll. Marked "deceased" on 12/17/63 clothing roll.

EDWARDS, JOSEPH W.: Only record is a parole as a member of Co. H at Winchester 5/3/65, age 22, resid. Fauquier Co., near Orleans, signs by mark.

EHART, ROBERT W.: Only record in the regiment is 7-8/63 roll of Co. I, which says "returned to his company in 59 Va. Inf." 8/18/63. Name is "Eheart" on rolls of Co. D, 59th Va. Inf. Resid. Orange Co. Paroled 5/23/65 at Gordonsville.

ELGIN, JAMES WILLIAM: b. 10/21/37 in Loudoun Co. enl. 6/26/61 in Co. K. Thirty days furlough from 2/11/62. Present until detailed as courier for Gen. W. E. Jones 7/10/63. Courier for Gen. L. Lomax on 11-12/64 roll. Present with co. on 12/27/64 roll. Courier for Gen. W. H. F. Payne on 9-10/64 roll and 1-2/65 final roll. Paroled 4/27/65 at Edwards Ferry, Md. Farmer and Commissioner of Revenue for Leesburg Dist. postwar. d. 3/1/00 at Evergreen Mills, near Leesburg. Wid. Sue A., m. 1867.

ELGIN, JOHN FRANCIS: b. 12/29/34 in Loudoun Co. enl. 4/10/62 in Co. K. "Absent, supposed to have been captured" on 6/30/62 roll. To Cpl. on 12/12/62 roll, present. In General Hosp., Charlottesville, with scabies 12/7/63-1/11/64. "Absent on duty" on final 1-2/65 roll. Farmer postwar. m. Anna Jackson 1866. d. 4/12/82.

ELIASON, RUTLEDGE HOMES: b. on Old Point Comfort. enl. 7/24/61 in Co. A. Absent with leave on 5-6/62 roll. Absent on detached service with Gen. Jeb Stuart 8/21/62-8/31/63. With Medical Dept., Cavalry Corps, 8/31-12/5/63. With co. on 11-12/63 roll. Wded. 5/5/64 in right leg at Spotsylvania and thereafter absent wded. thru 3/27/65 final roll. Retired 3/13/65 to Invalid Corps, stationed at Statesville, N.C. Paroled 5/12/65 at Greensboro, N.C. Postmaster at Bower, Oklahoma, postwar. d. 1/4/16 near Colbert, Ok., age 76 in 1913. Wid. Lutie G., m. 1877.

ELLIS, JOHN EVAN: b. 5/5/46 at "Ellisville," Orange Co. Att. VMI. enl. 3/15/64 in Co. I. Absent on horse detail on 9-10/64 roll. Present on 3/20/65 final roll. d. 1905, bur. family cem. at "Ellisville."

ELLIS, WILLIAM T.: b. 1840. enl. 3/1/64 in Co. I. Present until transferred 3/1/65 to Co. A, 39th Bn. Va. Cav. Paroled 4/9/65 at Appomattox. d. 1905, bur. family cem. at "Ellisville," Orange Co.

ERGENBRIGHT, GEORGE RICHARD: b. 1/2/40. enl. 5/28/61 in Co. C. On detail for horses 10/23-11/1/63. Present on every roll thru ca. 3/30/65 final roll. d. 2/15/96, bur. Mt. Olivet Cem., McGaheysville.

ERGENBRIGHT, P. H.: enl. 2/10/64 in Co. C. Present thru ca. 3/30/65 final roll.

ERGENBRIGHT, RICHARD B.: b. 5/12/42. enl. 5/28/61 in Co. C as Sgt. To Pvt. on 9-10/62 roll. Present until POW 6/9/63 at Beverly Ford. Paroled 6/25/63 at Old Capitol Prison. In Chimborazo Hosp., Richmond, on 5/2/64 roll. In Charlottesville General Hosp. with typhoid fever 9/14/63 until furloughed 10/23/63, then absent sick thru 9-10/64 roll. Present on final ca. 3/30/65 roll. Paroled 4/9/65 at Appomattox. d. 4/17/16, bur. Mt. Olivet Cem., McGaheysville.

EVANS, OLIVER PERRY: b. in Fairfax Co. enl. 4/20/61 in Co. F. Artist. Absent sick at Centreville since 7/23/61 on 7-8/61 roll. Wded. ca. 5/25/62 at Winchester in neck "and left there." Discharged 8/3/62 at Camp Madison for gunshot wd. partially paralyzing left arm, age 23. Claimed later service in Mosby's 43d Bn. Va. Cav. Paroled 5/13/65 at Charleston, W.Va. Discharged 11/5/13 from Lee Camp Soldiers' Home, Richmond.

EVANS, ROBERT F.: enl. 9/12/62 in Co. A. Wheelwright. Detailed as wagonmaker at brigade HQ 12/12/63 and so shown until POW 12/26/64 at Paris. In hosps. at Petersburg and Richmond with remittent fever and diarrhea 7/24-8/4/64. Took the oath 5/13/65 at Pt. Lookout. Resid. "Perriton, Ohio." Transportation ordered to Winchester. Wrote on 3/18/65 "I was conscripted and put in the service against my will."

EVANS, WILLIAM F.: enl. 10/15/62 in Co. F. Present until drowned 4/24/63 crossing South Branch of Potomac at Petersburg, (W.) Va., during Jones's W. Va. raid. See report of Lt. Col. John Shac Green 5/26/63 in *Official Records*.

EVANS, WELLINGTON F.: enl. 10/15/62 in Co. F. Absent with leave on 11/62 return. Otherwise present until d. 6/15/63 of typhoid fever at General Receiving Hosp. (Charity Hosp.), Gordonsville. First name sometimes given as "Willington."

EVERETT, _____: enl. 6/1/62 in Co. G. Substitute for N. L. Wade. AWOL from 6/62 and marked as a deserter. Never shown as present.

EVERHART, JAMES BENNETT: b. 8/10/40 near Berryville. enl. 4/18/61 in Co. D. On extra duty as teamster from 10/2 (or 12)/61. AWOL from 11/19/61. Teamster on 4/30/62 roll. Arrested as deserter 12/22/62. Present from 1-2/63 roll to 11-12/63 roll, when absent on duty in regimental QM dept. Thereafter present until 3/22/65 final roll, when absent with leave. Paroled 4/15/65 at Winchester, resid. Clarke Co. d. 5/8/89, bur. Green Hill Cem., Berryville. Wid. Martha E.

EVERHART, JOHN NEWTON: b. 2/12/38 in Clarke Co. enl. 4/18/61 in Co. D. On extra duty as teamster from 10/21/61. Wagonmaster in regiment on 9-10/62 thru 8/31/63 rolls. Absent in brigade commissary dept. from 11-12/63 roll thru 3/22/65 final roll. Also in the 12th Va. Cav. Paroled 4/20/65 at Winchester. Farm laborer postwar. d. 5/16/18, aged 80 years, 3 months, 4 days, bur. Green Hill Cem., Berryville.

FANT, WILLIAM D.: enl. 4/22/61 in Co. B, age 29. Farmer. Home on sick leave on 6/30/61 roll. AWOL for 3 months on 9/1/61 roll. To Sgt. on 5-6/62 roll. Assistant forage master on 11/62 return. Detached to commissary dept. grazing cattle 10/29/63 thru 9-10/64 roll. Absent in brigade commissary dept. buying cattle on 3/21/65 final roll. Paroled 5/8/65 at Winchester. Reportedly d. before 5/07.

FARLEY, ROBERT FRANCIS: enl. 3/17/62 in Co. G. Substitute. On 20 day horse detail on 7-8/63 roll. Otherwise always present thru 3/22/65 final roll. POW 4/5/65 near Richmond. Took the oath 6/12/65 at Pt. Lookout, resid. near Danville. d. 6/24/94, age 50, bur. Greenhill Cem., Danville.

FARMER, A. T.: enl. 7/21/62 in Co. B. Conscript. Absent sick, sent to hosp. on 11-12/62 roll. Discharged 2/2/63 by substituting William Lillis.

FARMER, J. H.: Shown in Co. G clothing book as discharged.

FAULKNER, ABSALOM W.: enl. 10/1/63 in Co. I. Absent on horse detail on 9-10/64 roll. AWOL on 3/20/65 final roll. Also shown as Faulconer.

FAULKNER, JAMES THOMAS: enl. 4/1/62 in Co. I. Farmer. Absent with leave on 5-6/62 roll. Twelve day furlough from 12/20/62. Detailed as co. wagoner on 1-2/63 roll. Absent sick and sent to hospital at Culpeper 8/19/63 on 7-8/63 roll. POW 5/5/64 at Spotsylvania C.H. Took the oath 5/15/65 at Pt. Lookout.

FAULKNER, J. W.: A man who gave this name, and identified as in Co. B, was a POW 3/20/65 at Hillsboro. Federal records note "belongs to Mosby's Gang," and there are no Confederate or postwar records on him in the 6th. Apparently refers to a member of Mosby's 43d Bn. Va. Cav., perhaps using a ruse.

FAULKNER, JOHN BENJAMIN: b. near Germanna Ford, Orange Co. 1/28/44. enl. 6/12/61 in Co. I. Previously in 9th Va. Cav. Present until absent on horse detail on 9-10/64 roll. Reported by Richmond as deserter 3/1/65. AWOL on final 3/20/65 roll. d. 1/9/25. Also shown as Faulconer.

FAUNTLEROY, THOMAS KINLOCH: b. 1837 at White Post in Clarke Co. enl. 6/1/62 in Co. D. Shown as discharged by promotion on 9-10/61 roll. Appointed Lt. in 1st Regular Battery, Confederate Lt. Art. 5/19/62 in Trans-Mississippi Dept. To Capt. 9/15/63 on staff of Gen. Henry W. Allen. Paroled 6/14/65 at Shreveport, La. Resid. near White Post. Methodist minister postwar, resid. Ruston, La.

FELTNER, JOSEPH: enl. 9/17/62 in Co. A. Present thru 1-2/63 roll. No further record. Reportedly resid. Clarke Co. Postwar roster says d. 4/63.

FERGUSON, THOMAS SEWELL: enl. 11/10/62 in Co. A. Absent with leave on 9-10/64 roll. Absent on furlough on 3/27/65 final roll. Paroled 4/22/65 at Winchester, age 23, resid. Paris. m. Mary E. Page 1869. d. 1882 in Madison Co. "from a sabre wound" in face.

FERGUSON, WILLIAM D.: enl. 3/10/62 in Co. G. Absent since 11/10/62 to procure horses on 11/62 return. Discharged by substituting Michael O'Day on 1-2/63 roll. Conscripted 9/24/64. Absent on horse detail on 9-10/64 roll. Present on final 3/22/65 roll. Resid. Glenland, age 66 on 6/19/01. d. 4/27/03. Wid. Elizabeth L., m. 1856.

FERGUSON, WILLIAM M.: b. 10/4/26. enl. 3/15/63 in Co. A. AWOL since 6/10/63 on 8/31/63 roll. Thereafter present until 3/27/65 final roll, when shown AWOL since 1/22/65. Paroled 4/22/65 at Charles Town, (W.) Va. d. 1/2/12, bur. Nalley-Strother Cem., near Paris.

FERRELL, CHILES HUTCHERSON: enl. 8/19/61 in Co. G, age 22. Discharged 11/8/61 by substituting Arthur McGinnis. Postwar roster says discharged for ill health.

FEWELL, BENJAMIN FRANKLIN: b. 1837. enl. 3/23/62 in Co. H. Shoemaker. POW 10/29/62 near Petersburg, (W.) Va. Paroled 12/2/62 near Vicksburg, Miss. Absent with leave, gone home for horse on 11-12/62 roll. Absent sick and AWOL since 2/1/63 on 2/28/63 roll thru 7-8/63 roll. Transferred to 8th Va. Inf. 11/23/63. d. 1898, bur. Marshall Cem.

FIELD, CHARLES WILLIAM: b. 4/6/28 at "Airy Mount," in Woodford Co., Ky. Grad. USMA. USA, 1849-61. Resigned as Capt. 5/30/61. Commissioned Lt. Col. Va. forces 6/17/61. To Col. 6th Va. Cav. 9/11/61. To Brig. Gen. of infantry 3/9/62. To Maj. Gen. 2/12/64. Paroled 4/9/65 at Appomattox. Resid. Baltimore, Md., and Savannah, Ga., postwar. Col., Egyptian army, 1875-78. Doorkeeper, U.S. House of Representatives; civil engineer; Supt. U.S. Reservation at Hot Springs, Ark. m. Monimia Mason 1857. d. 4/9/92 in Washington, D.C., bur. Loudoun Park Cem., Baltimore, Md. "Of vigorous intellect and indomitable will, of superb physique, Field was the *beau sabreur*" (*Dictionary of American Biography*).

FIELD, PHILIP B.: enl. 3/1/61 in Co. B. Student. KIA 5/23/62 near Front Royal. Brother of William. "A tall, slender boy of some eighteen years, with a face as delicate, as gentle, and as refined as a woman's, but with a shade of sadness, which but added to the attractiveness of his expression" (D. A. Grimsley). bur. family cem., Culpeper Co.

FIELD, RICHARD Y.: enl. 4/1/62 in Co. B, age 29. Wded. 5/23/62 near Front Royal. Detached in commissary dept. of Gen. A. P. Hill's Division 10/26/62 and so shown thru final 3/21/65 roll. Paroled with unattached men as courier, date and place not shown. Reportedly alive in 5/07.

FIELD, WILLIAM G.: Att. U.Va. enl. 4/1/62 in Co. B, age 22. Student. Wded. 5/23/62 near Front Royal. Reportedly KIA in Seven Days near Malvern Hill, bur. family cem., Culpeper Co. Brother of Philip. "Tall and well-developed, with a bright and cheery disposition" (D. A. Grimsley).

FINDLEY, CHARLES M.: enl. 1/1/64 in Co. F. POW 8/5/64 in Fauquier Co. (another source says near Burke Station) while detached to obtain horses. d. 7/3/65 at Elmira of chronic diarrhea and bur. there. Middle initial sometimes shown as "L."

FIRESHEETS, CHARLES B.: enl. 8/19/61 in Co. G, age 33. In Chimborazo Hosp. No. 2, Richmond, with icterus (jaundice) 3/17-4/15/62. In General Hosp., Charlottesville, with debility 5/25-5/29/62. Nurse at Halifax C.H. on 9-10/62 roll. In General Hosp., Danville, with debility, 1/10-11/16/63, much of which time he was a nurse. Present on co. rolls 11-12/63 thru final 3/22/65 roll. d. 3/28/92 in North Danville. Wid. Nannie.

FISHER, DAVID F.: Appears in Federal records as in Co. C, POW 5/30/62 at Front Royal, and exchanged 8/5/62 at Aiken's Ldg. No Confederate records.

FISHER, MARTIN: enl. 7/15/61 in Co. K. Sick on 12/1 on 12/62 return. Horse KIA 8/21/64 at Berryville. Present on all rolls thru 1-2/65 final roll. POW 4/1/65 at Five Forks. Took the oath 6/12/65 at Pt. Lookout. Resid. Montgomery Co., Md.

FISHER, THOMAS H.: b. in Rappahannock Co. enl. 7/1/62 in Co. B. Severely wded. 8/22/64 at Berryville, and absent wded. on final 3/21/65 roll. Postwar roster says enl. 3/62, age 18. Resid. Hawlin, age 64, on 6/28/10.

FITZGERALD, A. H.: Conscripted 2/1/64 and assigned to Co. F 2/25/64. No further record.

FITZGERALD, R. A.: Conscripted 2/1/64 and assigned to Co. F 2/25/64. No further record.

FITZGERALD, WILLIAM ROBERT: b. 12/15/42. enl. 4/1/62 in (2d) Co. E. In General Hosp., Charlottesville, with typhoid fever 7/17-8/5/62, and again, complaint unspecified, 11/15/62 thru 1-2/63 roll. Afterward present on all rolls thru final 3/4/65 roll. 1913 roster gives his address at that time as Monroe, N.C.

FITZHUG, E. T.: Only record is 8/31/63 muster roll of Co. A which shows him deserting 10/1/62. This is presumably an error, meaning E. T. Fitzhugh.

FITZHUGH, CHAMPE SUMMERFIELD: enl. 7/24/61 in Co. A. Fifteen days leave from 12/31/61. In Chimborazo Hosp. No. 5, Richmond, with dysentery 3/17/62. Returned to duty 10/8/62 with 15 day furlough but "refused to return to his co." and marked as deserting at Paris 10/17/62. May be identical to the man of this name in Co. D of Mosby's 43d Bn. Va. Cav., who was from Loudoun Co.

FLEMING, JOSEPH FRANKLIN: b. 10/13/34 in Loudoun Co. enl. 9/25/62 in Co. A. Present on every roll until final 3/27/65 roll, when reported absent, accidentally shot 3/1/65. Paroled 4/21/65 at Summit Pt., (W.) Va. Farmer postwar, resid. Pleasant Valley, Fairfax Co., on 3/26/09. d. 8/2/13, bur. Ivy Hill Cem., Upperville.

FLETCHER, ALPHEUS: b. 1/7/27. enl. 11/64 in Co. A. AWOL since 1/1/65 on 3/27/65 final roll. Paroled 4/28/65 at Winchester, resid. Fauquier Co. m. Tibatha Browning Wheatley. d. 9/12/08, bur. Fletcher Cem. at "Oak Spring" near Upperville.

FLETCHER, GEORGE W.: enl. 5/8/61 in Co. B, age 31. Farmer. d. 9/5/61 in Rappahannock Co. of disease contracted in service.

FLETCHER, TOWNSEND: enl. 10/18/62 in Co. H. Deserted 11/10/62 near Rectortown. Paroled 5/7/65 at Winchester, age 24, resid. Fauquier Co., signs by mark.

FLETCHER, WILLIAM H.: b. 9/18/30. enl. 10/30/62 in Co. F. Overseer. Deserted 11/1/62 at Upperville. Next record is of capture by Federals 4/23/63 near Leesburg. Paroled 4/28/63 at Ft. McHenry, Md. Paroled again 5/7/65 at Winchester, signs by mark. Reportedly served 3 months as wagonmaster for 11th Va. Inf. d. 11/15/92, bur. Fletcher Cem. at "Oak Spring" near Upperville.

FLOURNOY, CABELL EDWARD: b. 6/30/40 in Halifax Co. Att. Washington College. enl. 2/16/62 in (2d) Co. E. To Capt. 4/20/62. To Major 7/16/62. KIA 5/31/64. Resid. Pittsylvania Co. Tendered services to South Carolina on 12/6/60, in the event Virginia did not secede. Never married. Son of Col. Thomas S. "A gallant young officer, he was a little too fond of the bottle, not very choice in his language, rather reckless" (Luther W. Hopkins).

FLOURNOY, HENRY WOOD: b. 6/6/46 in Halifax Co. enl. 3/20/62 in Co. G. Detailed as orderly to the Col. (his father) on 9-10/62 roll. Orderly to Major Flournoy on 12/62 return. POW 7/12/63 at Hagerstown, Md. Paroled 3/16/64 at Pt. Lookout. Wded. 10/8/64, sent to hosp. at Staunton. Transferred 11/12/64 to 3d Co., Richmond Howitzers. m. Rosa B. Wood 1872. Postwar lawyer, businessman, secretary of the commonwealth, resid. Danville, Southwest Va., Richmond, and Farmville. d. 10/23/02 in Houston, Tex., bur. Hollywood Cem., Richmond.

FLOURNOY, THOMAS STANHOPE: b. 12/15/11 in Prince Edward Co. Grad. Hampden-Sydney College. Appointed Capt. Co. G 8/18/61. Lawyer. U.S. House of Representatives 1847-49. American Party candidate for governor 1855. Member of Va. secession convention. To Major 4/15/62. To Col. 7/16/62. Resigned 10/15/62 because of "domestic affliction." Unsuccessful candidate for governor 1863. Lawyer in Danville postwar. Delegate to Democratic convention of 1876. m. 1) Susan Ann Love 1835, 2) Mildred H. Coles 1852. d. 3/12/83 at his estate in Halifax Co. and bur. there. "His power in swaying a crowd from the stump was second only to his effectiveness before a jury" (Alexander Brown).

FLYNN, JAMES BLAIR: b. 3/10/39 near The Plains in Fauquier Co. enl. 4/22/61 in Co. K. Wded. in foot between Lovettsville and Berlin on 7-8/61 roll. Wagon driver on 12/7/61. Absent on sick leave since 1/10 on 1-2/62 roll. AWOL 6/3/63 until POW 7/20/63 in Loudoun Co. Exchanged 11/1/64 from Pt. Lookout. AWOL on final 1-2/65 roll. Paroled 4/25/65, resid. Loudoun Co. Farmer postwar, claimed two wds. d. 10/10, bur. Warrenton Cem. Wid. Rachel P., m. 1865, who gave his middle name as Benjamin.

FLYNN, WILLIAM AUSTIN: b. 1821 in Fauquier Co. enl. 4/24/61 in Co. H. Undertaker. Absent detailed at QM at Manassas on 9-12/61 rolls. Carpenter at Manassas on 12/61 return. m. Juliette Davis 1843 "in middle of Potomac near Leesburg." d. 1/24/62 at Salem, Fauquier Co., bur. Marshall Cem.

FOGG, CHARLES E.: enl. 3/1/62 in Co. B. Wded. severely in hip and spine and POW 7/3/63 at Fairfield, Pa. Paroled ca. 9/16/63 from De Camp General Hosp., Davids Island, N.Y. Harbor. Still absent due to Fairfield wd. on final 3/21/65 co. roll. Resid. Washington, Rappahannock Co., age 47, on 5/14/88. d. 1/22.

FOLEY, BENJAMIN FRANKLIN: b. 9/12/43 in Loudoun Co. enl. 3/8/62 in Co. K. Wded. 8/22/62 at Catlett's Station, returned to co. 2/16/63. POW 6/7/63 at Miller's Factory. Paroled at Old Capitol Prison 6/25/63. POW 3/20/64 in Loudoun Co. Held as hostage with 59 others for Ulric Dahlgren's men for 9 weeks. Took the oath 6/20/65 at Ft. Delaware. Farmer, stock dealer, and postmaster at Berryville postwar. m. Sarah Jane Rust 1869. d. 6/16/15 at Richmond during a reunion, bur. Green Hill Cem., Berryville.

FOLEY, JAMES OSWALD: Reportedly in Co. K, KIA 1861 at Kelly's Island, the 3d man killed in the war.

FONTAINE, NATHANIEL C.: enl. 3/28/62 in Co. G. Present on all rolls thru 3/22/65 final roll. Alive 12/18/88 at Marrowbone, Henry Co.

FORD, JAMES: enl. 3/20/62 in Co. G. Horse KIA 6/9/63 at Brandy Station. Except for absence on horse detail on 9-10/64 roll, present on all rolls thru 3/22/65 final roll. Signs by mark.

FORD, WILLIAM A.: enl. 8/19/61 in Co. G. Present thru 6/25/63 roll. Co. clothing book has discharged 8/19/62. d. 8/90, bur. Shady Grove Cem., near South Boston. Name spelled Foard in some Confederate records.

FOSTER, McKENDREE T.: enl. 9/2/61 in Co. I. Transferred 6/10/62 to 9th Va. Cav. Resid. Culpeper Co.

FOSTER, THOMAS HUNTON: enl. 8/27/61 in Co. H. To Lt. 2/6/63. POW 9/13/63 at Brandy Station. d. 8/21/64 at Pt. Lookout of chronic diarrhea, age 29, bur. Foster Cem., The Plains. His prison diary is at this writing in possession of Mr. James Mejdrich of Wheaton, Ill.

FOULKS, WILLIAM E.: enl. 8/19/61 in Co. G, age 35. Absent with leave since 11/23 on 11/61 return. In Petersburg General Hosp. 5/1-5/28/62 with debilitas. Present on 5-6/62 roll. Co. clothing book says discharged 8/19/62. May be identical to William E. Foulkes, Co. I, 18th Va. Inf., KIA 5/16/64 at Drewrys Bluff.

FOUT, JOHN D. B.: enl. 5/22/61 in Co. K as Cpl. To Sgt. on 6/30/62 roll. To Lt. 5/19/64. In Richmond hosps. 7/31-8/12/64 with chronic diarrhea. Absent to bring in absentees since 2/8 on 2/28/65 inspection report. Present on 1-2/65 final roll. Paroled 5/8/65 at Conrad's Ferry, Md., and 5/11/65 at Harpers Ferry. Took the oath 8/4/65 in Maryland, resid. Frederick Co., Md.

FOWLE, ROBERT ROLLINS: b. 3/20/32 in Alexandria. enl. 4/24/61 in Co. F as Lt. Resigned 6/7/61 because of hernia. Later served in Kemper's Battery and 2d Va. Cav. Paroled 4/22/65 at Fairfax C.H. m. Barbara Saunders. d. 3/20/73, bur. Christ Church Cem., Alexandria.

FOWLER, EVERETT: enl. 7/24/61 in Co. A. Present on 7-8/61 roll. No further record. Resid. Clarke Co.

FOX, THOMAS: b. 4/30/17. enl. 8/19/61 in Co. G, age 45. To Cpl. 12/26/61. To Sgt. 1/15/62. 11/61 return says in QM Dept. since 9/25/61. Discharged 6/9/62. d. 4/30/90, bur. Greenhill Cem., Danville.

FRANCIS, HENRY J.: enl. 4/24/61 as Sgt. in Co. H. Merchant. Sent home sick 8/9/61 with typhoid fever and never returned to the regiment.

FRANKLIN, JOHN BENJAMIN: b. 12/17/39. enl. 6/20/61 in Co. K. Lost one month to typhoid fever on 7-8/61 roll. Absent sick since 11/25 on 11-12/62 returns. AWOL 12/15/62-1/8/63. To Cpl. on 7-8/63 roll. Wded. in calf and horse KIA 10/11/63 at Brandy Station. In Charlottesville General Hosp. 11/9/63-2/16/64. Absent wded. until present on final 1-2/65 roll. d. 5/18/92, bur. Leesburg Union Cem. Wid. Eliza D., m. 1867.

FRANKLIN, WILLIAM W.: enl. 9/18/62 in Co. H. Absent sick at Linden since 11/13 (or 15)/62. No further record.

FRAZIER, HEROD T.: enl. 10/1/61 in Co. A. On extra duty as herdsman since 10/21/61 on 10/61-2/62 rolls. Present on 5-6/62 roll. On pay rolls dated 2/11 and 4/30/62 as forage master. Postwar roster says discharged, over age.

FRAZIER, JOHN S.: Conscript assigned 5/15/64 to Co. I. In Richmond hosps. 5/29-5/30/64. In Charlottesville General Hosp. 9/20-9/25/64 with chronic diarrhea. Absent sick on all rolls thru 3/20/65 final roll.

FRENCH, LEWIS JACOB: b. in Loudoun Co. enl. 10/15/62 in Co. K. In hosp. 5/21/63. Absent on sick leave on 7-8/63 roll. In Charlottesville General Hosp. 1/7/64 with morbi cutis, transferred 1/8/64 to Lynchburg. AWOL on 9-10/64 roll thru final 1-2/65 roll. Paroled 4/27/65 at Winchester, age 27. Laborer postwar, resid. Leesburg. d. 3/27/11, bur. Leesburg Union Cem. Wid. Josephine, m. 1868.

FRENCH, ROBERT: enl. 10/10/62 in Co. K. Present thru 11-12/62 roll. No further record.

FREW, WILLIAM: enl. 9/17/61 in (1st) Co. E, age 18. Resid. Savannah, Ga. MWIA 8/1/63 at Brandy Station. d. 8/9/63. On Roll of Honor 12/10/64 for Battle of Upperville.

FRIEDENSTEIN, GODFREY: enl. 8/10/61 in Co. G as farrier, age 35. Detailed in QM Dept. since 12/4/61 on 11-12/61 roll. Present thru 5-6/62 roll. Co. clothing book has discharged. Described in postwar roster as "a Dutchman living in Halifax." Probably identical to the man who signed himself "Godfrey Fridenstin," deserted from Co. M, 2d Va. State Reserves about 3/8/65 to U.S. steamer *Freeborn*, and took the oath 3/9/65 at Pt. Lookout.

FRISTOE, WILLIAM S.: enl. 4/22/61 in Co. B as Lt., age 31. Farmer. Submitted resignation 11/25/61 for reasons unknown. Absent sick since 2/5 on 1-2/62 roll. Dropped 4/20/62. Postwar roster says "not elected at reorganization." S. Bassett French Papers show an officer of this name, b. 1838 in Rappahannock Co., who "died of wounds received in battle, 1864."

FULLER, JESSE T.: enl. 1/15/64 in (2d) Co. E. Present on 1-2/63 roll. Pay records show him paid for service covering 3/1-4/30/63. Probably identical to Jesse Thomas Fuller, Co. B, 13th Bn. Va. Lt. Art. (Ringgold Battery), b. Pittsylvania Co., farmer, discharged 7/21/62 for "general disability resulting from indigestion."

FULLER, MONROE MADISON: b. 1839. enl. 5/27/61 in (2d) Co. E. Wded. in right arm 8/25/62 at Waterloo Bridge. Absent wded. until 12/9/62. Detached guarding bridge on 11-12/62 roll. In Chimborazo Hosp. No. 5, Richmond, 7/14-7/16/64 with intermittent fever. On detached service with commissary and QM officers on rolls for 7-10/64. Present on final 3/4/65 roll. Paroled 5/5/65 at Greensboro, N.C. d. 5/27/79 in Pittsylvania Co. Wid. Sallie A., m. 1867.

FULLER, WILLIAM L.: enl. 5/27/61 in (2d) Co. E. To Cpl., age 26, on 2/16/62 roll. To Lt. 4/20/62. "Absent with squadron ordered by Gen. Jackson" on 11/62 return. Commanding Co. on 7-8/63 roll. MWIA 5/7/64 near Spotsylvania C.H., bur. Spotsylvania Confederate Cem., where he is identified as "W.L.F."

FULTON, JOHN H.: enl. 9/17/61 in (1st) Co. E, age 18. Resid. Savannah, Ga. In Moore hosp., Danville, with typhoid fever 12/29/61, sent to hosp. at Front Royal. d. 1/27/62 at Savannah, Ga., of disease.

FUNSTEN, OLIVER RIDGEWAY: b. 3/22/45. enl. 6/1/62 in Co. D. On horse furlough on 11-12/62 roll. Otherwise present until transferred 11/1/63 to 11th Va. Cav. d. 11/6/94, bur. Thornrose Cem., Staunton.

FURR, JAMES: enl. 10/12/62 in Co. A. Wded. 9/13/63 at Brandy Station. Forty day furlough from 10/6/63 for gunshot wd. of left thigh from General Hosp. No. 1, Richmond. Shown as deserter since 4/1/64 on 7-8/64 roll, but as absent due to 9/13/63 wd. on 9-10/64 roll. No further record. Resid. Clarke Co.

FURR, JOHN WILLIAM THOMPSON: b. 9/26/45. enl. 1/1/64 in Co. A. Present on all rolls thru 3/27/65 final roll. Paroled 4/22/65 at Winchester, resid. Loudoun Co. d. 9/17/19, bur. Ebenezer Cem. near Round Hill.

GALLEHER, GEORGE T.: enl. 3/1/62 in Co. A. POW 10/17/62 at Upperville. Exchanged ca. 10/31/62 from Old Capitol Prison. Sent to hosp. 10/3/63. Present on 7-8/64 roll. In Charlottesville hosp. 1/3-1/21/65 with scabies. AWOL since 2/1/65 on 3/27/65 final roll. Paroled 4/20/65 at Winchester, age 20, resid. Leesburg.

GALLOWAY, WILLIAM H.: enl. 4/1/62 in (2d) Co. E. Twenty days horse leave from 12/17/62. Wded. 6/21/63 at Upperville. To Chimborazo Hosp. No. 2, Richmond, 6/18/64 with debility, transferred to Lynchburg 7/9/64. Present on 3/4/65 final roll.

GALT, ROBERT: b. 6/8/36 in Richmond. Grad. Princeton B.A., U. of Pa. M.D. Appointed assistant surgeon 10/18/61. Previously Pvt. in Co. F, 4th Va. Cav. POW 10/9/64 in Shenandoah Valley. Paroled 10/14/64 at Winchester as on staff of Gen. William H. Payne. In Richmond 10/24/64. Gen. Payne wrote 3/18/65 that Galt "has been very faithful and efficient" and "fully deserves promotion." Paroled at Greensboro, N.C., no date. d. 3/15/77 at Columbia, Va.

GANT, WILLIAM: enl. 4/1/64 in Co. B. Absent wded. 5/5/64 on all rolls thru 3/21/65 final roll. Admitted 5/7/64 to Chimborazo Hosp. No. 1, Richmond, with gunshot wd. Sixty day furlough from 6/1/64.

3/16/12

GARDNER, ALEXANDER ZACHARY: enl. 4/1/62 in Co. I as substitute for Baldwin Pannill. Absent on horse detail on 9-10/64 roll. Otherwise present on all rolls thru 3/20/65 final roll. d. 4/30/12 at Mine Run, age 64, bur. Antioch Baptist Church Cem., Orange Co. Wid. Elizabeth W., m. 1900.

GARDNER, JAMES M.: b. 9/24/44. enl. 5/4/61 in Co. I as substitute for M. A. Jones. Detailed as courier for Gen. Fitzhugh Lee 10/1/63. Shown as wded. 8/21/64, returned on 7-8/64 roll. Present on 3/20/65 final roll. Paroled 5/12/65 at Fredericksburg. Resid. Lahore in 7/03. d. 3/18/12, bur. Waugh Family Cem. on Bush Mountain Farm, Orange Co.

GARDNER, WILLIAM B.: enl. 1/15/63 in (2d) Co. E. Twenty-five day horse detail from 8/25/64. Otherwise present on all rolls thru 3/4/65 final roll.

GARTH, LEWIS T.: enl. 6/23/61 in Co. I, age 23. d. at his home in Greene Co. of bilious fever 8/4/61. Postwar roster gives middle initial as "L."

GATEWOOD, JAMES E.: b. 12/26/39 in Pittsylvania Co. enl. 5/27/61 in (2d) Co. E. Twenty days horse leave from 12/17/62. POW 9/13/63 near Culpeper. Paroled 10/11/64 from Pt. Lookout. Present at Camp Lee, Richmond, 10/17/64. Present on final 3/4/65 roll. General merchandising postwar, resid. Dry Fork 2/10/23. d. 5/22/30, bur. Chatham Cem.

GATEWOOD, JOHN T: b. 2/13/38 in Pittsylvania Co. Att. Richmond College. enl. 1/15/63 in (2d) Co. E. Present on all rolls thru 3/4/65 final roll. Paroled 4/9/65 at Appomattox. Farmer, resid. near Callands postwar. Claimed fever and exposure during war. m. Ella White 1868. d. 3/13/17.

GATEWOOD, ROBERT MONROE: b. 11/24/42 in Pittsylvania Co. enl. 5/27/61 in (2d) Co. E. Detached at pasture with horses on 7-8/63 roll. Twenty-five day horse detail from 8/23/64 and 22 days from 10/27/64. Otherwise present thru 3/4/65 final roll. Moved to Kentucky 1867. Farmer postwar. Wife Katherine M. Resid. Covington, Ky., on 8/20/26, when he applied to enter Soldiers' Home at Pewee Valley, Ky. d. 1/10/29.

GATEWOOD, WALTER T.: enl. 7/7/61 in (2d) Co. E. On sick leave on 2/16/62 roll and absent missing on 5-6/62 roll. On horse leave 9/19-10/9/63. Thereafter present until reported POW 5/30/64 at Cold Harbor. Admitted to Columbian College Hosp., Washington, D.C., 6/8/64 with breast wd. reportedly received 6/3/64 at Cold Harbor. d. 6/12/64, age 45.

GATHRIGHT, STAFFORD H.: enl. 10/20/62 in Co. C. Ten days furlough from 10/27/62. Wded. slightly in head and POW 7/3/63 at Fairfield, Pa. Paroled 8/24/63 at DeCamp Hospital, Davids Island, N.Y. Harbor. Present as Cpl. on 7-8/64 roll. Horse KIA 8/21/64 at Berryville. Thereafter present thru 3/30/65 final roll. Paroled 4/20/65 at Richmond, resid. Goochland Co.

GEORGE, WILLIAMSON CHURCHILL: b. 1/19/27. enl. 3/1/64 in Co. B. Farmer. Previously Capt. and commissary, 13th Va. Inf., "until this office was abolished by law." Present on all rolls thru 3/21/65 final roll. Resid. Culpeper on 4/14/00, age 73. m. Maria Louisa Turner, 1848. d. in Culpeper 8/24/06, bur. Culpeper Masonic Cem.

GERST, EMANUEL: enl. 8/19/61 in Co. G as Sgt., age 43. Present until 1-2/62 roll, when marked absent on sick furlough since 2/16/62. Co. clothing book says got H. E. West as substitute. Postwar roster says discharged, age limit, 1862, and spells his name Ghirst.

GIBSON, BRUCE: b. 8/30/30 in Loudoun Co. enl. 7/24/61 in Co. A as Sgt. Acting as Lt. from 10/18/61. To Lt. 11/14/61. To Capt. on 12/5/62 roll. Absent on court-martial duty on 11-12/63 roll. POW 5/11/64 at Yellow Tavern. "Immortal 600," held under hostile fire in South Carolina. Took the oath at Ft. Delaware 5/30/65. d. 2/20/01 at Winchester.

GIBSON, GILBERT B.: b. 4/19/42. enl. 9/7/61 in Co. A. On detached service with Gens. Walker and Jackson 10/10/62-1/1/63. Absent on clothing detail since 12/31/63 on 11-12/63 roll. Detailed as forage agent in QM Dept. on 9-10/64 roll. Present on final 3/27/65 roll. Paroled at Appomattox 4/9/65. d. 3/14/07, bur. Ivy Hill Cem., Upperville.

GIBSON, HENRY C.: enl. 7/24/61 in Co. A. Absent sick since 10/17/61 on 9-10/61 roll. Shown as discharged on 11-12/61 roll, furnished Isaac N. Broy as substitute.

GIBSON, HERMAN DOUGLAS: enl. 9/12/61 in Co. A. To Sgt. on 11-12/63 roll. On detached service since 8/25/63 on 8/31/63 roll. Pvt. on 11-12/63 roll. Absent, detailed to buy cattle on 7-8/64 roll thru 3/27/65 final roll. Paroled 4/24/65 at Winchester, age 25, as Sgt. d. 10/29/20, bur. Ivy Hill Cem., Upperville. Known as Douglas.

GIBSON, JOHN EMORY: b. in Loudoun Co. enl. 2/14/64 in Co. A. Transferred from unknown unit. In Chimborazo Hosp. No. 3, Richmond, with rheumatism 5/25-7/30/64. Absent with leave on 9-10/64 roll. AWOL since 3/7/65 on 3/27/65 final roll. Paroled 4/20/65 at Winchester, age 27, resid. Upperville. Farmer postwar. d. 9/25/10, age 74, at Lee Camp Soldiers' Home, Richmond, bur. Hollywood Cem.

GIBSON, JOHN NELSON: b. 9/1/35. enl. 7/24/61 in Co. A. To Sgt. 1/1/62. Absent on detached service as Commissary Sgt. since 8/15/62, but generally shown as Pvt., on rolls from 12/5/62 thru 11-12/63. To Commissary Sgt. 7/15/64, present on rolls for 7-8 thru 9-10/64. Paroled 4/9/65 at Appomattox with detailed and hired men of QM Dept. d. 5/10/89, bur. Ivy Hill Cem., Upperville.

GIBSON, JOSEPH ANDREW: b. 12/13/33. enl. 9/25/61 in Co. A. To Cpl. on 1-2/62 roll. To Lt. on 11/62 return. Present on all rolls until POW 9/24/64 at Luray. Took the oath 5/30/65 at Ft. Delaware, resid. Fauquier Co. Postwar roster says wded. at Yellow Tavern. d. 7/13/07, bur. Ivy Hill Cem., Upperville.

GIBSON, WILLIAM A.: b. 1839. enl. 6/21/61 in Co. D as Sgt. KIA and horse killed 10/15/61 near Annandale, bur. Leesburg Union Cem.

GIDDINGS, CHARLES GLENN: b. 12/3/34. enl. 4/22/61 in Co. K as Lt. Furlough 12/3/61 from Gen. N. G. Evans to see sick family. Present on 1-2/62 roll. Dropped 4/20/62. d. 1/4/10, bur. Leesburg Union Cem.

GILBERT, GEORGE H.: b. in Pittsylvania Co. enl. 5/27/61 in (2d) Co. E. Age 25 on 2/16/62 roll. Sick in camp on 5-6/62 roll. To Sgt. 10/28/62. POW 6/9/63 at Beverly Ford. Paroled 6/25/63 at Old Capitol Prison, and released same day from U.S.A. hosp. to which he had been admitted for erysipelas (presumably from wd. at Beverly Ford). Admitted to Petersburg General Hosp. 6/30/63 with wd. of right leg. Forty day furlough from 7/31/63 as paroled prisoner. KIA 5/8/64 near Spotsylvania C.H. bur. Swansonville Methodist Church Cem., northwest of Danville. Brother of William P.

GILBERT, GEORGE W.: enl. 5/27/61 in (2d) Co. E. Age 24 on 2/16/62 roll. Horse KIA 7/3/63 at Fairfield, Pa. Admitted 4/4/64 to Chimborazo Hosp. No. 2, Richmond, with syphilis. Present with co. on 7-8/64 roll. POW 9/19/64 at Winchester. Exchanged 2/10/65 from Pt. Lookout. Absent, exchanged POW on furlough, on final 3/4/65 roll.

GILBERT, JOHN E.: enl. 6/23/61 in Co. I, age 25. Died of bilious fever 8/12/61 at his home in Greene Co.

GILBERT, WILLIAM P.: enl. 5/27/61 in (2d) Co. E. Age 23 on 2/16/62 roll. Twenty days leave from 12/17/62. Detached as courier for Gen. W. E. Jones on 1-2/63 roll. KIA 7/3/63 at Fairfield, Pa., bur. Swansonville Methodist Church Cem., northwest of Danville. Brother of George H.

GILES, WILLIAM D.: enl. 9/23/63 in (2d) Co. E. Farmer. Previously in 57th Va. Inf. Wded. in left thigh 5/7/64 at Spotsylvania C.H. In Chimborazo Hosp. No. 2, Richmond, 5/9-5/23/64, transferred to Danville hosp. and furloughed, age 27. Present on all rolls thru 3/4/65 final roll. Resid. Cascade and Vance postwar, minnie ball still in his hip on 4/16/94. d. 8/14/14 in Pittsylvania Co.

GILL, CHARLES C.: enl. 8/19/61 in Co. G, age 32. Teamster since 9/1/61 on 11/61 return. POW 2/7/62 near Fairfax C.H., but no record of parole. "Deserter, taken prisoner in January and exchanged. Never reported to the company" on 11-12/62 roll. Sent to Provost Marshal at Guiney's Station as deserter 5/27/63. Present on 7-8/63 roll. In Petersburg hosp. 12/9/63 with acute rheumatism, furloughed 30 days 12/17/63. Absent on 20 days horse leave from 10/7/63 on 11-12/63 roll and marked AWOL. Shown in clothing book as Christopher C. Gill. No further record.

GILLILAND, JOHN W.: enl. 8/19/61 in Co. G, age 21. Absent on sick furlough since 2/25 on 1-2/62 roll. Absent, POW and paroled 9/22/62 on 9-10/62 roll. Absent, ordered to co. on 11-12/62 roll. Thereafter present until POW 6/9/63 at Beverly Ford, held at Old Capitol Prison 6/25/63. Transferred to Co. C, 1st Va. Lt. Art. 10/12/63.

GLASSCOCK, JAMES R.: enl. 11/1/62 in Co. H. Wded. 6/21/63 at Upperville. Present on all rolls until KIA 9/19/64 at Winchester.

GLENN, JOHN D.: enl. 7/31/62 in Co. G. Transferred from 21st Va. Inf. Absent sick, sent home by surgeon on 11-12/62 roll. On 20 days horse leave on 7-8/63 roll. Eighteen days horse leave from 12/10/63. In Chimborazo hosp. No. 2, Richmond, with debility 6/17-6/28/64. On horse detail on 9-10/64 roll. Present on final 3/22/65 roll.

GOGGIN, PLEASANT M.: enl. 4/1/62 in (2d) Co. E. Absent on detached service on 5-6/62 roll. Teamster in regiment on 11-12/63 roll. In Richmond hosps. with constipation ca. 6/30-8/13/64. In Staunton hosp. on 7-8/64 roll. Teamster in regiment on 9-10/64 roll. Present on final 3/4/65 roll. POW 4/4/65 near Appomattox. Took the oath 6/13/65 at Pt. Lookout, resid. Pittsylvania Co.

GOOCH, ARCHIBALD THOMAS: Conscript enl. 10/16/64 in Co. G. AWOL on final 3/22/65 roll. Resid. 2222 Venable St., Richmond, on 9/3/15, age 70, wife Susan E. Gooch. Dropped from applicants to Lee Camp Soldiers' Home, Richmond, in 1916.

GOODING, ARTHUR W.: Told Federals he enl. 7/15/64 in Co. A to avoid conscription. POW 8/19/64 at Waterford. Age 18 on 12/16/64, when he wished to go to Washington, D.C., where he had relatives. Took the oath 5/29/65 at Elmira, resid. Harpers Ferry, signs by mark. No Confederate records. May be the man of this name, 6/27/46-9/3/13, bur. Fairfax City Cem.

GORAM, JOHN B.: enl. 5/1/62 in Co. F. Committed to Old Capitol Prison 3/27/63, no parole shown. POW 4/23/63 in Fairfax Co. and still held at Old Capitol 5/19/63, again no parole shown. Wded. 11/27/63 at Raccoon Ford, sent to Orange hosp. Absent on horse detail on final 2/24/65 roll. POW yet again 3/19/65 near Richmond. Took the oath 6/12/65 at Pt. Lookout, resid. Fairfax Co., signs by mark. Postwar roster says wded. in Wilderness.

GORAM, WILLIAM: b. near Fairfax C.H. Conscript enl. 7/15/64 in Co. F. POW 9/19/64 at Winchester. Exchanged 3/15/65 from Pt. Lookout. Resid. near Burke Station 9/21/07, with name recorded as "Gorham," but signs by mark, age 76. Nursery business and farming postwar. Claimed injury when his horse was KIA 9/19/64 and fell on him.

GORDON, EDWARD: enl. 9/17/61 in (1st) Co. E, age 35. Resid. Savannah, Ga. Discharged 11/1/62 for physical disability.

GORDON, EDWARD HARRISON: enl. 3/15/64 in Co. I. Wded. 6/11/64 at Trevillian's Station. Present on final 3/20/65 roll.

GORDON, GEORGE ALEXANDER: b. 1840. enl. 10/1/61 in Co. F. To Sgt. on 7-8/62 roll. Horse KIA 6/26/63 at Fairfax C.H. Detailed to get clothing 12/31/64 at Winchester. Exchanged ca. 2/20/65 from Pt. Lookout. Furloughed 30 days at Camp Winder Hosp., Richmond, on 3/3/65. Paroled at Alexandria 4/24/65, resid. Fairfax Co. near Munson's Hill. Took the oath 6/17/65 at Alexandria. d. 1909, bur. Fairfax City Cem. A postwar roster also has him in Co. A.

GORDON, JOHN T.: On postwar "original list" of Co. F.

GORDON, WILLIAM WASHINGTON, II: Att. Yale Univ., enl. 9/17/61 in (1st) Co. E as Lt., age 27. Cotton factor. Resid. Savannah, Ga. To Cpt. on staffs of Gens. Hugh W. Mercer and Robert H. Anderson. m. Eleanor Kinzie 1857. President Savannah Cotton Exchange and Central R.R. and Banking Co. of Ga. postwar. Ga. State House of Reps., 1884-89. d. 1912. Father of Juliette Gordon Low, founder of Girl Scouts of America.

GOSSOM, WILLIAM: enl. 11/20/61 in Co. A, according to a 11/61 return, but another document shows him dying *the day before* of typhoid fever. Postwar roster gives his first name as Edward or Edwin, and says he d. in 1861 in hosp.

GOUGH, JOSEPH: enl. 9/17/61 in (1st) Co. E, age 23. Resid. Savannah, Ga. Detached at Tredegar Works, Richmond, and Government Foundry at Macon, Ga., from 4/30/62, and shown as detailed there by order of Secretary of War until 8/31/64 roll, where he appears as a deserter. Postwar published roster says deserter from 10/63.

GOULDING, FRANCIS R.: enl. 9/17/61 in (1st) Co. E, age 19. Resid. Darien, Ga. To Cpl. 6/62, resigned same 12/63. Paroled at Greensboro, N.C., 5/1/65.

GRADY, CUTHBERT POWELL: b. 7/16/40 in Loudoun Co. Grad. M.A., U.Va. enl. 7/24/61 in Co. D. Sick since 9/18 on 10/61 return. To Cpl. on 5-6/62 roll. To Sgt. on 9-10/62 roll. Absent, clerk for Gen. W. E. Jones on 11/62-2/63 rolls. On duty at brigade HQ on 8/31/63 roll, and at Gen. L. L. Lomax's HQ on 11-12/63 roll. Appointed Capt. and Acting Assistant Adjutant General 2/11/64, to rank from 12/19/63. To Gen. Lomax's staff 3/5/64. In Richmond hosp. with wd. of left arm 5/6/64. On Gen. Payne's staff 3/24/65. Professor of Latin at W. & L. postwar. Teacher in Baltimore, Md., ca. 1878. m. Susan Gordon Armistead 1867. d. 12/4/22, bur. Arlington Nat. Cem.

GRADY, EDWARD K.: b. ca. 1838 in Loudoun Co. enl. 7/17/61 in Co. D. Sick furlough for 10 days from 11/7 on 11/61 return. Otherwise present on all rolls until shown absent as scout for Gen. Fitzhugh Lee on final 3/22/65 roll. Paroled at Lynchburg 4/15/65. Known as Ned, resid. near Snickersville. Living at 919 Elm St., Baltimore, Md., in 1894. d. 3/14/13 at Lee Camp Soldiers Home, Richmond, bur. Hollywood Cem.

GRADY, TEMPLE: enl. 4/18/61 in Co. D. AWOL since 11/1 on 11/61 return. Sentenced to forfeit a month's pay on 11-12/61 roll. Otherwise present until d. 11/4 (or 6)/63 at Woodville of disease. Resid. near Snickersville.

GRAHAM, ARCH W.: b. in Telfair Co., Ga. enl. 9/17/61 in (1st) Co. E, age 24. Planter. d. 1/5/62 of typhoid fever at Warrenton General Hosp. Resid. Telfair Co., Ga.

GRANDLE, CHRISTIAN: Conscript enl. 2/10 (or 25)/64 in Co. C. Absent, detailed in brigade QM Dept. on all rolls thru final ca. 3/30/65 roll. May be identical to Cris C. Grandle, 1827-1910, bur. Beaver Creek Brethren Church Cem.

GRANT, WILLIAM A.: Shown on a postwar roster as enl. in Co. B in 3/64, age 18, severely wded. at Spotsylvania C.H. and unfit for service afterwards. It was not known if he was alive or dead in 5/07. Compare with William B. Grant, below.

GRANT, WILLIAM B.: enl. 9/18/62 in Co. H. Absent sick since 11/10 on 11-12/62 roll. d. 1/28/63 near Sperryville. Not on postwar rosters.

GRAVELEY, JABEZ B.: enl. 5/27/61 in (2d) Co. E. d. 9/18/61 at Monterey.

GRAVES, JACOB P.: enl. 5/27/61 in (2d) Co. E. Present thru 5-6/62 roll, but no further record in 6th Va. Cav. enl. 8/16/64 in Co. H, 21st Va. Inf. Transferred 2/25/65 to Co. G, 53d Va. Inf. Postwar roster says resid. Danville.

GRAVES, JEREMIAH HUNT: enl. 3/10/62 in Co. G. Absent sick on 9-10/62 roll. Deserted on 11/62 return, returned and furnished surgeon's certificate on 12/62 return. Duty as Ordnance Sgt. on 11-12/63 roll. POW 5/11/64 in Hanover Co. Paroled 10/29/64 at Elmira. Present on 3/22/65 final roll. In Petersburg hosps. 4/1-4/11/65. POW in hosp. 4/3/65. Records are contradictory, but he may have been released from Elmira 6/27/65 as Cpl. d. 1/29/08 at home in Hurt. Wid. Amanda M., m. 1867.

GRAY, ROBERT F.: Shown in Federal records as a member of Co. F, POW 1/26/63 at Middleburg, and exchanged at City Point 3/29/63 from Old Capitol Prison. Unofficial sources identify him as Robert F. Gray (Gary), b. 1825/30 in New Kent Co., m. Lucy Ann Taylor 1855. No Confederate records. Not on postwar roster.

GRAY, SAMUEL J.: enl. 4/22/61 in Co. K. Thirty days furlough from 2/11/62. Absent sick with leave on 7-8/63 roll. In Richmond hosps. 4/20-6/10/64 with onychia. Otherwise present until AWOL on final 1-2/65 roll. Paroled 4/18/65 at Edwards Ferry, Md.

GREEN, ARTHUR C.: enl. 6/1/62 in Co. B. Absent on sick leave from Harrisonburg hosp. since 2/11 on 11-12/62 roll. Absent on horse detail on 7-8/64 roll, and thereafter AWOL thru final 3/21/65 roll. Paroled 5/18/65 at Winchester, age 21, resid. Rappahannock Co. Reportedly d. before 5/07. Postwar roster says "captured, escaped."

GREEN, BENJAMIN: enl. 9/17/61 in (1st) Co. E. Age 23 on 10/16/61. Sgt. on 11/1/61 roll. On sick leave since 11/26 on 11/61 return. Discharged for physical disability 1/13/62. Appointed Lt. and Adjutant, 21st Ga. Cav. Bn. Later aide de camp and Capt. with Gen. J. F. Gilmer, Chief of Engineers. Resid. Savannah, Ga.

GREEN, BENJAMIN FRANKLIN: b. in Warren Co. enl. 7/23/62 in Co. H. Farmer. POW 10/29/62 near Petersburg, (W.) Va., age 21. Exchanged at Vicksburg, Miss., from Camp Chase 12/2/62. With his co. and under arrest in camp on 2/28/63 roll. AWOL since 7/1 on 7-8/63 roll. Shown as POW 10/31/63 at Martinsburg, (W.) Va., but as deserter on other records. Took the oath at Ft. Mifflin, Pa., 12/2/63 and enl. in U.S. Marine Corps same day. Signs by mark. Deserted USMC 10/19/64.

GREEN, BENJAMIN RUSSELL: b. in Fauquier Co. enl. 4/24/61 in Co. H as musician. Fifteen days sick furlough from 2/16/62 on 1-2/63 roll. Absent sick since 3/1/65 on 3/22/65 final roll. Paroled 4/21/65 at Winchester as bugler, age 27. Gardner and carpenter postwar. Resid. near Mt. Jackson on 2/14/03. Claimed exposure, fever, and yellow jaundice in service. d. 1/16/12 near Quicksburg. Wid. Marthy.

GREEN, GEORGE R.: enl. 5/8/61 in Co. B, age 24. Farmer. Receipt rolls show him paid as teamster on 12/31/61 and 4/30/62. Present on all rolls thru 5-6/62 roll. Postwar roster says "put in a substitute in 1862 Deserted."

GREEN, HUGH RUSTIN: b. 4/7/42. enl. 4/24/61 in Co. H. Physician. In Charlottesville hosp. 3/23-8/16/62 with bilious fever. Absent from co., detailed as hosp. steward on rolls for 9-10/62 thru 2/28/63. Appointed regimental hosp. steward 8/3/63. In Charlottesville hosp. with chronic diarrhea 1/31-2/28/64. Absent sick since July on 9-10/64 roll. Paroled 4/22/65 at Winchester, resid. near Piedmont. d. 10/28/16, bur. Westminster Presbyterian Church Cem., Delaplane. m. Sarah Catherine Smith.

GREEN, JAMES: enl. 3/1/62 in Co. B. Shown as deserter on 11/62 return. In Charlottesville hosp. for surditas (deafness) 2/20-3/6/63. Otherwise present until reported as deserter by Richmond on 2/28/65. AWOL on final 3/21/65 roll. 5/07 roster has him alive, age 27 on enlistment, slightly wded. at Winchester 9/19/64, and with middle initial "W."

GREEN, JAMES WILLIAM: enl. 4/21/61 in Co. B as Lt., age 31. Farmer. Resigned 7/24/61 at Union Mills. Reportedly d. before 5/07.

GREEN, JOHN SHACKLEFORD: b. 6/9/17 in Rappahannock Co. enl. 4/22/61 in Co. B as Capt. Farmer. On recruiting duty since 2/4 on 1-2/62 roll. Dropped 4/20/62. To Major 4/30/62. To Lt. Col. 7/16/62. Wded., POW and paroled 9/22/62 at Paris. Acquitted by court-martial of disobedience of orders and breach of arrest 9/17/63. Resigned 4/23/64 for the good of the service. On this Gen. Jeb Stuart wrote that Green "deserves credit for his patriotism. *The service will be benefitted beyond a doubt by its acceptance.*" Resignation recorded as of 5/9/64. Lived in Norfolk postwar, d. there 1/1/91.

GREEN, ROBERT RUSSELL: b. at Woodville, Rappahannock Co. enl. 5/8/61 in Co. B, age 21. Absent in Rappahannock on 9/1/61. On extra duty in QM Dept. as teamster since 10/23 on 10/61 return. In confinement on 1-2/62 roll. Sick since 3/20 on rolls for 5-10/62. Confined by Federals 8/9/62, date and place of capture not shown. Paroled 9/7/62 on steamer *Juniata*. Courier for Gen. Payne since 12/20/64 on final 3/21/65 roll. Farmer, resid. Richardsville postwar. Claimed typhoid fever, frozen feet, and POW 8 weeks. d. 3/8/20, bur. Arlington National Cem. Wid. Margaret E.

GREEN, WILLIAM WIRT: b. in Clarke Co. enl. 11/10/62 in Co. A. Absent with leave on 9-10/64 roll. Otherwise present on all rolls thru 3/27/65 final roll. Paroled 4/21/65 at Winchester, age 24, resid. Fauquier Co. near Paris, as in (2d) Co. E. Alive in Fauquier Co. 11/18/22, age 81. bur. Ivy Hill Cem., Upperville. Postwar roster says wded. at Fairfield, Pa.

GREGG, WILLIAM H.: b. in Loudoun Co. enl. 4/11/63 in Co. A. Present on all rolls thru 3/27/65 final roll. Paroled at Winchester 4/22/65, age 28, resid. Loudoun Co. Took the oath 7/12/65 at Alexandria, "paroled prisoner voluntarily surrendered his parole." Dentist postwar, resid. near Philomont on 3/29/05. AWOL from Lee Camp Soldiers' Home, Richmond, 9/28/14. d. 3/6/15.

GREIVER, A. W.: Conscript assigned to the regiment 4/20/64, no company shown. No further record. Compare with Phillip Greiver.

GREIVER, PHILLIP: Conscript assigned to the regiment 4/20/64, no company shown. No further record. Probably identical to conscript Philip Grever, detailed for QM service with Maj. H. M. Bell at Staunton ca. 6/10/63-3/24/64, and Philip Greaves. Co. L, 62d Va. Mtd. Inf., paroled at HQ Army of the Shenandoah 4/30/65, age 36, resid. Augusta Co. Correct name apparently Philip Grever.

GRIFFITH, JOHN W.: enl. 9/14/62 in Co. H. On detached service at Gen. Jeb Stuart's since 12/27 on 11-12/63 roll. AWOL on 9-10/64 roll. Otherwise present thru final 3/22/65 roll. POW 4/1/65 at Five Forks. Took the oath at Pt. Lookout when sick 6/8/65 and released.

GRIFFITH, WILLIAM E.: enl. 10/18/62 in Co. H. AWOL on 11-12/62 roll, but 12/62 return says absent on furlough after horse. Absent on horse detail on 9-10/64 roll. Otherwise present thru final 3/22/65 roll. Reported by Richmond as deserter on 2/28/65, to be found in Loudoun Co. on ca. 1898 Fauquier Co. veterans census, age 59.

GRIFFITH, WILLIAM H.: enl. 7/24/61 in Co. A. Sentenced to forfeit $12 of his pay by regimental court-martial on 9-10/61 roll. Absent sick since 12/29 on 11/62 roll; 12/61 return has him AWOL from 12/29. Present, but then AWOL on 12/5/62 roll. Deserted, probably on 11/12/62 near Paris. Doubtless identical to the man of this name, 9/10/40-4/13/19, bur. Edge Hill Cem., Charles Town, (W.) Va.

GRIGGS, JAMES LEE: enl. 7/24/61 in Co. D. Absent on duty in Ordnance Dept. on rolls for 8/31/63 and 11-12/64. In Richmond hosp. with dysentery 4/19-6/4/64 and on 5/4/64. Wded. 9/22/64 near Luray. Otherwise present thru 3/22/65 final roll. d. 7/25/85, age 57 (another source says 61), bur. Edge Hill Cem., Charles Town, W.Va.

GRIMES, JOHN T.: Only record is a return for 11/62, which has him in Co. A, transferred in Oct. to Capt. Grubb's Co., White's 35th Bn. Va. Cav., identified only as "Grimes."

GRIMES, WILLIAM HENRY: b. 8/5/48 in Fauquier Co. enl. 10/1/62 in Co. K. Ten days leave from 8/29/63. AWOL since 9/11/63 on 11-12/63 roll. Federal records state that he purposely arranged to be arrested on 9/12/63 at Point of Rocks, at first declined to take the oath, then did 9/25/63 at Ft. McHenry, Md., signing by mark. Present on 12/27/64 roll. POW 2/13/65 at Leesburg, "guerilla, not to be exchanged." Released from Ft. McHenry 5/6/65. Farmer postwar, m. Lucy A. Kernes, (Kearnes, Kearns, Kerns), 1869. d. 9/10/29, bur. Sharon Cem., Middleburg.

GRIMSLEY, DANIEL AMON: b. 4/3/40 in Rappahannock Co. enl. 4/22/61 in Co. B as Cpl. Farmer. To Sgt. 6/20/61. To Capt. 4/20/62. Horse KIA 5/23/62 at Front Royal. In Charlottesville hosp. 12/19/63-1/14/64 with "closure of lacrymal ducts." Detailed for court-martial duty 11/28/62 and 8/19, 11/25, and 12/31/63. To Major 9/3/64, confirmed 1/5/65 to rank from 6/4/64. Paroled at Winchester 5/9/65. Culpeper lawyer and circuit judge postwar, in Va. legislature. m. Bettie Browning. d. 2/5/10, bur. Culpeper Cem., Route 522.

GRIMSLEY, THOMAS F.: b. 12/20/35. enl. 5/8/61 in Co. B. Teacher. Absent to get clothing since 12/10 on 11-12/63 roll, and on extra duty in regimental ambulance corps on 7-8/64 roll. Otherwise present on all rolls thru 3/21/65 final roll. Postwar roster says severely wded., but place not shown. d. 3/6/13, bur. Culpeper City Cem.

GROVES, TOBIAS M.: enl. 5/28/61 in Co. C. To Cpl. 1/1/63, but on 7-8/63 roll as Pvt. Absent with leave from 12/29 on 11-12/63 roll. Otherwise present thru final ca. 3/30/65 roll. Paroled 5/2/65 at Harrisonburg, age 25, resid. Rockingham Co.

GRUBB, BURWELL S.: enl. 5/27/61 in (2d) Co. E. Twenty days leave to get horse from 12/7/62. To Cpl. on 7-8/63 roll. On details to get a horse beginning 12/16/63, 8/23/64, and 10/27/64. Present on final 3/4/65 roll.

GRUBB, SAMUEL E.: enl. 7/16/61 in Co. K. Absent sick at home with leave from 11/15/61 on 1-2/62 roll. Transferred by promotion to Lt. Co. C, 35th Bn. Va. Cav. d. 8/4/67 in Texas.

GRUBB, WILLIAM E.: b. 8/2/38 in Loudoun Co. enl. 7/16/61 in Co. K. Killed on picket at Waterford 10/22 (or 24)/61, "by some enemy," bur. Salem Church on Route 671.

GUERARD, ROBERT C.: enl. 9/17/61 in (1st) Co. E. To Cpl. in 9/61, age 18. Transferred to QM Dept. at Savannah, Ga., for clerical work, probably early in 1863. To Sgt. 2/11/63. Postwar roster says "discharged on account of health." Resid. Savannah, Ga.

HACKEL, _____: Shown as in Co. G, absent sick on 11/62 return. No other record.

HACKLEY, GEORGE: enl. 10/15/62 in Co. H. Reported as deserter 12/12/62. Under arrest in camp on 11-12/62 roll. KIA 9/13/63 at Culpeper.

HADDOX, JOHN D.: enl. 4/22/61 in Co. B, age 23. Farmer. Absent sick in Rappahannock Co. on 9/1/61 roll. Otherwise present until he and his horse KIA 5/23/62 near Front Royal.

HAGGERTY, PATRICK: Recorded as a deserter from Co. G, received by Federals at Culpeper 8/23/63. Took the oath 9/26/63 and released from Old Capitol Prison to go to Philadelphia 9/28/63. Residence: Pottsville, Schuylkill Co., Pa. No Confederate records; probably a bogus claimant to membership in the regiment.

HALL, ALFRED: enl. 4/24/61 in Co. H. Farmer. Shown AWOL from 5/20/62, but substituted John C. Pearson on that date.

HALL, BRYANT: On postwar "original list" of Co. F.

HALL, SNOWDEN COWMAN: b. 9/30/35 in Loudoun Co. enl. 4/4/62 in Co. A. Absent with leave to get clothing on 11/62 return. Granted furlough of indulgence 12/21/63. Wded. 6/11/64 and absent wded. thru 3/27/65 final roll. m. Lucinda Hedgeman 1867. d. 1/31/93 at Bluff Point, Northumberland Co.

HALLY, S. P.: Shown as in Co. C in register of C.S. Military Prison Hospital, Richmond, age 22, admitted 4/22/64 with remittent fever. No other record; probably a mistake.

HALSEY, JOSEPH JACKSON: b. 4/5/23 in New Jersey. B.A. and M.A. Princeton. Lawyer. enl. 5/4/61 in Co. I. To Capt. and Acting Commissary of Subsistence 11/16/61. Generally present except for sick furloughs until dropped 2/4/63 for prolonged AWOL. Reinstated from 3/10/63. Detailed on duty for brigade on 2/28/65 report. m. 1) Mary Jane Glassell 1845, 2) Mildred Jackson Morton 1846. Resid. "Lessland," Raccoon Ford. d. 2/25/07, bur. Graham Cem. west of Orange.

HALT, J. M.: Only record is 11/62 return, which has him in Co. G, absent at hosp. in Staunton.

HAMDEN, C. H.: Only record is a register of General Hosp. No. 9, Richmond, which shows him in Co. B, admitted 5/29/64, and sent to Jackson Hosp. 5/30/64. Probably an error, referring to Charles Henry Houghton.

HAMILTON, ELI JANNEY: enl. 7/24/61 in Co. A. On extra duty in QM Dept. since 10/6/61 on 9-10/61 roll: Shown as discharged on 11-12/61 roll, furnishing James Ball as substitute. To Capt. and AQM, 39th Bn. Va. Cav.

HAMMOND, WILLIAM TAYLOR: Att. Episcopal High School, Alexandria. enl. 5/25/61 in Co. D. Sick in quarters with phthisis 3/21/62 at Orange. On sick furlough on 5-6/62 roll. Otherwise present until detailed as scout on 11-12/63 roll. d. of wounds received 7/5/64 at Reams Station. Horses KIA 6/21/63 near Upperville and 6/12/64 at Trevillian's Depot.

HAMRICK, WILLIAM P.: enl. 9/15/62 in Co. B. Absent sick in private quarters since 12/20/61 on 11-12/62 roll, but present on 1-2/63 roll. No further record. Reportedly alive in 5/07. Name also shown as Hambrick.

HANCOCK, SAMUEL H.: enl. 1/16/62 in Co. G. Absent sick (for "incipient phthisis pulmonalis, with chronic diarrhea") on 1-6/62 rolls. Detailed as teamster on 9-10/62 roll. Accidentally wded. before 12/22/62. Absent in hosp. at Staunton on 11/62-8/63 rolls. On extra duty as ambulance driver on later rolls thru 3/22/65 final roll. Resid. Pen Hook, age 71 on 4/1/01. Claimed wd. in foot. d. 2/28/17 in Pittsylvania Co.

HANCOCK, WILLIAM HENRY: enl. 8/19/61 in Co. G. Age 40 on 9/10/61. Present until marked "absent on sick furlough over 3 months" on 5-6/62 roll. Co. clothing book has discharged 8/19/62. d. 6/13/74 at Riceville. Wid. Alice W., m. 1844.

HAND, EASTHAM: enl. 3/1/64 in Co. B. Absent on horse detail on 7-8/64 roll. Otherwise present thru 3/21/65 final roll. Postwar roster says d. before 5/07. Probably the man of this name who d. 1/22/89 at his home near Slate Mills, age 55, and was bur. "at home."

HAND, WILLIAM: enl. 6/1/64 in Co. B. Absent sick on 9-10/64 roll and AWOL since 3/8/65 on 3/21/65 final roll. d. 5/5/10 at Woodville, age 84. When his widow, Mary V., m. 1875, applied for pension in 1923 she was apparently denied because of the AWOL record.

HANNAVAN, JOHN: b. at Langley. enl. 11/16/61 in Co. A. Absent in arrest on 12/5/62 roll. Otherwise present until 8/31/63 roll, when absent with led horses since 8/13/63. Wded. 6/12/64 at Trevillian's Station and absent due to wd. thru 3/27/65 final roll. Postwar roster says wded. at Fairfield and Trevillian's. Resid. Lewinsville, age 67, on 3/21/11, a stone mason, signs by mark. Name also appears as Hanovan and Hannovan.

HANSFORD, WILLIAM A.: enl. 5/4/61 in Co. I, age 35. AWOL on rolls for 5/62-2/63. Discharged 4/9/63. Dropped from pay roll and name sent to enrolling officer on 7-8/63 roll. POW 12/1/63 at Mitchells Ford. Paroled 3/9/64 at Pt. Lookout. Wded. 6/29/64 at Cold Harbor in right thigh and thereafter absent wded. thru 3/20/65 final roll.

HARDEN, AUSTIN: On a postwar roster of Co. F. No official record.

HARDEN, GILBERT: enl. 11/1/61 in Co. F. Discharged 7/26/62.

HARDEN, LEWIS: b. in Loudoun Co. enl. 9/8/61 in Co. C. Extra duty as teamster since 10/22/61 on 9-10/61 roll. Deserted 9/25/62, re-joined 4/28/63. Deserted again ca. 5/5/63, "tired of service." POW at Edwards Ferry 5/23/63, age 38, after turning himself in. Took the oath 6/24/63 at Washington, D.C.

HARDESTY, CHARLES WESLEY: b. 12/22/30. enl. 10/7/62 in Co. D. Absent with leave on 11-12/62 roll. Otherwise present on all rolls until AWOL on final 3/22/65 roll. d. 7/12/06, bur. Green Hill Cem., Berryville. Wid. Jane L., m. 1852, who gave his middle name as "Westley" on pension applications.

HARDIE, RICHARD T.: b. 8/25/25 in Halifax Co. enl. 8/19/61 in Co. G. Farmer. Discharged 9/19/61 for heart disease and chronic bronchitis. Stated on 3/9/08 that after discharge he was "buying food and shipping in the Quartermaster Department until called into service December 1864." On postwar roster of Co. E. d. 8/12/09, bur. Woodland Cem., Chase City. Resid. Halifax and Lunenberg Cos. postwar.

HARE, JEFFERSON: Shown on postwar roster of Co. I. 12/61 return shows a man of this surname in Co. H, on leave since 5/20/61.

HARFORD, ANDREW J.: enl. 4/18/61 in Co. D. Discharged on surgeon's certificate 10/19/61 (another record says 10/3/61). Released as civilian 12/23/64 from Ft. McHenry, Md. Resid. Clarke Co.

HARLEY, WILLIAM H. H.: b. 11/29/40. enl. 6/1/62 in Co. D. "Absent with leave. One month's pay deducted by court-martial carbine lost in action 912/63" on 11-12/63 roll. Otherwise present until AWOL on final 3/22/65 roll. d. 8/24/86, bur. Episcopal and Masonic Cem., Middleway, W.Va.

HARPER, JAMES M.: enl. 8/19/61 in Co. G, age 28. To Sgt. on 5-6/62 roll. Absent on sick furlough since 2/25/62 on 1-2/62 roll. Otherwise present on all rolls thru 3/22/65 final roll.

HARRELL, BENJAMIN S.: enl. 3/15/62 in Co. H. Absent sick since 10/21/62 on 11-12/62 roll. Otherwise present until POW 1/31/64 in Madison Co. Tonsilitis at Old Capitol Prison. d. 5/7/65 at Ft. Delaware of inflammation of lungs, bur. Finn's Pt. Cem., N.J.

HARRELL, FREDERICK L.: enl. 4/24/61 in Co. H. Present 6/30/61. No further record.

HARRELL, JOHN A.: b. in Fauquier Co. enl. 3/7/62 in Co. H. On horse furlough on 12/62 return. Absent on horse detail on 9-10/64 roll and AWOL since 3/6/65 on 3/22/65 final roll. Paroled 4/25/65 at Winchester, age 24, resid. near Salem, Fauquier Co. Carpenter postwar. Alive 7/18/11 in Manassas. Said he left service when Lee surrendered, signs Harrell, but brother signs as Herrall.

HARRELL, LEWIS S.: b. near Salem (Marshall) 3/6/33. enl. 3/15/62 in Co. H. Reported as deserter 12/14/62. Present on 2/28/63 roll. Detailed as wagoner in regiment on 11-12/63 roll. AWOL since 3/6/65 on 3/22/65 final roll. Farmer postwar, claimed rheumatism from wartime exposure. d. 4/18/14, bur. Marshall Cem. Spelled Herrell on tombstone.

HARRELL, MIDDLETON D.: enl. 4/24/61 in Co. H. Reported AWOL 9/22-10/31/61, but this was later changed to sick at home with doctor's certificate, in which status he appears thru 5-6/62 roll. Present on 9-10/62 roll. Deserted 11/25/62 near Markham.

HARRELL, THEORICK LEITH: b. 8/3/39. enl. 4/24/61 in Co. H. Courier at Madison C.H. on 5-6/62 roll. Numerous AWOL charges at various times. In Charlottesville Hosp. 1/7/64 with morbi cutis, transferred to Lynchburg. Deserted 1/1/65 on 3/22/65 final roll. Paroled 4/21/65 at Winchester, resid. near Markham. d. 7/9/05 at Thornhill, bur. Unionville Christian Church Cem., Orange Co. Wid. Nannie B. First name also appears at Theodrick, Thdororick, Theodore.

HARRELL, THOMAS: enl. 3/1/62 in Co. B. In confinement since 11/1 on 11-12/62 roll. On extra duty as teamster since 2/1 on 1-2/63 roll. Orderly for Lt. Col. Green on 11-12/63 roll. AWOL on 7-8 and 9-10/64 rolls. No further record. Age 69 on 6/8/00. Alive in Rappahannock Co. on 3/17/04. Reportedly d. before 5/07. Middle initial given as "H" and "G", surname spelled many ways.

HARRIS, ALEXANDER H.: enl. 5/28/61 in Co. C. Teamster at Camp Harrison on 4/30/62 payroll. AWOL since 5/6 on 9-10/62 roll. Reported as deserting at Elk River in 5/62 on 11/62 return.

HARRIS, FREDERICK J.: b. at Fishersville, Augusta Co. enl. 10/20/62 in Co. C. Blacksmith on 12/62 return. Detailed with Asst. QM on 11-12/63 roll. Detailed as blacksmith in division ordnance train on 7-8/64 roll thru 3/30/65 final roll. Blacksmith postwar. Resid. McGaheysville, age 65, on 5/27/09. d. 9/26/21.

HARRIS, GEORGE: b. in Jefferson Co., (W.) Va. enl. 8/16/61 in Co. D. To Cpl. on 5-6/62 roll. Horse KIA 6/9/63. To Sgt. on 7-8/64 roll. Horse KIA 10/9/64 near Woodstock. Present on every roll thru 3/22/65 final roll. d. 2/28/05 near Myerstown, W.Va., age 73, bur. Edge Hill Cem., Charles Town, W.Va.

HARRIS, JAMES H.: In U.S. records as in Co. A. POW 12/5/62 by home guards in Wayne Co., (W.) Va. Farmer, age 21, resid. Kanawha Co. Released 3/11/63 at Camp Chase, Ohio. No Confederate records, not on postwar rosters, and probably an error.

HARRIS, JOHN: On postwar rosters of Co. D.

HARRIS, THOMAS: In Federal records as in Co. I, POW 5 (or 7)/24/64 at Culpeper. Wheelwright. Previously Capt. 7th Va. Inf., but resigned 2/24/64. Exchanged from Elmira 10/29/64. No Confederate records in 6th Va. Cav.

HARRIS, WILBER F.: Previously in 10th Va. Inf. On roll of the River Rangers (which became Co. C) published in *Rockingham Register* on 5/31/61.

HARRISON, BENJAMIN: b. in Fauquier Co. enl. 4/24/61 in Co. H. Farmer. Sick at home with consumption 5/4/61 thru 1-2/62 roll. Present on 5-6/62 roll, the only one on which he is so shown. Discharged 8/18/62 for phthisis, age 33.

HARRISON, DANIEL BURR: b. 1825 at Salem, Fauquier Co. enl. 5/18/62 in Co. H. To Cpl. 9/1/64. Wded. 9/22/64 at Milford: "I was struck by a musket ball in the centre of the forehead, the ball passing out back of the right eye." Part of brain exuded from wd. Totally incapacitated until he d. in 1903. Bur. Harrison-Hume-Rector-Bowersett Cem., Marshall, Va.

HARRISON, J. B.: This name appears on a published postwar roster of Co. H.

HARRISON, JULIEN: b. 2/6/27 in Richmond. Appointed Lt. Col. 9/11/61. AWOL sick since 11/25/61 on 11-12/61 roll. To Col. 4/15/62. Resigned 7/28/62 due to chronic hemorrhoidal tumor. To Col. 9/23/62. Wded. 10/11/63 in left thigh at Brandy Station. Found unfit because of wd. 1/15/64. Retired to Invalid Corps 3/6/65. To court duty in defenses of Richmond and Petersburg 3/23/65. Paroled 5/3/65 at Columbia. m. 1) Lavina Heth, 2) Lillie Johnston. d. 7/17/77.

HARRISON, LUTHER DAWSON: enl. 5/20/61 in Co. F. Detailed for special service in QM Dept. 8/21/61 and so shown thru 1-2/62 roll. Discharged 7/26/62.

HARRY, T. A.: Shown as in Co. G, admitted 7/16/64 on a register of General Hosp. No. 9, Richmond. Probably an error.

HART, H. W.: b. in Halifax Co. On a pay roll of Co. G as teamster 4/30/63. Admitted 10/29/63 to Chimborazo Hosp. No. 4, Richmond, with chronic diarrhea, returned to duty 11/27/63. Railroad worker and wheelwright in Danville postwar, age 66 on 7/26/02. d. 1/2/23. Sometimes spelled Heart.

HART, MALCOLM: enl. 5/4/61 in Co. I, age 34. At home with bilious fever on ca. 6/19/61 roll. To Commissary Sgt. 12/9/61. Present thru 5-6/62 roll. No further record in regiment. Purchasing agent at Danville 1-4/64.

HART, ROBERT: On postwar rosters as in Co. I. One of these states he was detailed to another co. in 1862.

HARTLEY, THOMAS JEFFERSON: enl. 5/4/61 in Co. I, age 22. Transferred to Co. B 5/1/62. Reported as deserter by Richmond 2/28/65. Otherwise present on all rolls thru final 3/21/65 roll. Postwar rosters have him wded. at Five Forks. Reportedly alive in 5/07.

HARVEY, BENJAMIN P.: b. 7/10/33. enl. 3/10/62 in Co. G. Absent, on sick furlough over 30 days on 5-6/62 roll. To Cpl. 12/17/62. POW 5/11/64 at Yellow Tavern. Paroled 10/11/64 at Elmira. Absent sick on final 3/22/65 roll. Paroled 4/9/65 at Appomattox. d. 3/1/06, bur. Cub Creek Cem., Charlotte C.H.

HARVEY, HENRY CLAY: b. 10/11/31 in Pittsylvania Co. enl. 8/19/61 in Co. G as Cpl. To Lt. 4/20/62. Generally present until severely wded. 6/321/63 at Upperville. Detailed to QM Dept. at Lynchburg 12/29/63. QM agent in Pittsylvania Co. on 2/17/65, and detailed on 3/22/65 final roll. d. 3/14/08, wid. Sallie A., m. 1899.

HARVEY, JAMES DOUGLAS: enl. 10/20/63 in Co. G. Absent on horse detail on 9-10/64 roll. Present on final 3/22/65. Paroled 4/9/65 at Appomattox. Resid. Charlotte Co.

HATE, J. W.: On postwar "original list" of Co. F.

HAVEN, W. B.: On postwar "original list" of Co. F.

HAVENER, JOSEPH R.: b. 1839. enl. 7/16/61 in Co. K. Detailed as wagoner 4/10/62 and so employed for most of his service thru 1-2/65 final roll. Courier on 8/62 pay roll. Laborer on farm at Sterling on 11/30/03. d. 1909, bur. Chestnut Grove Cem., Herndon.

HAWES, WILLIAM F.: b. in Greene Co. enl. 4/1/62 in Co. B. Miller. On extra duty in QM Dept. as teamster on most rolls from 6/9/62 thru 9-10/64. Provost guard from 10/1/63 on 11-12/63 roll. Reported by Richmond as deserter 2/28/65. Resid. Wayland's Mill, Culpeper Co., age 70, a miller, on 11/26/04. Still living 3/28/11. bur. Bethel Baptist Church Cem., Culpeper Co.

HAWKINS, ARTHUR: enl. 4/1/62 in Co. B. Injured in fall from horse and horse KIA 5/23/62 at Cedarville. Absent on scout with Lt. Duncan on 11-12/63 roll. Reported by Richmond as deserter 2/28/65. Otherwise present thru 3/21/65 final roll. Resid. Oma, Culpeper Co., age 73 on 4/14/00, claiming wd. at Cedar Creek. d. 3/9/11 at Leon, Madison Co. Wid. Evaline, m. 1871.

HAWKINS, JOHN: enl. 10/1/62 in Co. B. On detached service at various times including from 2/6/63 as shoemaker on 1-2/63 roll, horse detail on 7-8/64 roll. AWOL on 9-10/64 roll and on final 3/21/65 roll since 2/7/65. d. 11/17/78 near Slate Mills. Wid. Laura N., m. 1860. Sources give his middle initial as "D" or "J." Postwar roster says age 28 on enlistment.

HAWKINS, MORTIMORE: Conscript assigned 4/25/64 to Co. B. In Chimborazo Hosp. No. 3, Richmond, with dysentery 5/28-5/31/64. Absent sick on 7-8/64 roll. Wded. 11/12/64 and absent wded. on 3/21/65 final roll. Postwar roster gives age 28 on enlistment. d. 7/7/98, wid. Mary M., m. 1869.

HAWKINS, MUSCOE L: b. 9/9/37 near Slate Mills, in Rappahannock Co. enl. 10/1/62 in Co. B. Mechanic. On extra duty as brigade teamster on 7-8/64 roll. Otherwise present on all rolls thru final 3/21/65 roll. Resid. Olive, Culpeper Co., postwar, as builder and miller. Claimed typhoid fever and exposure in war. m. Mary Elizabeth Bushong. d. 7/13/24.

HAWKINS, WILLIAM L: enl. 10/1/62 in Co. B. Reported by Richmond as deserter 2/28/65, but otherwise present on every roll thru 3/21/65 final roll. Postwar roster says age 22 on enlistment, wded. at Yellow Tavern, resid. Culpeper Co., alive in 5/07.

HAWLEY, M. R.: Shown as a member of the regiment, no company shown, in postwar roster of Culpeper Co. veterans.

HAWS, P. H.: On a postwar roster of Co. C, from Fairfax. A Fairfax Co. veterans roster ca. 1898 has him in Co. C, 6th Va. Inf., age 65.

HAYCOCK, E. MOSS: enl. 5/1/62 in Co. C. Absent sick 7/15/62, since 1/10/63 on 1-2/63 roll, and with morbi cutis at Charlottesville Hosp. 1/7-1/8/64, transferred to Lynchburg. d. of lung wd., pyemia 6/5/64 at St. Francis de Sales Infirmary, Richmond. Presumably identical to Edgar Haycock, Co. K, on monument to dead of Fairfax Co.

HEATON, AMBROSE B.: enl. 4/22/61 in Co. B, age 19. Farmer. Wded. 5/23/62 at Cedarville and absent wded. remainder of 1862. Wded. slightly 7/3/63 at Fairfield, Pa. To Cpl. on 11-12/63 roll, sick since 12/21. Absent sick from 8/20/64 thru 9-10/64 roll. Present on final 3/21/65 roll. Paroled 5/9/65 at Winchester. Postwar roster says wded. at Spotsylvania and d. before 1/5/07.

HEDGMAN, PETER DANIEL GRAYSON: enl. 8/20/62 in Co. A. Absent with leave 12/10/62 to 1/5/63. Transferred to Co. A, 15th Va. Inf., reported to that unit 9/7/63 but left same day. In Richmond hosp. with lumbago 9/14/63, transferred to Castle Thunder 9/19/63, resid. Stafford. Paid for service 9/1-10/31/63. Known as Grayson. Records for C. G. and B. Hedgeman appear to be for this man.

HEDRICK, CHARLES L: enl. 5/28/61 in Co. C. To Sgt., at home wded., on 9-10/62 roll. Evidently identical to F. H. Headrick, Co. C, Sgt., d. 11/8/62 on 11-12/62 roll.

HEDRICK, GEORGE W.: b. 4/26/34. enl. 5/28/61 in Co. C. Farmer. Present only on 9-10/61 roll. Rockingham Co. enrolling book at Va. Hist. Soc. states he got Charles Murphy as substitute, ca. 1863. d. 3/16/00, bur. Mt. Olivet Cem., McGaheysville.

HEDRICK, WILLIAM W.: b. 12/24/22. Shown as in Co. C on 5/31/61 published roster. Farmer. Rockingham Co. enrolling book at Va. Hist. Soc. states he got A. B. Whipple as substitute. No Confederate record otherwise. d. 7/19/03, bur. Mt. Olivet Cem., McGaheysville.

HEFFESTY, RICHARD: enl. 5/28/61 in Co. C. Deserted 9/15/62. Teamster on 4/30/62 payroll, signs by mark. Alternate spellings: Hefisty, Hefferty, Hefesty, Heffestay.

HEIDT, THOMAS G.: enl. 10/7/61 in (1st) Co. E. Resid. Effingham Co., Ga. Mortally wded. 12/4/61 in Fairfax Co. d. 12/22/61 at Charlottesville.

HEINE, JOSEPH: Shown as in Co. A, paroled 5/8/65 at Winchester, age 16, resid. Loudoun Co. No other record. cf. Edward Hennie.

HENDERSON, THOMAS W.: enl. 4/1/64 in Co. G. In Chimborazo Hosp. No. 4, Richmond, with chronic rheumatism 5/14-5/24/64. d. of debilitas 12/11/64 at General Hosp., Harrisonburg.

HENNIE, EDWARD: enl. 7/24/61 in Co. A. Absent on sick furlough since 12/28 on 11-12/61 roll. "Accidentally shot at Martinsburg" on 5-6/62 roll. No further official record. Name also given Henne. Postwar roster of Co. A has Edward Henry, discharged, over age.

HENRY, _____: Shown as in Co. H, absent sick since 8/19 on 12/61 return. No other record.

HENRY, THOMAS: enl. 3/25/63 in Co. F. Reported AWOL from 7/1/63. No further record.

HENSON, CHARLES: b. 1846 in Fauquier Co. enl. 5/24/63 in Co. H. Reported AWOL from 11/30/63, and as deserter on 9-10/64 roll. Farmer postwar at Clifton. d. 7/24/20, bur. Payne Cem., (Clifton Town Cem.). Wid. Eliza Ellen, m. 1868. Name also spelled Hinson.

HENSON, GEORGE W.: enl. 6/9/61 in Co. H. Merchant. Sick with jaundice from 10/27 on 9-10/61 roll. Courier to Gen. Stuart on 5-6/62 roll. Desertion 11/25-12/3/62 "excused by Maj. Flournoy." AWOL since 12/28 on 11-12/63 roll. Absent wded. 6/29/64 and so shown thru final 3/22/65 roll. Paroled 4/27/65 at Winchester, age 29, resid. Fauquier Co.

HERNDON, DUDLEY: enl. 9/18/62 in Co. H. Absent on horse furlough on 12/62 return and absent with leave on 2/28/63 roll. No further record. May be the man of this name 8/7/29-1/14/09, bur. Triangle Community Cem., Prince William Co.

HERNSBURGER, ALFRED L.: enl. 5/28/61 in Co. C as Cpl. Present on 9-10/61 roll. No further record. Surname also given as Harnsberger.

HERNSBURGER, WILLIAM MICHAEL: b. 5/23/35 at Port Republic. Grad. Dickinson College, Pa. enl. 5/28/61 in Co. C. Teacher. Unofficial source states that he was Sgt. when KIA 9/23/62 at Paris. bur. Port Republic Cem. on Hill.

HERRELL, WILLIAM S.: b. 4/25/45 in Fauquier Co. enl. 8/16/63 in Co. H. Absent sick on 9-10/64 roll. Otherwise present on all rolls thru 3/22/65 final roll. Paroled 4/22/65 at Winchester, when shown in Co. A. Shoemaker postwar. d. 8/14/10, bur. Cedar Grove Cem., Bealton.

HESSER, ANDREW MASON: enl. 7/24/61 in Co. A. Detailed to guard baggage at Manassas on 1-2/62 roll. POW 7/14/64 at Petersburg. Exchanged 3/10/65 from Elmira. Absent, paroled prisoner on final 3/27/65 roll. Paroled 5/8/65 at Harpers Ferry, age 28. Known as Mason Hesser.

HESSER, COLBERT CRAWFORD: b. near Snickersville, Loudoun Co. enl. 6/27/63 in Co. A. Absent with leave to get clothing since 12/31 on 11-12/63 roll. POW 5/31/64 at Cold Harbor. Released 5/31/65 at Elmira. Resid. Bluemont, age 72, in 1911. Clerk postwar. d. 11/4/13 at Lee Camp Soldiers' Home, Richmond. bur. Hollywood Cem., Richmond. Known as "Bud."

HEWLETT, WILLIAM H.: enl. 9/17/61 in (1st) Co. E, age 20. Discharged 1/10/62 for physical disability. Resid. Beaufort Dist., S.C.

HEYL, WILLIAM H.: enl. 4/24/61 in Co. H. Painter. Exceeded leave since 6/27 on 6/30/61 roll. AWOL since 10/6 on 9-10/61 roll. AWOL since 4/23 on 5-6/62 roll. Ordered transferred to infantry 11/14/62, but absent sick since 12/25 on 11-12/62 roll. Present on 2/28/63 roll. Postwar roster says deserted.

HEYWARD, THOMAS W.: enl. 9/17/61 in (1st) Co. E. Discharged 8/9/64 for physical disability. Resid. Savannah, Ga.

HIBBS, SOLOMON: enl. 7/23/61 in Co. D. AWOL on 8/31/63 roll. Absent sick in hosp. on 11-12/63 roll. Absent with leave on 7-8/64 roll. AWOL on 9-10/64 roll. Absent at hosp. for final 3/22/65 roll. Not present on any roll. Living in Loudoun Co., age 79 (also given as 81) on 4/29/00.

HICKS, WILLIAM N.: enl. 10/1/63 in (2d) Co. E. In Richmond hosp. with catarrh 5/5-5/23/64. Sick at Danville with chronic rheumatism 5/29-7/26/64. Absent sick at Liberty hosp. on 9-10/64 roll. Present on final 3/4/65 roll.

HILL, JAMES D.: enl. 7/1/62 in Co. B. POW 8/20/62 at 2d Manassas. Exchanged at Aiken's Ldg. 9/21/62. Otherwise present until final 3/21/65 roll, when marked AWOL since 2/7/65. Postwar roster says age 18 on enlistment. d. before 5/07.

HILL, J. M.: Only record is of parole as Sgt. in Co. A at Winchester 6/5/65, age 27, resid. Augusta Co.

HILL, JOSEPH R.: b. 1840. enl. 10/1/63 in Co. A. Previously deserted Co. A, 8th Va. Inf. POW 1/31/64 in Madison Co. Took the oath 6/20/65 at Ft. Delaware. Resid. Loudoun Co. d. 1928, bur. Ebenezer (Bloomfield) Cem.

HILL, LABAN LODGE: b. 1838 in Loudoun Co. enl. 10/1/62 in Co. A. POW 7/14/64 at Petersburg. Paroled 3/10/65 at Elmira. Absent, paroled prisoner on 3/27/65 final roll. Laborer, resid. Loudoun and Clarke Cos., Washington, D.C., and Lee Camp Soldiers' Home, Richmond postwar. d. 7/14/23, bur. Green Hill Cem., Berryville.

HILL, VOLNEY PURCELL: Shown as a member of Co. A only on Union POW records. Actually a member of Co. A, 8th Va. Inf.

HILT, JOHN: enl. 3/14/62 in Co. H. AWOL since 5/25/62 and marked as a deserter from that date on 2/28/63 roll. No other record.

HILTON, N. THOMAS: enl. 10/6/62 in Co. K. Detailed to go to horse hosp. with led horses on 7-8/63 roll. AWOL 9/11/63 on 11-12/63 roll. "Deserted" on 7-8/64 roll, dated 12/27/64. Absent, wded. in 10/63 on 9-10/64 roll. No further record. Postwar sources says wded. in leg in Loudoun 1864, and wded. by Sam Means' men.

HINKLE, SAMUEL: b. in Rockingham Co. enl. 12/10/62 in Co. C. Present until killed 9/13/63 in Culpeper Co. Also shown as Henkel. Previously in 52nd Va. Inf.

HINES, CAROLIN CLAY: b. 12/29/40 in Bryan Co., Ga. Grad. Trinity College, N.C. enl. 9/17/61 in (1st) Co. E. m. Margaret Galbreath 1870. Teacher and Methodist minister postwar. d. 11/20/23, bur. Oak Ridge Cem., McRae, Ga.

HISLE, DANIEL W.: enl. 9/1/62 in Co. B. Wded. 10/11/63. Reported by Richmond as deserter 2/28/65, but not so shown on rolls. Present on final 3/21/65 roll. POW 4/3/65 at Hatcher's Run. Took the oath 6/14/65 at Pt. Lookout, resid. Rappahannock Co. Postwar roster spells name Hysle. Another such roster says age 28 on enlistment, severely wded. 10/10/64 at Brandy Station.

HISLE, LLOYD AYLETTE: b. 12/2/32. enl. 9/1/62 in Co. B. Wded. 6/29/64 at Reams Station and therefore absent on rolls for 7-8/64 thru final 3/21/65 roll. Admitted 7/4/64 to Richmond hosp. with flesh wd. of right breast, 30 day furlough from 7/12/64. d. 4/1/12, bur. Sperryville Cem.

HITE, CORNELIUS BALDWIN: b. 8/5/42 at "Belle Grove" in Frederick Co. Conscript assigned 3/26/64 to Co. D. Sick in hosp. on 9-10/64 roll. AWOL on final 3/22/65 roll. Stated postwar that he "volunteered tho' went through Conscript Bureau," was discharged 12/7/61 from Co. F, 1st Va. Cav., and resigned acting Lt. of Topographical Engineers in 1863. Farmer, teacher, surveyor, and in real estate postwar. m. Margaret Lewis 1871. d. 10/9/43 at Washington, D.C., bur. Hollywood Cem., Richmond.

HITE, IRVINE E.: On postwar rosters as in Co. D. d. of disease contracted in service in Clarke Co. 7/1/61.

HITE, JAMES MADISON: On postwar rosters as in Co. D. Discharged on surgeon's certificate. d. 1903.

HITE, THORNTON FONTAINE: enl. 4/28/62 in Co. D. Present on all rolls until KIA 1/11/65 by shot in chest at Beverly, (W.) Va. Resid. Frederick Co.

HITE, WILLIAM M.: Shown on a register of deceased soldiers as in Co. D, KIA 10/11/63 at Brandy Station. Postwar roster says resid. Albemarle Co.

HITT, ALBERT H.: b. in Rappahannock Co. enl. 11/20/64 in Co. B. Present on final 3/21/65 roll. Farmer postwar, resid. Amissville, age 69 on 3/26/15. There is confusion on postwar rosters between this man and William A. Hitt, Co. B, KIA at Middletown.

HITT, JAMES D.: enl. 6/1/62 in Co. B. Absent sick since 10/1 on 9-10/62 roll. Absent with leave on 11-12/63 and 9-10/64 rolls. In Richmond hosps. with diarrhea 6/8-6/18/64. Present on final 3/21/65 roll. Reportedly alive 5/07.

HITT, WILLIAM A.: enl. 3/1/64 in Co. B. KIA 10/19/64 at Middletown. Confused on a postwar roster with Albert Hitt.

HIXSON, WILLIAM: At least one person of this name enl. 10/7/62 in Co. A. There is great confusion between persons reported POW ca. 12/29/63 at Middleburg (or Vienna), POW 6/5 or 11/15/64 at "Shipyard," d. 10/27/64 of diarrhea at Pt. Lookout and bur. there, and paroled 2/18/65 at Pt. Lookout. One postwar roster has "Hixson, William, killed at Aldie." Middle initial may be "A."

HODNETT, JOHN: enl. ca. 4/30/62 in Co. G. Discharged 1/31/63. Co. clothing book has transferred. Again in Co. G 9/24/64 thru final 3/22/65 roll. Also shown as Hodinett.

HODNETT, THOMAS: enl. 3/22/62 in Co. G. Present until discharged 2/2/63 by substituting William Collins, but shown on 9-10/64 roll as absent on horse detail. No further military record. AWOL 8/13/95 from Lee Camp Soldiers' Home, Richmond. d. 9/22 (or 26)/95 in Danville. Wid. Harriet G., m. 1851. Sometimes shown as Hodinett.

HOFFMAN, A. J.: Only record (no company shown) is as POW 4/15/64 by Provost Marshal, Cavalry Corps, Army of the Potomac. Sent to Washington, D.C., 4/21/64. Probably an error.

HOFFMAN, JOHN D.: enl. 4/1/62 in (2d) Co. E. Absent sick on 5-6/62 roll. Paid as teamster 1/11-1/20/63. KIA 6/9/63 at Brandy Station. On 1913 roster as John Hoofman. Another postwar roster has "John Huffman, Chatham C.H."

HOGANS, JOSEPH: enl. 4/1/62 in (2d) Co. E. Discharged 5/8/62.

HOGANS, OBEDIAH: enl. 4/1/62 in (2d) Co. E. Detached as regimental blacksmith for much of service. POW 9/14/63 near Culpeper. Paroled 3/10/65 at Elmira, signs by mark. Transferred 9/15/63 to 57th Va. Inf. but never reported and marked "deserted." Resid. Pittsylvania Co. 5/1/00, age 76. d. 6/15/01, wid. Catherine, m. 1866. Sometimes spelled Hogan.

HOGE, GEORGE DICKSON: b. 3/21/46. enl. 2/25/64 in Co. A. Persent on final 3/27/65 roll. Paroled 4/22/65 at Winchester. Identified as "Dr." on tombstone. d. 9/19/18, bur. Ebenezer Cem. (Bloomfield).

HOGE, RICHARD H.: Shown as enl. 2/25/62 (presumably meaning 1864) in Co. A, last paid 12/31/63, absent with leave on 9-10/64 roll, which is his only record.

HOLBROOK, G. J.: enl. 6/1/62 in Co. C. To Sgt. 10/1/62. In Charlottesville hosp. with morbi cutis 1/7-1/8/64, transferred to Lynchburg. Absent wded. on 9-10/64 roll. Absent on sick furlough in Wythe Co. on final 3/30/65 roll. May be identical to Garland J. Holbrook, Co. A (Wythe Grays), 4th Va. Inf.

HOLMES, JOHN S.: enl. 4/24/61 in Co. H as Sgt. Carpenter. Sent home sick with dysentery 6/30/61. d. 10/2/61 of typhoid fever.

HOLMES, WASHINGTON CARTER: b. 6/18/42 in Fauquier Co. enl. 4/24/61 in Co. H. Tobacconist Absent with typhoid fever 8/21/61 thru 5-6/62 roll. POW 6/2/62 in Hardy Co. (W.) Va., and paroled. POW 10/29/62 near Petersburg, (W.) Va., paroled 12/2/62 near Vicksburg, Miss. On horse leave before marked AWOL since 2/1 on 2/28/63 roll. On horse leave again before being marked AWOL since 3/6 on 3/22/65 final roll. Paroled 4/22/65 at Winchester. Postmaster of Marshall postwar. d. 1/2/30, bur. Marshall Cem.

HOLTZCLAW, CHARLES W.: enl. 3/28/65 in Co. H. Absent sick with fever 9/1/62 thru 7-8/62 roll. POW 2/28/65 in Fauquier Co. Took the oath at Ft. Delaware 6/20/65. Resid. Warrenton, age 73 on 5/26/00. Still alive 9/18/08.

HOLTZCLAW, GEORGE W.: enl. 3/16/62 in Co. H. AWOL since 4/16 on 5-6/62 roll. Detailed as wagoner 10-12/62. AWOL since 8/8/63 on 7-8/63 roll. In Richmond hosp. with catarrh 12/2-12/10/63, but present on 11-12/63 roll. Sentenced for desertion 3/7/64 to 12 months hard labor and 6 months with ball and chain, with leniency for "extenuating circumstances." Deserted 3/23/65.

HOMER, ALEX: On postwar rosters as in Co. A. No official record.

HOOD, CHARLES BARBOUR: b. in Culpeper. Conscript enl. 3/14/64 in Co. B. Absent on horse detail on 7-8/64 roll (m. 7/22/64 in Augusta Co.). Absent sick since 2/25/65 on final 3/21/65 roll. Age 79 on 3/20/11. d. 11/27/15 at Culpeper, wid. Jeanie K.

HOOKE, ABRAHAM SCOTT: b. 12/14/30. enl. 5/28/61 in Co. C as Cpl. Farmer. To Sgt. on 1-2/63 roll. Six day furlough from 2/24/63. Wded. 5/7/64 in left shoulder. Otherwise present on all rolls thru 3/30/65 final roll. m. S. Frances Null 1865. d. 4/20/12. bur. Port Republic Cem.

HOOKE, GEORGE W. K.: b. 2/21/42 (or 1845). enl. 4/15/63 in Co. C. Admitted 9/16/63 to Charlottesville General Hosp. d. there 10/15/63 of typhoid fever, bur. Hooke Cem. near Port Republic.

HOOKE, ROBERT J.: b. 4/1/35. Enl. 5/28/61 in Co. C. Admitted to hosp. 10/14/61. d. 11/22/61 as Sgt. at Charlottesville of typhoid fever, bur. Hooke Cem. near Port Republic.

HOOKE, ROBERT W.: b. 1/7/40. Sgt. in Co. C on 9-10/61 roll. d. 9/13/61, bur. Cross Keys Cem..

HOOPER, GEORGE W.: enl. 7/24/61 in Co. A. Discharged 9/24/61 on furnishing an acceptable substitute.

HOPE, THEODORE J.: b. 10/22/47 in Va. enl. 1/1/64 in Co. A. In Charlottesville hosp. with scabies 1/3-1/17/65. AWOL since 3/7/65 on 3/27/65 final roll. m. Cora Ankrom (5/30/74-1/1/1964)/1898. d. 10/15/10 at Marshall, Mo.

HOPKINS, LUTHER WESLEY: b. 1843 in Loudoun Co. enl. 9/1/62 in Co. A. POW 10/17/62 at Upperville. Paroled from Old Capitol Prison ca. 11/2/62. POW at Yellow Tavern 5/11/64. Paroled and exchanged from Pt. Lookout 9/18/64. In Richmond hosp. with rheumatism 9/23-10/1/64, then 40 days furlough. Absent on parole on 9-10/64 roll, and absent sick since 11/64 on final 3/27/65 roll. Wholesale commission merchant postwar. Resid. Baltimore, Md., from 1875. Author *Bull Run to Appomattox*. d. 7/4/20 at son's home at Sewickley, Pa.

HOPKINS, ZEBULON M.: enl. 5/4/61 in Co. I, age 19. Fifteen day furlough of indulgence from 8/31/63. Absent sick at hosp. on 9-10/64 roll. Present on all other rolls thru final 3/20/65 roll. Claimed wd. at High Bridge in 4/65, and hernia from resulting fall from horse. d. 12/15/18, bur. Unionville Christian Church Cem., Orange Co., wid. Harriet A., m. 1865.

HORNER, DAVID H.: enl. 9/1/62 in Co. F. POW ca. 6/20/63 at Seneca Mills, Md. Later records are hopelessly confused, but probably include other captures and paroles. Absent on horse detail on final 2/24/65 roll. POW 4/1/65 at Centreville. Took the oath 7/7/65 at Elmira. Resid. Montgomery Co., Md. or Washington, D.C.

HORNER, RICHARD HENRY: b. 8/20/39. enl. 7/24/61 in Co. A. Re-enlisted 8/16/62 in Co. H. POW 8/16/62 at Thoroughfare Gap. Paroled 12/24/63 at Pt. Lookout. Various hospitalizations for dysentery, icterus, scabies. Present on final 3/22/65 roll. Paroled 4/22/65 at Winchester, resid. Fauquier Co. d. 12/8/99 near Marshall, bur. Warrenton Cem.

HORTON, PALATINE A.: b. in Campbell Co. grad. Va. Medical College 1859. enl. 4/1/62 in (2d) Co. E. Physician. Discharged 5/4/62 with chronic inflammation of lungs, age 30. Contract physician and Acting Assistant Surgeon at General Hosp. No. 1, Lynchburg, 9/1-11/28/62.

HOSKISS, WILLIAM: On postwar rosters as in Co. A, regimental blacksmith. No official record. One roster says d. 7/96.

HOTCHKISS, ELIJA J.: enl. 7/24/61 in Co. A. To Sgt. on 9-10/61 roll. Reduced to ranks 1/1/62. Absent sick on 5-6/62 roll. No further record.

HOUCHIN, CAMBIAS: enl. 9/1/64 in Co. F. Present until final 2/24/65 roll, when absent on horse detail.

HOUGHTON, CHARLES HENRY: b. 1844 in Rappahannock Co. enl. 9/1/63 in Co. B. Absent, wded. 10/11/63 on 11-12/63 roll. Absent sick until present on final 3/21/65 roll. Paroled 5/18/65 at Winchester, signs by mark. Claimed "ruptured while in the service (on both sides) by the fall of a horse." Farmer, alive 3/26/04 at Hartwood. Bur. Grove Presbyterian Church Cem., Goldvein.

HOUGHTON, JACKSON W.: enl. 4/22/61 in Co. B, age 25. Farmer. Wded. by accidental shot through hand 5/11/61 at Centreville. Sick since 12/1 on 12/61 return. Absent sick since 2/4/62 on 1-2/62 roll. Sick at hosp. since 11/1/62 on 11-12/62 roll. Absent as pioneer on 7-8/64 roll and until present on final 3/21/65 roll. Reportedly alive 5/07.

HOUGHTON, MARSHALL: enl. 7/19/61 in Co. B. Absent sick since 12/1 on 1-2/62 roll. KIA 6/21/63 at Upperville. Postwar roster gives age as 20 on enlistment.

HOUGHTON, THOMAS: enl. 1/1/63 in Co. B. Wded. slightly at Fairfield, Pa., 7/3/63. Absent to get clothing on 11-12/63 roll. Absent sick on 9-10/64 roll. Present on final 3/21/65 roll. Postwar roster says age 18 on enlistment, alive 5/07.

HOUGHTON, WILLIAM JACKSON: b. in Rappahannock Co. enl. 6/1/62 in Co. B. Accidentally wded. by discharge of his gun on picket 6/26/62. Marked as deserter "not having reported recently" on 11-12/62 roll. Absent sick since 1/1 on 1-2/63 roll. No further official record. Claimed "on detail from about 1st Feb. '65." Farmer in Culpeper Co., age 67, 3/19/03. Stated he had fever during war, horse fell on him in 1863. d. 1/3/09, wid. A. Elizabeth, m. 1859.

HOWDERSHELL, HUMPHREY: b. 9/30/44 near Hopewell in Fauquier Co. enl. 11/24/62 in Co. A. On clothing detail since 12/31 on 11-12/63 roll. Absent, frost-bitten on Beverly Raid in Jan. on final 3/27/65 roll. Paroled 4/25/65 at Winchester. Farmer near Waterfall, Prince William Co., postwar. m. Armenia Peak 1869. d. 11/7/14.

HOWISON, JAMES BENJAMIN: enl. 8/1/61 in Co. H. Absent sick on 9-10/62 roll, then present until elected Lt. 7/23/64. Commanding co. on 9-10/64 roll. Absent, wded. in fight at Beverly on final 3/22/65 roll.

HUBBARD, JOHN F.: b. in Pittsylvania Co. enl. 4/1/62 in (2d) Co. E. Farmer. Discharged 6/23/62 for partial paralysis and mental disorder. Middle name may be Fuller.

HUBBARD, OBADIAH H.: enl. 4/1/62 in (2d) Co. E. Absent on detached service thru 11-12/62 roll. POW ca. 9/14/63 near Culpeper. Paroled 4/27/64 at Pt. Lookout. In Richmond hosp. with scurvy 5/1-5/8/64, then 60 day furlough. Absent at Staunton hosp., wded. at Winchester on 9-10/64 roll. Present on final 3/4/65 roll. POW ca. 4/6/65 at Southside R.R. Took the oath 6/15/65 at Newport News. 1913 roster says resid. Chatham RFD.

HUBBARD, RAWLEY THOMPSON: enl. 3/22/62 in Co. G. Present on every roll thru 3/22/65 final roll. Pension record says age 17 on enlistment. d. 7/8/16 at Mt. Airy. Wid. Emma S., m. 1885.

HUBBARD, THOMAS C.: b. 12/7/33. enl. 5/27/61 in (2d) Co. E. To Cpl. on 5-6/62 roll. Absent several times on horse leave or detached service. Absent wded. in Pittsylvania Co. on 9-10/64 roll. Present on final 3/4/65 roll. 1913 roster has "accidentally shot himself." d. 4/23/23 in Campbell Co.

HUDSON, RICHARD O.: b. in Rappahannock Co. enl. 1/1/63 in Co. B. Present until reported by Richmond as deserter 3/1/65. Absent sick since 2/25 on final 3/21/65 roll. Farmer, resid. Ohio, Texas, Kansas, and Washington postwar. Age 78 on 7/19/23. d. in Rappahannock Co., near Boston, obituary printed 5/30/33.

HUFF, EDWARD H.: enl. 4/22/61 in Co. B, age 28. Farmer. Absent sick 8/27 thru 1-2/62 roll. POW 5/12/64 at Spotsylvania. Took the oath 6/14/65 at Elmira, resid. Rappahannock Co.

HUFF, JACKSON: b. in Clarke Co. enl. 7/24/61 in Co. A. Farmer. AWOL since 11/25 on 12/61 return. Discharged 6/30/62 for diseased lungs, age 45. Also shown as Hoff, Hough.

HUFF, JAMES R.: b. in Rappahannock Co. enl. 4/22/61 in Co. B, age 23. Farmer. Sick at home on 9/1/61 roll. On furlough on 1-2/62 roll. Horse KIA 5/23/62 near Front Royal. Extra duty in QM Dept. as teamster since 5/25 on 5-6/62 roll. AWOL on 11-12/63 and 9-10/64 rolls. Teamster on final 3/21/65 roll. Said he was "detailed a few days before surrender to come home after a horse & was at home at time of surrender." Postwar roster says wded. in hand at Spotsylvania. d. 2/2/17.

HUFF, THOMAS HUMPHREY: enl. 2/2/65 in Co. B. Present on final 3/21/65 roll. Paroled 4/9/65 at Appomattox with men detailed and hired in QM Dept. of Cavalry Corps. Previously in infantry. Farmer, age 72, in Rappahannock Co. on 4/25/16. d. 8/23/17, wid. Eliza Ellen, m. 1875.

HUFF, WILLIAM J.: enl. 3/1/62 in Co. B. Teamster on extra duty in QM Dept. 5/25/62 thru 11-12/62 roll. AWOL on 9-10/64 roll and AWOL since 3/1 on 3/21/65 final roll. Paroled 5/18/65 at Winchester, age 25, resid. Rappahannock Co. Apparently identical to John Huff on postwar roster, reportedly alive 5/07.

HUFFMAN, BURRIS: enl. 5/28/61 in Co. C. Present on 9-10/61 roll. No further record. Given name also spelled Burrus.

HUGHES, ENEAS JESSIE: b. 10/27/22 in Prince Edward Co. enl. 8/19/61 in Co. G. Lawyer. On sick furlough from 2/16 on 1-2/62 roll. On extra duty in commissary as clerk from 10/28 on 11/61 return. Discharged 8/3/62 for chronic diarrhea. d. 3/15/83, bur. Halifax Town Cem.

HUGHES, GEORGE H.: enl. 4/1/62 in Co. I. POW 10/9/64 at Fisher's Hill, sent to Pt. Lookout. Federal authorities received an order from President Lincoln for release of "George R. Houghes" or "G. W. Houghes," Co. I. George H. Hughes told them he had not applied to Lincoln for release, and refused to take the oath unless sent to his home within Confederate lines. d. 2/10/65 of acute dysentery, bur. Pt. Lookout. Not on postwar rosters. cf. Richard Hughes.

HUGHES, JEFFERSON: b. 5/26/25 in Orange Co. enl. 5/4/61 in Co. I. Farmer. Absent on sick furlough since 2/5 on 1-2/62 roll. In Orange hosp. with diarrhea 2/24/62. AWOL or deserter on later rolls. Dropped from payroll and name sent to enrolling officer on 7-8/63 roll. Later in 13th Va. Inf. m. Mary Ann Herndon 1853. d. 1/1/96, bur. on farm in Rhoadsville.

HUGHES, MELCAJAH: Conscript enl. 11/4/63 in Co. G. POW 5/11/64 at Yellow Tavern. d. 10/19/64 at Elmira of chronic diarrhea, bur. there. Wid. Lucy, m. 1859.

HUGHES, RICHARD: enl. 4/1/62 in Co. I. AWOL on 5-6/62 roll. Present on 11-12/62 roll. No other record. Postwar roster says "Prisoner till close of war." Another such roster has POW 1863 at Winchester, held at Pt. Lookout, d. 1863 in prison. cf. George H. Hughes.

HUGHLETT, JAMES A.: enl. 5/1/62 in Co. F. POW 6/5/62 at Middletown. Exchanged from Ft. Delaware 8/5/62. AWOL on 7-8/63 roll. Detailed to herd cattle 11/20 on 11-12/63 roll. POW 2/29/64 in Fauquier Co. Took the oath 6/20/65 at Ft. Delaware, resid. Fauquier Co.

HULVEY, JOHN H.: enl. 11/15/62 in Co. C. Wded. slightly 7/3/63 at Fairfield, Pa. Deserted 5/16/64.

HUME, CHARLES: enl. 11/1/64 in Co. I. Present on final 3/20/65 roll.

HUME, JAMES N.: enl. 5/28/61 in Co. C. To Lt. 4/20/62. With squadron under Gen. T. J. Jackson on 11/62 return. To court-martial duty 1/16/64. Badly wded. in shoulder ca. 8/24/64. Commanding Co. B on 7-8/64 roll. Present on final ca. 3/30/65 roll. Paroled 5/10/65 at Charlottesville. Known as "Tip."

HUMMER, BRADEN EZRA: b. 12/12/35. enl. 7/16/61 in Co. K. Had typhoid fever 6 weeks on 7-8/61 roll. Sick at home with leave since 12/27 on 1-2/62 roll. Transferred 5/1/62 to Co. A, 35th Bn. Va. Cav. d. 3/18/24, bur. Lewinsville Presbyterian Church Cem. near McLean.

HUMMER, GEORGE WASHINGTON FOX: b. 1827. enl. 5/26/61 in Co. K. Detached as courier to Col. Eppa Hunton 7/21 on 11/61 return. Transferred 1/31/62 to 8th Va. Inf. d. 1917, bur. Herndon.

HUMMER, JOHN P.: b. 11/14/32. enl. 9/25/62 in Co. A. Court-martial announced 12/26/63. Otherwise present on all rolls until absent sick on 9-10/64 roll. AWOL since 9/64 on final 3/27/65 roll. Paroled 4/22/65 at Winchester, resid. Clarke Co. d. 4/20/17, bur. Ebenezer Cem., Bloomfield.

HUMMER, MASON HARRISON: b. 1/3/82. enl. 9/25/62 in Co. A. Present until deserted 9/15/63. Paroled 4/27/65 at Winchester. d. 8/23/19, bur. Green Hill Cem., Berryville.

HUNT, LEWIS H.: enl. 2/1/64 in Co. A. POW 6/1/64 at Cold Harbor. Told Federals he was conscripted 3/17/64, and wished to remain North. Took the oath 5/29/65 at Elmira, resid. Mechanicsburg, Ohio. Postwar roster has a man of this surname, "died in prison."

HUNT, THOMAS W.: enl. 4/24/61 in Co. H. Reported sick at home from 6/25/61, but this was later changed to AWOL when he did not return. No further record.

HUNTER, ROBERT ALEXANDER: Conscript enl. 2/20/64 in (2d) Co. E. Farmer. Previously in 2d Va. Cav. Wded. 5/6/64 near Spotsylvania in head. In Richmond hosp. 5/9, age 26, transferred to Lynchburg 5/21/64. Applied for retirement 2/25/65. Absent wded. on final 3/4/65 roll. m. Susan Payne. Resid. Campbell Co.

HUNTER, TALIAFERRO: enl. 10/1/63 in Co. D. On duty at Gen. L. L. Lomax's HQ on 11-12/63 roll. Otherwise present thu final 3/22/65 roll. Paroled 4/24/65 at Ashland, resid. Caroline Co. Member of R. E. Lee Camp No. 1, Confederate Veterans, Richmond, 1900.

HUNTON, HENRY M.: enl. 7/24/61 in Co. A. AWOL since 12/18 on 11-12/61 roll. In Charlottesville hosp. with acute bronchitis 8/6-8/7/62. POW 8/26/62 at Manassas. Exchanged 9/21/62 at Aiken's Ldg. Detailed to Engineer Bureau, Richmond, as draughtsman 11/4/62. Transferred 12/9/62 to Treasury Dept. with Keatinge and Ball, contractors, at Columbia, S.C. Paroled 4/26/65 at Winchester as in Topographical Engineers, age 25, resid. Prince William Co.

HUNTON, JAMES W.: enl. 7/24/61 in Co. A. AWOL since 8/30 on 7-8/61 roll and since 9/23 on 9-10/61 roll. 11-12/61 roll says discharged, got John Hannavan as substitute. Postwar roster has him in Co. F. Probably identical to James W. Hunton, 1838-1903, bur. Buckland Methodist Church Cem., Prince William Co.

HURLEY, DANIEL B.: enl. 8/19/61 in Co. G as Cpl., age 44. Tailor. Discharged 5/2/62 for "anchylosis and enlargement of the ancle joint cause by scrofulous ulceration" near Conrad's Store, when his age was given as 40. Resid. Pittsylvania Co.

HURT, JOHN LINN: b. 3/10/38 in Carroll Co., Tenn. Att. Samuel Davies Institute, Halifax. enl. 5/27/61 in (2d) Co. E as Sgt. To Lt. on 2/16/62 roll, where he is shown as absent, POW, not re-enlisted. In Va. Senate 1877, 1881-82, one of the leaders of the anti-Mahone Democrats. m. 1) Nannie Kate Clement, 2) Sallie T. Douglas. Resid. Pittsylvania Co. in 1915.

HURT, RUFUS: enl. 2/10/64 in Co. C. Absent, detailed to brigade QM Dept. on all rolls thru final ca. 3/30/65 roll. On extra duty roll for 1/65 as teamster.

HUTCHERSON, GEORGE P.: enl. 4/1/62 in (2d) Co. E. Detached as teamster on all rolls thru 11-12/63 roll. Shown as deserted on 7-8/64 roll, but present on final 3/4/65 roll. Alive 4/28/00 in Pittsylvania Co., age 55.

HUTCHINSON, LOMUS: Federal records show a man of this name in Co. C, POW 7/21/64, captured by Gen. Sheridan and sent to Washington, D.C., 8/24/64, thence to Ft. Delaware. No further record and no Confederate records.

HUTCHISON, ELIJAH: enl. 4/22/61 in Co. K. POW 10/16/62 at Mountsville, Loudoun Co., and horse KIA. Paroled 11/2/62 at Aiken's Ldg. and returned to co. 2/24/63. Absent on account of injuries received 12/2/63 and 11-12/63 roll. Deserted 12/1/63 at Morton's Ford.

HYATT, JEFF: enl. 10/15/61 in (1st) Co. E. Wded. 8/25/64 at Reams Station. Resid. Meriwether Co., Ga.

IDEN, SAMUEL: b. in Fauquier Co. enl. 9/25/62 in Co. K. Farmer. d. 12/16/62 near Orange of typhoid pneumonia, age 19. Survived by Elizabeth Iden, his mother.

INGRAM, MARCELLUS G.: enl. 8/19/61 in Co. G, age 23. Present until 5-6/62 roll, when shown absent on sick furlough over 3 months, "no report." d. 7/62.

INSKIPP, JEFFERS B.: Conscript assigned 4/1/64 to Co. F. Employed as laborer at Orange 4/1-4/18/64. Deserted and took the oath 12/6/64 at Washington, D.C. Probably identical to John Inskip, shown on a postwar roster of Co. F.

IRVINE, ROBERT: Conscript assigned 2/25/64 to Co. F. No further record.

IRWIN, CHARLES F.: enl. 9/17/61 in (1st) Co. E, age 29. Present until taken to Richmond hosp. 11/30/61. Discharged 12/11/61. Apparently re-enlisted, because he is shown on a postwar roster of the Georgia Hussars as AWOL and dropped 2/20/63. Resid. Tatthall Co., Ga.

JACKSON, PHILIP M.: enl. 10/15/64 in Co. I. Absent, detailed as blacksmith on 9-10/64 roll and final 3/20/65 roll.

JACKSON, SAMUEL, C.: b. 12/1/35. enl. 4/22/61 in Co. K. Absent on 12/12/62 roll. In Petersburg hosp. with anasarca 8/1-8/4/64, transferred to Danville. Otherwise present on all rolls until final 1-2/65 roll, when absent sick. Paroled 4/24/65 at Harpers Ferry, (W.) Va. d. 10/21/20, bur. Leesburg Union Cem.

JACKSON, WILBAR LITTLETON: b. 7/31/44 near Markham, Fauquier Co. enl. 9/14/62 in Co. H. In Richmond hosp. with catarrh and hemorrhoids 11/28/63-4/9/64. Absent sick on rolls for 7-10/64. Present on final 3/22/65 roll. Paroled 4/24/65 at Winchester, m. Mrs. Sallie Fleming Winecoff 1882. d. 12/12/11 at Archer, Fla., with a "host of friends, black and white." Obituary gives name as William Littleton Jackson.

JAMES, F. B.: enl. 10/2/63 in Co. A. "Returned to 8th Va. Reg." 12/28/63.

JAMES, FLEET H.: b. 12/3/44. enl. 4/20/63 in Co. A. Present until 3/27/65 final roll, when absent sick, ordered to Charlottesville hosp. 2/7/65. Paroled 5/8/65 at Winchester, resid. Loudoun Co. d. 4/27/19, bur. Ketoctin Free Baptist Church Cem., where he is shown as "Rev."

JAMES, ROBERT M.: b. 1844. enl. 7/24/61 in Co. A. Sentenced to forfeit ½ month's wages on 11-12/61 roll. Sick since 2/10 on 1-2/62 roll. Courier for Gen. L. L. Lomax on 7-10/64 rolls. In Charlottesville hosp. 1/15-3/24/65 and on 3/27/65 final roll. Paroled 6/2/65 at Winchester, resid. Jefferson Co. d. 1892, bur. Ketoctin Cem.

JAMESSON, WILLIAM S.: enl. 6/15/61 in Co. F. Absent on horse furlough on 7-8/63 roll. Absent under arrest since 12/3 on 11-12/63 roll. Present on all other rolls except final 2/24/65 roll, when absent on horse detail. Paroled 4/25/65 at Fairfax C.H., age 23. Postwar roster spells name "Jamieson," and says captured and exchanged.

JANNEY, ASBURY: b. in Loudoun Co. POW 3/4/64 at Hamilton, and shown as both in Co. K and as Forage Agent (one record has 3/4/63). Occupation clerk, age 31, resid. Loudoun Co. Paroled 10/30/64 at Ft. Delaware. Paroled 4/21/65 at Edwards Ferry, Md., as in QM Dept. Paid as courier for Maj. Gen. D. H. Hill 6/1-8/4/62.

JANNEY, WILLIAM WALTER B.: b. 9/20/43. enl. 4/23/61 in Co. D. Student. Courier for Gen. Jeb Stuart on 9-10/61 roll. 5-6/62 roll has POW while on furlough and paroled. In Richmond hosp. with dysentery 6/10-6/17/64. POW 7/20/64 at Winchester. d. 3/5/65 at Camp Chase of chronic diarrhea and bur. there, but reinterred in Episcopal and Masonic Cem., Middleway, W.Va. Known as Walter B.

JAVINS, THOMAS: enl. 5/20/61 in Co. F. Dishonorably discharged 10/1/61 by order of Secretary of War at Fairfax C.H. Resid. Alexandria on 2/24/62, at about which time a Unionist denounced him as "a bitter determined Rebel."

JEFFERSON, THOMAS B.: enl. 5/27/61 in (2d) Co. E. Present on 7-8/61 roll. No further record. May be identical to the man of this name in Co. B, Booker's Regiment (3d) Va. Reserves.

JEFFRIES, ADDISON T.: enl. 4/24/61 in Co. H. Farmer. AWOL 9/21-10/31/61. Present, detailed as wagoner 11/22 on 11/62 thru 2/28/63 rolls. AWOL since 8/8 on 7-8/63 roll. Present on 11-12/63 thru 9-10/64 rolls. Absent, detailed as wagoner in regiment on final 3/22/65 roll.

JEFFRIES, ENOCH: b. 2/14/37. enl. 4/24/61 in Co. H. Farmer. AWOL 9/1-9/17/61. POW ca. 10/15/62 near Salem, paroled from Old Capitol Prison 10/31/62. Absent sick from 12/19/62 and marked as deserter. POW 6/9/63 at Beverly Ford, paroled 6/25/63 at Old Capitol. Thereafter generally present thru 3/22/65 final roll. Reported by Richmond as deserter 3/1/65. Paroled 5/7/65 at Winchester. d. 10/29/21, bur. Marshall Cem. Wid. Nannie J., m. 1859.

JEFFRIES, GEORGE H.: Name cancelled on 7-8/63 roll of Co. H. No further record. George A. Jeffries, age 64, Co. H, discharged, shown on ca. 1898 Fauquier Co. veterans census.

JEFFRIES, WILLIAM ROUZIE: enl. 4/24/61 in Co. H as Cpl. Saddler. Confined for AWOL and place as Cpl. filled by "Rust" on 6/30/61 roll. detailed as artisan in QM Dept. 11/22/61 thru 11-12/63 rolls. Absent sick on 7-10/64 rolls. Absent sick since 3/1 on 3/22/65 final roll. Paroled 4/22/65 at Winchester, age 39, resid. Fauquier Co.

JENKINS, BANKS: enl. 3/1/62 in Co. B. AWOL from 5/24 and 10/15/62 on rolls. In Culpeper hosp. with rubeola 10/1-10/30/62. Deserter on 11-12/62 roll. POW 4/22/64 in Culpeper Co. U.S. records state "left his regiment more than a year ago and don't want to go back." Took the oath 6/20/65 at Ft. Delaware, resid. Culpeper Co., signs by mark. Pensioned in Shenandoah Co. d. 8/6/01, bur. Massanutten Cem., Woodstock. Wid. Martha A., m. 1859.

JENKINS, EDWARD: b. 1836 in Berryville. Conscript enl. 9/20/62 in Co. A. AWOL on 12/5/62 roll. In Richmond hosp. with scabies 11/18/63-1/13/64. POW 2/1/65 in Clarke Co. Took the oath 6/30/62 at Elmira, resid. Charles Town, (W.) Va. Resid. Mt. Savage, Md., postwar. d. 1/19/02 at Johns Hopkins Hosp., Baltimore.

JETT, WILLIAM ARMISTEAD LANE: b. in Rappahannock Co. enl. 4/22/61 in Co. B. Farmer. Hip injured in fall from horse 9/15 and sent home. Discharged 1/9/62 for spinal and pelvic lesion from fall, occupation clerk. Present again on 7-8/64 roll thru final 3/21/65 roll. Paroled 5/17/65 at Winchester. m. Alice Hopper. Episcopal rector 30 years in Murray Hill, N.J. d. 5/24/31, bur. Hollywood Cem., Richmond. Postwar roster has wded. at Spotsylvania.

JOHNS, ARTHUR S.: On postwar "original list" of Co. F.

JOHNSON, EDWIN: enl. 8/7/61 in Co. K. Present on rolls for 7-8/61 thru 6/30/62. Not on reliable postwar rosters and probably identical to Lawson E. Johnson.

JOHNSON, GEORGE A.: enl. 4/22/61 in Co. B, age 29. Plasterer. Absent sick since 1/26 on 1-2/62 roll. Wded. 5/23/62. Horse KIA 6/29/64 in Dinwiddie Co. AWOL on 9-10/64 roll and on final 3/21/65 roll since 3/1/65. Postwar roster says deserted, reportedly alive 5/07. Bur. Elk View Cem., Clarksburg, W.Va. Signature appears to be "Johnston," but all other sources have Johnson.

JOHNSON, HENRY CLAY: enl. 3/1/63 in Co. B. Absent on scout under Lt. Duncan on 11-12/63 roll. AWOL on 9-10/64 roll and on final 3/21/65 roll since 3/1/65. 5/07 roster says age 30 on enlistment. Still alive 6/28/10. Probably identical to H. C. Johnson, 7/26/35-4/20/18, búr. Sperryville Cem.

JOHNSON, ISAAC W.: Reportedly in Co. C in 1861.

JOHNSON, JAMES A.: enl. 7/18/61 in Co. K. On sick leave at home since 1/10 on 1-2/62 roll. Detailed to horse hosp. with disabled horses on 7-8/63 roll. Wded. 9/19/64 near Luray. AWOL on final 1-2/65 roll. Signs by mark. Paroled 4/24/65 at Edwards Ferry, Md.

JOHNSON, JAMES DALLAS: enl. 3/1/64 in Co. B. In Richmond and Farmville hosps. 5/24-7/27/64 with debility from attacks of remittent fever and chronic diarrhea, then 60 days furlough. AWOL since 12/1/64 on 3/21/65 final roll. Reported by Richmond as deserter 2/28/65. Reportedly alive 5/07, age 18 on enlistment.

JOHNSON, JAMES MADISON: b. 1841. enl. 3/15/62 in Co. I. AWOL on 11-12/62 roll and shown as tried for it on next roll, sentence not read. Wded. 7/3/63 in leg at Fairfield, Pa. In Richmond hosps. with typhoid fever 5/3-7/1/64, then 30 days furlough. On horse detail on 9-10/64 roll. Present on final 3/20/65 roll. Claimed loss of hearing from fever. d. 2/22/27, bur. Zoar Baptist Church Cem., Orange Co.

JOHNSON, JOHN W.: b. in Orange Co. enl. 10/15/64 in Co. I. Present thru final 3/20/65 roll. Farmer, resid. Locust Grove, Orange Co., age 57 on 9/1/02.

JOHNSON, JOHN MORGAN: b. 11/21/47 in Alexandria. enl. 9/20/64 in Co. D. AWOL on final 3/22/65 roll. Paroled 5/2/65 at Harrisonburg, resid. Alexandria. Lawyer at Alexandria postwar, m. Constance C. Beach 1887. Alive in Alexandria 1893. Also claimed service in 13th N.C. Inf.

JOHNSON, J. W.: enl. 6/25/61 in Co. C. Sick in hosp. since 10/20 on 9-10/61 roll. AWOL 5/28 on 9-10/62 roll.

JOHNSON, LAWSON E.: b. 12/3/41 in Fairfax Co. enl. 10/1/62 in Co. K. In Charlottesville hosp. with bronchitis 9/14-10/13/63. Othewise shown as present until found guilty of AWOL by courtmartial, which led to a public reprimand on dress parade. AWOL sick since 9/15 on 9-10/64 roll and AWOL on final 1-2/65 roll. Paroled 4/26/65 at Edwards Ferry, Md. Farmer at Vienna postwar. d. 12/3/25, bur, Flint Hill Cem., Oakton. Probably identical to Edwin Johnson.

JOHNSON, MIDDLETON MARIAN: b. 10/18/43 in Rappahannock Co. enl. 3/1/62 in Co. B. Absent with leave on 11-12/63 roll, but AWOL on 9-10/64 roll and AWOL since 3/1/65 on final 3/21/65 roll. Resid. a few years in Kansas postwar, later in Va. House of Delegates. m. Eliza McKay Compton 1865. d. 3/9/13, bur. Prospect Hill Cem., Front Royal.

JOHNSON, WILLIAM: b. in Fairfax Co. Conscript enl. 3/26/63 in Co. K. Present until AWOL sick since 10/29 on 9-10/64 roll and AWOL on final 1-2/65 roll. Paroled 4/25/65 at Edwards Ferry. Day laborer, resid. Sterling, age 65, on 9/24/02.

JOHNSON, W. R.: Shown on a regimental return for 11/62 as in Co. C, "deserted, over 40 years." No further record.

JOHNSTON, JAMES W.: enl. 7/24/61 in Co. A as Sgt. AWOL sick near Middleburg from 10/17/61 thru 1-2/62 roll, shown as Pvt. Absent sick on 5-6/62 roll. No further record. Confederate records spell the name Johnson. Reportedly alive in 1917.

JOHNSTON, SAMUEL R.: enl. 4/20/61 in Co. F as Lt. Detached by Gen. Jeb Stuart for outside service on 1-2/62 roll. Otherwise present until dropped 4/20/62 at reorganization.

JONES, CHARLES SAMUEL: b. 3/8/35 in Culpeper Co. enl. 4/30/62 in Co. H. Courier at Madison C.H. on 5-6/62 roll. Detailed at horse hosp. on 7-8/63 roll. Otherwise numerous absences for sickness, but present on final 3/22/65 roll. Paroled 4/22/65 at Winchester. d. 7/2 (or 6/21)/91, bur. Culpeper City Cem. Also in 13th Va. Inf.

JONES, EDWARD THOMPSON: Grad. U.Va. in law. enl. 4/22/61 in Co. B as Cpl., age 29. Lawyer. To Sgt. 7/26/61. To regimental QM Sgt. 1/1/62. Absent, wded. in hand on 11-12/62 roll. Sick in Lynchburg hosp. on 1-2/63 roll. Otherwise present thru 9-10/64 roll. Paroled 4/9/65 at Appomattox with QM Dept. of Cavalry Corps. In Va. legislature pre-war. Farmer in Rappahannock Co. postwar. Alive in 1913.

JONES, EDWARD T., JR.: enl. 5/17/61 in (2d) Co. E. Present thru 5-6/62 roll. No further record. Resid. Chatham, age 59, suffering from exposure in war on 5/11/00. d. 1903, bur. Chatham Cem.

JONES, EDWARD THOMAS, SR.: b. 8/18/26 at "Ellerslie" in Pittsylvania Co. enl. 5/27/61 in (2d) Co. E as Cpl. To Sgt. on 2/16/62 roll. d. 6/4/62 at home of sickness, when shown as Pvt., bur. Sheva Church of Christ, Rt. 685 & Rt. 649, Pittsylvania Co., m. Frances Henry 1852.

JONES, GEORGE: Shown in Federal records as in Co. G, POW 9/3/63 at Rappahannock River. Took the oath 9/26/63 at Old Capitol Prison, "deserter released & sent to Philadelphia, Pa." Resid. Rochester, N.Y. No Confederate records.

JONES, J. HENRY: enl. 5/15/62 in Co. C. Apparently the Pvt. Jones shown on 11/62 return as Commissary Sgt. in the company. Deserted 1/15/63.

JONES, JAMES S. T.: b. in Pittsylvania Co. enl. 5/27/61 in (2d) Co. E. Age 27 on 2/16/62 roll. Absent on sick leave on 5-6/62 roll. Sick with diarrhea in Danville 8/24-10/24/62 and 12/18/62-3/7/63. KIA 5/11/64 at Yellow Tavern. Brother of John Thomas Jones.

JONES, JOHN M. E.: b. in Pittsylvania Co. enl. 10/11/63 in (2d) Co. E. POW 5/11/64 at Yellow Tavern. Exchanged ca. 9/18/64 from Pt. Lookout. Died as paroled prisoner of acute dysentery at Receiving and Wayside Hosp. (General Hosp. No. 9), Richmond, 9/24/64, bur. Oakwood Cem., Richmond.

JONES, JOHN T.: enl. 4/24/61 in Co. H. Farmer. On leave of absence since 6/26 on 6/30/61 roll. Went home sick with pulmonary disease 9/19/61. No further record.

JONES, JOHN THOMAS: b. 7/24/36 in Danville. Att. Pineville Academy. enl. 5/27/61 in (2d) Co. E. Absent guarding baggage at Gordonsville on 11-12/62 roll. Sick in Pittsylvania Co. on 7-10/64 rolls. Discharged, elected magistrate on final 3/4/65 roll. Brother of James S. T. m. Mary A. Lanier. d. near Chestnut Level 7/30/66, bur. family cem.

JONES, LUTHER M.: enl. 5/4/61 in Co. I, age 36. On detached service at Culpeper hosp. on ca. 6/19/61 roll. Shown as AWOL from 5-6/62 roll. Dropped from payroll and name sent to enrolling officer of Orange Co. on 7-8/63 roll. Postwar rosters say discharged in 1862.

JONES, MONTGOMERY A.: enl. 5/4/61 in Co. I, age 29. Discharged by furnishing James M. Gardner as substitute 6/23/62.

JONES, ROBERT: enl. 5/23/62 in Co. D. Shown as absent sick from 7/20/62 until POW 5/9/63 at Newtown. "Braxton (a colored man) a witness, says Jones is notorious rascal Bushwacker & c." Held for a time as a "political prisoner of war." Paroled 9/28/64 at Ft. Delaware. In Richmond hosp. 11/20-11/21/64. Shown as POW on final 3/22/65 roll. Resid. Frederick Co.

JONES, ROBERT: enl. 6/16/61 in Co. K. Absent on sick furlough from 2/25/62, and thereafter shown as AWOL thru 1-2/63 roll. No further record.

JONES, THOMAS: Federal records show a man of this name in Co. K, POW 9/28/64 at "Wadesboro" (presumably meaning Waynesboro), and sent to Pt. Lookout 10/12/64. No Confederate records.

JONES, WILLIAM A.: enl. 4/1/62 in (2d) Co. E. Reported missing, but POW 6/15 (or 22)/62 at Port Republic. Paroled at Winchester in 6/62, age 17, and exchanged from Ft. Delaware 8/5/62. Sick in Pittsylvania Co. on 1-2/63 roll, but present on 7-8/63 roll. Transferred to Co. I, 53d Va. Inf., d. 3/27/65 at Elmira of diarrhea and bur. there.

JONES, WILLIAM R.: enl. 6/16/61 in Co. K. Sick one month with typhoid fever on 7-8/61 roll. Absent by permission of Gen. Lee 10/1/62 on 12/12/62 roll. AWOL from 12/1/62 until shown as deserted on 9-10/63 roll. Later in 35th Bn. Va. Cav. Reportedly living in Oregon in 1907.

JORDAN, ROBERT: b. 1830. enl. 10/15/63 in Co. B. Absent, detailed to get clothing 12/5/63 on 11-12/63 roll. Reported by Richmond as deserter 2/28/65 but shown as present on rolls thru final 3/21/65 roll. Paroled 5/2/65 at Winchester, age given as 44, resid. near Flint Hill. d. 1909 at Flint Hill.

JUDD, JACOB: enl. 9/15/62 in Co. B. "Deserted" on 11/62 return and in confinement on 11-12/62 roll. On extra duty as teamster in QM Dept. 2/10/63 thru 11-12/63 roll. In Petersburg and Richmond hosps. with gunshot wd. and diarrhea 6/25-8/26/64, then 50 days furlough. d. of disease 2/24/65. Resid. Rappahannock Co. Postwar roster says age 30 on enlistment.

JUSTIS, JAMES L.: enl. 4/22/61 in Co. B as Sgt., age 30. Wheelwright. On extra duty in QM Dept. as wagonmaster and forage master 1/10/62 thru 3/21/65 final roll. To Pvt. on 5-6/62 roll. Paroled 4/9/65 at Appomattox with men detailed and hired in QM Dept. of Cavalry Corps. Resid. Amissville 4/26/00 claiming disability from "affliction of hardship of war ever since 1867." Reportedly d. before 5/07.

KAGEY, JACOB P.: b. 4/26/36. Conscript assigned 4/25/64 to Co. C (the enlistment date of 2/10/64 on one muster roll appears to be incorrect). Previously enlisted 10/22/62 as Cpl. in Guards and Scouts, Rockingham Co. AWOL on 7-8/64 roll, and deserted 8/20/64 on 9-10/64 roll. d. 4/10/13, bur. Massanutten Cross Keys Cem.

KAYLOR, SAMUEL HENRY: b. 3/20/43. enl. 5/28/61 in Co. C. Sick in hosp. since 9/4 on 9-10/61 roll. Discharged 11/26/61 with otalgia and otirrhea. m. Mary (Mollie) Rebecca Baker 1876. d. 11/16/13, bur. Mt. Horeb Presb. Church Cem., Augusta Co.

KEARFOOT, JAMES W.: On postwar roster of Co. D.

KEARNS, MARSHALL: b. ca. 1825 in Fauquier Co. enl. 4/24/61 in Co. H. Stonemason. AWOL thru Sept. and Oct. on 9-10/61 roll, but present on 11-12/61 roll. Went home on sick leave with surgeon's certificate 2/8/62. No further record. m. Mary Cathy Gill 1841. Also spelled Kearnes, Kerns, Kernes.

KEATTS, JAMES MADISON: enl. 8/19/61 in Co. G, age 33. Absent on sick furlough over 30 days on 5-6/62 roll. Sick in Staunton hospital on 11-12/62 roll. Wded. 6/9/63 at Brandy Station. In Richmond and Danville hosps., then on furlough until return 8/19/63. Reported as deserter 8/23, but present on 11-12/63 roll thru 3/22/65 final roll. Paroled sometime after with unattached men cut off from their commands, no place shown. d. 1876, bur. Chatham Cem.

KEATTS, WILLIAM C.: enl. 5/27/61 in (2d) Co. E. Age 26 on 2/16/62. Detailed 4/12/62. In Danville with chronic diarrhea 10/18/62-2/18/63, shown as deserted on latter date. Present on 7-8/63 roll. Transferred 8/29/63 to Co. I, 53d Va. Inf.

KEELER, JOHN MILTON: b. in Clarke Co. enl. 8/1/63 in Co. D. Present on all rolls thru 3/22/65 final roll. Resid. Millwood, age 60, on 10/3/04. Wheelwright and gardener postwar. d. 2/11/26.

KEEN, JOHN: enl. 7/24/61 in Co. A. Absent with sick leave since 12/23 on 11-12/61 roll. KIA 5/23/62 at Front Royal, bur. Mountain Ebenezer Church Cem., Clarke Co., near Bluemont.

KEERAN, ROBERT H. G.: enl. 2/20/63 in Co. C. To Richmond hosp. 11/9/63 with stab wd., furloughed 12/26/63 40 days. Absent sick on 11-12/64 roll. Received medical certificate of unfitness and on duty in provost marshal's office, Harrisonburg, 9/5/64 and 60 days preceding. Present on 9-10/64 roll, but AWOL on final ca. 3/30/65 roll.

KEERAN, THOMAS J. R.: enl. 5/28/61 in Co. C. Farmer. Shown as co. QM Sgt. on 10/61 return. Paid as teamster for 3/23-4/30/62. Got Lewis Harden as substitute. Enl. 4/1/64 in Co. B, 41st Bn. Va. Cav.

KEMP, JOSEPH D.: Conscript enl. 7/1/64 in Co. C. Absent, detailed at brigade HQ as teamster on 7-8/64 and final ca. 3/30/65 rolls. Present on 9-10/64 roll. Paroled 5/1/65 at Staunton, age 20.

KEMPER, CHARLES MARK: enl. 5/28/61 in Co. C. To Lt. 7/1/61. To Capt. on 9-10/62 roll. Various absences for sickness and wds. Wded. 9/22/62 at Paris. Horse KIA 10/10/63 at Brandy Station. Wded. 8/21/64. Absent wded. on final ca. 3/30/65 roll. Postwar roster says twice wded. and POW, but no U.S. records on capture. Signs testimonial for J. E. Burkett 8/21/12 in Rockingham Co. d. Mecham's River, Albemarle Co., 4/28/19, bur. White Hall, Albemarle Co.

KEMPER, FONTAINE LLEWELLYN: enl. 3/1/65 in Co. C. Present on final ca. 3/30/65 roll. Paroled 4/30/65 at Staunton, age 18.

KENDALL, BRAXTON: enl. 8/1/63 in Co. B. In Richmond hosp. with catarrh 4/20-6/11/64. AWOL on 7-8/64 roll. Deserted 9/19/64 on 9-10/64 roll. Reportedly age 18 on enl. and alive in 5/07. Some sources have middle initial as "J" or "C".

KENDALL, CHARLES S.: enl. 3/19/61 in Co. D. AWOL on 5-6/62 roll. Present as teamster in regiment on 9-12/62 rolls, but shown on returns as deserter 11/26/62, returned 12/3/62 and excused by Capt. 3 day horse furlough from 8/31/63. Deserted to the enemy ca. 9/6/63.

KENDALL, SUWARROW: enl. 3/1/62 in Co. B. Horse KIA and Kendall MWIA 5/23/62 near Front Royal. d. 5/26/62. Postwar roster says age 18 on enl. Father Enoch W.

KENNARD, GEORGE: Paroled 5/7/65 at Winchester as in Co. F, signs by mark, age 35, resid. Fauquier Co. No other record. Doubtless identical to George Canard. A George Canard, no dates, is bur. Marshall Cem.

KENNEDY, DANIEL L.: b. in Tattnall Co., Ga. enl. 9/17/61 in (1st) Co. E, age 22. Physician. Appointed hosp. steward 11/27/61. In Danville hosp. 12/29/61, sent to Front Royal. To Lt., Co. G, 47th Ga. Inf. 8/10/62. Paroled as Capt., Co. H, 1st Ga. Regulars at Greensboro, N.C., 5/1/65. Resid. Tattnall Co., Ga.

KENNERLY, JOSEPH McKENDREE: b. 3/23/26 at Greenway Court, Clarke Co. Att. Dickinson College, Pa. enl. 4/18/61 in Co. D as Cpl. Farmer. To Lt. 4/20/62. Always present until wded. 6/29/64 in left leg at Reams Station, thereafter absent wded. thru final 3/22/65 roll. WIA 10/28/64. To Capt. on 7-8/64 roll. Paroled 4/19/65 at Winchester. Postwar source says wded. twice in same battle. In constitutional convention 1867-68. d. 7/6/93 at Greenway Court.

KERFOOT, HENRY DODGE: b. 1/10/46 in Clarke Co. enl. 7/23/62 in Co. D. Previously in 2d Va. Inf. and 17th Bn. Va. Cav. Almost always present thru final 3/22/65 roll. Wded. in right forearm and sent to Charlottesville hosp. 5/26-6/20/64. Paroled 4/15/65 at Lynchburg. Postwar source says wded. at Milford and twice at Five Forks. Grad. U.Va. 1868. M.D. at Bellevue College and Hosp., N.Y., then in Fauquier and Clarke Cos. m. Minnie Hunton Moss 1874. d. 4/9/03, bur. Green Hill Cem., Berryville.

KERFOOT, JAMES FRANKLIN: b. 9/2/32. enl. 6/16/62 in Co. B. Transferred from 2d Va. Inf. Farmer. POW 2/10/63 at Upperville, exchanged 3/16/63 from Old Capitol Prison. Detailed to get clothing 12/5 on 11-12/63 roll. Detailed as scout for Gen. W. W. Wickham on 9-10/64 roll and for Gen L. L. Lomax on 3/21/65 final roll. Paroled 4/22/65 at Winchester, resid. Clarke Co. d. 1/20/15, bur. Berryville Baptist Church Cem.

KERFOOT, JOHN DAVID: b. 1835 in Clarke Co. Grad. U.Va. enl. 8/24/61 in Co. D. Lawyer at Dallas, Texas, from 1855. AWOL 11/9 on 11/61 return, forfeit 1 month's pay on 11-12/61 roll. Otherwise present on all rolls until final 3/22/65 roll, when AWOL. Paroled 4/21/65 at Winchester. Judge, justice of peace, and mayor of Dallas postwar. d. 1903, bur. Old Oak Cliff Cem., Dallas, Texas.

KERFOOT, JUDSON G.: b. 6/12/34. enl. 6/1/62 in Co. B. Transferred from 2d Va. Inf. Detailed as courier for Gen. W. E. Jones on 11/62-2/63 rolls. Absent detailed on 11-12/63 roll. In Richmond hosp. with neuralgia 5/27-6/6/64, transferred to Lynchburg. Absent wded. on 9-10/64 roll. AWOL since 12/1 on final 3/21/65 roll. Paroled 4/19/65 at Winchester, resid. White Post. d. 12/22/07, bur. Old Bethel Church Cem., end of Rt. 625, Clarke Co.

KERFOOT, WILLIAM F.: enl. 12/1/62 in Co. B. Present on 11-12/62 roll. Discharged by order of Gen. W. E. Jones, being improperly attached to co. on 1-2/63 roll.

KERFOOT, WILLIAM TURNER: b. at "Granville," in Clarke Co. Att. Columbian College, Washington, D.C. enl. 12/1/62 in Co. B. Farmer. Previously in 7th Va. Cav. Sabre wd. in head and finger cut off in Pa. campaign, 7/63. Detailed to hosp. duty 1/22/64 and detailed on 11/63-10/64 rolls. In Charlottesville hosp. with old wd. 1/15-1/30/64, ca. 2/5/64, and 7/6-7/7/64, then 60 day furlough. Retired to Invalid Corps 1/4/65 at Charlottesville. Farmer, school trustee, road overseer, in House of Delegates postwar. m. Ella Moshier Chapin 1869, d. 6/7/36 at Front Royal, age 93, bur. Prospect Hill Cem.

KETTLE, JAMES M.: b. 3/12/39. enl. 10/5/62 in Co. K. Farmer. Present wded. slightly at Fairfield, Pa., 7/3/63. In Richmond hosp. 5/9-6/10/64 with gunshot wd. of right hip. POW 9/24/64 at Luray. Paroled at Pt. Lookout 3/7/65. Paroled 4/28/65 at Edwards Ferry, Md. d. 4/20/09, bur. Leesburg Union Cem.

KEYS, JOHN: Shown on postwar rosters as a member of Co. A, KIA at Cedarville 5/23/62. No official record.

KEYS, LANDON H.: enl. 9/9/62 in Co. A. On leave to get clothing on 10/62 return. Otherwise present until transferred 9/30/63 to Co. C, 35th Bn. Va. Cav. Known as "Bud."

KEYSTER, JOHN W.: enl. 5/28/61 in Co. C. AWOL since 7/23 on 10/61 return. Present on 11-12/62 roll, and shown as teamster on 12/62 return. Absent sick at Harrisonburg hosp. since 2/16/63 on 1-2/63 roll. AWOL 8/25/63 on 7-8/63 roll and deserter on 11-12/63 roll.

KIDWELL, CHARLES W.: enl. 8/16/64 in Co. F. Absent sick since 10/25 on 9-10/64 roll. Present on final 2/24/65 roll.

KIDWELL, GEORGE R.: enl. 3/25/64 in Co. K. POW 9/24/64 at Luray. Paroled 3/17/65 at Pt. Lookout. Paroled 4/27/65 at Edwards Ferry, Md. In some Federal records as Pike or P. M. Kidwell.

KIGER, JAMES: enl. 10/17/61 in Co. D. Horse KIA 6/9/63 near Brandy Station. Present until 7-8/64 roll, when marked AWOL. 9-10/64 roll has "deserted to the enemy" 9/1/64. Probably identical to James M. Kiger, arrested by Federals 8/20/64 at Berryville, and who took the oath 11/29/64 at Ft. McHenry.

KIMBALL, CHARLES E.: enl. 5/1/61 in Co. D. To Sgt. Maj. on 9-10/62 roll. Held "for examination" by Federals 10/14/63, age 22. Recommended for adjutant 11/25/63 by Col. J. Harrison: "Sgt. Kimball . . . is well qualified for the position, and familiar with the duties of the office, which he has performed since the vacancy in the regt." To Lt. and adjutant 1/18/64, to rank from 10/1/63. Reported present with staff officers with Lomax's Old Brigade 10/29/64.

KING, GEORGE: enl. 4/20/61 in Co. F. Present until 5-6/62 roll, when absent sick in Waynesboro on furlough. Discharged 7/26/62.

KING, WILLIAM H.: enl. 5/1/61 in Co. F. Present consistently until wded. 10/11/63 at Morton's Ford. To Cpl. on 7-8/64 roll, present, and so shown on 9-10/64 roll. Absent on horse detail on final 2/24/65 roll. "Wounded November in advance on Manassas" on postwar roster.

KINSEY, GEORGE M.: enl. 4/22/61 in Co. B, age 22. Farmer. Absent on furlough on 1-2/62 roll. Otherwise present on all rolls thru 1-2/63 roll, then no further record until U.S. records show him POW 2/3/65 in Loudoun Co. Held as "guerilla, not to be exchanged" until paroled 5/1/65 at Ft. McHenry, Md., signing by mark. Postwar roster says deserted.

KIRBY, F. ASBURY: enl. 3/8/62 in Co. K. Present until transferred 11/11/62 to (2d) Co. F, 5th Va. Cav. Took the oath 6/17/65 at Alexandria as Sgt., Co. I, 11th Va. Cav., resid. Fairfax Co.

KIRBY, GEORGE WILLIAM: b. in Fauquier Co. enl. 4/24/61 in Co. H. Farmer. Sent home sick 10/22/61. AWOL since 2/12/62 on 1-2/62 roll. To Cpl. on 5-6/62 roll. Otherwise usually present thru final 3/22/65 roll. Pleaded guilty to AWOL at 1/27/64 courtmartial and sentenced to reprimand at dress parade. Paroled 4/20/65 at New Market, age 24. Farmer, resid. Forestville, Shenandoah Co., postwar, claiming rheumatism in service. d. 11/15/11, wid. Delilah, m. 1901.

KIRBY, JAMES R.: b. in Fauquier Co. enl. 4/24/61 in Co. H. Farmer. Sick at home since 5/20 on 6/30/61 roll. Pronounced unfit and sent home by surgeon 8/14/61. Later in Co. C, Mosby's 43d Bn. Va. Cav. Manual laborer, resid. Rectortown 6/2/02, age 68, claiming bayonet stroke through right shoulder.

KIRBY, ROBERT: b. in Georgetown, D.C. Resid. Fairfax Co. since ca. 1825. enl. 4/20/61 in Co. F. To Cpl. on 5-6/62 roll. Discharged 6/23/62 on expiration of enlistment. Farmer resid. near Fredericksburg immediately after discharge. Signed statement for Federals at Alexandria 4/19/65.

KIRK, JAMES W. R.: b. in St. Mary's Co., Md. enl. 8/12/62 in (2d) Co. E, age 15. Discharged 12/20/62, "by reason of being too young, and having enlisted without his parents' knowledge, who now demand him to send to school." May be the man of this name enl. 2/20/64 in (2d) Co. B, 13th Va. Inf.

KIRKPATRICK, MARCELLUS: b. 3/20/42 in Fauquier Co. enl. 3/14/62 in Co. H. Absent sick since 12/24 on 11-12/62 roll. AWOL since 8/25/63 on 7-8/63 roll, and since 9/1/63 on 11-12/63 roll. Wded. 9/25/64 ("his leg had to be dressed throughout his life"). Present on 3/22/65 final roll. Farmer, resid. Opal postwar, claiming shot by pistol in thigh in charge at Brandy Station 6/9/63. d. 1929, bur. Marshall Cem. m. Nancy Ann Wines 1867.

KITCHEN, GEORGE W.: enl. 8/14/61 in Co. D. AWOL since 9/21 on 11-12/61 roll. Present, declined to re-enlist on 5-6/62 roll. Present on 9-10/62 roll. Returns show him transferred to 17th Va. Cav., but no record in that unit found. Briefly a scout for Union Gen. R. H. Milroy. Tried by U.S. military commission at Winchester as a spy and found not guilty 3/18/63. Confined at Ft. McHenry, Md., without charge 11/10/64, released 11/12/64. Told Federals he was a resident of Iowa and his family was there. Brother of John N.

KITCHEN, JOHN NEWTON: b. 11/25/38 in Berkeley Co. enl. 4/25/61 in Co. D. POW 3/23/62 in Winchester while AWOL. Exchanged 8/5/62 from Ft. Delaware, but AWOL on 9-10/62 roll. Present on rolls for 1/62-10/65. AWOL on final 3/22/65 roll. Paroled 4/20/65 at Winchester, age 27, resid. White Post. m. 1) Miss Gaunt, 2) Malinda (Minnie) C., 1866. d. 11/15/10 near Winchester, bur. Mt. Hebron Cem. Brother of George W.

KLEIN, JOHN ALEXANDER: enl. 7/24/61 in Co. A. On extra duty as hosp. steward since 10/17 on 9-10/61 roll. To Asst. Surgeon in regiment 11/16/61. Assigned to temporary duty with 2d Va. Cav. 12/13/61. Transferred to Baltimore Light Artillery 4/23/62. Physician postwar. d. 12/1/12 in 74th year, bur. Goose Creek Burying Ground, Lincoln.

KNAPP, A. CHAMPION: enl. 9/17/61 in (1st) Co. E, age 20. Resid. Savannah, Ga. Wded. at Upperville 6/24/63. Paroled as Sgt. at Greensboro, N.C., 5/1/65.

KNELLER, JACOB S.: enl. 9/25/62 in Co. D. Horse KIA 10/11/63 at Brandy Station. Fifteen days leave from 12/21/63. In Richmond hosp. 6/20-6/21/64. Otherwise present until AWOL on 9-10/64 roll and final 3/22/65 roll.

KNELLER, LEWIS C.: enl. 4/25/61 in Co. D. AWOL since 12/20 on 11-12/61 roll. To Pvt. on 7-8/64 roll. In Richmond hosp. with acute diarrhea 7/30-8/18/64. Otherwise present thru 3/22/65 final roll. Transferred to Thompson's Battery Horse Art. 3/24/65 "being hopelessly dismounted."

KNIGHT, DANIEL McC.: enl. 7/22/63 in Co. A. In Charlottesville hosp. with acute diarrhea 2/11/64. Absent with leave on 9-10/64 roll. AWOL since 1/23/65 on final 3/27/65 roll. Postwar records show him as resid. Clarke Co. May be identical to Daniel Knight, d. 1/27/17, bur. Green Hill Cem., Berryville.

KNIGHT, HENRY: b. in Clarke Co. enl. 10/1/62 in Co. F. Farmer. POW 2/19/64 in Clarke Co., age 30. Took the oath 6/20/65 at Ft. Delaware. Farm worker, resid. White Post 3/28/10, claiming hernia from riding horseback in army. d. 7/7/16.

KNIGHT, JOSEPH: enl. 10/30/62 in Co. F. Present until POW ca. 8/14/64 at White Post (or Front Royal). Took the oath at Elmira 6/21/65, resid. Winchester. Farmer postwar, d. 10/9/09 at Carper's Valley, Frederick Co., bur. Macedonia Methodist Church Cem., age 70 years and 9 months.

KRAMER, WILLIAM P.: enl. 6/21/61 in Co. D. Reported as deserting near Fairfax C.H. 10/6/61. Capt. H. M. Nelson wrote a comic reward notice for his apprehension 2/12/62. Kramer wrote Secretary of War J. A. Seddon from Bartow Co., Ga., ca. 2/63 that he was unaware he had been enlisted, and asking to be relieved of charges "upon the condition that I enter the Southern army and demean myself properly." He wrote that he was raised in Baltimore, and was vouched for by Cong. Augustus R. Wright. May be the man of this name in 2d (Duke's) Ky. Cav.

KUBE, LEWIS: enl. 5/4/61 in Co. I, age 21. Twenty days sick furlough from 12/28/61. Absent sick on 11/62-2/63 rolls. In Orange hosp. with typhoid fever 1/29-2/10/62. Wded. 10/11/63 at Brandy Station. Absent sick from 7/64 thru 3/20/65 final roll. d. 2/7/92, bur. family cem. near Locust Grove.

KYGER, GEORGE W.: enl. 5/25/63 in Co. C. POW 6/30/64. Inexplicably reported exchanged 11/15/64 at Venus Pt., Savannah River, "came in place of" Thomas Nevitt, Co. F. Also reported exchanged from Elmira 10/29/64. Present on 3/30/65 final roll.

KYLE, WILLIAM P.: enl. 5/28/61 in Co. C. Present, two pistols lost on 9-10/61 roll. Discharged 11/26/61 for fracture and dislocation of the ankle. d. Taylor's Springs, Rockingham Co., 12/19/75, age about 60.

LADD, ALFRED: enl. 9/17/61 in (1st) Co. E. Resid. Florida. Deserted to Federals while a courier 1/5/62 at picket post near Sangster's Crossroads.

LAKE, BLADEN D.: enl. 4/19/62 in Co. H as Sgt. Present on 6/30/62 roll. Unofficial source says d. of typhoid fever in 1863. The 1860 census for Fauquier Co. has farmer, age 21.

LAKE, MARSHALL: This name appears on a muster roll of Co. H for 9-10/61, presence or absence not stated. No other record in the regiment. Gen. William Smith described him on 5/28/63 as "Highly respectable in character — comfortable in fortune — cultivating his own land and managing his own affairs... An original secessionist." Appointed Capt. and Assistant QM 3/16/64, but vacated by virtue of non-confirmation. Paroled 4/22/65 at Winchester as Pvt. in commissary dept., age 39, resid. Fauquier Co.

LAKE, THOMAS H.: enl. 9/17/61 in (1st) Co. E. To Sgt. on 11/1/61 roll. Resid. Savannah, Ga. On Roll of Honor 12/10/64 for Battle of Upperville. Paroled 5/1/65 at Greensboro, N.C.

LANCASTER, JOSEPH O.: enl. 11/8/61 in Co. G. Clerk. To Sgt. on 5-6/62 roll. Present on all rolls until wded. in spine 5/7/64. d. 5/18/64 at Chimborazo Hosp. No. 2, Richmond, of disease, age 32.

LANCASTER, RICHARD: enl. 5/4/61 in Co. I, age 23. AWOL 8/31/63 on 7-8/63 roll. Absent sick at hosp. since 11/20/63 on 11-12/63 roll, and so absent thru 9-10/64 roll. Reported by Richmond as deserter 3/1/65, but present on 3/20/65 final roll. Resid. Orange Co. on 5/23/00.

LANDSTREET, ARISTIDES C.: b. 8/9/20. Moved from Md. to Fairfax Co. 9/60. enl. 4/20/61 in Co. F. POW 7/13/61 on scout near Falls Church. Paroled 12/61 from Old Capitol Prison. POW 1/15/62 at his home in Fairfax Co. Paroled from Old Capitol 3/24/62. POW 9/23-9/27/62, declared paroled 11/10/62. Clerk in 2d Auditor's Office, C.S. Treasury Dept. Paroled 6/13/65 at Baltimore as in 3d Va. Inf. Local Defense. m. Mary Margaret Reese. Resid. Fairfax Co. postwar. d. 3/14/10, bur. Pohick Church. Landstreet wrote a beautiful hand. He had brothers in both armies.

LANGLEY, JOHN WAYNE: enl. 9/17/61 in (1st) Co. E. Resid. McIntosh Co., Ga. POW 6/2/64 at Samaria Church. Drowned in James River trying to escape from Ft. Powhatan while held a prisoner.

LANIER, JOHN EDWARD: b. 1837. enl. 5/27/61 in (2d) Co. E. Acted as Sgt. Maj. on 7-8/61 roll. On horse leave on 11-12/62 roll. In Richmond and Danville hosps. with gunshot wd. 6/16-8/7/63. To Sgt. on 9-10/64 roll. Present on 3/4/65 final roll. d. 1894, bur. Chatham Cem.

LANTIN, JOHN: enl. 12/17/62 in Co. G, substitute for A. W. Thompson. Under arrest for desertion on 7-8/63 roll. Transferred to Co. K, "23d Va. Regt." 9/3/63, but no further record found.

LARKIN, J. H.: On a roster of Co. C as published in the *Rockingham Register* 5/31/61.

LARKIN, JOHN W.: enl. 9/10/62 in Co. H. To Cpl. on 11-12/63 roll. Present on all rolls until in Chimborazo Hosp. No. 2, Richmond, with typhoid fever 6/18/64. d. there 6/22/64, bur. Oakwood Cem., Richmond.

LARUE, CHRISTOPHER COLLINS: enl. 4/18/61 in Co. D. To Sgt. on 5-6/62 roll, but Pvt. on next (9-10/62) roll. Wded. 6/9/63 at Brandy Station and 10/9/64. Present as Cpl. on 3/22/65 final roll. Paroled 4/9/65 at Appomattox, resid. Clarke Co. Sent from Lee Camp Soldiers' Home, Richmond, to asylum 6/14/99. d. ca. 1900. m. Maria Osborne LaRue. Postwar rosters show wds. 9/13/63 at Brandy Sta. 12/20/64 at Lacey Springs, and 4/65 at Five Forks.

LARUE, GILBERT: enl. 3/1/63 in Co. D. Austrian rifle lost in action on 11-12/63 roll. Present on final 3/22/65 roll. POW 4/2/65 at Dinwiddie C.H. Took the oath 6/14/65 at Pt. Lookout, resid. Clarke Co. Transportation furnished by Federals at Washington, D.C., to Winchester 6/15/65. On U.S. record as William G., and postwar rosters as Gilbert C.

LARUE, JOHN JAMES: b. 8/26/35 in Clarke Co. enl. 4/19/61 in Co. D. Absent sick with chronic rheumatism since 8/1/61 in Clarke Co. until shown as discharged on 11/62 return. m. Catharine Grantham 1863. Resid. Rippon, W.Va., postwar. d. 8/8/14, bur. Green Hill Cem., Berryville.

LARUE, WILLIAM A. M.: b. 2/2/31. enl. 4/19/61 in Co. D. Sentenced to forfeit 1 month's pay and allowances on 9-10/61 roll. AWOL since 12/25 on 11-12/62 roll and on 5-6/62 roll. On sick furlough on 9-10/62 return, "has not been with the comp. for a year." m. Cornelia Grantham 1863. d. 1895.

LAUCK, JOHN H.: enl. 7/24/61 in Co. A. Absent sick on 9-10/62 roll. Otherwise present thru 11-12/63 roll. Apparently identical to "Jack Lock" on a postwar roster, marked "deserted." cf. J. Howard Locke.

LAUGHLIN, WILLIAM P.: enl. 7/4/62 in Co. D. Absent sick on all rolls until he deserted to enemy 11/1/63 at Gordonsville. Received at Philadelphia, Pa., 12/31/63, age 22. Postwar roster says resid. Jefferson Co., (W.) Va.

LAUK, WILLIAM: enl. 7/24/61 in Co. A. Absent sick with leave 12/9/61 thru 1-2/62 roll. Present on 5-6/62 roll, but absent sick on 9-10/62 roll. Deserted 12/16/62 at camp near Harrisonburg. Postwar roster spells name "Lock." cf. John H. Lauck, J. Howard Locke. One roster has d. since the war.

LAWRENCE, JAMES R.: enl. 4/24/61 in Co. H. Farmer. Sent home sick 9/10/61, returned 10/22/61. d. of typhoid fever 12/30/61 at home in Fauquier Co.

LAWRENCE, JOHN W.: Conscript enl. 10/8/62 in Co. A. Absent guarding Mt. Jackson bridge on 12/62 return, relieved 1/10/63. Gave himself up to Federals at Berlin, Md., 7/24/64, but made POW. On 8/64 list of men desirous of taking the oath at Elmira and release ordered 11/30/64. d. of pneumonia at Elmira 12/3/64, bur. there at Woodlawn Cem.

LAWS, JOEL NEWTON: b. 8/5/42 at Paris, Fauquier Co. enl. 7/24/61 in Co. A. To Cpl. on 5-6/62 roll. Absent sick 9/1/62 thru 1-2/63 roll. To Sgt. 11/1/63. Absent with leave 12/31/63 thru 9-10/64 roll. Present on final ca. 3/27/65 roll. Paroled at Winchester 4/18/65, resid. Fauquier Co. m. Georganna Kerfoot 1869. d. 12/8/09 at Front Royal, bur. Prospect Hill Cem. there. Postwar roster says wded. at Stoney Creek.

LAWS, NORVAL W.: enl. 10/7/62 in Co. A. To Cpl. on 11/62 return, absent sick. POW 6/22/63 at Ashby Gap as Pvt. Paroled 3/3/64 at Pt. Lookout. In Richmond hosp. 5/29-5/30/64. Present with co. on later rolls until absent sick since 3/8 on ca. 3/27/65 final roll. Paroled 4/21/65 at Winchester, age 20, resid. Fauquier Co.

LAYCOCK, SAMUEL: enl. 4/22/61 in Co. K. Sick on 12/61 return. To Sgt. on 6/30/62 roll. Paroled 9/22/62 at Paris, no record as POW. Wded. 9/14/63 near Rapidan Station. In Richmond hosps. with gunshot wd. 9/21-10/27/63. Absent with leave on 11-12/63 roll. Missing in action 10/19/64 near Strasburg and AWOL on final 1-2/65 roll. POW 4/1/65 at Five Forks. Took the oath at Pt. Lookout 6/14/65. d. 1927 near Woodburn. Wid. Susan A., m. 1882, said Laycock was wded. through neck and by sabre cut on head.

LAYTON, SAMUEL L.: b. in Rockingham Co. enl. 4/15/63 in Co. C. POW 5/11/63 in Hanover Co. Inexplicably shown present on final ca. 3/30/65 roll. Took the oath at Elmira 6/19/65. Resid. Huntington, W.Va., and North River, Va., postwar. Age 79 on 8/16/24. d. 5/16/27, Frankford, W.Va., age 84, bur. Mt. Horeb Cem., Augusta Co.

LEE, ALEXANDER HAMILTON: b. 5/29/39. enl. 3/8/62 in Co. K. Present on all rolls until POW 2/16/65 in Fauquier Co. Took the oath at Ft. Warren, Mass., 6/16/65, resid. Loudoun Co. d. 6/19/04, bur. Mt. Zion Old School Baptist Church on Route 50, Loudoun Co.

LEE, JAMES H.: b. in Campbell Co. enl. 3/10/62 in Co. G. Clerk. Ordered discharged for external piles 8/3/62, age 38, but sent to Culpeper hosp. 8/19/63. In Richmond and Danville with hemorrhoids 5/4/64-7/27/64. Sixty days medical furlough from 8/21/64. Later in Danville and Raleigh, N.C., hosps. with his usual problem. Present (amazingly) on final 3/22/65 roll. Paroled 4/22/65.

LEE, LAFAYETTE: enl. 5/4/61 in Co. I, age 36. Detailed as teamster 11/21/61 and so shown until absent sick from 1/20 on 1-2/62 roll. Present on 5-6/62 roll, but thereafter AWOL or deserter thru 1-2/63 roll. No further record. Bur. Massey Cem. south of Mine Run.

LEE, WARFIELD: enl. 5/28/61 in Co. C. Courier to Gen. Jeb Stuart since 10/10 on 10/61 return. POW ca. 9/7/62 near Manassas. Exchanged 9/21/62 at Aiken's Ldg. Sick at Mt. Jackson since 2/21 on 1-2/63 roll. AWOL since 8/23 on 7-8/63 roll. In Charlottesville hosp. with gonorrhea 12/3-12/29/63. Wded. 9/19/64. Present on final ca. 3/30/65 roll.

LEE, WILLIAM H.: enl. 2/12/63 in Co. F. POW 5/11/63 near Strasburg. Name cancelled on roll of POWs sent to Baltimore, Md., from Winchester 5/14/63. No further record.

LEIGH, ALFRED: b. 1816. POW 7/13/63 in Fairfax Co. (another record says Montgomery Co., Md.), as member of Co. A. Took the oath at Old Capitol Prison 9/19/63. No Confederate records. d. 3/99, bur. Andrew Chapel Cem., Leesburg Pike at Trap Rd. On ca. 1898 Fairfax Co. Veterans' roster. m. Mary Ashby Oliver 1845. In House of Delegates 1883-84.

LEITH, JAMES DALLAS: enl. 9/15/62 in Co. A. Absent with leave since 7/24 on 8/31/63 roll. Otherwise present until MWIA 5/5/64 in the Wilderness, d. 5/8/64. Cousin of Luther W. Hopkins, whose book describes his death.

LEITH, LAURENCE L.: b. 10/31/42 in Loudoun Co. enl. 7/24/61 in Co. A. After horses in Fauquier 12/21/62-1/1/63. Otherwise present on all rolls thru 3/27/65 final roll. Farmer at Middleburg 10/1/10. Postwar roster says wded. near Culpeper. m. Louisa Anna Asbun 1867.

LEITH, THEODRICK B.: b. 7/7/33. enl. 7/24/61 as Cpl. in Co. A. To forfeit 1 month's pay on 11-12/61 roll. In Charlottesville hosp. with scabies 1/29-2/4/64. Otherwise present until 3/27/65 final roll, when AWOL since 2/7/65. Paroled 4/24/65 at Winchester. d. 5/15/96, bur. Sharon Cem., Middleburg. Postwar roster says wded. at Fairmont. First name also shown as Theodoric.

LEONARD, JOHN T.: enl. 4/20/61 in Co. F. Present until discharged 6/23/62.

LESLIE, THOMAS MARTIN: enl. 7/24/61 in Co. A. On extra duty as teamster 9/1-10/1/61. Ten days sick leave from 1/11/62. Otherwise present until killed accidentally at Strasburg by discharge of his own pistol, shown on 5-6/62 roll.

LESTER, A. J.: Only reference is in registers for Chimborazo Hosp. No. 3, Richmond, in which a man of this name from Co. G is shown for 3/14-4/13/62, suffering from diarrhea. Doubtless an error meaning another man named Lester.

LESTER, D.: Only record is a postwar roster of Co. G, which shows a man of this name enl. 1861.

LESTER, JAMES W.: b. 3/14/14 in Halifax Co. (another source says Lunenburg Co.), enl. 8/19/61 in Co. G. Farmer. Discharged 2/13/62 because of "an attack of erysipelas and a want of strength consequent on sickness of 3 mos. standing." d. 7/6/01.

LESTER, JAMES W.: enl. 4/1/62 in (2d) Co. E. "Joined from desertion and now absent in arrest" on 11-12/62 roll. Charged with desertion and sentenced to 4 years at hard labor 10/31/64. Shown as discharged and sentenced to penitentiary on final 3/4/65 roll. In hosp. at Salisbury, N.C., with pneumonia 3/6-3/22/65. May be the man of this name b. 5/9/13 in Pittsylvania Co. and who reportedly d. at age 78.

LESTER, JOHN J.: enl. 8/19/61 in Co. G, age 18. Horse KIA 9/23/62 while courier for Col. A. H. Colquitt. In Richmond hosp. 12/8-12/18/63. POW 5/12/64 at Hanover C.H. d. 7/5/64 at Pt. Lookout.

LEWIS, HENRY L. DANGERFIELD: b. 4/25/41. Att. VMI. enl. 8/11/61 in Co. D. Student. Previously drill master in 27th Va. Inf. Detailed as courier to Gen. Jeb Stuart throughout his service with the 6th. Stuart wrote "he is zealous, capable, & deserving" and R. E. Lee on 11/16/63 "he is a youth of unexceptionable character, of good principles & gentlemanly deportment. He has frequently come under my observation during the war." To Lt. on staff of his brother Col. J. R. C. Lewis 1/7/64. Later adjutant at Mobile, Ala., and in Liddell's Division, Dist. of the Gulf. POW 4/8/65 at Blakely, Ala. d. 12/17/93, bur. Grace Episcopal Church, Berryville.

LEWIS, JAMES S.: Appointed surgeon in regiment 8/2/62 from La. POW 4/63 at Greenland Gap. Paroled 5/14/63 at Ft. Monroe. POW at Camp Hamilton 8/6-8/8/64. Reported as Major and surgeon on staff of Gen. L. L. Lomax 10/29/64. Relieved from duty with ANV 12/20/64, to report at Montgomery, Ala. At Macon, Ga., hosps. from 2/65. Described 6/7/62 as "of New Orleans."

LEWIS, JOHN HENRY: b. 11/18 (or 28)/28. enl. 4/22/61 in Co. K. Detached as brigade blacksmith on 7-8/61 roll and as regimental blacksmith for most of his subsequent service. Paroled 4/9/65 at Appomattox and again 4/28/65 at Harpers Ferry. d. 3/10/13, bur. Leesburg Union Cem.

LEWIS, ROBERT H.: enl. 3/10/63 in Co. G. In Chimborazo hosp. No. 3, Richmond, with acute diarrhea 6/24-7/12/64. Otherwise present on all rolls thru 3/22/65 final roll. May be identical to Robert Henry Lewis, 8/30/43-3/29/77, bur. Lynchburg.

LEWIS, ROBERT HUME: b. 11/12/43 in Alexandria. Att. VMI. enl. 10/1/62 in Co. D. Student. In Charlottesville hosp. with scabies 12/4/63. Found guilty of AWOL by court-martial 3/7/64. Courier for Gen. T. L. Rosser on 9-10/64 roll. Scout for Gen. Fitzhugh Lee on final 3/22/65 roll. Paroled 4/20/65 at Winchester, resid. Jefferson Co., (W.) Va. Farmer and insurance agent in Charles Town and Winchester postwar. m. Ann Cary Randolph Jones 1879. d. 12/12/21 in Baltimore, Md. VMI records say POW twice but escaped both times, slightly wded. in right leg at Cool Spring.

LILLARD, WILLIAM J.: enl. 4/22/61 in Co. B, age 28. Farmer. POW 5/27/61 while on picket duty. Paroled 6/18/61. Horse KIA at Fairfield, Pa., 7/3/63. On scout in Rappahannock Co. on 11-12/63 roll. On detail in same county 12/28/63-1/14/64. Reported by Richmond as deserter 2/28/65, but present on final 3/21/65 roll. Alive at 1927 Culpeper reunion.

LILLIS, WILLIAM: enl. 1/7/63 in Co. G. Farmer. Present until in Richmond hosp. wded. 12/1-12/7/63. Absent on horse detail on 7-8/64 roll. Absent wded. on final 3/22/65 roll. Paroled 5/11/65 in Staunton, signs by mark. Took the oath 8/28/65 in Richmond, age 30, resid. New Orleans.

LILLY, J. HARVEY: Conscript assigned 4/25/64 to Co. C. Present until ca. 3/30/65 final roll, when AWOL. Also shown as Harvey J. Lilley and variants. May be John H. Lilly, 3/8/46-8/10/18, bur. Mt. Horeb Cem., Rockingham Co.

LINDSEY, JAMES W.: enl. 3/18/62 in Co. D. AWOL since 6/1/62 on 5-6/62 roll. POW 6/7/62 at Middletown. Exchanged 8/5/62 from Ft. Delaware. KIA 6/20/63 near Upperville.

LIPSCOMB, ROBERT DICKSON: b. 1843. enl. 5/28/63 in Co. A. Present until POW 1/31/64 in Madison Co. Took the oath at Ft. Delaware 5/5/65, resid. Baltimore Co., Md. d. 1925, bur. Stone Chapel in Garrison Forest, Baltimore Co., Md.

LLOYD, JAMES W.: enl. 3/7/62 in Co. H. POW 6/2/62 at Woodstock. Exchanged from Ft. Delaware 8/5/62. To Cpl. on 9-10/62 roll. Marked as deserter 12/20/62-2/28/63. Pvt., present again on 7-8/63 roll. Detailed as brigade wagoner from 12/23 on 11-12/63 roll. Thereafter present until AWOL since 3/6/65 on final 3/22/65 roll.

LOCKE, J. HOWARD: enl. 4/1/64 in Co. A. Shown as POW 3/1/64 on 7-8/64 roll, as deserter on 9-10/64 roll, and as POW since 3/1/64 on final 3/27/64 roll. No Federal records. Probably identical to Jack Lock and John H. Lauck, q.v.

LONG, JOHN FARISH: b. 5/15/28. Conscript enrolled 1/30/64 in Co. F. In Richmond hosp. with diarrhea 5/24-6/7/64. Later detached as nurse in General Hosp. No. 2, Lynchburg. AWOL on final 2/24/65 roll. d. 1895, bur. Presbyterian Church, Mitchells.

LONG, JOHN S.: In Federal records as a deserter from Co. C, surrendered 2/65 at New Creek, W.Va. Confined at Wheeling 2/13/65, age 20, farmer, resid. Rockingham Co. Took the oath and sent North. No Confederate records. d. 1/31/04, age 59 years, 3 months, 21 days, bur. Millcreek Church of Brethren Cem. near Port Republic.

LONGER, FRANCIS: In Federal records as a deserter from Co. D who gave himself up and was made POW 10/6/63 near Martinsburg, (W.) Va. Took the oath 1/7/65 at Ft. McHenry, Md., as an alien and released. No Confederate records. Not on postwar rosters.

LOVETT, LANDON T.: enl. 7/24/61 in Co. A. Sick in hosp. on 7-8/61 roll. AWOL since 12/23 on 12/61 return. In confinement or under arrest 1/24/62 thru 5-6/62 roll. Postwar roster says "dropped from the roll." Later in 35th Bn. Va. Cav., where he was shown as a deserter from the U.S. Army. Released from Ft. Delaware 6/20/65. Postwar roster says "killed 1897."

133

LOVETT, MORTIMER C.: enl. 7/24/61 in Co. A. Forfeited $12 pay by regimental court-martial on 9-10/61 roll. AWOL since 12/23 on 11-12/61 roll. In confinement or under arrest 1/24/62 thru 5-6/62 roll. Postwar roster says "dropped from the roll." Arrested by Federals ca. 3/26/63 and sent to Ft. McHenry, Md. "Served 2 months in the Rebel Army and confined nearly one year before deserting. Broke jail and returned a second time. Refused to take the oath. Charge Treason." Release ordered from Ft. Delaware ca. 2/22/64. Resid. Loudoun Co.

LUCIUS, CHARLES: enl. 7/24/61 in Co. A. Discharged 9/9/61 when he provided a substitute.

LUCK, ROBERT: enl. 11/1/64 in Co. I. Present on final 3/20/65 roll.

LUCK, WILLIAM AUSTIN: b. 2/1/34. enl. 11/9/61 in Co. I. Forty-two day furlough from 2/12/62. To Cpl. on 5-6/62 roll. Back to Pvt. on 11-12/62 roll, absent sick. To Cpl. on 1-2/63 roll. To Sgt. on 7-8/63 roll. Absent sick at hosp. on 9-10/64 roll. AWOL on final 3/20/65 roll. d. 9/26/86, bur. Unionville Christian Church Cem. Wid. Ella S., m. 1879.

LUCKET, JOHN: enl. 4/30/63 in Co. C. Deserted 5/63.

LUCKET, SEYMOUR: Shown as deserter from Co. C on the only roll with his name, which is for 11-12/63.

LUCKETT, COOKE DINWIDDIE: b. 1841. Att. U.Va. enl. 9/7/63 in Co. A. Previously in 8th Va. Inf. In hosps. with neuralgia 10/26/63-1/30/64. In Charlottesville hosp. with hemorrhoids 5/19-6/3/64. Thereafter present thru final ca. 3/27/65 roll. Paroled 4/22/65 at Winchester, resid. Loudoun Co. d. 1913.

LUNCFORD, WILLIAM A.: enl. 10/30/62 in Co. F. Absent on horse furlough on 7-8 and 11-12/63 rolls. Otherwise present until KIA 10/12/64 in skirmish at Castleman's Ferry on Shenandoah River, bur. Stonewall Cem., Winchester. Name also appears as Lunsford and Lunceford.

LYLES, JOSEPH: On postwar "original list" of Co. F.

MABY, ALPHEUS: Shown on printed postwar roster as in Co. A, resid. Clarke Co. May be identical to Mackabee, Othias.

MACKABEE, OTHIAS: enl. 9/24/61 in Co. A as substitute for George Hooper, who was a poor rider. Sick in quarters on 1-2/62 roll. "Left at Martinsburg to nurse Henne [Edward Hennie]" on 5-6/62 roll. No further record. Also shown as McAbee, Mackabe.

MACRAE, GEORGE H. FORREST: b. 1832. enl. 4/20/61 in Co. F as Cpl. Farmer. On sick leave 9/9-10/28/61. To Pvt. on 11-12/62 roll. Wded. 4/26/63 at Rowlesburg, (W.) Va., in lung, and left there. POW at Rowlesburg 5/23/63. Paroled 3/9/64 at Pt. Lookout. Detailed to Medical Purveyor, Richmond, 6/10/64. Certificate of medical disability granted 3/22/65. Paroled 5/6/65 at Winchester, resid. Fairfax Co. Resid. Centreville 5/21/88, claiming wd. through right shoulder and left breast. d. 1917, bur. Manassas City Cem.

MACRAE, JAMES: enl. 7/1/62 in Co. F. Farmer. AWOL on 9-10/62 roll, but absent sick since 8/25 on 11/62 return. POW 4/30/63 at Rowlesburg, (W.) Va., resid. Prince William Co. Paroled 5/13/63 at Camp Chase. Wded. 9/19/64 at Winchester in left foot. In Charlottesville hosp. 9/26/64. Paroled 5/3/65 at Fairfax C.H., age 22.

MACRAE, JOHN ROBERT WALLACE: b. 7/19/27. enl. 4/30/61 in Co. H. Present on rolls until discharged 2/21/62 by furnishing Charles Padgett as substitute. d. 4/1/87, bur. Macrae Cem., Old Tavern, Warrenton. "One honest man very much given to hospitality." m. Hannah Blanchmore Tomlin.

MAGNER, MATHEW FERRELL: enl. 6/27/61 in Co. D. Previously in Co. B, 11th Miss. Inf. Present until absent on sick furlough on 9-10/62 roll. Discharged on expiration of service. Paroled 5/7/65 at Winchester as Lt. in Mosby's 43d Bn. Va. Cav., age 25. d. 1866 of cholera. See Nancy Chappelear Baird, ed., *Journals of Amanda Virginia Edmonds*.

MALLORY, JOHN: enl. 5/4/61 in Co. I as Cpl., age 42. To Pvt., on 5-6/62 roll. Detailed to repair ambulance 8/27/63 and as wagon maker for 90 days on 11-12/62 roll. Present on final 3/20/65 roll. Paroled 5/15/65 at Lousia C.H.

MALLORY, ROBERT: enl. 5/4/61 in Co. I, age 38. Present on all rolls thru 3/20/65 final roll.

MALLORY, WILLIAM M.: b. in Orange Co. enl. 5/4/61 in Co. I, age 24. Always present until final 3/20/65 roll, when absent wded. Farm worker, resid. True Blue 8/11/02, claiming wd. through thigh 11/12/64 at Newtown. d. 12/8/20.

MANN, CHARLES HOWELL: b. 2/1/44 in Tattnall Co., Ga. enl. 9/17/61 in (1st) Co. E. On Roll of Honor 12/10/64 for Cold Harbor. m. Nancy Cooper Mobley 1865. Attorney and judge postwar. d. 12/28/12, bur. Providence Church Cem., Toombs Co., Ga.

MANN, JONATHAN TAYLOR: b. 6/14/21 in Salisbury, N.H. enl. 4/1/62 in Co. I. Farmer and watchmaker, resid. Va. from ca. 1849. Exchanged 9/21/62 in vicinity of Ft. Monroe, no record as POW. To Lt. from Cpl. 12/4/62. KIA 6/9/63 at Brandy Station. Supposedly bur. at base of Clark's Mountain. m. Sarah Joseph Spencer 1849.

MANN, JOHN T.: b. 1835 in Tattnall Co., Ga. enl. 9/17/61 in (1st) Co. E. Physician. Discharged 9/3/62 from Jeff Davis Legion to accept lieutenancy in Co. K, 54th Ga. Inf. KIA 7/4/64 at Kenesaw Mountain, Ga., bur. Green Wood Cem., Atlanta, Ga.

MANUEL, ISAAC NEWTON: enl. 12/15/64 in Co. D. Present on final 3/22/65 roll. POW 4/1/65 at Five Forks. Took the oath 6/15/65 at Pt. Lookout, resid. Clarke Co. Transportation ordered to Winchester.

MARCUS, SPENCER: enl. 7/24/61 in Co. A. Absent from 8/18/61 with dislocated shoulder on all rolls until discharged 2/20/62 for that ailment.

MARDERS, WILLIAM L: On postwar "original list" of Co. F.

MARILLA, JOHN: enl. 9/6/62 in (2d) Co. E, age 23. Miller. Twenty-two days horse leave from 10/27/64. Otherwise present on all rolls thru 3/24/65 final roll. Wife Jane. d. 6/28/91 in Pittsylvania Co.

MARLOW, GEORGE W.: enl. 9/13/62 in Co. A. On clothing detail from 12/31/63 on 11-12/63 roll. Absent sick from 8/4/64, which was changed to AWOL on final 3/27/65 roll. Paroled 4/21/65 at Winchester, age 25, resid. Clarke Co.

MARLOW, JAMES: enl. 9/13/62 in Co. A. Deserted 8/27/63 at Snickersville. Resid. Clarke Co. Postwar roster says deserted to Ohio.

MARR, WILLIAM T.: b. 7/1/38 in Pittsylvania Co. enl. 4/1/62 in (2d) Co. E. Carpenter. Previously in Co. I, 18th Va. Cav. Shown absent until POW 6/9/63 at Beverly Ford. Paroled 6/25/63 at Old Capitol Prison. Twenty days horse leave from 8/13/63. Transferred 12/16/63 to Capt. Shoemaker's Co., Va. Horse Art. Resid. Staunton, age 54, on 1/9/93. d. 3/18/12, bur. Thornrose Cem.

MARSHALL, EDWARD C., JR.: enl. 9/1/64 in Co. D. Detailed at Division Commissary Dept. on the 2 rolls of the unit on which his name appears (thru 3/22/65 final roll). Postwar roster says Commissary Sgt.

MARSHALL, FIELDING LEWIS: b. 3/29/19 at Weyanoke, Charles City Co. Att. U.Va. enl. 4/24/61 as Sgt. in Co. H. Farmer. Absent on recruiting service from 2/18/62 on 1-2/62 roll. To Lt. of art. 5/17/62. On ordnance duty at Lynchburg. Paroled 4/15/65 at Lynchburg as Capt. m. 1) Rebecca Frances Coke 1843, 2) Mary Newton Thomas 1867. In House of Delegates 1869-71. d. 6/30/02 at Orange, bur. Graham Cem., Route 20 West, Orange. Author of *Recollections and Reflections* (1911). Father of Richard Coke Marshall.

MARSHALL, RICHARD COKE: b. 7/5/44 at Oak Hill. Claimed to have served in Co. H, but not so shown on Confederate or postwar records. Later in Co. A, 7th Va. Cav. Attorney postwar. d. 4/5/14, bur. Cedar Grove Cem., Portsmouth. Son of Fielding Lewis Marshall.

MARSHALL, ROBERT A. M.: b. 1828. enl. 10/1/62 in Co. A. Present until POW 5/11/64 in Hanover Co. Cpl. on Union records. d. 3/4/65 at Elmira of pneumonia and bur. there at Woodlawn Cem. Memorial stone in Ebenezer Cem., Bloomfield.

MARSTON, E. I.: Only record is of parole as in Co. D 4/9/65 at Appomattox. Not on postwar rosters and probably an error of transcription.

MARTIN, JAMES: enl. 1/1/63 in Co. C. Deserted 1/3/63.

MARTIN, ROBERT M.: b. in Orange Co. enl. 5/4/61 in Co. I, age 23. Carpenter. Absent at home with measles on ca. 6/19/61 roll. Discharged 2/19/62 for "debility and want of strength, consequent on an attack of chronic bronchitis." Signs by mark. d. 9/20/19 at Lee Camp Soldiers' Home, Richmond.

MARTIN, THOMAS J.: b. in Orange Co. enl. 5/4/61 in Co. I, "age 38." Laborer. Discharged 6/21/62 near Harrisonburg for secondary syphilis, "age 45."

MARTZ, ALBERT: enl. 10/8/62 in Co. A. On detached service guarding bridge at Mt. Jackson from 12/62 return thru 1/10/63. Absent sick on surgeon's certificate on 11-12/63 roll. No further record. Postwar roster says deserted. Also shown as Marts.

MARTZ, SAMUEL THORNTON: b. 1830. enl. 7/24/61 in Co. A. Sick leave since 2/2/62 on 1-2/62 roll. Detailed as teamster in ordnance dept. 7/14/62 until POW 10/9/64 at Fisher's Hill. Paroled 3/28/65. Paroled 4/22/65 at Winchester. m. 1) Anna Furr, 2) Emily Gaver. d. 2/17/01 at Marionville, Loudoun Co., bur. Ebenezer Cem., Bloomfield.

MASON, GEORGE: b. 12/24/39 in Frederick Co. enl. 4/18/61 in Co. D. To Lt. 7/1/61. Dropped to Pvt. 4/20/62. Absent on leave on 11-12/63 roll. Otherwise present on all rolls thru final 3/22/65 roll. Paroled 4/19/65 at Winchester, resid. Frederick Co. near White Post. Resid. Fauquier Co. ca. 1898. d. 12/7/16 at Baltimore, Md.

MASON, HORATIO P.: enl. 5/4/61 in Co. I, age 20. Detailed for road service in Western Va. 10/3/61, and so shown thru 1-2/63 roll, except for furlough for disability on 12/61 return. No further record. Postwar roster says discharged in 1862.

MASON, JOHN T.: On postwar "original list of Co. F.

MASON, JOSEPH GAMBLE: b. in Clarke Co. enl. 4/18/61 in Co. D. Two weeks sick furlough from 12/1/61. Absent sick on 11/62 return and on 8/31/63 roll. Otherwise present thru final 3/22/65 roll. Paroled 4/19/65 at Winchester, age 23, resid. Frederick Co. near White Post. d. 1/3/16 at Clarksburg, W.Va., bur. Masonic Cem., Clarksburg.

MASON, WILLIAM DAVID: b. in Rappahannock Co. enl. 4/22/61 in Co. B. Farmer. Four absences on sick leave before being slightly wded. 7/3/63 at Fairfield, Pa. Absent with leave since 3/6/65 on final 3/21/65 roll. Paroled 5/8/65 at Winchester, age 26, resid. near Sperryville. Lived in Missouri several years postwar. Pensioner 5/17/16 at Castleton, Va.

MASON, WILLIAM DOUGLAS: b. in Frederick Co. enl. 4/18/62 in Co. D. Farmer. Present on 5-6/62 roll. Otherwise absent sick on rolls and returns until discharged 3/11/63 at Staunton, age 16, because "his general health is greatly impaired; has chronic diarrhea & organic disease of the heart."

MASSEY, ED: On a postwar roster Sgt. Maj., transferred from Co. A, 7th Va. Cav. No Confederate records.

MASSEY, JOHN: In a postwar source as enl. 4/10/61 in Co. I, resid. Culpeper Co. This source says he d. 12/18/83 in Texas. No Confederate records.

MASSEY, THOMAS C.: enl. 11/20/62 in Co. I. In Chimborazo Hosp. No. 3, Richmond, with acute diarrhea 6/24-6/27/64. Sick in hosp. on 9-10/64 roll. Absent sick on final 3/20/65 roll. Postwar source says wded. 11/15/63 at Stevensburg and 11/1/64 at Winchester, resid. Culpeper. Also spelled Massie.

MATHERS, WILLIAM: enl. 4/11/64 in Co. K. Detailed as teamster on 9-10/64 roll. AWOL on final 1-2/65 roll.

MATTHEWS, JAMES: enl. 4/22/61 in Co. K. Thirty days furlough from 2/1/62. POW 6/8/63 in Fauquier Co. (or near Winchester), age 35. Paroled at Ft. McHenry, Md., 6/26/63. Otherwise present on all rolls until AWOL on final 1-2/65 roll. Paroled 4/26/65 at Harpers Ferry, signs by mark. Also spelled Mathews.

MATTHEWS, JOHN H.: enl. 4/22/61 in Co. K. Generally present on all co. rolls. To Lt. 9/25/62. Signs as commanding dismounted men of regiment 8/31/63. To Capt. 9/8/64. Absent seeking absentees 2/28/65. MWIA 3/31/65 at Dinwiddie C.H. (or Five Forks). In Petersburg hosp. 4/1/65. POW 4/3/65 at hosp. d. 7/24/65 from gunshot wd. of right thigh, bur. near hosp.

MATTHEWS, WILLIAM: enl. 4/22/61 in Co. K. Thirty days furlough from 2/11/62. Confederate records show him POW 3/9/62, with following roll (dated 12/12/62) stating he was AWOL until 10/5/62. No U.S. records on this capture. POW 6/26/64 at Leesburg while home wded. Took the oath 6/14/65 at Elmira, resid. Point of Rocks, Md. Signs by mark.

MAUCK, GEORGE FRANKLIN: Conscript enl. 4/4/64 in Co. C. Absent with leave on 9-10/64 roll and AWOL on final ca. 3/30/65 roll. Previously in 146th Va. Militia.

MAUPIN, JAMES A.: b. in Port Republic. Pensioner claiming service in Co. C. No Confederate records. Said he later served in Capt. Woodson's Independent Co. Resid. Texas 1867-72. Age 81 on 5/20/26. Brother of Lt. W. H. H.

MAUPIN, WILLIAM HENRY HARRISON: enl. 5/28/61 in Co. C. To Sgt. 9/1/61. To Lt. 10/1/62. Wded. 10/19/64. Present on final ca. 3/30/65 roll. At Gilmore, Upshur Co., Texas in 1868. Brother of James A.

MAUZY, JOSEPH NICHOLAS: b. 3/21/45. enl. 5/25/63 in Co. C. Present until final ca. 3/30/65 roll, when AWOL. Resid. Montevideo in 1908. d. 12/6/10, bur. Mt. Olivet Cem., McGaheysville.

MAXWELL, ALEXANDER: b. Rectortown, Fauquier Co. enl. 4/24/61 in Co. H. Merchant. POW 12/2/61 at Annandale. Exchanged ca. 2/14/62. Absent on sick furlough before POW 9/22/62 at Paris as Sgt., no record of parole. Present on 11-12/62 roll. AWOL or sick 8/25/63 thru 9-10/64 roll. To Pvt. on 11-12/63 roll. In Charlottesville hosp. 1/9-3/8/64 with secondary syphilis. In Richmond hosp. with contused wd. of breast 5/9-5/29/64, age 23. Took the oath ca. 11/28/64 at Berlin, Md. Arrested 12/6/64 near Queenstown, Md., in dress coat of Federal staff officer. Took the oath 12/28/64 at Baltimore City Jail and sent North of Philadelphia.

MAY, GEORGE WESLEY: Conscript enl. 9/64 in Co. C. Present on final ca. 3/30/65 roll. d. 6/6/81 at Port Republic. Wid. Eliza A., m. 1857.

MAY, JAMES HARRISON: b. 1842 in Rockingham Co. Claimed on pension application to have served in Co. C, as well as Co. B, 10th Va. Inf., and Avis Guard. Said he was accidentally wded. outside picket post near Fairfax Station. No Confederate records. Mechanic postwar. d. 1918, Port Republic Cem. on Hill.

MAYS, THOMAS TERRY: enl. 4/1/62 in (2d) Co. E. Farmer. Reported MWIA 7/3/63 at Fairfield, Pa., but POW and paroled 8/24/63 at DeCamp General Hosp., N.Y. harbor. In Richmond hosp. with gunshot wd. of right side from Gettysburg 12/2-12/16/63, age 39. Thereafter present until wded. at Winchester and absent at Lynchburg hosp. on 9-10/64 roll. Present on final 3/4/65 roll.

McARTOR, HENRY T.: enl. 9/14/62 in Co. A. Farmer. Present until POW 2/20/64 at Upperville, age 20. Took the oath 6/15/65 at Ft. Delaware. d. 1/27/09. Wid. Addie Lon applied for pension in Miller Co., Ark., 1928.

McARTOR, THOMAS W.: b. at Upperville. enl. 9/24/62 in Co. A. On detached service as scout in Loudoun and Fauquier Cos. 11/24-12/18/62. Furloughed 8/29/63. Transferred 2/14/64 to Co. A, 39th Bn. Va. Cav. Silversmith postwar. Resid. Stephens City, age 75, on 4/7/11. "I supplied myself with eight horses that were broken down in service."

McATEE, FRANKLIN: enl. 9/13/62 in Co. A. Sent to hospital 8/28/63 and so shown thru final 3/27/65 roll. Farmer postwar. d. in Loudoun Co. Postwar roster shows Frank McArtor.

McCARTY, RICHARD CHICHESTER: b. in Middleburg, Loudoun Co. enl. 10/15/62 in Co. K. Present on all rolls to 9-10/64 roll, when shown AWOL sick since 10/15/64. Present on final 1-2/65 roll. Paroled 4/24/65 at Edwards Ferry. Farmer postwar in Loudoun Co., Fauquier Co. after 1881. Age 78 on 9/14/18, resid. Rectortown. d. 7/10/19. m. Martha Megeath.

McCARTY, SAMUEL S.: b. 7/28/42. enl. 10/15/63 in Co. K. Present until wded. at Winchester 9/9/64 and absent wded. on final 1-2/65 roll. d. 7/12/70, bur. Leesburg Union Cem.

McCAULY, R. PETER: enl. 5/28/61 in Co. C. Shown as teamster on 12/62 return. POW 5/13/63 in Warren Co. Sent from Ft. McHenry, Md., for exchange 5/17/63. Otherwise present until shown as deserter on 11-12/63 roll. Also shown as McCauley, McCaully.

McCLAIR, VALENTINE: Told Federals he deserted from Co. B. Farmer. Surrendered at Paw Paw, (W.) Va., 2/65, took the oath and sent North. No Confederate or postwar records.

McCLAREN, ROBERT: enl. 5/4/61 in Co. I, age 20. Found guilty of drunkenness on duty, sentenced to forfeit 6 months' pay, and to serve at hard labor 2 months 1/23/62. In arrest for insubordinate conduct by order of Gen. Robertson 6/28/62. Detailed as teamster on 11-12/62 roll thru final 3/20/65 roll.

McCLELLAN, ROBERT MILLER: enl. 9/17/61 in (1st) Co. E, age 28. To QM Sgt. 4/1/62. To Capt. and AQM 5/21/63. Resid. Savannah, Ga.

McCLURE, JAMES NICHOLAS: enl. 5/29/61 in Co. D. Usually on extra duty as clerk on QM Dept. from 10/22/61. Absent as clerk in regimental QM Dept. on final 3/22/65 roll. Paroled 4/26/65 at Winchester, age 27, resid. Jefferson Co., (W.) Va. Salesman in Baltimore, Md., postwar. In Maryland Line Confederate Soldiers' Home, Pikesville, Md., 1894. d. 1/20/94, bur. Loudon Park Cem., Baltimore.

McCORD, HENRY D.: enl. 10/1/63 in Co. ?. d. 8/11/64.

McCORMICK, CYRUS: b. 4/27/45 at "Frankford," Clarke Co. Att. VMI and U.Va. enl. 7/25/62 in Co. D. In Charlottesville hospital with gunshot wd. 11/20-12/13/63. POW 9/4/64 at Berryville. Paroled 5/23/65, to remain within limits of Camp Chase, Ohio. Took the oath 6/3/65 at Camp Chase. Grad. in medicine U. of Md. Physician at Berryville postwar. m. Anne Elizabeth Taylor 1869. D. 1/12/05, bur. Green Hill Cem., Berryville.

McCORMICK, EDWARD: b. 10/26/24. enl. 5/25/61 in Co. D. To Capt. in QM Dept. 9/11/61. Post QM at Lynchburg from 10/3/61. Paroled 4/19/65 at Berryville. Wrote to Federals on 6/3/65 "I was not an original secessionist . . . I struggled to prevent the war, so long as I saw any probability of doing so." d. 3/18/70, bur. Grace Episcopal Church Cem., Berryville. m. Ellen Lane Jett, d. 1908.

McCORMICK, HUGH HOLMES: b. 12/21/44. Att. VMI. enl. 7/25/62 in Co. D. In Charlottesville hosp. with gunshot wd. 10/13-10/19/63, returned to duty 12/13/63. In Petersburg hosp. with acute dysentery 8/1-8/4/64, then 30 day furlough. Absent as scout for Gen. Fitz Lee on final 3/22/65 roll. Paroled 4/15/65 at Winchester. Lawyer at Berryville postwar, never married. d. in fall from window in Alexandria 5/11/70, bur. Grace Episcopal Church Cem., Berryville.

McCORMICK, PROVINCE, JR.: b. 2/18/47 at Berryville, Clarke Co. enl. 5/11/64 in Co. D. Present thru 3/22/65 final roll. Unofficial source states he was courier for Gen. R. S. Ewell before enlistment in Co. D. att. U.Va. postwar. Farmer, inspector in Indian Service, served 20 years as county supervisor, 50 years as director of Berryville Turnpike. Food administrator of Clarke Co. in WWI. m. Elizabeth Taylor 1871. d. 1936, bur. Green Hill Cem., Berryville.

McCULLOCH, ROBERT S.: enl. 6/26/61 in Co. I, age 21. Sick with measles on ca. 7/61 roll. Wded. 7/3/63 at Fairfield, Pa. Otherwise present until absent sick in hosp. on 9-10/64 roll. AWOL on final 3/20/65 roll. Paroled 5/17/65 at Charlottesville.

McDANIEL, GEORGE: Only record is a postwar roster which has him in Co. F.

McDONALD DONALD: enl. 9/17/61 in (1st) Co. E, age 26. To Cpl. on 11/1/61 roll. To Sgt. on 7-8/62 roll. MWIA 8/1/63 at Brandy Station. d. 8/28/63 after amputation for gunshot wd. at Florida Hosp., Richmond. Resid. Savannah, Ga.

McDONALD, WILLIAM: enl. 7/1/64 in Co. F. Confederate records show him POW 8/17/64 in Clarke Co., and he is so shown thru final 2/24/65 roll, but no Federal records confirm this.

McDONALD, W. NORMAN: enl. 9/17/61 in (1st) Co. E as Cpl., age 22. Postwar source says he resigned office of Sgt. in 1/62. Paroled 5/1/65 at Greensboro, N.C., as Pvt. Resid. McIntosh Co., Ga.

McFARLAND, FRANCIS W.: enl. 4/20/61 in Co. F. To Sgt. 8/19/61. Shown as Ordnance Sgt. on 9-10/61 roll. Absent on sick leave from 12/4/61, "not since reported, considered a deserter." Postwar roster says "put in a substitute."

McGINNIS, ARTHUR: enl. 11/8/61 in Co. G as substitute for Charles H. Ferrell. Discharged 11/8/62 at Newtown because he was a Marylander.

McGREGOR, THOMAS: b. in Pittsylvania Co. enl. 8/19/61 in Co. G, "age 34." Farmer. Absent on sick furlough from 11/27/61 until discharged at "age 38" 7/20/62 at Camp Ashby, Orange C.H., for "permanently diseased lungs & chronic enlargement of the testicle." Postwar roster says resid. Pittsylvania Co.

McGREGOR, THOMPSON L.: b. in Halifax Co. enl. 3/22/62 in Co. G. Physician. Previously in Co. G, 38th Va. Inf. Discharged 5/8/62 at camp near Conrad's Store for tuberculosis, age 34. His only record in the regiment is a certificate of disability for discharge filed under Thomas McGregor's name, and there is much chance for confusion of the two. Also spelled McGrigor, McGregor on rolls of 38th Va.

McGUIRE, BURWELL: b. 1846. enl. 6/16/64 in Co. D. Present until AWOL on final 3/22/65 roll. d. 1/12, bur. Old Chapel Cem., Millwood.

McGUIRE, DAVID HOLMES, JR.: b. 1843. enl. 9/1/62 in Co. D. Previously in 2d Va. Inf. Shown detailed as scout and a month's pay deducted by court-martial on 11-12/63 roll. Scout for Gen. Fitzhugh Lee on 7-8/64 roll. POW. 10/21/64 at Warrenton, mysteriously "acknowledged captaincy 42 Va." Took the oath 6/4/65 at Ft. Delaware as Capt., 6th Va. Cav. (which he was not). Lawyer and editor postwar. A photograph in the courthouse at Berryville shows him in an officer's uniform, which must have an interesting explanation. d. 3/29/74, bur. Old Chapel Cem., Millwood. Lawyer and newspaper editor.

McGUIRE, M. F.: Shown in Federal records as Sgt. in Co. D. POW 7/17/64 at "Percersville, Va.," and sent to Ft. Delaware. No Confederate records and not on several postwar rosters. Probably an error.

McINTOSH, JOHN McCOY: enl. 9/17/61 in (1st) Co. E, age 23. Postwar roster says wded. 12/4/61 at Bog Wallow ambuscade, Fairfax Co. Resid. McIntosh Co., Ga. Paroled 5/1/65 at Greensboro, N.C.

McINTOSH, R. E.: Only record is of parole at Harper's Ferry, (W.) Va., 4/28/65, as in Co. F, age 37. Signs by mark.

McKIMMEY, CHARLES F.: b. 7/29/38 in Loudoun co. enl. 4/22/61 in Co. K. Farmer. To Cpl. on 6/30/62 roll, sick at hosp. In Charlottesville hosp. with morbi cutis 1/7-1/8/64, transferred to Lynchburg. Otherwise present until POW 2/21/64 in Loudoun Co. "whilst disbanded." Took the oath at Ft. Delaware 6/20/65. d. 1/29/26, bur. Lovettsville Union Cem.

McKIMMEY, JOHN THORNTON: enl. 4/22/61 in Co. K. Always present until MWIA 5/9/64 near Spotsylvania C.H. d. in field hosp. 5/11/64.

McLAUGHRY, JOHN: enl. 9/15/62 in Co. A. Detached as teamster to "headquarters" 1/12/63. Deserted 1/23 (or 27)/63 at Snickersville. Many spellings of surname. Postwar roster gives John McClaughrey, resid. Clarke Co. Apparently identical to "John McLeary, deserted" on another postwar roster.

McLEARY, JOHN: On a postwar roster of Co. A, deserted. See John McLaughry. Another such roster says substitute, deserted to Ohio.

McLENDON, DUNCAN F.: enl. 9/17/61 in (1st) Co. E, age 26. To Cpl. 10/1/62. KIA 6/21/63 at Upperville. Resid. Telfair Co., Ga. This spelling of surname is from a certificate given by his mother. Confederate and postwar records spell it McLennan.

McLWAIN, VANBUREN: Federal records show a man of this name in Co. B, b. in Braxton Co., (W.) Va., farmer, enl. 9/61, POW 3/20/65 at Bulltown, (W.) Va., age 30. He was classed as a deserter, awaiting his friends to join him to go North while held at Clarksburg. Certainly a mistake of some kind referring to some other unit. No Confederate or postwar records.

McMILLAN, WARREN J.: enl. 8/19/61 in Co. G, age 27. D. at General Hosp. No. 1, Lynchburg, of icterus 5/14/62, bur. City Cem., Lynchburg. Also shown as McMillen.

McMURRAN, E. M.: On postwar "original list" of Co. F.

McMURRAY, JOHN P.: enl. 4/18/61 in Co. D as Sgt. To Pvt. on 5-6/62 roll. On duty at Gen. Jeb Stuart's HQ on the two 1863 rolls. Present with co. on later rolls thru 3/22/65 final roll. Paroled 4/15/65 at Winchester, age 28, resid. Clarke Co. Some postwar rosters spell name McMurry.

McMURREIN, C. H.: On postwar "original list" of Co. F.

McNEALY, THOMAS: enl. 4/22/61 in Co. K. Present, wded. accidentally, absent one month on 7-8/61 roll. Discharged 1/12/62 for gunshot wd. of right breast, the ball passing through the lung and fracturing the right scapula.

McQUEEN, HENRY C.: enl. 1/13/63 in Co. B. Present until AWOL on 9-10/64 roll. Dropped from rolls as deserter 3/10/65 on final 3/21/65 roll. Reportedly alive in 5/07. Postwar roster says age 18 on enlistment.

McRAE, ALEXANDER C.: b. 3/21/43 in Telfair Co., Ga. enl. 9/17/61 in (1st) Co. E. Paroled at Greensboro, N.C., 5/1/65. d. 8/74 of tuberculosis.

MEAD, WILLIAM WORSLY: b. 4/4/36 in Loudoun Co. enl. 4/22/61 in Co. K as Lt. To Capt. 7/1/61. Absent on sick furlough 2/5-2/26/62. On recruiting duty from 2/26/62. Dropped 4/20/62. Refugee at Emaus, Bedford Co., 12/8/62 when he wrote he was "completely broken down" and had retired and sought a position. Raised a co. for Mosby which was disbanded, then in Co. G, 2d Va. Cav. Wded. and erroneously reported KIA 5/16/63 at Berry's Ferry. Merchant, farmer, and postmaster in Bedford Co. postwar. m. Cornelia Francis Mead 1867. d. 9/1/94, bur. family cem. Moneta, Bedford Co.

MEADE, DAVID, JR.: b. 10/30/40. enl. 4/18/61 in Co. D. Absent with leave on 11-12/63 roll. Otherwise present on all rolls thru 3/22/65 final roll. POW 4/1/65 at Dinwiddie C.H. Took the oath 6/15/65 at Pt. Lookout. Resid. White Post postwar. d. 7/23/17, bur. Meade Memorial Episcopal Church, White Post.

MEADE, FRANCIS KEY: b. 3/1/44. enl. 9/22/62 in Co. D. Present until in Charlottesville hosp. with morbi cutis 11/14/63-1/12/64. Horse KIA 6/11/64 near Trevillian's Station, POW 10/10/64 at Edinburg. Took the oath 6/15/65 at Pt. Lookout, resid. Clarke Co. d. 3/19/27, bur. Old Chapel Cem., Millwood. Known as Frank.

MEADE, HENRY: enl. 6/19/64 in Co. D. Present thru 3/22/65 final roll. Paroled 4/25/65 at Winchester, age 19, resid. Clarke Co. Also known as Harry. Middle initial "V". or "Y." d. 2/27/26, at Lee Camp Soldiers' Home, Richmond.

MEADOWS, WILLIAM WADE: enl. 4/1/62 in (2d) Co. E. Paid as teamster 4/30/63. Absent sick in hosp. at Staunton on 11-12/63 roll. Otherwise present until missing in action at Cold Harbor 5/30/64.

MEANS, GEORGE F.: b. in Prince William Co. enl. 4/22/61 in Co. K as Cpl. Sick on 12/61 return. To Lt. 4/20/62. KIA 10/9/62 at Aldie, bur. Sharon Cem., Middleburg. Name on monument to dead heroes of Fairfax Co.

MENEFEE, HENRY ST. CYR: b. 6/18/44 at Washington, Va. Att. VMI. enl. 9/1/62 in Co. B. Absent as courier for Gen. W. E. Jones on 11-12/62 roll. In Richmond hosp. 7/30-7/31/64. AWOL on 7-8/64 roll. Absent sick on 9-10/64 roll. AWOL on final 3/21/65 roll. Lawyer and farmer in Rappahannock and Bedford Cos. postwar. In Va. legislature in 1880's. Never married. Postwar source says "served throughout the war without a scratch." d. 12/20/13, bur. private cem. at Washington.

MERCER, JESSE: enl. 9/8/62 in Co. A. AWOL since 8/26/63 on 8/31/63 roll. Found guilty of AWOL 11/20/63, sentenced to guard house 20 days and to carry a 30 pound billet of wood 4 hours each day while confined. Deserted 4/64. Postwar source says resid. Clarke Co.

MERCER, NATHANIEL: enl. 9/25/62 in Co. A. AWOL since 10/8/63 on 11-12/63 roll. "Deserted gone home 4/64" on 7-8/64 roll. Paroled 4/21/65 at Winchester, age 34, signs by mark, resid. Loudoun Co. d. 1896 near Bluemont. Wld. Lydia Jane, m. 1853. Postwar source says resid. Clarke Co.

METCALF, GEORGE: enl. 3/7/62 in Co. H. Deserted 11/25/62 near Salem (Marshall), under arrest on 12/62 return. Thereafter present until AWOL on 7-8/64 roll. AWOL since 8/31/64 on final 3/22/65 roll.

METCALF, PRESSLY G.: enl. 4/24/61 in Co. H. Carpenter. AWOL 9/1-9/21/61. Wded. on picket 10/23/61 "is yet unfit for duty" on 9-10/61 roll. AWOL since 11/21 on 11/61 return, still AWOL on 12/61 return. AWOL since 5/20/62 on 5-6/62 roll. Marked as a deserter from 10/1/62 and no further Confederate records. POW 5/3/63 near Fredericksburg. Paroled at HQ Army of the Potomac 5/4/63 and sent to City Point for exchange 5/10/63.

MICHAEL, RIEL D.: Conscript enl. 10/10/64 in Co. C. Present thru final ca. 3/30/65 roll.

MICHIE, HENRY BOWYER: b. 2/12/39. enl. 1/20/63 in Co. D. Transferred from Capt. Garber's Battery, Va. Lt. Art. In Staunton hosp. with scabies 7/25-8/6/63. Absent sick at hosp. on 11-12/63 roll. Absent sick in Staunton hosp. on 9-10/64 roll. Otherwise present until shown absent, POW, on final 3/22/65 roll, but no Federal records on capture. d. 3/15/95, bur. Thornrose Cem., Staunton.

MICKLE, WILLIAM: enl. 3/5/63 in Co. C. KIA 7/3/63 at Fairfield, Pa.

MILAM, GEORGE P.: enl. 9/25/64 in Co. G. Absent on horse detail on 9-10/64 roll. Absent sick on final 3/22/65 roll. d. 5/3/09 at Richmond hosp. Wld. Hattie A., m. 1874, resid. Pittsylvania Co.

MILBURN, JOHN: enl. 8/11/61 in Co. D. Fifteen day sick furlough from 12/25/61. Absent at hosp. on 9-10/62 roll. 11/62 return says discharged, spinal affection. Postwar rosters say d. of smallpox in hosp. at Harrisonburg, 1863.

MILEY, HEROD THOMAS: b. 10/4/44. enl. 9/15/62 in Co. A. On detached service after deserters 12/21/62-1/1/63. AWOL since 8/26 on 8/31/63 roll. In Staunton hosp. 11/8/63 with contusion. Found guilty of AWOL 11/20/63, to be publicly reprimanded: "The court are thus lenient, on account of the youth of the accused, and the circumstances under which he left his command." POW 5/12/64 in Hanover Co. At Elmira 8/15/64, date of parole unknown. Absent with leave on final ca. 3/27/65 roll, "having been exchanged & not yet notified." Paroled 4/21/65 at Winchester, resid. Clarke Co. Resid. Gaithersburg, Md., 1934. d. 7/29/36, bur. Edge Hill Cem., Charles Town, W.Va. Some letters he received are at Duke Univ.

MILLAN, JOHN W.: enl. 4/22/61 in Co. B, age 25. Farmer. On special duty at Manassas on 1-2/62 roll. Otherwise present until transferred 4/5/63 to Co. F. He never reported to Co. F and was marked a deserter.

MILLER, _____: Shown as enl. 11/1/62 in Co. B on a 11/62 return. No other record and probably a mistake, perhaps referring to John Byron Miller.

MILLER, ALBERT: enl. 11/64 in Co. C and shown as AWOL on the ca. 3/30/65 roll, the only one with his name.

MILLER, B. F.: enl. 10/20/62 in Co. C. Present until POW in Fairfield, Pa. vicinity, ca. 7/3/63. d. 3/19/64 at Pt. Lookout.

MILLER, EASTHAM J.: enl. 4/22/61 in Co. B, age 25. Farmer. d. 5/11 (or 16)/61 at Centreville.

MILLER, GEORGE FRANCIS: b. 6/20/46. enl. 4/1/64 in (2d) Co. E. Furlough 40 days for fever 7/7/64 at Chimborazo Hosp. No. 1, Richmond. Absent sick at Lynchburg hosp. on 7-8/64 roll. Thereafter present thru 3/4/65 final roll. Resid. Alfalfa Co., Oklahoma, in 1925. d. 7/29/47 at Carmen, Ok., age 101 years, 1 month and 9 days, bur Carmen Cem.

MILLER, HENRY P.: enl. 9/17/61 in (1st) Co. E, age 18. Resid. Savannah, Ga. POW 5/3/62 between Yorktown and Williamsburg. Exchanged 8/6/62.

MILLER, JOHN BYRON: b. 9/26/44 in Rappahannock Co. Att. VMI. enl. 10/20/62 in Co. B. POW 7/7/63 at Williamsport, Md. Paroled 5/3/64 at Pt. Lookout and exchanged. Wded. 10/19/64 at Cedar Creek. Absent wded. on final 3/21/65 roll. Farmer, lumber merchant, bank director postwar. Two terms in Va. legislature. d. 10/12/15 at Richmond, bur. family cem. in Rappahannock Co.

MILLER, ROBERT E.: b. 1/2/48 at Sperryville. May have served previously in Co. B, 7th Va. Inf. enl. 2/1/64 in Co. B. Shown on 11-12/63 roll (sic) as absent, detailed. Otherwise present until absent buying cattle for brigade on final 3/21/65 roll. d. 3/2 (or 8)/1928). One source gives his middle name as Emmett, another as Edward. A postwar roster gives his age on enlistment as 21!

MILLER, SILAS PETER: b. 1/7/36 in Rockingham Co. enl. 10/4/63 in Co. C. In Petersburg hosp. with gunshot wd. of right leg 7/1/64, transferred to Richmond (where he was given 40 days furlough from 7/7/64). Present on final ca. 3/20/65 roll. Farmer at Montevideo 9/29/02, claiming wd. in thumb at Yellow Tavern and in leg in raid below Petersburg. d. 4/10/19, bur. Mt. Olivet Cem., McGaheysville. Wld. Georgia L., m. 1872.

MILLER, THOMAS P.: b. at Alexandria. enl. 7/15/61 in Co. K. Farmer. Discharged 6/14/62, age 20, near Harrisonburg for "diseased testacles." Discharge gives date of enl. as 4/20/62.

MILLER, W. INMAN: enl. 9/17/61 in (1st) Co. E, age 27. Paroled 5/1/65 at Greensboro, N.C. Resid. Liberty Co., Ga.

MILLETTE, SAMUEL MORGAN: b. in Georgia. enl. 9/17/61 in (1st) Co. E. Taken sick at Richmond 10/7/61. Resid. Savannah, Ga. bur. Natchez City Cem., Miss. Name spelled Millett on some records.

MILLIRON, GEORGE W.: enl. 4/1/62 in (2d) Co. E. Absent sick on 5-6/62 roll, his only record.

MILLNER, WILLIAM P.: Conscript enl. 2/19/64 in Co. F. In Richmond and Danville hosps. with debility and chronic diarrhea 5/28-6/21/64. In Danville hosp. with chronic rheumatism 10/26-11/15/64. Present on final 9-10/64 roll dated 2/24/65. Postwar roster spells name Millener.

MILLS, ALEXANDER S.: enl. 5/4/61 in Co. I, age 36. To Sgt. 2/12/62. Absent with leave on 5-6/62 roll. To Pvt. on 11-12/62 roll, AWOL, "over 35." AWOL or deserter on 1-2/63 roll, name cancelled on roll. "Dropped from Pay Roll and name sent to Enrolling officer Orange Co." on 7-8/63 roll. One roll and a postwar roster gives middle initial as "H." The latter adds "discharged 1862."

MILLS, JOHN: enl. 10/20/61 in Co. F. Present until discharged 7/30/62.

MILSTEAD, GEORGE W.: enl. 5/1/61 in Co. H. Farmer. Sick at home 9/1-10/15/61. On furlough 2/12-3/16/61. AWOL from 12/12/62 and marked deserter on 12/62 return. Absent sick since 2/13 on 2/28/63 roll, and with disabled horse on 7-8/63 roll, but present on 11-12/63 roll. Absent, detailed as forager on final 3/22/65 roll. Paroled 4/22/65 at Winchester, age 29, resid. Fauquier Co., signs by mark.

138

MILSTEAD, JAMES: b. in U.S. enl. 9/29/62 in Co. H. Present on all rolls thru 3/22/65 final roll, but reported by Richmond as deserter 2/28/65. Wded. and POW 4/1/65 at Hatcher's Run. d. 5/23/65 at Lincoln General Hosp., Washington, D.C., of chronic diarrhea, age 20, resid. Charles Town, (W.) Va. Single, effects given to his aunt Ann Bean.

MILTON, WILLIAM TAYLOR: b. 7/17/38 at "Galloway," Jefferson Co., (W.) Va. enl. 8/1/62 in Co. D. Previously Lt. in 2d Va. Inf. POW 6/9/63 at Beverly Ford. Paroled 6/25/63 at Old Capitol Prison, Washington, D.C. Fifteen days leave from 12/21/63. Thereafter present until acting as Sgt. Maj. on final 3/22/65 roll. Farmer, Commissioner of Revenue for Clarke Co. 22 years, then insurance agent. Resid. Berryville 2/15/18. m. Frances Calendar Duncan 1867. d. 1923, bur. Green Hill Cem., Berryville.

MINE, WILLIAM H.: Only record is of parole as in Co. H at Winchester 4/24/65, age 25, resid. Fauquier Co. May refer to William Henry Wines.

MINOR, ALBERT G.: enl. 5/24/61 in Co. F. Present until discharged 7/26/62. Apparently identical to Absalom Minor, shown on postwar roster.

MITCHELL, ALFRED: enl. 12/20/61 in Co. F as substitute for Thomas C. Stevens. AWOL on rolls for 5-8/62, then no further record. Postwar roster says killed.

MITCHELL, EDWARD Y.: enl. 8/24/64 in Co. I. POW 9/24/64 at Luray. Paroled ca. 11/1/64 at Pt. Lookout. Absent sick on final 3/20/65 roll. On Gordonsville hosp. roll 3/20/65 with gelatis. Middle initial on some rolls shown as Z. and T.

MITCHELL, JAMES SHIPP: On postwar rosters of Co. D. No official record in 6th Va. Cav. Apparently identical to the man of this name in Co. I, 12th Va. Cav.

MITCHELL, PHILIP E. CARY: enl. 4/20/61 in Co. D. Absent on duty as courier for Gen. Jeb Stuart on 11/61 return. d. 3/9/63 at Mt. Jackson hosp. of disease, probably bur. at Mt. Jackson Confederate Cem.

MITCHELL, ROBERT B.: enl. 4/3/62 in Co. D. Horse reported KIA 8/21/62. Absent sick on 9-10/62 roll and 11/62 return. POW 6/7/63 in Clarke Co., age 20. Paroled 6/26/63 at Ft. McHenry, Md. Postwar roster says KIA 8/21/62.

MITCHELL, WILLIAM T.: enl. 5/26/61 in (2d) Co. E as Sgt. Age 26 on 2/16/62 roll. To Lt. 4/20/62. To Capt. on 11-12/62 roll. In Danville wded. 6/18/63. To court-martial duty 1/16/64. POW 5/11/64 at Yellow Tavern. Sent to Hilton Head, S.C., to be placed under fire 8/20/64. Took the oath at Ft. Delaware 6/16/65, resid. Pittsylvania Co. d. 10/25/95 near Alchie. Wid. Mahala E., m. 9/16/63. 1913 listing noted "Capt. Mitchel was a very brave man."

MOFFETT, JESSIE EPHRAIM: b. 1836. enl. 3/12/62 in Co. H as Cpl. Sick at hosp. since 10/23 on 11-12/62 roll. Generally present after 2/28/63 roll. To Sgt. on 11-12/63 roll. Horse KIA 11/12/64 at Newtown. Reported by Richmond as deserter 3/1/65. Present on final 3/22/65 roll. Paroled 4/22/65 at Winchester. resid. Warrenton. d. 1913, bur. Camp Branch Church near Sedalia, Mo. "Jessee" in wartime signature.

MOFFETT, JOHN T.: enl. 9/10/62 in Co. H. To Sgt. on 11-12/62 roll. On detached service as scout with Frank Stringfellow 12/28/63-4/10/64. Present on final 3/22/65 roll. Paroled 4/22/65 at Winchester, age 33. Resid. The Plains on ca. 1898 Fauquier Co. veterans census.

MOFFETT, WALTER FRANKLIN: b. 9/21/45 at Washington. Att. VMI. Conscript enl. 3/26/64 in Co. B. Prior service reportedly with Major Jed Hotchkiss in engineer party. KIA 5/11/64 at Yellow Tavern.

MOGAN, CHARLES F.: On postwar "original list" of Co. F.

MONROE, JAMES: enl. 9/25/62 in Co. A. Deserted 11/5/62 at Ashby's Gap, Fauquier Co.

MONROE, WILLIAM: Shown in Federal records as in Co. H, POW 7/21 (or 23)/63 at Chester Gap. Took the oath 9/23/63 at Old Capitol Prison and sent to Philadelphia, Pa., resid. Fauquier Co. No Confederate or postwar records.

MOON, ELDRIDGE BRECKENRIDGE: b. 1841. enl. 4/1/64 in Co. G. Present until absent sick on final 3/22/65 roll. May be the E. B. Moon previously in Montague's Bn. Va. Inf. Unofficial source says POW at Winchester, but no U.S. records on this. d. 3/15/19 at Roanoke.

MOON, ELLIS M.: b. 1849 in Halifax Co. Att. Hillsboro Mil. Academy, N.C. enl. 4/1/64 in Co. G. POW 5/12/64 in Hanover Co., no parole record. In Richmond hosp. with debility ca. 6/30/64. Present on rolls for 7-8/64 thru final 3/22/65 roll. Postwar sketch says went to Greensboro, N.C., to join Johnston, and paroled 4/65 in Danville. In tobacco business in Richmond 1877-99. Brother of Thomas A.

MOON, THOMAS A.: enl. 8/19/61 in Co. G as Lt., age 27. Ten days leave to get co. clothing from 12/14/62. To Capt. 3/9/64. POW 5/11/64 at Yellow Tavern. Sent to Hilton Head, S.C., to be placed under fire 8/20/64. Took the oath 6/13/65 at Ft. Delaware. Known as "Sandy." Accidentally killed 1869. Brother of Ellis M.

MOON, WALTER LEAKE: b. 1/3/43 in Halifax Co. enl. 4/1/64 in Co. G. Clerk. Previously in Montague's Bn. Va. Inf., Co. A, 53d Va. Inf., then att. VMI. Wded. near Spotsylvania 5/7/64 by shell, right arm amputated. In Richmond hosp. 5/9-5/21/64. Retired to Invalid Corps 8/30/64. Farmer and in tobacco business at South Boston postwar, sheriff of Halifax Co. 1887. m. 1) Mary H. Russell 1865, 2) Eliza Chastain Carrington 1873. d. 12/30/09 at South Boston.

MOORE, AMMISHADDAI, JR.: b. 5/30/46 at "Upton," Clarke Co. enl. 7/25/62 in Co. D. In Charlottesville hosp. with bronchitis 1/16-1/26/64. POW 5/12/64 at Yellow Tavern, escaped between Pt. Lookout and Elmira. Present on 9-10/64 roll and final 3/22/65 roll. Grad. U.Va. in law. Lawyer at Berryville 1870-1921. House of Delegates, presidential elector 1892, counsel and director Northern Va. Power Co., Pres. Bank of Clarke Co. m. 1) Cornelia Daniel Ellet, 2) Annie B. Cabell. d. 1/18/29, bur. Green Hill Cem., Berryville. Wrote history of Clarke Cav. in Gold's *History of Clarke Co.* Brother of Sgt. William Moore, Co. D.

MOORE, FRANCIS: b. 10/22/42. enl. 6/26/61 in Co. D. AWOL since 12/3 on 11-12/61 roll. d. 3/6/62 of disease contracted in service, bur. Green Hill Cem., Berryville. Known as "Frank."

MOORE, FREDERICK: enl. 3/24/63 in Co. K. Detailed as courier and scout for Gen. R. E. Lee 3/24/63 thru 7-8/64 roll. AWOL on 9-10/64 roll and final 1-2/65 roll. Paroled 4/9/65 at Appomattox.

MOORE, JOHN: enl. 9/1/63 in Co. B. Absent wded. since 5/11/64 on 7-8/64 roll. Absent with leave on next roll, but AWOL since 12/16/64 on final 3/21/65 roll. Reported as deserter by Richmond 3/1/65. Paroled 4/29/65 at Winchester, age 21, resid. Flint Hill. Reportedly d. before 5/07.

MOORE, ROBERT P.: On a postwar roster of Co. D.

MOORE, NICHOLAS P.: b. 2/18/41. enl. 4/21/61 in Co. D. Present until wded. 6/9/63 at Brandy Station. In Charlottesville hosp. 6/17-7/19/63, then nurse there and furloughed. Retired to Invalid Corps 10/25/64. Paroled 4/19/65 at Winchester. Farmer near Berryville postwar, "have a ball in my hyp." d. 7/25/38, bur. Green Hill Cem., Berryville.

MOORE, WILLIAM BREWER: b. 10/9/39. enl. 5/15/61 in Co. D. To Cpl. on 5-6/62 roll. To Sgt. on 9-10/62 roll. Horse KIA 6/9/63 at Brandy Station. Always present until MWIA 3/30/65 at Five Forks. d. 4/1/65, bur. Green Hill Cem., Berryville. Postwar roster says promoted to Lt. Brother of Ammi Moore.

MOORE, WILLIAM F.: enl. 4/20/61 in Co. F as Cpl. Detached to QM Dept. 8/13/61 thru 1-2/62 roll. Pvt., AWOL, on 5-6/62 roll. No further record.

MOORHEAD, A. H.: On a postwar roster of (2d) Co. E as enl. 1861. No official record.

MOORMAN, C. S. A.: enl. 4/1/62 in (2d) Co. E. Discharged 8/16/62, age 22. Probably identical to Charles Moorman on postwar roster.

MOORMAN, SAMUEL A.: enl. 5/26/61 in (2d) Co. E as Sgt. Age 24 on 2/16/62 roll. Present on 5-6/62 roll. No further record.

MORAN, JOHN: enl. 10/1/62 in Co. K. Present until he deserted 11/21 or 12/21/62.

MOREHEAD, JAMES MILTON: enl. 4/24/61 in Co. H. Farmer. To Lt. 7/1/61. Absent with leave on 9-10/61 roll. Sick furlough 1/1/63. Numerous absences until resignation 8/13/63 for fistula in ano. Major C. E. Flournoy wrote on 7/20/63 "he has done no duty for nearly a year with his co., & a much better man can be elected to fill his place. The service will be decidedly benefited by his resignation."

MOREL, CHARLES H.: b. in Savannah, Ga. enl. 9/17/61 in (1st) Co. E, age 22. Clerk. Discharged for disability 7/22/62. Later in Co. B, 22d Bn. Ga. Art. and detailed to Signal Corps.

MORELAND, JEREMIAH: enl. 7/24/61 in Co. A. Detailed as hosp. attendant since 11/25 on 11/61 return. Detailed as teamster in QM Dept. or at brigade HQ 12/11/62 thru 3/27/65 final roll. Paroled 4/21/65 at Winchester, age 36, signs by mark. Resid. Loudoun Co. Postwar sources say resid. Clarke Co., "discharged for inability after three years of faithful service."

MORELAND, JOSEPH: enl. 10/1/62 in Co. F. Absent on furlough from 1/30/63, "supposed to have been taken prisoner." Absent on furlough to get horse on 7-8/63 roll. Present on 11-12/63 roll and 5/2/64 clothing roll. AWOL on 9-10/64 roll.

MORELAND, WILLIAM: enl. 9/10/62 in Co. A. Horse KIA 7/3/63 at Fairfield, Pa. Absent on furlough since 8/29 on 8/31/63 roll. Present on 11-12/63 roll. Postwar roster says KIA at Yellow Tavern.

MORGAN, DANIEL HENRY: enl. 4/28/62 in Co. D. POW 7/14/63 at Falling Waters, Md. (or 7/15/63 at Shepherdstown) as Sgt. Paroled 12/24/63 at Pt. Lookout. Present as Pvt. on 9-10/64 roll. AWOL on final 3/22/65 roll. MWIA 4/1/65 at Five Forks. d. 4/8/65, age 30 years, 7 months, 6 days, bur. Elmwood Cem., Shepherdstown, (W.) Va.

MORGAN, JOHN: enl. 4/18/61 in Co. D. Present until POW 5/16/61 at Berry's Ferry. Paroled 5/20/63 at Ft. McHenry, Md. POW 2/22/64 at Berryville, age 26. Took the oath at Ft. Delaware 6/9/65.

MORGAN, ROBERT P.: On a postwar roster of Co. D.

MORGAN, THOMAS J.: enl. 4/22/61 in Co. K. Absent sick at hosp. on 6/30/62 roll. Absent sick at hosp. from 12/16/62 until he d. at the General Receiving Hosp., Gordonsville, 3/30/63. Father: John Morgan.

MORGAN, WILLIAM CASTLEMAN: b. 1835 in Clarke Co. Att. U.Va. enl. 4/25/61 in Co. D. To Sgt. on 5-6/62 roll. Pvt. on 9-10/62 roll. Horse KIA 10/11/63 at Brandy Station. Absent at brigade HQ on 9-10/64 roll. POW 1/17/65 near Berryville. Took the oath 6/10/65 at Elmira. Grad. U.Va., lawyer postwar. d. 12/17/09 in Martinsburg, W.Va., bur. Green Hill Cem., Berryville.

MORRIS, AUGUSTINE M.: enl. 2/1/63 in Co. G. Absent, detailed as teamster at division HQ 11-12/63 roll thru final 3/22/65 roll.

MORRIS, E. S.: Only record is as member of Co. C, admitted to Richmond hosp. 2/5/65 and given 15 days furlough.

MORRIS, WILLIAM G.: enl. 2/64 in Co. K. Deserted 3/25/64 while disbanded. Paroled 4/20/65 at Millwood, age 33.

MORRISON, GABRIEL: enl. 9/26/62 in Co. K. In Richmond hosp. with intermittent fever 12/13-12/26/62. AWOL sick on 7-8/63 roll. Otherwise present until AWOL on final 1-2/65 roll. Paroled at Winchester 5/6/65, age 26, resid. Rappahannock Co.

MORTON, WILLIAM J.: enl. 5/4/61 in Co. I as Sgt., age 31. Farmer. In Orange hosp. 9/28-11/1/61 with remittent fever. To Lt., date unknown. To Capt. on 11/62 return. On detached service on 12/62 return. Wded. in left index finger 5/31/64, and sent to Richmond hosp. 6/1-6/4/64 ("age 28"). In Richmond hosp. with chronic diarrhea 9/1/64 and Charlottesville hosp. with debility 9/2-9/19/64. KIA 10/9/64 at Tom's Brook.

MOSES, W. A.: Only record is of parole as a member of Co. F 5/15/65 at Staunton, age 28.

MOUNTJOY, ALEXANDER: enl. 9/18/62 in Co. H. Present on rolls thru 2/28/63. No further record.

MOUNTJOY, CHARLES: In Federal records as a member of Co. H, POW 7/2/64 at Berryville. Took the oath 5/11/65 at Ft. Warren, Mass., resid. Fauquier Co. No Confederate records.

MOUNTJOY, JOHN WILLIAM: b. 1/7/40. enl. 6/26/61 in Co. H. Farmer. At home sick 9/1-10/23/61. On furlough 2/11-3/15/62. To Cpl. on 9-10/62 roll, which has him absent, POW 9/22/62 at Paris (but no U.S. record of capture). Present on 11-12/63 roll. To Pvt. on 11-12/63 roll. Absent sick since 3/1 on 3/22/65 final roll. Paroled 4/25/65 at Winchester. On ca. 1898 Fauquier Co. veterans census. d. 12/11/23, bur. Warrenton Cem.

MOUNTJOY, WILLIAM E.: enl. 9/18/62 in Co. H. Present until detailed 11/15/62 to nurse William W. Franklin, who was sick at Linden. No further record.

MUNNERLYN, JOHN D.: b. at Georgetown, S.C. enl. 9/17/61 in (1st) Co. E, age 18. Clerk. Discharged 12/26/62 for stricture of urethra, enlarged prostate, and irritability of the bladder, from which he had suffered for several years. Resid. Savannah, Ga. Later Pvt., Co. C, 18th Bn. Ga. Inf.

MURPHY, CHARLES: Shown on enlistment book for Rockingham Co. in Va. Hist. Soc. as in Co. C, a substitute for George W. Hedrick. Probably identical to Samuel C. Murphy.

MURPHY, SAMUEL C.: enl. 5/28/62 in Co. C. Ten days furlough from 12/27/62. Reported missing in 5/63 while on West Virginia trip. No further record. Probably identical to Charles Murphy.

MURRAY, JOHN C.: Shown in Federal records as in Co. C, a deserter who became a POW 8/26/63 at the Rappahannock River. Took the oath 9/26/63 at Old Capitol Prison, giving residence as Alleghany Co., Pa., and was forwarded to Philadelphia, Pa. No Confederate records.

MURRAY, REUBIN J.: b. in Fauquier Co. enl. 4/24/61 in Co. H. Farmer. AWOL 1/20-1/29/62. Detailed as courier at Madison C.H. on 5-6/62 roll. AWOL since 8/25/63 on 7-8/63 roll. Deserted and POW by Federals 12/3/63 in Fauquier Co. Joined USA 4/8/64 at Pt. Lookout and assigned to Co. G, 1st U.S. Vol. Inf., age 27. Mustered out 5/21/66 at Ft. Leavenworth, Kan. Farmer postwar at Springvale, Fairfax Co. d. 4/04.

MURRAY, ROBERT P.: enl. 6/25/61 in Co. C. POW 9/22/62 at Paris and paroled. Absent paroled on 11/62 return. AWOL since Nov. on 12/62 return. To Cpl. 1/1/63. POW and wded. In flesh of right leg at Barnett's Ford, Rapidan River 2/6/64. Took the oath 1/11/65 at Ft. Delaware. Absent, POW, on final ca. 3/30/65 roll. Railroad Engineer 1870. d. 7/12/89, age 52, bur. Thornrose Cem., Staunton.

MURRY, JAMES: enl. 3/5/63 in Co. C. Present until AWOL on 9-10/64 roll. Present on final ca. 3/30/65 roll. Also shown as Murrey, Murray, Mury.

MUSE, JOHN M.: Only mention is in a record of paroled prisoners of the Federal Middle Military Dept., which shows a man of this name, no company given, surrendered at Cynthiana, Ky., paroled 5/8/65 at Danville, Va., former residence Independence, Mo., and destination Somerset, Ky.

MYERS, FREDERICK: enl. 12/8/61 in Co. A. Present until shown as "missing since fight at Strasburg" on 5-6/62 roll. Shown as deserting at Woodstock 6/3/62 on 11/62 return. Shown as deserted, but name cancelled on 11-12/62 roll. Presumably identical to "Miers or Myuers, Henry, killed at Strasburg" on postwar roster.

MYERS, FREDERICK W.: enl. 4/1/62 in (2d) Co E. d. 5/12/62 at General Hosp. No. 1, Lynchburg, of rubeola.

MYERS, GEORGE R.: enl. 4/1/62 in (2d) Co. E. Absent sick on 5-6/62 roll. Twenty days horse leave from 12/17/62. Wded. in left knee and sent to Charlottesville hosp. 9/30/64. d. 10/10/64 from hemorrhage resulting from his wd., bur. Confederate Soldiers' Cem., U.Va., Charlottesville.

MYERS, JACOB: enl. 10/24/62 in Co. C. Absent with leave on 11/62 return. To Cpl. 1/1/63. On detail for horses 9/17-9/25/63. Absent with leave since 12/29 on 12/63 return. POW 6/11/64 at Louisa C.H. Paroled 10/11/64 at Elmira. Received for exchange 11/15/64 at Venus Pt., Savannah River.

MYERS, JACOB: enl. 4/1/62 in (2d) Co. E. Absent sick on 5-6/62 roll. Thereafter present until d. of disease at Morton's Ford 9/29/63, leaving neither wife, child, father, or mother.

MYERS, JAMES W.: enl. 4/22/61 in Co. K. Present until shown on clothing rolls as in hosp. 5/21, 9/8, and 12/17/63. In Charlottesville hosp. with morbi cutis 1/7/64, transferred to Lynchburg 1/8/64. In hosp. 5/2/64. Wded. near Trevillian's Station 6/6/64. Present on 9-10/64 roll. AWOL on final 1-2/65 roll. Paroled 4/21/65 at Edwards Ferry, Md. A man of this name (7/36-2/6/10) is bur. Leesburg Union Cem.

MYERS, JOHN H.: enl. 4/10/64 in Co. K. AWOL in Loudoun Co. on 7-8/64 roll. Present on 9-10/64 roll. AWOL on final 1-2/64 roll. Paroled 4/25/65 at Harpers Ferry, (W.) Va., age 20, signs by mark.

MYERS, JOHN T.: enl. 5/28/61 in Co. C. Absent with leave from 2/27/63 on 1-2/63 roll. POW 6/9/63 at Beverly Ford. Paroled 6/25/63 at Old Capitol Prison. POW 1/31/64 in Madison Co. Took the oath 6/10/65 at Ft. Delaware, resid. Rockingham Co. Many spellings of surname, including Meyers and Myars.

MYERS, MAHLON L.: b. 1/30/40. enl. 5/22/61 in Co. K. POW 8/5/61 at Point of Rocks. No record of parole, but paid by Confederates 3/9/62. POW again near Leesburg 10/3 (or 9)/62, paroled 10/13/62 at Ft. McHenry, Md. In Richmond hosp. 10/24-10/30/62, then detailed as nurse. Present on 11-12/62 roll thru 9-10/63 roll. AWOL on final 1-2/65 roll. Paroled 4/18/65 at Edwards Ferry, Md., and again paroled and took the oath 4/22/65 at Harpers Ferry, (W.) Va. Farmer at Araby, Md., in 1886. d. 12/6/11, bur. Mt. Olivet Cem., Frederick Md.

NALL, JAMES WILLIAM: b. 1/1/44. enl. 9/14/62 in Co. H. Previously enl. in Co. C, 8th Va. Inf. Detailed as courier on 9-10/62 roll. Absent sick since 12/15/62 on 11-12/62 roll. Ordered to report to 8th Va. Inf. 1/30/63. d. 9/6/21, bur. Antioch Baptist Church, Prince William Co.

NEILL, DANGERFIELD FAUNTLEROY: b. 6/30/38. enl. 7/24/61 in Co. A as Sgt. Shown absent sick from 10/23/61 until present as Pvt. on 5-6/62 roll. Absent sick since 6/15/63 on 8/31/63 roll. Otherwise present until "deserted staying in Culpeper" on 7-8/64 roll. d. 3/18/17, bur. Sharon Cem., Middleburg. Known as Faunt Neill.

NELSON, HUGH MORTIMER: b. 10/20/11 at "Mt. Air," Hanover Co. Grad. M. A. U.Va. Member Va. Secession convention. Appointed Capt. Co. D 7/21/61. Farmer. Dropped 4/20/62 when not re-elected. To Lt. and aide de camp to Gen. R. S. Ewell 5/4/62. Sometimes referred to as Capt. and Major on Ewell's staff, but no official documentation found. d. 8/6/62, bur. Old Chapel Cem., Millwood.

NELSON, THOMAS A.: b. in Fauquier Co. enl. 3/12/62 in Co. H. Wded. 7/3/63 at Fairfield, Pa. POW 7/21/63 at Chester Gap. Exchanged 2/13/65 from Pt. Lookout. Paroled 4/22/65 at Winchester, age 29. Farmer postwar at Dudie. d. 8/14/15 at Lee Camp Soldiers' Home, Richmond.

NEVITT, HENRY CLAY: enl. 4/20/61 in Co. F. POW 5/24/61 opposite Georgetown, D.C., while acting as vidette on Potomac. Shown as returned on parole on 9-10/61 roll, and as having taken the oath on 11-12/61 roll.

NEVITT, JOHN EDWARD: enl. 10/7/61 in Co. A. POW 6/9/63 at Brandy Station, paroled 6/25/63 at Old Capitol Prison. POW 9/13/63 near Culpeper. d. 9/7/64 at Pt. Lookout of chronic diarrhea, "some person unknown having assumed the name E. Nevitt was transferred to Elmira, N.Y.," 8/16/64. Appears as Edward Nevitt on monument to Fairfax Co. dead.

NEVITT, NAPOLEON B.: On postwar "original list" of Co. F.

NEVITT, RICHARD L.: On postwar "original list" of Co. F.

NEVITT, SAMUEL E.: On postwar "original list" of Co. F.

NEVITT, THOMAS WILLIAM: b. in Fairfax Co. enl. 4/20/61 in Co. F. POW 3/18/62 at Manassas. Exchanged 8/5/62 at Aiken's Ldg. To Cpl. on 7-8/64 roll. POW 6/11/64 at Louisa C.H. Transferred for exchange 10/11/64, but George W. Kyger came in his place. Took the oath 6/8/65 at Pt. Lookout. Postwar source states he allowed his brother to be released under this name. Resid. Pulaski Co. postwar. d. 9/18/21 at Lee Camp Soldiers' Home, Richmond, age 80, bur. Hollywood Cem., Richmond.

NEVITT, WILLIAM HENRY: b. at Newington, Fairfax Co. enl. 4/20/61 in Co. F. POW 9/13/63 in Culpeper Co. Paroled 3/10/65 at Elmira, "unable to travel." Records show him paroled 4/20/65 at Appomattox and at New Market same day. Resid. Newington 9/6/02, age 64 years 6 months. d. 2/23/20 at Lee Camp Soldiers' Home, Richmond, bur. Pohick Church Cem., Fairfax Co.

NEWBY, JAMES M. P.: enl. 4/22/61 in Co. B, age 45. Farmer. Absent sick since 2/26/62 on 1-2/62 roll. Present on 5-6/62 roll. No further record. Reportedly d. before 5/07.

NEWBILL, JAMES H.: enl. 1/18/62 in Co. G. Farmer. Detailed as teamster on 9-10/62 roll and 11 and 12/62 returns. Transferred 11/14/63 to Co. A, 53d Va. Inf. Wded. 5/10/64, d. 5/23/64, age 37.

NEWELL, _____: Only record is of absence from Co. H on furlough after horse on 12/62 return. Probably an error, meaning John A. Harrell (or Herrell).

NEWMAN, HAMDEN A.: enl. 7/24/61 in Co. D. AWOL since 11/1/61 on 11-12/61 roll, sentenced to lose $36. Absent sick on several later rolls. AWOL since 10/20/62 on 1-2/63 roll. A letter of 12/31/61 stated that he lived in Kentucky before 1851, and might return there. Postwar roster says deserted.

NEWMAN, JOHN T.: enl. 4/24/61 in Co. H. Clerk. AWOL from 10/13/62 on 9-10/62 roll. Sick, absent "in the country" since 2/18 on 2/28/63 roll. POW 8/18/63 in Fauquier Co. Paroled 3/3/64 at Pt. Lookout. Paid as paroled prisoner 3/7/64, but shown as AWOL on later rolls thru 9-10/64.

NEWMAN, JULIUS E.: att. U. Va. enl. 7/13/61 in Co. D. Present, except for 20 day sick furlough from 12/25/61, thru 5-6/62 roll. Absent sick in hosp. in 9-10/62 roll. In Charlottesville hosp. 12/3/62 with "spermatorrhea," and thereafter at Charlottesville hosp. as nurse, ward master, or other capacity thru hosp. roll dated 3/14/65. Erroneously on company rolls as POW from 7-8/64 roll, and as deserter on postwar rosters.

NICHOLAS, GEORGE M.: b. 3/1/43. enl. 5/28/61 in Co. C as Cpl. Farmer. In Harrisonburg hosp. 8/29/64. Otherwise present on all rolls until wded. and POW 1/11/65 at Beverly, W.Va. Lost leg at Beverly. Paroled 4/24/65 at Clarksburg. d. 8/5/12, bur. Port Republic Cem. on hill.

NICHOLAS, SILAS C. K.: b. 9/2/41 at Port Republic. enl. 5/28/61 in Co. C as Cpl. AWOL on 9-10/62 roll. To Sgt. 1/1/63. POW 2/1/64 in Madison Co. Paroled 9/28/64 at Ft. Delaware. On clothing roll as paroled prisoner 10/11/64. KIA 3/15/65 at Ashland, bur. Port Republic Cem. on Hill. At this writing his terse prison diary is in the collection of William Turner of Clinton, Md. Brother of George M.

NICHOLAS, GEORGE WASHINGTON: enl. 3/1/61 in Co. B. He and his horse KIA 5/23/62 at Front Royal. Wife Melvina.

NIGHTINGALE, WILLIAM A.: enl. 11/14/61 in Co. A. Present until AWOL on 5-6/62 roll.

NUCKLE, WILLIAM: Only records are a report of casualties dated 7/18/63 which shows him in Co. C, KIA 7/3/63 at Fairfield, Pa., and a register of casualties with the same information.

NUCKOLS, JESSE: enl. 4/1/62 in (2d) Co. E. Sick in camp on 5-6/62 roll. d. 7/15/62. Brother of Josiah J.

NUCKOLS, JOHN EDWARD: b. 1836 in Pittsylvania Co. enl. 5/27/61 in (2d) Co. E. Present on all rolls thru final 3/4/65 roll. d. 8/9/18 in Pittsylvania Co.

NUCKOLS, JOSIAH JOSEPH: b. in Pittsylvania Co. enl. 4/1/62 in (2d) Co. E. In Richmond hosp. 4/9/64. Horse KIA at Winchester 9/19/64. On scout for 12 days beginning 10/28/64. Otherwise present on all rolls thru final 3/4/65 roll. Resid. Rondo, age 70, on 5/1/00, claiming exposure and slight wd. d. 4/25/24 at Lee Camp Soldiers' Home, Richmond, bur. Hollywood Cem., Richmond.

NUNN, WILLIAM: Shown in Co. G clothing book as discharged.

NUNNALLEY, JOHN A.: b. in Halifax Co. enl. 3/16/62 in Co. G, age 30. Farmer. Resid. Wolftrap, Halifax Co. d. 4/24/62 at Richmond of pneumonia. Wid. Mary E., m. 1855 or 1856.

OAKES, CHRIST. C.: b. in Halifax Co. enl. 3/6/62 in Co. G. Farmer. Absent on sick furlough until discharged on surgeon's certificate of disability 12/8/62, age 24. Applied for pension in Danville, age 62, claiming exposure in service, 7/21/02.

O'BANNON, HENRY CLAY: enl. 3/1/62 in Co. B. On sick furlough since 6/17/62 on 5-6/62 roll. Courier for Gen. W. E. Jones on Nov. and Dec. returns. On extra duty as orderly for Capt. D. A. Grimsley on 7-8/64 roll. Absent with leave on 9-10/64 roll and absent sick since 3/1/65 on final 3/21/65 roll. Postwar roster says age 20 on enlistment. Resid. Fredericksburg. d. 7/21/16 at Ft. Stanton, N.M., and bur. there.

O'BANNON, WALTER: b. 9/17/35. enl. 4/22/61 in Co. B as Lt. Farmer. Sick in quarters on 12/61 return. Dropped as Lt. when not re-elected 4/20/62. To regimental Ordnance Sgt. on 9-10/62 roll. Otherwise present thru 9-10/64 roll. Paroled 5/17/65 at Winchester, resid. Rappahannock Co. d. 5/12/93 in Va.

O'BRIEN, WILLIAM: Only record is of parole as in Co. A 5/11/65 at Charleston, W.Va., age 19.

O'CONNEL, TERRY: enl. 1/1/63 in Co. D as substitute for George H. Sowers. Missing on 7/3/63, supposed to be POW, but no Federal records. Postwar rosters give name as P. O'Connel, P. O'Connell.

O'DAY, MICHAEL: enl. 1/9/63 in Co. G. Laborer. POW 5/1/63 at Fairmont, (W.) Va. Released 6/3/63 from Camp Chase, Ohio. Age 43, resid. Fairfax.

ODEN, JAMES S.: enl. 7/15/61 in Co. K. AWOL on 7-8/61 roll. Detached as courier since 11/1 on 11/61 return, and detached since 12/3 on 12/61 return. POW 5/30/62 at Front Royal. Exchanged 8/5/62 at Aiken's Ldg. Signs as in Co. K on 8/7/62. Appointed Capt. and AQM from Louisiana as of 6/5/63. Paroled at Edwards Ferry, Md., 5/65 as Capt. and AQM, Stuart Horse Art. Unofficial sources also state he served as aide to Gen. Micah Jenkins and as ordnance officer with Gen. R. B. Garnett.

ODEN, JOHN BEVERLY: b. 2/23/39. enl. 7/15/61 in Co. K. Appointed Assistant Surgeon 9/13/61 (or 10/9/61), most of which subsequent service seems not to have been with the regiment. To Surgeon 11/26/63. Retired 5/28/64, suffering from phthisis pulmonalis. d. 1/25/11, bur. Sharon Cem., Middleburg.

O'DONNELL, J.: enl. 9/17/61 in (1st) Co. E, but name cancelled on 10/16/61 roll, "failed to join. Horse reported to belong to the captain." No further record.

O'GRADY, MICHAEL C.: b. in Ireland. enl. 9/17/61 in (1st) Co. E, age 34. Teacher. Resid. Savannah, Ga. Discharged 8/31/62 for hernia.

OLIVER, GEORGE Y.: enl. 10/11/62 in (2d) Co. E. Twenty day horse detail from 12/16/63. POW 1/31/64 on Robinson River, Madison Co. Took the oath 6/20/65 at Ft. Delaware, resid. Pittsylvania Co. Farmer postwar, age 55 on 5/15/00, resid. Acorn and Nathalie, Halifax Co. d. 4/17/24.

OPIE, HIEROME LINDSAY, JR.: b. 1837. enl. 12/28/62 in Co. D. Previously in Capt. Garber's Co. (Staunton Artillery) Va. Lt. Art. Present until appointed drill master with rank of Lt. as of 11/3/63 on staff of Col. W. L. Jackson. Capt. John D. Imboden wrote 3/20/62 "his estate of some $40,000 was all at Wheeling. The Yankees have it all." Brother of John N. d. Covington, Ky., 5/25/92.

142

OPIE, JOHN NEWTON: b. 3/14/44 at Millview, Jefferson Co., (W.) Va. Att. VMI. enl. 10/15/62 in Co. D. Previously in 5th Va. Inf. Horse KIA 6/9/63 at Brandy Station. Wded. 10/11/63 at Brandy Station, and absent wded. on rolls until POW on final 3/22/65 roll. Retired to Invalid Corps 1/8/65. POW 2/6/65 in Clarke Co. Paroled 3/14/65 at Elmira. Paroled Winchester 5/8/65. Grad. U. Va. law school 1885. House of Delegates 1882-84, State Senate 1896-1904. m. 1) Belle Harmon 1866, 2) Ida Walton Fletcher 1878. Wrote *A Rebel Cavalryman* . . . (1899). d. at Staunton 1/26/06, bur. Thornrose Cem., Staunton.

ORISON, FREDERICK: b. 1840 in Loudoun Co. enl. 4/22/61 in Co. K. Thirty day furlough from 8/5/61. Confederate records show POW 3/1/62, but there are no U.S. records of this. The 12/12/62 roll states AWOL until 9/1/62. Accidentally wded. 6/20/63. Otherwise present until final 1-2/65 roll when AWOL. Paroled 4/18/65 at Edwards Ferry, Md. d. 1905 in Loudoun Co. Confederate records also spell name Orrison.

ORRISON, GEORGE G.: b. 10/4/32 in Loudoun Co. Reported KIA 8/5/61 at Point of Rocks in Co. K, bur. New Valley Church Cem., Lucketts.

ORRISON, JONAH L.: enl. 7/15/61 in Co. K. POW 8/5/61 opposite Point of Rocks, Md. Held at Ft. Lafayette, N.Y., and paroled 3/24/62. POW 6/9/63 at Brandy Station. Paroled 6/25/63 at Old Capitol Prison. Otherwise present until POW 7/1/63 at Waterford. d. 10/4/64 of chronic diarrhea at Elmira and bur. there. Name also appears as Orison.

OSBORN, EDWARD: enl. 5/31/61 in Co. D. Reported as AWOL from 12/12/61, "sentenced to loose $24 . . . had joined another company" and "said to be lieut. to some compy. unknown." No further record. Postwar rosters spell name Osborne, one stating he resid. Loudoun Co.

OSBORN, W. P.: Conscript assigned 3/7/64 to Co. G. d. 5/5/64 of typhoid pneumonia at General Hosp. No. 9, Richmond. Never taken up on rolls of company. Also shown as Osbourne, Osburn, etc.

OSBORNE, JOSEPH: Shown in Co. G clothing book as discharged.

OSBURN, HERBERT: b. 2/14/43. enl. 7/24/61 in Co. A. Present until POW 9/14/63 near Culpeper. Paroled 3/10/65 at Elmira. Absent, paroled POW since 3/10 on final ca. 3/27/65 roll. Paroled 4/24/65 at Charles Town, (W.) Va. d. 2/2/90, bur. Leesburg Union Cem.

OSBURN, JAMES MILLER: b. 1846 at Snickersville, Loudoun Co. enl. 9/22/62 in Co. A. Absent with leave on 9-10/64 roll. Otherwise present thru final ca. 3/27/65 roll. POW 4/3/65 at Appomattox. Took the oath 6/15/65 at Pt. Lookout, resid. Loudoun Co. Postwar source says never wded., 2 horses shot under him. Moved to Shelbyville, Ky., 1876. Businessman in Louisville since 1881 in Ohio.

OVERFIELD, MARSHALL: Arrested 5/10/64 by Federals in Jefferson Co., (W.) Va., who recorded him as "guerilla and horsethief" of Co. H. He appears actually to have been a member of Mosby's 43d Bn. Va. Cav., as there are no records for him in the 6th Va. Cav.

OWEN, HENRY E.: enl. 8/19/61 in Co. G, age 20. d. 11/21/61 at Ashland of typhoid fever.

OWEN, RUFUS H: b. 9/24/30. enl. 8/19/61 in Co. G as Sgt. To Lt. 12/26/61. On recruiting service since 2/16 on 1-2/62 roll. To Capt. 4/20/62. Several absences for sickness in 1862. On detached service in Culpeper and Albemarle Cos. 4-6/63. Requested retirement for mumps and hemorrhoids 10/29/63. Last present on 11-12/63 roll. Honorably retired 3/9/64. d. 3/19/92 at home near Houston of grip, bur. "Green's Folly," Hwy. 654, Centerville, Halifax Co. Wid. Eliza J., m. 1853.

OWEN, THOMAS HOWERTON: b. 6/11/33 in Halifax Co. Grad. VMI. enl. 8/19/61 in Co. G as Lt. Resigned 12/25/61. In Danville hosp. 12/26/61. Elected to Capt., 3d Va. Cav., later Lt. Col. Civil engineer and farmer at South Boston postwar. d. 5/8/94.

OWENS, CUTHBERT, JR.: b. 7/12/43. enl. 3/9/62 in Co. H. Detailed as courier to Gen. L. L. Lomax on 7-8/63 roll. Detached service at Gen. Jeb Stuart's HQ since 8/1 on 11-12/63 roll. Otherwise present until KIA 5/11/64 at Yellow Tavern, bur. Owens Cem., The Plains.

OWENS, JOHN: This name appears as a member of Co. D on a register of a Petersburg hosp. for 2/14-9/10/64. However, there is no other record, official or unofficial, of this man in the regiment, and it is doubtless an error.

OWENS, P. W.: POW 12/6/63 in Fauquier Co. as in Co. A. Paroled 5/3/64 at Pt. Lookout. In Richmond hosp. 5/8-5/20/64 with chronic diarrhea, then furloughed 30 days. Not on company rolls or postwar rosters. No further record. One record shows middle initial "L."

OWENS, SIMON KENTON: b. 3/22/39. enl. 4/24/61 in Co. H. Student. Transferred 8/21/61 to 8th Va. Inf. KIA 5/6/62 at Williamsburg, bur. Owens Cem., The Plains.

OWENS, WILLIAM MASON: b. 2/22/41. enl. 5/20/61 in Co. H. Farmer. To Sgt. on 5-6/62 roll. Transferred 8/16/62 to Co. A. Pvt. on 12/5/62 roll. Detailed to go on scout with Lt. Stringfellow 12/12 on 11-12/63 roll. KIA 1/10/64 at Loudoun Heights, bur. Owens Cem., The Plains. See L. Hopkins, *Bull Run to Appomattox* (1908), pp. 201-203. Known as Mason Owens.

PADGETT, CHARLES P.: enl. 2/21/62 in Co. H. Substitute for J. R. W. Macrae. Detailed as courier for Gen. Jeb Stuart on 5-6/62 roll. d. 6/62, bur. 6/10/62 at Oakwood Cem., Richmond.

PADGETT, JOSEPH: enl. 4/20/61 in Co. F. Sent to Richmond hosp. sick 4/20/62. d. 6/62, bur. 6/10/62 at Richmond. Possible middle initial is P. or H.

PAGE, ARCHIE C.: enl. 9/3/61 in Co. D. Ten days leave from 12/18/61. Reported as AWOL on 9-10/62 roll and returned from desertion 12/10/62 with surgeon's certificate. Absent sick at hosp. on 8/31/63 roll. Absent on duty in QM Dept. at Harrisonburg as clerk 9/27/63 thru 3/22/65 final roll. Otherwise present. Paroled 4/19/65 at Winchester, age 35.

PAGE, GEORGE RANDOLPH: b. 1824. enl. 7/10/61 in Co. D. Ten days sick furlough from 12/17/61. AWOL on 5-6/62 roll. No further record. d. 3/14/03, bur. Mt. Hebron Cem., Winchester.

PAGE, WILLIAM BYRD: att. Episcopal H.S., Alexandria. enl. 5/17/61 in Co. D. Courier for Gen. Jeb Stuart on 11/61 return. Absent sick with broken leg 11/25/62 thru 1-2/63 roll. Wded. 9/13/63 at Culpeper and permanently disabled. Absent wded. at hosp. on final 3/22/65 roll. One postwar source says KIA.

PAINTER, JACOB M.: Conscript enl. 2/24/64 in Co. F. Shoemaker. Paroled 5/26/65 at Charleston, W.Va., age 44, resid. Rockbridge Co.

PALMER, JAMES FRANK: b. 6/14/35. enl. 7/24/61 in Co. A. Farmer. Twelve days sick furlough from 2/25/62. On furlough since 8/29/63 on 8/31/63 roll. To Cpl. 11/1/63. Wded. 5/31/64 at Cold Harbor and left arm lost, thereafter absent (Pvt.) due to wd. thru 3/27/65 final roll. Paroled 5/9/65 at Charles Town, (W.) Va. d. 3/4/05, bur. Ebenezer Cem. near Round Hill.

PALMER, JOHN WILLIAM: b. in Loudoun Co. Enl. 3/9/62 in Co. F. Absent on sick furlough on 5-6/62 roll. Thereafter present until AWOL on 9-10/64 roll. Farmer, resid. Archie, Culpeper Co., age 61 on 6/4/04. Claimed wd. at Brandy Station, typhoid pneumonia, "left in Fall 64 on acct. illness." d. 5/25/21.

PALMER, LEWIS FRANKLIN: b. 10/3/28 (or 1829) in Loudoun Co. enl. 7/15/61 in Co. K. On sick furlough from 2/17/62 on 1-2/62 roll. POW 8/20/64 while on horse detail near Leesburg. Paroled 3/14/65 at Elmira. Present as paroled POW in hosp. and at Camp Lee, near Richmond, 3/18-3/20/65. Paroled 4/28/65 at Edwards Ferry, Md. In mercantile business at Arcola postwar. d. 2/13/94 (or 1892), bur. Mt. Zion Old School Baptist Church Cem. on Route 50.

PANNIL, JAMES BRUCE: On a 1913 roster of (2d) Co. E. No official record.

PANNILL, BALDWIN: enl. 4/1/62 in Co. I. Present on 5-6/62 roll. Got Alexander Z. Gardner as substitute. Postwar roster says discharged 1863.

PARKER, STAFFORD H., JR.: b. 1846. enl. 9/10/62 in Co. G. Discharged 10/27/62 by order of Secretary of War, he being a minor enlisted without the consent of his parents. Son of Capt. John H. Parker, CSN. Later cadet and Lt. in Parker's Co. Va. Lt. Artillery. Lost an arm from wd. at Spotsylvania. Living in California in 1885.

PARNELL, ARTHUR F.: enl. 3/1/62 in Co. B. POW 6/14/62 at Sperryville "by a scouting party of the enemy whilst on his way from Rappk. Co. to join his company." Exchanged from Old Capitol Prison 8/1/62. On extra duty in QM or Commissary Dept. as teamster from 11-12/62 roll thru 9-10/64 roll. Reported as deserter by Richmond 3/1/65. Deserted and dropped from rolls on final 3/21/65 roll. Paroled 5/2/65 at Winchester, age 29. Reportedly d. before 5/07.

PARRISH, ABRAHAM N.: enl. 4/1/62 in (2d) Co. E. Sick at home in Pittsylvania on 11-12/62 roll. Detached as teamster for brigade on 7-8/63 roll. Order transferred to Co. I, 21st Va. Inf. in exchange for "Josephus Parrish" of that unit 9/1/63. Always absent sick on rolls of 21st. Resid. Axton, age 70, on 11/19/88. Claimed wded. in battle near Petersburg in 1863, thigh bone broken. Also shown as Abram.

PARRISH, ABRAM P., SR.: enl. 5/27/61 in (2d) Co. E. d. 8/10/61 at Monterey. Possibly identical to Peck or Perk Parrish shown on postwar rosters.

PARRISH, JOHN W.: enl. 2/8/63 in (2d) Co. E. Fifteen days furlough on 1-2/63 roll. POW 5/11/64 at Yellow Tavern. Took the oath at Elmira 6/16/65, resid. Danville.

PARRISH, JOSEPH MADISON: b. 1833 in Pittsylvania Co. enl. 5/27/61 in (2d) Co. E as Sgt. Farmer. Present until POW 5/11/64 at Yellow Tavern. Took the oath 6/16/65 at Elmira, resid. Danville. d. 7/5/97 near Chatham. Wid. Sallie S., m. 1892.

PARRISH, PECK: On 1913 roster of (2d) Co. E. Another postwar roster shows Perk Parrish (Parish). Perhaps identical to Abram P. No official record.

PARRISH, WILLIAM C.: enl. 9/8/62 in (2d) Co. E. POW 9/13/63 near Culpeper. Paroled 3/10/65 at Elmira for exchange.

PARRISH, WILLIAM S.: b. in Pittsylvania Co. enl. 5/27/61 in (2d) Co. E. Age 36 on 2/16/62 roll. On detached service on 5-6/62 roll. Shown as AWOL, exchanged POW on 12/62 return, no other record of capture. POW 10/11/63 at Brandy Station. d. 7/9/64 at Pt. Lookout.

PARTLOW, JOHN M.: b. in Rappahannock. enl. 5/4/61 in Co. I, age 19. Sick at home with measles on ca. 6/61 roll. Absent sick with pneumonia 2/10-4/4/62. To Cpl. on 5-6/62 roll. AWOL since 10/23/63 on 11-12/62 roll. Found not guilty of AWOL 3/7/64 by court-martial: "being found not guilty, Captain [sic] Partlow will resume his sword." Present 7-8/64 roll thru 3/20/65 final roll, but back to Pvt. on final roll. Paroled 4/65 at Lynchburg. Postwar roster says badly wded. at Five Forks. Farmer, resid. near Washington, Rappahannock Co. 4/16/08. d. 7/21/20.

PARTLOW, WILLIAM E.: b. at Washington, Va. enl. 8/15/64 in Co. I. Present thru 3/20/65 final roll. Justice of the Peace at Sanger, Denton Co., Texas, age 78 on 7/11/25. Resid. in Texas for 49 years prior to 1925. d. 8/20/26.

PATE, MATTHEW H.: enl. 8/19/61 in Co. G, age 26. Absent on sick furlough since 2/16 on 1-2/62 roll. Present on 5-6/62 roll. Shown as having obtained substitute (William Clark) on 9-10/62 roll.

PATRICK, DENNIS M.: enl. 9/17/61 in (1st) Co. E, "age 39," as farrier. On 5/62 sick report of Chimborazo Hosp. No. 3, Richmond, "Disease: For being 57 years old." Discharged for disability 5/15/62. His certificate reads "Great disability from a long attack of typhoid pneumonia. He is 40 years of age & of broken down constitution." Teamster from 11/18 on 11/61 return. Resid. Savannah, Ga.

PATTIE, JAMES S.: enl. 9/1/62 in Co. H. Clerk. Previously in Co. K, 17th Va. Inf. 12/1/62 transfer to 17th Va. Inf. was aborted. In Charlottesville hosp. 6/14-6/26/63 with chronic diarrhea and 8/29-9/20/63 with acute gonorrhea. Absent sick on 7-8/63 roll. AWOL from 12/28/63. Took the oath 3/12/64 at Old Capitol Prison and sent to New York, age 21, resid. Warrenton. Voluntarily came in to the pickets of the 1st N.J. Cav. 1/25/64 near New Baltimore. Told Federals he "belonged to a Military Comp. before the war, was called out by the Governor in 4/62, never in favor of secession."

PATTON, JOHN W.: enl. 7/24/61 in Co. A. Present until marked absent sick since 12/9 on 1-2/62 roll. Present on 5-6/62 roll. Postwar roster says "discharged," no date.

PAXSON, THOMPSON M. C.: b. 11/23/23. enl. 7/15/61 in Co. K. Absent on sick furlough from 2/17 on 1-2/62 roll. Detailed in QM Dept. from 12/12/62 roll thru 11-12/63 roll. Transferred 2/10/64 to Co. A, 39th Bn. Va. Cav. Paroled 4/24/65 at Winchester. Resid. Peonia 1896. d. 6/8/07, bur. Union Cem., Leesburg. Cousin of Union Gen. John R. Kenly.

PAYNE, AMOS PARKER: b. 8/14/37 in Fairfax Co. enl. 10/1/61 in Co. F. In Richmond hosp. wded. 5/18-6/2/64. Otherwise present until absent on horse detail on final 2/24/65 roll. Paroled at Appomattox 4/9/65. Took the oath at Alexandria 6/17/65. Farmer in East Falls Church 5/28/18. d. 1/5/29 at Chesterbrook, bur. Arlington National Cem. Wid. Elizabeth Catherine, m. 1891.

PAYNE, CHARLES R.: b. in Campbell Co. enl. 5/27/61 in (2d) Co. E. Age 19 on 2/16/62 roll. d. 2/28/62. Left no widow or child; father Philip M. Payne.

PAYNE, EDWARD SCOTT: enl. 4/2/62 in (2d) Co. E. AWOL on 5-6/62 roll and in arrest on 11-12/62 roll. Present on 1-2/63 roll. Gave himself up to Federals 9/12/64 at Point of Rocks, took the oath at Harpers Ferry, (W.) Va., 9/14/64, age 22, resid. Culpeper. Transportation furnished to Philadelphia, Pa. Stated his captain's name was "West." In C.S. records as Edward S. or Ned S., but in U.S. records as Edwin, of Co. H. An unreliable postwar roster says he d. in Pittsylvania Co.

PAYNE, ROBERT C.: enl. 5/27/61 in (2d) Co. E. Age 25 on 2/16/62 roll. AWOL on 5-6/62 roll. No further record.

PAYNE, THOMAS: Shown in Federal records as in Co. H. Gave himself up to them 9/12/64 at Point of Rocks, age 21, resid. Culpeper. Took the oath 9/14/64 at Harpers Ferry, (W.) Va. and transportation furnished to Philadelphia, Pa. Said his captain's name was "West." No Confederate records. Not in postwar rosters.

PAYNE, WALTER C.: enl. 4/1/62 in (2d) Co. E. Absent on 5-6/62 roll. In Charlottesville hosp. 9/30, d. there 10/1/62 of typhoid fever, age 17. One death record puts him in Co. F, which seems erroneous. His father was Fullington Payne of Pittsylvania Co. Walter C. is bur. Confederate Soldiers' Cem., U. Va., Charlottesville.

PEAKE, BENJAMIN FRANKLIN: b. 1842 in Fauquier Co. enl. 7/24/61 in Co. A. To Cpl. on 11-12/63 roll. POW 5/11/64 in Hanover Co. Exchanged ca. 11/15/64 at Venus Pt., Savannah River, from Elmira and Pt. Lookout (erroneously reported as 3/15/65). Sick at home since 1/65 on 3/27/65 final roll. Paroled 5/8/65 at Millwood. Resid. Alexandria postwar. Merchant at The Plains in 1914. d. 1921 in Baltimore, Md., bur. family cem. at "Rockdale," Fauquier Co. Brother of John W.

PEAKE, JOHN W.: b. in Fauquier Co. enl. 3/1/62 in Co. A. Present until shown as absent sick 8/64 thru final 3/27/65 roll. Paroled at Winchester 4/25/65, age 19. Known as "Tip" or "Tippy." Claimed service as courier for Gens. Jeb Stuart and L. L. Lomax. m. Alwilda Marshall Brooke. Wrote "Recollections of a Boy Cavalryman" in 7/26 *Confederate Veteran*. d. 10/12/25 at Washington, D.C., bur. family cem. at "Rockdale," Fauquier Co. Brother of Benjamin F.

PEARSON, JAMES MASTIN, JR.: enl. 1/15/63 in (2d) Co. E. Sick at Orange hosp. on 11-12/63 roll. POW 5/11/64 at Yellow Tavern. Paroled 9/18/64 at Pt. Lookout. In Richmond hosp. with scorbutis 9/22-9/27/64, then 45 day furlough. Drew clothing at Richmond 11/11/64. Present on final 3/4/65 roll. d. 1899, bur. Pearson family cem., Chatham.

PEARSON, JOHN C.: b. in Fauquier Co. enl. 5/20/61 in Co. H. Farmer. On furlough 2/10-3/14/62. To Cpl. on 5-6/62 roll. To Pvt., AWOL since 12/28/63 and on 11-12/63 roll. Thereafter generally absent sick and so absent since 3/1 on final 3/22/65 roll. Paroled 4/22/65 at Winchester, age 25. Farmer at Selone on 3/28/11. d. 7/13/16 in Fauquier Co. of tuberculosis. Wid. Mary E., m. 1863. Claimed frostbite on Rosser's raid resulting in leave of absence.

PEARSON, WILLIAM H.: enl. 6/26/61 in Co. K. Previously in Co. F, 5th Va. Cav., in which records his name appears as Pierson or Person. Detailed to drive baggage wagon 11/20/61 thru 12/61 return. Paid for 90 days service as butcher 3/31/62. Detailed as regimental wagoner on 6/30/62 roll.

PEARSON, WILLIAM MALBARRY: enl. 4/1/62 in (2d) Co. E. Paid as teamster 12/4-12/31/61, 4/1-4/20/62. Sick at home since 10/28 on 12/62 return. Otherwise present thru final 3/4/65 roll. Resid. Red Eye, age 56, claiming flesh wd. in left leg at Spotsylvania ca. 3/11/64 on 5/2/00 pension application. d. 6/22/28, wid. Josephine, m. 12/21/65.

PEMBERTON, J. O.: Shown as a member of Co. I, from Culpeper, on a postwar roster. No Confederate service record.

PENCE, JOHN T.: enl. 2/10/64 in Co. C. Present thru final 3/30/65 roll. POW 4/1/65 at Five Forks. Took the oath 6/11/65 at Pt. Lookout, resid. Rockingham Co.

PENCE, PETER: Only record in the regiment is of parole as in Co. I, 5/18/65 at Staunton, age 25. Previously in Co. I, 33rd Va. Inf.

PENCE, SYLVESTER HARRISON: b. 10/10/36. enl. 5/28/61 in Co. C. Absent sick since 10/21 on 9-10/61 roll. Thereafter present thru 11-12/63 roll and drew clothing 5/2/64. Presumably identical to "Pvt. S. A. Ponce, Co. C," listed in Richmond *Sentinel* of 5/27/64 at KIA between 5/4 and 5/13/64. KIA Wilderness 5/6/64.

PENDLETON, DUDLEY DIGGES: b. 1840 in Louisa Co. Grad. Washington College. enl. 9/24/61 in Co. D. Teacher. Transferred from Rockbridge Artillery. Present until appointed Capt. and Adjutant on staff of his uncle, Gen. William N. Pendleton 5/22/62. Personally recommended for Lt. by Gen. T. J. Jackson and by Col. Charles Field, Capt. Hugh M. Nelson and Gens. W. N. Pendleton and Jeb Stuart. Paroled 4/9/65 at Appomattox. Principal, postwar, of Shepherd College, Shepherdstown, W.Va. d. 8/25/86, bur. Elmwood Cem., Shepherdstown.

PENDLETON, ROBERT NELSON: b. 2/4/42 in Lousia Col. Att. Washington Coll. enl. 3/19/62 in Co. D. Horse wded. 5/23/62 near Front Royal. Absent as clerk at brigade HQ 12/5/63 thru final 3/22/65 roll. To Lt. and drillmaster on staff of Gen. W. H. Payne 3/28/65. Recommended by Gen. Payne 2/26/65 for "intelligence, good habits, courage and usefulness on the field." Paroled 4/25/65 at Summit Pt., (W.) Va. Farmer and civil engineer postwar, resid. Jefferson and Clarke Cos. and Wytheville. m. Fannie Gibson 1869. d. at Wytheville 1905. Nephew of Gen. W. N. Pendleton.

PENICK, ROBERT: enl. 8/19/61 in Co. G as bugler, age 36. Absent on sick furlough since 11/28/61 on 11-12/61 roll. Thereafter present thru 5-6/62 roll. Co. clothing book has discharged 8/19/62. Postwar roster says "served part time as bugler."

PENNYBACKER, FRANCIS STRIBLING: b. 9/26/40 at "The White House." Att. Roanoke College. enl. 11/15/63 in Co. D. Transferred from Co. F, 10th Va, Inf. In Charlottesville hosp. 12/19/63 with morbi cutis, transferred to Staunton. Absent sick at hosp. on 11-12/63 roll. Courier for Gen. T. L. Rosser on 9-10/64 roll. Present on final 3/22/65 roll. In Richmond hosp. with scabies 3/31/65. m. Lucy Elizey White 1867. In insurance business at Mt. Jackson 1903. d. 1925, bur. New Mount Jackson Cem., Mt. Jackson. Known as "Frank."

PERKINS, A. H.: Only record is as a member of Co. C, in Richmond hosp. with bronchitis 3/5-3/15/65, then given 60 days furlough.

PEYTON, HAMILTON: enl. 9/20/64 in Co. B. Present on 9-10/64 roll, but reported by Richmond as deserter 3/1/65, to be found in Rappahannock Co., and shown as deserted and dropped from the rolls on final 3/21/65 roll.

PHILLIPS, GRANVILLE D.: enl. 3/5/62 in Co. C. Present on all rolls thru 11-12/63 roll, and drew clothing in 1/64. No further official record, but Annie L. Winegord (who had m. Isaac Winegord in 1874) stated on a pension application that she m. Phillips in 1863 and that he d. of a gunshot wd. on the battlefield of Spotsylvania C.H.

PHILLIPS, JOHN: enl. 3/24/62 in Co. H. Present until paid as discharged soldier 7/31/62.

PHILLIPS, THADDEUS W.: enl. 10/10/34 in Co. C. In Richmond hosp. with diarrhea 11/28-12/24/63. Present on 11-12/63 roll. Drew clothing in 1/64. No further record. Known as "Shad."

PHILLIPS, WILLIAM HIRAM: b. 3/2/41. enl. 3/5/62 in Co. C. Absent with leave on 9-10/64 roll. In Richmond hosp. with dysentery 10/11-10/17/63. In Charlottesville hosp. with scabies 1/12-2/11/64. Otherwise always present thru final ca. 3/30/65 roll. Paroled 5/2/65 at Harrisonburg, age 24, resid. Rockingham Co. d. 5/7/08, bur. Goshen Baptist Ch. Cem.

PIERCE, WILLIAM G.: enl. 4/18/61 in Co. D. On extra duty as teamster in QM Dept. 10/21/61 thru 12/61 return. AWOL since 6/1 on 5-6/62 roll, but present on 9-10/62 roll. Deserted 12/3/61 at Harrisonburg.

PILLOW, SAMUEL B.: enl. 3/10/62 in Co. G. Absent sick on 9-10/62 roll, and charge of AWOL removed on 12/62 return when he furnished a surgeon's certificate. Transferred 2/16/63 to Co. I, 53d Va. Inf. POW at Gettysburg and exchanged. POW at Five Forks, d. 4/28/65 at Pt. Lookout of chronic diarrhea and bur. there. Resid. Pittsylvania Co., signs by mark.

PINE, GEORGE: enl. 11/25/62 in Co. A. On horse and clothing leave in Fauquier Co. 12/10/62-1/16/63. Present on 1-2/63 roll, but AWOL since 6/27/63 thru 11-12/63 roll. No further record. Postwar listing says resid. Clarke Co.

PIRKEY, ALBERT H.: b. 4/22/38. enl. 5/28/61 in Co. C. Absent sick since 10/21 on 10/61 return. Sick at Mt. Jackson hosp. since 2/27/63 on 1-2/63 roll. POW 6/5/64 at Piedmont. Paroled 3/4/65 at Camp Morton, Ind. Still POW on final ca. 3/30/65 roll. d. 8/9/15, bur. Frieden's United Church of Christ, east of Harrisonburg.

PIRKEY, OSCAR F. A.: enl. 5/28/61 in Co. C. Sick in hosp. since 10/1 on 9-10/61 roll. Present, joined from desertion 10/62 on 9-10/62 roll. Absent wded. on 9-10/64 roll. Otherwise present thru final ca. 3/30/65 roll. Paroled 5/2/65 at Harrisonburg, age 29.

PLASTER, GEORGE EMORY: b. 5/12/26. enl. 7/24/61 in Co. A. Physician. To Lt. 7/30/61. POW 3/14/62 at Upperville. Paroled from Old Capitol Prison 8/1/62. Thirty days leave from 9/13/63. Acting regimental adjutant since 10/20/63 on 12/31/63 roll. Recommended by Gen. L. L. Lomax for valor and skill 7/23/64. Wded. 10/9/64. To Capt., Co. H, 10/27/64. Detailed to bring in absentees 2/28/65. Present on final 3/22/65 roll. POW 4/1/65 at Dinwiddie C.H. Took the oath 6/19/65 at Johnson's Island, Ohio. Resid, "Glenmeade," near Bluemont, which he bought with money made in California in 1849. m. Sallie Meade Taliaferro. d. 3/1/25, bur. Ebenezer Cem., Bloomfield.

PLASTERS, ROBERT E.: Only record is a register of commissioned officers, which shows him as Lt. in Co. A, appointed 8/1/61, dropped 4/20/62.

POLLARD, E. W.: enl. 5/28/63 in Co. C. Absent, detailed with brigade QM on all muster rolls with his name (thru 9-10/64 roll). Forage master with brigade forage master on 2/64 clothing roll. Paroled 5/31/65 at Harrisonburg, age 32.

PORTER, DAVID: enl. 4/20/61 in Co. F. POW 5/24/61 as vidette on Potomac opposite Georgetown, D.C. Released on parole by Federals 2/61, and then employed at Norfolk Navy Yard. Signed receipt for pay 11/30/61 (covering period 4/20-10/31/61), but apparently did not return to the regiment. Shown as "released by federals on parole, not heard from since" on 7-8/62 roll.

PORTER, MARCELLUS: Only record is as a member of Company I on a 1909 roster. This may be a confused reference to Marcellus Proctor, but both names are on the roster.

POTTER, JOHN: On postwar "original list" of Co. F.

POWELL, A. H.: On postwar "original list" of Co. F.

POWELL, BENJAMIN R.: enl. 5/28/61 in Co. C. Absent sick since 10/21 on 9-10/61 roll. Next appearance is on 9-10/62 roll, where he is absent, sent to hosp. in Sept. Shown as deserting 10/15/62 at Rippon on 11/62 return. Present on rolls for 11/62-2/63. Absent sick since Aug. on 12/62 return. Absent under arrest since 5/1/63 on 11-12/63 roll. enl. 23rd Va. Cav., 1/14/64.

POWELL, EDWARD BURR: b. 1822. enl. 4/20/61 in Co. F. Merchant. To Capt. 7/1/61. Sick 10 days from 12/30/61. Dropped 4/20/62. J. R. Tucker wrote G. W. Randolph, Secretary of War, "He was a gallant officer left out in the re-organization." Appointed enrolling officer for Loudoun, Fauquier, Fairfax, Prince William, Alexandria and Culpeper 7/25/62. Paroled 4/24/65 at Fairfax C.H. Took the oath 5/29/65 at HQ, Defenses South of the Potomac. Originally from Alexandria. Commissioner in chancery at Leesburg postwar. d. 12/1/97 at his home at Annapolis Junction, Md., bur. Union Cem., Leesburg.

POWELL, GEORGE W.: enl. 5/28/61 in Co. C. Present on extra duty in QM Dept. as teamster since 10/12 on 9-10/61 roll. AWOL on rolls for 9-12/62. Present on 1-2/63 roll, but AWOL since 8/1 on 7-8/63 roll and since 12/14 on 11-12/63 roll. No further record.

POWELL, JOSIAH H.: b. in Franklin Co. enl. 4/1/62 in (2d) Co. E. Farmer. Absent sick in Staunton hosp. on rolls until discharged for casies of tibia 11/12/62, age 35, signs by mark. Claimed wd. at Brandy Station on right shin in 1862 on 4/18/92 pension claim. At that time he gave his middle initial as "F," and his age as 67.

POWELL, ROBERT N.: enl. 4/1/61 in (2d) Co. E as Cpl. Farmer. To Sgt., guarding bridge at Mt. Crawford, on 12/62 return. Wded. 5/7/64 at Spotsylvania in right thigh, age 41, then in Richmond and Danville hosps. and at home in Franklin Co. until returned to duty 7/26/64. Present on final 3/4/65 roll.

POWELL, THOMAS L.: Only references is as a member of Co. K, "served 1 year," enl. 4/61, on ca. 1898 Fairfax Co. veterans census, on which his age is given as 66.

POWELL, WILLIAM L.: enl. 7/24/61 in Co. A. Seven days sick from 1/29/62. Otherwise present thru 5-6/62 roll. Transferred ca. 10/62 to 11th Va. Cav. d. 1/8/15 at his home near Woodburn, age 73. Wid. Fannie W., m. 1872.

POWER, JOHN A.: b. in Ireland. enl. 9/17/61 in (1st) Co. E, age 23. Merchant. In Richmond hosp. sick 10/7/61 thru 11/61 return. Discharged 1/20/62 on surgeon's certificate of disability. Resid. Savannah, Ga.

POWER, JOHN W.: enl. 8/19/61 in Co. G, age 26. Present until absent in Danville hosp. on 1-2/63 roll. Shown as Cpl. on 12/9/63 receipt roll, but not elsewhere. In General Hosp. No. 9, Richmond 5/11/64, transferred to Chimborazo 5/20, no complaint shown. Otherwise present thru final 3/22/65 roll. Resid. Riceville in 1888.

POWER, WILLIAM QUARLES: enl. 6/10/63 in Co. G. On detached service in pasture with horses on 7-8/63 roll. Twenty days horse leave from 12/16/63. Wded. 5/11/64 at Yellow Tavern in left ankle. In Richmond hosps. until given 40 days furlough 6/10/64. Otherwise present thru 3/22/65 final roll. Age 53 on 1/17/98, when he applied for pension claiming disability from wd. d. 10/19/07 at Gretna. Wid. Drucilla C., m. 1871.

POWERS, BURR W.: enl. 4/22/61 in Co. K. Present on 7-8/61 roll. No further record.

POWERS, GEORGE: Only record is as a member of Co. C, absent sick on 11/62 return.

POWERS, R. W.: Shown in Co. G on a postwar roster. No Confederate records.

PRESGRAVE, THOMAS LUDWELL: b. in Loudoun Co. enl. 10/1/63 in Co. K. Present until POW 9/14/63 near Brandy Station. Paroled 3/10/65 at Elmira. Paroled again 4/26/65 at Edwards Ferry, Md. Farmer postwar, resid. Herndon 4/2/12, age 69. d. 6/23, bur. Chestnut Grove Cem., Herndon.

PRESGRAVES, RICHARD: Shown in Federal records as in Co. A, POW 10/1/62 in Fairfax Co. by troops of Gen. Franz Sigel. Paroled 10/31/62 at Old Capitol Prison, D.C. No Confederate records; not found on postwar rosters.

PRICE, ABRAHAM N.: enl. 5/27/61 in (2d) Co. E. Age 31 on 2/16/62 roll. Twenty days horse detail from 12/16/63. Otherwise present on every roll thru 3/4/65 final roll.

PRICE, DAVID E.: enl. 4/1/62 in (2d) Co. E. In Lynchburg hosp. 9/63. Admitted to Charlottesville hosp. for debility 6/23/64. Thereafter absent sick until he d. 1/6/65 of chronic dysentery in Pittsylvania Co.

PRICE, JOHN B.: Conscript, no company shown, enrolled 2/20/65 at Camp Lee near Richmond and assigned 3/14/64 to 6th Va. Cav. No further record.

PRICE, LENT CRANE: enl. 4/1/62 in (2d) Co. E. Absent sick on 5-6/62 roll. Thereafter present until POW 7/17/64 at Snicker's Gap. Exchanged from Pt. Lookout 2/10/65. Paroled prisoner at Camp Lee near Richmond 2/17/65. Paroled 4/9/65 at Appomattox, resid. Pittsylvania Co.

PRICE, NAT N.: enl. 4/1/62 in (2d) Co. E. d. 5/14/62 in general hosp. at Liberty of pneumonia. Probably identical to Nicholas Price, shown on postwar rosters.

PRICE, NATHANIEL COLEMAN: enl. 7/1/61 in (2d) Co. E. Age 26 on 2/16/62 roll. AWOL on 5-6/62 roll. POW 6/9/63 at Beverly Ford. Paroled 6/25/63 at Old Capitol Prison, D.C. POW 10/11/63 near Brandy Station. Exchanged from Pt. Lookout 11/1/64. Present on final 3/4/65 roll.

PRICE, STEPHEN D.: enl. 4/1/62 in (2d) Co. E. On 15 day furlough on 1-2/63 roll. POW 7/4/63 near Fairfield, Pa. Paroled 8/24/63 at DeCamp General Hosp., N.Y. Harbor. Present on 11-12/63 roll. KIA on picket near Orange C.H., 2/64. Wid. Nancy P., m. 1858.

PRICE, WILLIAM P.: enl. 4/1/62 in (2d) Co. E. Sick in camp on 5-6/62 roll. Twenty days horse leave from 12/17/62. In hosps. or absent wded. 6/16/63 thru 11-12/63 roll. On detached duty arresting deserters and conscripts in Pittsylvania Co. on 7-8/64 roll thru final 3/4/65 roll.

PRITCHETT, ROBERT HENRY: b. 11/10/26 in Pittsylvania Co. enl. 8/19/61 in Co. G as Cpl. Farmer. Present until admitted to Chimborazo Hosp. No. 3, Richmond, 3/20/62 with typhoid fever. d. 3/26/62 of pneumonia. Wid. Martha A.

PROCTOR, AUSTIN: On a postwar roster of Co. I. No Confederate records.

PROCTOR, MARCELLUS: enl. 5/4/61 in Co. I, age 20. Sick at home with measles on ca. 6/19/61 roll. To Cpl., sick at home since 8/22 on 7-8/63 roll. Horse KIA 10/19/64 at Cedar Creek. Absent on horse detail on 9-10/64 roll. Present on final 3/20/65 roll.

PROCTOR, ORLANDO: b. 4/3/37 in Orange Co. enl. 4/1/62 in Co. I. "Tried by gen. court martial at New Market for absence without leave sentence not read" on 1-2/63 roll. Absent on horse detail on 9-10/64 roll. In Charlottesville hosp. with scabies 1/5-1/11/65. Absent sick on final 3/20/65 roll. Farmer at Verdiersville on 2/9/12, claiming wd. at Winchester in 1863. m. Mildred H. d. 12/29/13, bur. Maplewood Cem., Orange Co.

PROCTOR, OSWALD OLIVER: b. in Orange Co. enl. 5/4/61 in Co. I, age 40. At home AWOL 11/20/61 thru 1-2/62 roll. On sick leave on 5-6/62 roll. AWOL on 11-12/62 roll. Thereafter present until absent sick on 9-10/64 roll thru final 3/20/65 roll. Paroled 5/15 and 5/20/65 at Louisa C.H. Carpenter postwar at Thorn Hill. d. 11/26/03 at home in Orange Co., wid. Frances Ann, m. 1851.

PROCTOR, WALTER R.: enl. 5/26/61 in Co. I, age 26. Sick at home with measles on ca. 6/19/61 roll. AWOL 8/31/63 on 7-8/63 roll. Otherwise present thru 7-8/64 roll. Postwar roster says KIA at Middletown.

PRYOR, JAMES N.: Conscript enrolled 2/12/64 at Camp Lee near Richmond. Assigned 3/17/64 to 6th Va. Cav., no company shown. No further record.

PULLEN, BRUCE ALBERT: b. 4/4/44. enl. 4/1/62 in (2d) Co. E. Absent, detached as orderly to Maj. C. E. Flournoy on 11-12/62 roll. Present on 1-2/63 roll and drew clothing 4/1/63. No further record. d. 4/16/84, bur. Pullen Cem., Pittsylvania Co.

PULLEN, JOHN A.: b. in Warren Co. enl. 4/1/63 in Co. B. Present thru final 3/21/65 roll. Farmer, resid. Piedmont Magisterial District, Rappahannock Co., age 63 on 3/1/08, claiming wd. in head. Postwar roster says wded. at Beverly 1/65. d. 12/19/20.

PULLEN, JOSEPH, JR.: enl. 4/22/62 in Co. B. He and his horse KIA 5/23/62 at Cedarville, near Front Royal. Postwar roster says age 30 on enlistment.

PULLEN, JOSEPH, SR.: b. in Richmond Co. enl. 4/1/62 in Co. B. Farmer. Previously in Co. B, 7th Va. Inf., from which he was discharged 11/26/61 at age 60 for advanced age. Absent with leave on 11-12/62 roll. On extra duty in medical dept. as hospital steward on 1-2/63 roll. Cook in hosp. on 12/62 return. Drew clothing 5/2/64. No further record. Reportedly d. before 5/07.

PULLEN, JAMES: Only record is of parole as in Co. B at Winchester 5/31/65, age 17, resid. Rappahannock Co.

PUTMAN, JOHN B.: enl. 4/1/62 in Co. B. In Charlottesville hosp. with debility 8/20/62-1/3/63. Paid as teamster for 1/1-3/28/63. Otherwise present on all rolls until final 3/21/65 roll, when shown absent sick since 3/1/65. Resid. Orlean, age 70, on 5/4/00. d. 5/24/06, wid. Elizabeth Ann, m. 1854.

PUTNAM, RICHARD: enl. 3/16/62 in Co. H. d. 5/20/62.

QUARLES, DAVID WALKER: enl. 6/10/63 in (2d) Co. E. Twenty day horse detail from 12/16/63. POW 5/11/64 at Yellow Tavern. Paroled as invalid 10/11/64 at Elmira. Exchanged 10/29/64. Present on final 3/4/65 roll. d. 3/2/21, bur. Patmor Cem., near Bedford.

QUARLES, HENRY: enl. 5/4/61 in Co. I, age 39. Present thru 1-2/62 roll. AWOL on 5-6/62 roll. No further Confederate record, but postwar roster says "Killed near Richmond."

QUARLES, JOHN B.: enl. 4/1/62 in (2d) Co. E. On detached service on 5-6/62 roll. Twenty days horse leave from 12/17/62. Found not guilty of AWOL 1/30/64. Absent sick at Richmond hosps. on records for 6-10/64. Absent sick in Pittsylvania Co. on surgeon's certificate on final 3/4/65 roll. Sent to hosp. by examining board 3/18/65, ill 10 months. Present on 3 rolls during service. d. 7/15/93, bur. in "a country cemetery" at Penhook, near Gretna.

QUISENBERRY, BENJAMIN: enl. 4/1/62 in Co. I. Absent sick in hosp. on 9-10/64 roll. Otherwise present on all rolls thru 3/20/65 final roll. Postwar roster says wded. 4/2/65. May be the man of this name 3/10/24-1/25/03, bur. Antioch Baptist Church Cem., Orange Co.

QUISENBERRY, DANIEL: b. 8/17/38 in Orange Co. enl. 4/1/62 in Co. I. Present on every roll thru 3/20/65 final roll. Farmer at St. Just postwar. d. 5/14/21, bur. Antioch Baptist Church Cem., Orange Co.

RAGAN, J. H.: enl. 2/10/64 in Co. C. In Richmond hosp. with inverted toe 4/23/64, transferred to Danville 5/7/64; with chronic dysentery 5/28-5/31/64. Sick at hosp. in Harrisonburg on 9-10/64 roll. AWOL on final ca. 3/30/65 roll. On hosp. records as Reagan, Ragens.

RAGSDALE, CHARLES: b. 1825. enl. 5/27/61 in (2d) Co. E as Sgt. Discharged 7/21/61 by Gen. T. J. Jackson on account of disease. d. 1878, bur. Chatham Cem.

RAHN, JAMES WILLIAM: enl. 9/17/61 in (1st) Co. E, age 20. KIA 5/65 near Raleigh, N.C., in last engagement of his troop with the enemy. Resid. Effingham Co., Ga.

RAMBO, JOHN: enl. 9/17/61 in (1st) Co. E, age 36. Appointed surgeon in 47th Ga. Inf. 6/1/62. Resid. Lowndes Co., Ga.

RAMEY, ALFRED P.: enl. 4/1/62 in Co. H. Sick in hosp. since 12/9/62 on 2/28/63 roll. POW 8/2/63 at Flint Hill, Rappahannock Co. Paroled 1/17/65 at Pt. Lookout. In Richmond hosps. with chronic diarrhea 1/21-1/25/65, then 60 day furlough. Paroled 4/19/65 at Winchester, age 24, resid. Flint Hill.

RAMEY, EDWARD: enl. 9/21/62 in Co. H. Reported deserter, AWOL from 12/12 on 12/62 return and under arrest on 11-12/62 roll. Thereafter present until he deserted 3/23/64.

RAMEY, JAMES WILLIAM: b. 1842. enl. 4/1/62 in Co. H. Absent sick since 5/18 on 5-6/62 roll. POW 9/22/62 at Paris, paroled at unknown date. Present on 2/28/63 roll. At this point records become very confusing, showing him either a POW 8/1/63-3/10/65, or in various Confederate hosps. with veneral disease during this time. Shown sick at hosp. since 1/1/65 on 3/22/65 final roll. d. 11/25/15 at home in Vienna, Fairfax Co., bur. Andrew Chapel Cem.

RAMEY, THOMAS A.: enl. 4/1/62 in Co. H. AWOL from 10/16 on 9-10/62 roll. Absent on a scout since 11/24 on 11/62 return. Reported as deserter since 12/1 on 12/62 return, but present on 11-12/62 roll. AWOL sick from 8/1/63 (another record says 7/5/63) and eventually marked as deserter. No further record.

RAMEY, WILLIAM M.: enl. 4/1/62 in Co. H. POW 5/7/62 in Page Co. Exchanged from Ft. Delaware 8/5/62. Sick at home 9/1 thru 12/62 return. Marked as a deserter from 1/1/63. POW 8/2/63 in Rappahannock Co. d. 9/8/64 of chronic diarrhea at Elmira, bur. Woodlawn Cem. there.

RAMSAY, J. W.: Only record is as member of Co. H, in Chimborazo Hosp. No. 5, Richmond, 7/30-8/25/64. Probably an error meaning James W. Ramey.

RANDOLPH, CHARLES CARTER: b. 4/18/46 at "The Grove," near Warrenton in Fauquier Co. Att. VMI. enl. 5/1/62 in Co. F. Detailed as courier to Gen. T. J. Jackson on all rolls until discharged 12/3/62 on surgeon's certificate. Wded. at Battle of New Market. Grad. VMI 1870, Va. Theological Sem., Alexandria 1876. Episcopal priest from 1877 in Baltimore, Botetourt Co., Americus, Ga., and Campbell Co., Va. Retired 1916. m. 1) Sallie Turpin, 2) Sarah Blair McGuire. d. 5/14/25 at home in Richmond. Subject of *Stonewall's Courier* (1959), by Virginia Hinkins.

RANDOLPH, WILLIAM F.: enl. 5/1/62 in Co. F. Detailed on "special service" by Gen. R. S. Ewell. Reported on 12/62 return as transferred 12/2/62 to "White's" Bn., but evidently identical to the man elected Capt., 39th Bn. Va. Cav., 8/18/62. The latter's dates are 12/7/31-7/31/14, bur. Warrenton Cem.

RATRIE, HENRY H.: enl. 3/8/62 in Co. K. Always present until POW 3/20/64 near Aldie while disbanded. Took the oath 6/12/64 at Ft. Warren, Mass., resid. Loudoun Co. Living in Culpeper 1908.

RAWLINGS, RICHARD HERNDON: b. in Orange Co. enl. 9/22/63 in Co. I. Horse KIA 5/31/64 at Cold Harbor. In Richmond hosp. with back injury from fall from horse 6/1-6/7/64. Present on final 3/20/65 roll. Paroled 5/2/65 at Richmond. d. at Charlottesville.

RAYNES, HENRY E.: enl. 5/28/61 in Co. C. Horse KIA 7/21/61 at Manassas. Discharged 2/26/62. The spelling of this surname of 5 men in Co. C has been made uniform, but also appears at times as Rains and Raines.

RAYNES, JACOB: b. 7/20/40. enl. 4/18/63 in Co. C. AWOL since 4 on 7-8/63 roll. Wded. 5/30/64 at Cold Harbor (shot through left thigh). In Richmond and Charlottesville hosps. 6/6/64 until furlough ca. 6/21/64. AWOL on ca. 3/30/65 final roll. Signs by mark. Living at Port Republic in 3/04.

RAYNES, NOAH: b. 3/3/45. enl. 3/5/62 in Co. C. Recorded as deserting 11/25/62 at Woodstock, then as AWOL since 8/21/63 on 7-8/63 roll without being shown as present in interim. Absent under arrest on 11-12/63 roll. No further record. d. 1/23/14, bur. Port Republic Cem. on Hill.

RAYNES, REUBEN: enl. 5/28/61 in Co. C. Present until he deserted 11/25/62, either at Rippon or Woodstock. Applied for a pension in 1914 as Reuben Raines.

RAYNES, ZACK: enl. 3/5/62 in Co. C. Shown on all rolls and returns as absent at home, wded. July or Aug. 1862 near Brandy Station, until shown AWOL 8/1/63 on 7-8/63 roll. Last record is 11-12/63 roll, where he is absent sick, wded.

REAGER, GEORGE W.: enl. 10/20/62 in Co. B. Present thru 1-2/63 roll. No further record.

REAGER, LEWIS: enl. 4/1/62 in Co. B. Present on 5-6/62 roll. No further record. 1907 roster gives his age as 25 on enlistment.

RECTOR, ASA H.: b. 9/9/39. enl. 7/24/61 in Co. A. Absent sick since 2/19/62 on 1-2/62 roll. On furlough from 8/29/63 on 8/31/63 roll. To Sgt. 11/1/63. Wded. 5/5/64 at Spotsylvania. Sixty days furlough from Richmond hosp. 5/26/64. Still absent wded. on 3/27/65 final roll. Paroled 4/22/65 at Winchester, resid. near Middleburg. d. 1/24/11, bur. Sharon Cem., Middleburg.

RECTOR, BATTLE: b. 1843 in Fauquier Co. enl. 3/16/62 in Co. H. Absent sick since 11/25 on 12/62 return. AWOL since 8/25 on 7-8/63 roll. In Charlottesville hosp. with morbi cutis 1/7-1/8/64, transferred to Lynchburg. Otherwise present thru final 3/22/65 roll. Paroled 4/24/65 at Winchester. Resid. Marshall 3/31/11. d. 1918, bur. Harrison-Hume-Rector-Bowersett Cem., Marshall.

RECTOR, CALEB C.: enl. 7/24/61 in Co. A. To Cpl. on 5-6/62 roll. In charge of guard at Mt. Jackson bridge 11-12/62 roll thru 1/10/63. Otherwise present until POW 6/11/64 at Louisa C.H. d. 8/16/64 at Pt. Lookout.

RECTOR, CHANDLER P.: b. in Fauquier Co. enl. 2/15/63 in Co. F. POW 10/19/62. Exchanged 10/31/62 from Old Capitol Prison. Wded. 10/11/63 at Morton's Ford. Absent on detail on 7-8/64 roll. AWOL on final 2/24/65 roll. Paroled 4/25/65 at Winchester, age 25, resid. Fauquier Co. Farmer, resid. Belvoir, age 87, on 6/19/24. d. 2/19/28.

RECTOR, RICHARD H.: b. 3/9/33. enl. 7/24/61 in Co. A. To Sgt. on 5/62/62 roll. Detached to go after horses and deserters 12/21/62-1/12/63. Ordered to Charlottesville hosp. 2/8/65 on final 3/27/65 roll. Paroled 4/22/65 at Winchester, resid. near Middleburg. d. 6/9/88, bur. Sharon Cem., Middleburg. Apparently identical to Cpl. Harvey Rector, wded. at Cold Harbor, on postwar roster.

REDD, EDMOND M.: enl. 11/10/63 in Co. G. Present until admitted with flesh wd. of left leg to Richmond hosp. 5/14/64, furloughed 60 days from 5/30/64. Thereafter present thru final 3/22/65 roll. Paroled at HQ 6th Army Corps 5/13/65. Apparently identical to Mot (or Mat or Mort) Redd shown on postwar roster.

REDMAN, SAMUEL: enl. 9/14/62 in Co. H. Deserted 11/25/62 near Salem, but present on 2/28/63 roll. Present until shown AWOL since 9/13 on 11-12/63 roll. "Deserted in face of enemy" 8/20/64 on 9-10/64 roll. Paroled 5/10/65 at Winchester, age 27, resid. Fauquier Co., signs by mark. On ca. 1898 veterans census of Fairfax Co., age 60, surname spelled Redmond.

REDMAN, WELFORD: b. 4/20/32. enl. 10/8/62 in Co. A. Absent guarding Mt. Jackson bridge 12/62-1/10/63. Detailed at company horse hosp. 4/20/63. Deserted and gave himself up to Federals 7/25/64 at Berlin, Md., "claims to have been a Union man." Took the oath 12/2/64 at Elmira, resid. Loudoun Co., signs by mark. d. 3/8/19, bur. Sharon Cem., Middleburg. Given name shown in C.S. records as "Wilford." Surname on postwar roster as Redmond.

REED, JAMES W: b. 11/17/36 in Clarke Co. enl. 7/1/61 in Co. K. Farmer. Present until wded. 10/11/63 at Brandy Station. POW 10/20/63 near Snickersville, but other records show POW 10/12/63 at Charles Town. enl. 10/14/64 in Co. B, 3d U.S. Vol. Inf. at Rock Island, Ill., for frontier service. Mustered out 11/29/65 at Ft. Leavenworth, Kansas, as Sgt. Resid. Goresville, Loudoun Co. d. 3/31/05, bur. Monocacy Cem., Beallsville, Md.

REED, JOHN T.: b. 3/13/42. Enl. 7/24/61 in Co. A. Present until AWOL 7/15/64, afterward shown "deserted & staying." In Petersburg hosp. 7/2-7/15/64 with flesh wd. of thigh, then 30 days furlough. POW 12/29/64 at Leesburg for "shooting treacherously at an officer in Leesburg." Took the oath 6/16/65 at Ft. Warren, Mass. Postwar roster says wded. at Stoney Creek. d. 4/27/73, bur. Harmony Methodist Church, Hamilton.

REED, OSCAR: enl. 7/24/61 in Co. A as Cpl. To Sgt., absent sick, on 5-6/62 roll. Detached after horses and deserters 12/24/62-1/10/63. Horse KIA 6/9/63 at Brandy Station. POW and wded. 7/3/63 at Fairfield, Pa. Paroled at DeCamp hosp., N.Y. City, ca. 9/63. At Camp Lee near Richmond 9/14/63. POW 12/29/63 at Vienna (or Middleburg). Exchanged 2/13/65 from Pt. Lookout. Absent with leave, exchanged and not yet notified on final 3/27/65 roll. Paroled 4/25/65 at Winchester, age 26, resid. Fauquier Co. Also shown as Reid, which may be correct.

REED, WALTER H.: enl. 5/26/61 in Co. K. Present thru 6/30/62 roll. Also shown as Reid.

REED, WILLIAM J.: enl. 7/15/61 in Co. K. Present thru 6/30/62 roll. Also shown as Reid, Ried. Postwar rosters give middle initial as "H."

REGAN, W. B.: Only record is a roll of a detachment of paroled and exchanged POWs at Camp Lee, near Richmond, 3/20/65, which has him in Co. C. Probably an error.

REID, SAMUEL D.: enl. 4/24/61 in Co. H. Wheelwright. Absent sick 9/1-10/5, 11/10-12/30/61. To Sgt. on 5-6/62 roll. Wded. 7/3/63 at Fairfield, Pa. In Richmomd hosp. 5/1/64 and with erysipelas 5/24-6/10/64, then 30 days furlough. Absent sick since 5/23/64 on final 3/22/65 roll. Paroled 4/25/65 at Winchester, age 27, resid. Barbee's Crossroads. Claimed double hernia in fall from horse at Yellow Tavern. d. 7/11/14 at Washington, D.C., bur. Arlington National Cem.

REID, S. T.: On postwar "original list" of Co. F.

REID, WILLIAM H.: enl. 10/28/62 in Co. H. Absent sick since Oct. on 11/62 return. Absent sick since 11/25 on 11-12/63 roll. Thereafter shown AWOL until he d. 2/15/65 in Fauquier Co. on final 3/22/65 roll.

RENOE, HENRY: enl. 1/28/63 in Co. H. Found not guilty of desertion by court-martial 3/7/64. Present on all rolls until KIA 10/9/64. Postwar roster says KIA 10/30/64 at Backroad.

REYNOLDS, JOHN W.: b. in Orange Co. enl. 7/1/61 in Co. I, age 26. Miner. Fourteen days sick furlough from 12/19/61. Admitted to Orange hosp. 1/30/62 with pneumonia. AWOL on 5-6/62 roll. Discharged 7/28/62 for secondary syphilis with ulceration of throat and palate, completely debilitated. Postwar roster says wded. 1863 at Brandy Station and d.

REYNOLDS, JOSEPH B.: enl. 5/4/61 in Co. I, age 19. Thirty-four days furlough from 2/9/62. Sent to hosp. 8/5/63 and still there on 11-12/63 roll. Otherwise present until KIA 10/19/64. Postwar roster says wded. in 1863.

REYNOLDS, ROBERT W.: Conscript assigned 2/12/64 in Co. G. d. 5/17/64 of wds. through lungs received ca. 5/13/64. Richmond *Sentinel* of 5/27/64 shows him as Cpl.

REYNOLDS, STEPHEN E.: b. in Louisa Co. Conscript assigned 2/13/64 to Co. G. Farmer. In Petersburg and Richmond hosps. with diarrhea and fever 7/14-8/10/64. Present thru 9-10/64 roll. Deserted to Federals ca. 2/5/65, age 21, and sent to Ohio. Wife Sallie J.

REYNOLDS, VIVIAN S.: enl. 10/12/61 in Co. I. In Culpeper hosp. with fever 10/25-10/29/62, then 15 days furlough. Absent sick at home 11/9/62 thru 11-12/63 roll. Present on 7-8/64 roll thru final 3/20/65 roll.

RHOADES, ACHILLES: b. 7/6/35. enl. 5/4/61 in Co. I. Twelve days sick furlough from 2/13/62. To Cpl. on 11-12/62 roll. Sick in hosp. on 9-10/64 roll. Otherwise present thru final 3/20/65 roll. Absent sick on 1-2/63 roll. Postwar roster says wded. 5/17/05, bur. Salem Methodist Church Cem., Orange Co.

RICHARDS, DANIEL T.: b. 7/9/36. enl. 4/20/61 in Co. D. To Lt. 8/26/61. Fourteen days sick furlough from 12/1/61. To Capt. 4/20/62. Horse KIA 9/14/63 near Rapidan Station. Horse KIA 10/11/63 at Brandy Station. In Charlottesville hosp. with tonsilitis 11/28-12/15/63. WIA Yellow Tavern 5/11/64. Thirty days leave from 7/23/64. To Lt. Col. 9/3/64 to date from 6/4/64. Wded. 9/24/64 at Luray. Passed by board 11/19/64 as Lt. Col., but not for promotion, "capable of making a fine officer." In Richmond hosp. with acute bronchitis 3/10-4/2/65. Paroled 4/22/65 at Winchester. d. 8/3/72, bur. Presbyterian Cem., Gerrardstown, W.Va.

RICHARDS, GEORGE W.: enl. 5/4/61 in Co. I, age 28. Always present until POW 2/6/64 at Rapidan River. Took the oath at Ft. Delaware 6/21/65.

RIDGEWAY, RICHARD S.: enl. 4/18/61 in Co. D. AWOL since 9/15 on 9-10/61 roll. Discharged on surgeon's certificate 12/23/61 for injury to hip joint from accident on railroad.

RIELY, JAMES P.: enl. 7/24/61 in Co. D. Absent on sick furlough on 11-12/61 roll. AWOL on 5-6/62 roll and so shown until "deserted" at Richmond on 11/62 return. enl. Co. A, 1st Md. Cav. 5/15/62.

RIELY, WILLIAM A.: b. 11/7/29. enl. 4/18/61 in Co. D. On sick furlough 12/61 return thru 5-6/62 roll. Absent sick "on parole" (no record of capture) on 9-10/62 roll. Absent sick on 11-12/62 roll. Present on 1-2/63 roll. POW 10/31/63 in Clarke Co. Paroled 3/27/65 from Rock Island, Ill. d. 8/9/05, bur. Stone's Chapel Presbyterian Church Cem., Clarke Co.

RIPLEY, CHARLES P.: enl. 9/1/61 in Co. A. Absent, detached on special service with Cavalry Corps as courier or provost marshal 5-6/62 thru 9-10/64 rolls. Admitted to Richmond hosp. with gonorrhea 2/18/65. Absent, ordered to Richmond hosp. 2/23 on ca. 3/27/65 final roll.

RITENOUR, LEWIS C.: enl. 9/8/63 in Co. B. Transferred from Co. E, 49th Va. Inf. Absent wded. since 6/28/64 on 7-8/64 roll and since 5/20/64 on 9-10/64 roll. Detailed on light duty in brigade QM Dept. since 12/1/64 on final 3/21/65 roll. Paroled 5/18/65 at Winchester, age 34.

RITTER, GEORGE W.: b. in Frederick Co. enl. 7/23/63 in Co. D. Present until absent with leave on 9-10/64 roll. AWOL on final 3/22/65 roll. Paroled 4/15/65 at Winchester, age 39, resid. Frederick Co. Resid. Clarke Co. postwar. d. 7/13/00 at Lee Camp Soldiers' Home, Richmond, bur. Hollywood Cem.

149

ROACH, JAMES: b. 6/12/34 in Orange Co. enl. 5/4/61 in Co. I as Cpl. To Sgt. 2/12/62. On sick furlough since 2/24 on 1-2/62 roll. To Lt. 4/20/62. Resigned 12/1/62 because of election as Orange Co. sheriff (an office he held until 1869). Auctioneer, farmer, etc., postwar. d. 4/6/13 in Stafford Co., bur. Fredericksburg City Cem.

ROBERTS, GEORGE BROOKE: enl. 3/1/62 in Co. B. To Sgt. on 9-10/62 roll. Absent sick on 12/62 return. Otherwise present until he d. of wds. 11/23/64. Known as Brooke.

ROBERTS, JOHN A.: enl. 5/4/61 in Co. I, age 39. To Lt. 7/1/61. Absent on recruiting service since 2/23 on 1-2/62 roll. Dropped 4/20/62.

ROBERTS, LINDLEY M.: In Federal records as POW 4/4/63 at Aldie, in Co. A, "guide for Mosby." Record of exchange 4/17/63 from Old Capitol Prison cancelled. Also identified as in 4th Va. Cav. and 54th Va. Militia. No Confederate records and probably not 6th Va. Cav. Previously in 1st Va. Cav.

ROBERTS, ROBERT P.: enl. 10/1/63 in Co. B. In Petersburg and Richmond hosps. with dysentery 7/7-8/29/64. Absent sick on 9-10/64 roll. Present on final 3/21/65 roll. Paroled 5/18/65 at Winchester, age 43, resid. Rappahannock Co. Postwar roster says d. before 5/07.

ROBEY, JAMES G.: enl. 10/1/61 in Co. F. Absent sick at Staunton hosp. 5-6/62 roll thru 11-12/63 roll, "not heard from since 7/62." Postwar roster says d. 1862; name on monument to Fairfax Co. dead.

ROBINSON, ALPHEUS: b. in Fauquier Co. enl. 4/24/61 in Co. H. Farmer. Sick at home 9/21-10/23/61. Furlough 2/10-3/14/62. Otherwise present until discharged 8/18/62 for chronic pleurisy, age 25.

ROBINSON, JOHN G.: enl. 9/12/62 in Co. A. Absent sick on 11/62 return. Absent sick since 1/15/63 on 1-2/63 roll. In Charlottesville hosp. with scabies 5/1-5/3/64, transferred to Lynchburg. Otherwise present until absent sick on surgeon's certificate on final ca. 3/27/65 roll.

ROBINSON, MELBOURNE: enl. 9/12/62 in Co. A. Detached as nurse 1/29/63 on 1-2/63 roll. On furlough since 8/29 on 8/31/63 roll. Otherwise present until POW 5/11/64 at Yellow Tavern. d. 7/22/64 at Pt. Lookout. Apparently identical to "Milton Robinson" in postwar sources. Also shown as Robbinson.

ROBINSON, ROBERT E.: In Federal records as a member of Co. A, POW 9/13/63 at Mitchell's Station. Paroled 5/3/64 at Pt. Lookout, received at Venus Pt., Savannah River, 11/15/64. On Confederate extra duty rolls as courier for 1 and 2/65.

ROBINSON, WILLIAM HAMMET: b. in Fauquier Co. enl. 9/15/62 in Co. A. Horse leave 12/21/62-1/16/63. POW 9/13/63, but no Federal records or record of parole. Present on 7-8/64 roll. In Richmond hosps. with diarrhea 5/8-5/30/64, then 30 days furlough. Absent on light duty as orderly with brigade QM on final ca. 3/27/65 roll. Alive in Loudoun Co., age 87, on 2/14/21, formerly farmer. d. 10/31/23, bur. Ivy Hill Cem., Upperville.

RODGERS, BRANCH: Shown on two postwar rosters of Co. G. Son of John R. and brother of Stephen and William J. No Confederate records. Possibly identical to Branch A. Rodgers, Co. C, 25th Bn. Va. Inf.

RODGERS, JOHN H.: enl. 1/16/62 in Co. G. Absent wded. and paroled 8/12 on 11/62 return. Thereafter in Danville hosp. thru 1-2/63 roll. Absent on horse detail on 7-8/64 roll, but present on 9-10/64 roll. AWOL on final 3/22/65 roll. Middle name may be Henry.

RODGERS, JOHN H.: enl. 2/20/63 in Co. C. AWOL since 8/26 on 7-8/63 roll. In Richmond hosp. 4/22-4/23/64. In Danville hosp. with debility 5/8-7/26/64. Otherwise present until d. of wds. received in action 10/12/64.

RODGERS, JOHN R.: b. in Halifax Co. enl. 8/19/61 in Co. G. Present until AWOL on 5-6/62 roll. Discharged 7/24/62 for chronic rheumatism, with permanent contraction of muscles of limbs, age 45. Postwar roster says father of Stephen, William J., and Branch.

RODGERS, STEPHEN T.: enl. 8/19/61 in Co. G, age 20. Horse KIA 6/9/63 near Brandy Station. Detailed to take up conscripts under "Lt. Clay" on 11-12/63 roll. Otherwise present thru final 3/22/65 roll. Son of John R., brother of William J. and Branch.

RODGERS, WILLIAM J.: enl. 8/19/61 in Co. G, age 18. Present until d. 6/6/62 in Orange Co. Postwar roster says drowned in Rapidan River 1862. Son of John R., brother of Stephen and Branch.

ROGERS, RICHARD H.: b. 11/13/37. enl. 4/22/61 in Co. K. Detailed with baggage at Manassas on 1-2/62 roll. To Sgt. on 6/30/63 roll. On horse detail on 9-10/64 roll. Absent sick on final 1-2/65 roll. Paroled 4/29/65 at Edwards Ferry, Md. d. 8/10/12, bur. Leesburg Union Cem.

ROGERS, SAMUEL EDGAR: b. 6/20/45 at Hamilton, Loudoun Co. Federal records show him in Co. K, POW 4/10/65 at Burke Station, enl. 9/3/61, "desires to go to his home in Loudoun Co., Va.," released from Elmira 7/7/65. Not on Confederate or postwar rosters of 6th Va. Cav., and apparently actually in Mosby's 43d Bn. Va. Cav. 8/28/21 at Hamilton.

ROGERS, WILLIAM F.: On a usually accurate postwar roster of Co. K. No Confederate records. d. 3/12/97, bur. Rogers-Fisher Cem., Warren Co.

ROHRER, EDWARD A.: b. in Baltimore, Md. enl. 9/17/61 in (1st) Co. E. Clerk. Taken to Richmond hosp. 11/30/61. Discharged 7/15/62 for partial paralysis and atrophy of the muscles of the right leg of six months standing, age 27. Resid. Savannah, Ga. d. 5/6/03, bur. Mt. Hope Cem., Westchester Co., N.Y.

ROLLINS, JOHN H.: enl. 4/22/61 in Co. K as Sgt. Miller. Discharged 1/10/62 for valvular disease of left side of heart, age 26. d. 10/2/96 in Washington, D.C., from consumption. Wid. Frances L., m. 1863. Also appears as Rollings.

ROLLINS, JOSHUA: enl. 8/7/61 in Co. K. Present thru 6/30/63 roll. No further record. Also appears as Rollings.

ROLLINS, CHARLES: enl. 4/10/64 in Co. K. Deserted 5/20/64 while on horse detail. Also shown as Rawlings.

ROOT, GEORGE SAMUEL: b. 2/6/45 at Scott's Ford. enl. 11/64 in Co. C. Absent sick on final ca. 3/30/65 roll, the only one bearing his name. d. 8/5/25 at North River, bur. Frieden's United Church of Christ Cem. on Rt. 275, east of Harrisonburg.

RORCH, F.: Federal records show a man of this name in (2d) Co. E, POW confined 7/13/63 at Ft. McHenry, Md., and sent 7/18/63 to Ft. Delaware. No other record, and evidently an erroneous or garbled entry.

ROSE, CUTHBERT O.: enl. 7/24/61 in Co. A. Absent sick 10/12/61 thru 11-12/61 roll. On furlough since 8/29/63 on 8/31/63 roll. POW 9/13/63 near Culpeper. Paroled at Pt. Lookout 11/1/64. POW 12/22/64 at Hopewell Gap. Took the oath 7/19/65 at Elmira, resid. Hopewell Gap. Postwar roster gives Custis Rose, d. in prison.

ROSE, WILLIAM: Federal records show this man, possibly in Co. H, POW 6/6 (or 6/10)/64 in Prince William Co. He was a farmer, age 52, paroled ca. 9/18/64 at Pt. Lookout. Confederate records show a man of this name in a Richmond hosp. with chronic diarrhea 9/24-12/12/64, when he was turned over to the provost marshal.

ROSS, HENRY: enl. 10/2/61 in Co. D. Artificer, blacksmith, or farrier on 8-10/61 returns. POW 6/15/62 at Harpers Ferry (or Winchester). Exchanged 8/5/62 at Aiken's Ldg. POW 5/11/63 near Strasburg (or Winchester). Paroled 5/16 (or 17)/63 at Ft. McHenry. Present on 8/31/63 roll, but AWOL since 9/13 on 11-12/63 roll. Postwar roster says deserted.

ROSSER, GEORGE GILBERT: b. 1835. enl. 5/27/61 in (2d) Co. E. To Sgt. on 5-6/62 roll. Horse KIA 6/9/63 at Brandy Station. Sick at Orange hosp. on 11-12/63 roll. Wded. 5/11/64 at Yellow Tavern. In Richmond hosp. 5/14-5/23/65, left arm amputated, transferred to Danville. Retired to Invalid Corps 10/24/64, assigned 11/26/64 to Lynchburg post QM. d. 1900, bur. Green Hill Cem., Danville.

ROSZEL, DULANY DeBUTTS: enl. 9/4/62 in Co. A. POW and horse KIA 6/9/63 at Beverly Ford. Paroled 6/25/63 at Old Capitol Prison. POW 5/31/64 at Cold Harbor. Released 5/29/65 from Elmira. Paroled 4/27/65 at Harpers Ferry, age 19. On ca. 1898 Fauquier Co. veterans census.

ROUGH, B.: enl. 10/20/62 in Co. C. Present on 9-10/62 roll, his only record with the regiment. May be identical to Benjamin H. Ruff, Co. A, 37th Va. Inf., who was AWOL in this period.

ROW, GEORGE WASHINGTON ESTES: b. 6/21/43. enl. 3/15/62 in Co. I. Previously in 9th Va. Cav. Courier for Gens. Jeb Stuart or W. E. Jones 12/12/62 thru 1-2/63 roll. To Sgt. on 7-8/63 roll. AWOL since 12/10 on 11-12/63 roll. Found guilty of AWOL by court-martial and reduced to ranks 3/1/64. Horse KIA 6/29/64 near Stoney Creek Bridge. Courier to Gen. L. L. Lomax on 7-8/64 rolls. Present on final 3/20/65 roll. m. 1) Annie Daniel, 2) Mary Elizabeth Houston. d. 4/83, bur. "Greenfield," Spotsylvania Co.

ROW, JOHN SAUNDERS: b. 1/24/31. enl. 4/1/62 in Co. I. To Capt. 4/20/62. Absent on sick furlough since 7/1 on 5-6/62 roll [sic]. Resigned 10/7/62 to prosecute duties as deputy sheriff of Orange Co. and to "save those who are bound as security to me, for large sums." d. 4/10/92, bur. Graham Cem. on Rt. 20, west of Orange.

ROWE, ELKANON WINCHESTER: b. 11/10/36. Att. U.Va., U. Pa. enl. 5/4/61 in Co. I. Physician. Detailed for hosp. service at general hosp. at Orange thru 1-2/62 roll. Appointed assistant surgeon out of regiment 4/30/62 to rank from 3/8/62. To surgeon 14th Va. Cav. 3/14/63. Paroled 4/9/65 at Appomattox. Wife: Ida L. d. 5/23/00, bur. Graham Cem., Orange Co.

ROWLES, JOHN F.: enl. 5/8/61 in Co. B, age 34. Farmer. Wded. thru shoulder 6/1/61 at Fairfax C.H. Thereafter absent wded. in Rappahannock Co. until discharged 1/9/62 due to wd. Reportedly d. before 5/07.

ROWLETT, THOMAS M.: enl. 4/1/64 in Co. G. To Sgt. 10/1/64. Present thru final 3/22/65 roll.

ROYER, JAMES: Conscript enl. 5/64 in Co. C. AWOL on final ca. 3/30/65 roll, the only one with his name.

ROYER, JOHN H.: enl. 5/28/61 in Co. C as Sgt. To Lt. 4/20/62. Horse KIA 9/13/63 near Culpeper. Always present until KIA 8/21/64 at Berryville.

ROYSTON, GEORGE R.: enl. 4/19/61 in Co. D. Discharged on surgeon's certificate of disability 9/28/61.

RUCKER, JOHN: Only record is a postwar roster of Co. G, "enl. 1861."

RUCKER, SAMUEL BURKS, SR.: b. 3/26/45 in Amherst Co. Conscript assigned 3/26/64 to Co. F. POW 6/10 (or 11)/64 at Louisa C.H. Took the oath 6/4/65 at Elmira, resid. Lynchburg. Tobacco warehouse man for 60 years postwar. d. 3/8/31, bur. Presbyterian Cem., Lynchburg. Wrote a brief memoir of his wartime service now in Jones Memorial Library, Lynchburg.

RUDASILL, JAMES MIFFLIN: enl. 10/1/62 in Co. B. Present until POW 2/18/64 in Fauquier Co. Took the oath 6/20/65 at Ft. Delaware, resid. Fauquier Co. Postwar roster says age 18 on enl., wded. at Spotsylvania.

RUDASILL, JOHN WOOD: enl. 3/1/62 in Co. B. Wded. severely 5/23/62 at Cedarville. Absent on parole since 7/15/62 (no record of capture) on 9-10/62 roll. Absent, "accidentally shot" on Nov. and "wded." on 12/62 returns. AWOL on 11-12/63 roll. Otherwise present thru final 3/21/65 roll. Paroled 5/9/65 at Winchester, age 21, resid. Rappahannock Co. Reportedly alive in 5/07, may have resid. Texas postwar.

RUDASILL, THADDEUS A.: enl. 5/8/61 in Co. B, age 23. Farmer. "Never has mustered and now at home" on 6/30/61 roll. enl. again 10/1/62. Wded. 11/1/62 by accidental discharge of his pistol, absent wded. thru 1-2/63 roll. Wded. 5/8/64 at Spotsylvania and absent thru 9-10/64 roll. Present on final 3/21/65 roll. Farmer postwar, resid. Boston, Culpeper Co. 6/29/06, claiming wd. in right elbow and exposure. d. 3/3/26 at Lee Camp Soldiers' Home, Richmond.

RUDASILL, WILLIAM GALEN: b. 8/9/42 in Rappahannock Co. enl. 4/22/61 in Co. B. Farmer. Absent on furlough 1-2/62 roll. Wded. 12/12/63 and thereafter absent wded. thru 3/21/65 final roll. Reported by Richmond as deserter 3/1/65. d. 2/22/11 in Rappahannock Co., bur. Sperryville Cem.

RUDASILL, WILLIAM K.: b. 5/7/42. enl. 4/22/61 in Co. B. Farmer. Absent sick at hosp. on 11-12/62 roll. Absent with leave on 9-10/64 roll. Otherwise always present thru 3/21/65 final roll. Paroled 5/9/65 at Winchester, resid. Rappahannock Co. Farmer at Sperryville postwar. d. 6/28/25, bur. Sperryville Cem., wid. Rachel Scott. Middle name appears as Kelly, Kenley, and Kennerly.

RUDDER, GEORGE W.: enl. 8/19/61 in Co. G. Present until in Richmond hosp. with typhoid fever 12/2/63-1/4/64, then 30 days furlough. In Richmond hosp. with debility 2/11-2/23/64. Teamster in division ordnance train 7-8/64 roll thru final 3/22/65 roll. Resid. Perth, Halifax Co., 5/16/10, age 63, claiming rupture and general debility from accident while in army. d. 12/15/12, bur. family cem. at Nathalie.

RULE, DAVID: Conscript assigned 2/25/64 to Co. F from Camp Lee, near Richmond. No record showing he reached the regiment.

RUNNER, HENRY: enl. 1/28/63 in Co. H. AWOL since 6/19/63 on 7-8/63 roll, the only roll with his name.

RUSH, J. H. F.: Conscript enl. 10/10/64 in Co. C. Present thru final ca. 3/30/65 roll.

RUSSELL, _____: Pvt. in Co. K, KIA 10/9/62 at Aldie in a skirmish.

RUSSELL, BENNETT E., JR.: b. 1829. enl. 4/18/61 in Co. D. In QM Dept. as teamster 10/21/61 thru 12/61 return. Paid as teamster 2/11 and 4/30/62. Absent sick 8/15/62 thru 1-2/63 roll. d. 1863, bur. family cem. 2 miles west of Berryville.

RUSSELL, E. M.: On register of admissions to General Hosp. No. 9, Richmond, 5/13/64, as in Co. G, sent to Chimborazo Hosp. the next day. No other record. Not on postwar roster.

RUSSELL, GEORGE: enl. 5/1/61 in Co. F. In charge of company wagon and team on 11-12/61 returns. Present until under arrest at Charlottesville on 11-12/63 roll. Found guilty of AWOL by court-martial 1/30/65, sentenced to walk a ring 20 yards in diameter every alternate hour carrying a billet of wood for 10 days from reveille to retreat, and to be paraded with an AWOL placard. Present on 7-8/64 roll, absent on detail on 9-10/64 roll, and AWOL on final 2/24/65 roll.

RUSSELL, JESSE NEWTON: b. 9/7/38. enl. 4/18/61 in Co. D as Cpl. AWOL from 12/8/61 thru 9-10/62 roll. "Deserted," Clarke Co., on 11/62 return. d. 12/4/03, bur. Greenhill Cem., Berryville.

RUSSELL, JOHN W.: b. 6/4/21 in Frederick Co. Enl. 4/24/61 in Co. H. Bricklayer. At home sick 9/1-9/26/61, and from 2/7/62 on 1-2/62 roll. Present on 5-6/62 roll. Postwar source says left service when he reached age limit of 40, re-enl. with Mosby when age limit raised to 45. KIA 2/1/64 near Warrenton under Mosby. bur. Marshall Cem.

RUSSELL, THOMAS JEFFERSON: b. 7/11/40. enl. 4/19/61 in Co. D. On sick furlough 10/19 thru 11-12/61 roll. AWOL, "has joined another company" on 5-6/62 roll. Wded. and POW 6/9/63 at Brandy Station. Exchanged from Pt. Lookout 3/3/64. Retired to Invalid Corps 10/28/64. Absent wded. at hosp. on final 3/22/65 roll. Paroled 4/21/65 at Winchester, resid. near Berryville. d. 5/24/02 (or 1903) of paralysis at Berryville. Wid. Mary Elizabeth, m. 1873.

RUST, JAMES: enl. 3/18/62 in Co. H. Courier to Gen. Jeb Stuart on 9-10/62 roll and 11/62 return. To Cpl. on 11-12/63 roll. Otherwise always present until d. 8/9 (or 10)/64 at home in Fauquier Co.

RUST, JAMES WILLIAM: enl. 4/24/61 in Co. H. Student. Sent home with dysentery 6/30/61. Present as Cpl. on 9-10/61 roll. To Sgt. on 11-12/1 roll. Sick furlough 2/16/62 thru 5-6/2 roll. POW 5/16/63 at Piedmont, Fauquier Co. Paroled 5/20/63 at Ft. McHenry, Md. Horse KIA 8/22/63 near Hay Market, absent with disabled horse on 7-8/63 roll. Brief leave ca. 12/26/63. KIA 8/21/64 at Berryville (postwar roster says 9/1/64).

RUST, NIMROD ASHBY: b. in Fauquier Co. enl. 4/24/61 in Co. H. Schoolmaster. Sent home with dysentery 6/30/61. Sick at home 10/22-10/31/61. Absent sick on 5-6/62 roll. Discharged 8/3/61 ("merchant") for chronic diarrhea and irritation of stomach and bowels, but POW 5/16/63 at Piedmont, Fauquier Co. Paroled 5/20/63 at Ft. McHenry. Paroled 4/26/65 at Winchester, age 23. d. 2/7/09 at Luray, where he resid. 40 years.

RUST, ROBERT SINGLETON: b. 6/30/42 in Fauquier Co. enl. 4/24/61 in Co. H. Student. Several periods of sickness early in his service, absent with neuralgia on 7-8/63 roll. To Cpl. on 11-12/61 roll. To Sgt. on 11-12/63 roll. In Richmond hosp. with morbi cutis 4/9-5/4/64. Later present, but reported by Richmond as deserter 3/1/65. Present on final 3/22/65 roll. Paroled 4/26/65 at Winchester. On ca. 1898 Fauquier Co. veterans census. d. 1/18/15 at Front Royal, bur. Prospect Hill Cem. there. m. Mary Matilda Turner 1864.

RYAN, JOHN W.: b. in Shenandoah Co. enl. 4/22/61 in Co. B. Mechanic. POW 6/1/61 at Fairfax C.H., "took the oath of allegiance to the U.S. and now in Rappahannock" on 9/1/61 roll. Later in Co. G, 23d Va. Cav. and O'Ferrall's Bn. Va. Cav. Arrested 12/12/63 at Front Royal as in Co. K, 6th Va. Cav., age 18. Took the oath 6/7/65 at Ft. Delaware, resid. Shenandoah Co. Not on postwar roster.

SADDLER, WILLIAM: enl. 8/19/61 in Co. G, age 20. In Richmond hosp. with wd. in right shoulder joint 6/3-6/23/64, then furloughed 40 days. Otherwise present on all rolls thru final 3/22/65 roll. POW 4/2/65 at Petersburg. He asked to take the oath and go north 4/8/65, but did not take it until 6/19/65 at Pt. Lookout. Resid. Halifax Co.

SAFFER, WILLIAM THORNTON: b. 1825. enl. 7/15/61 in Co. K. Present on 7-8/61 roll. No further record. Known as Thornton Saffer. d. 1/17/94, bur. Mt. Zion Cem. near Aldie.

SALE, JOHN S.: enl. 5/4/61 in Co. I, age 33. To Lt. 7/1/61. Always present, sometime commanding company, until dropped 4/20/62. d. in Orange 6/30/05.

SAMS, D. A.: Shown as in Co. I, admitted to General Hosp. No. 9, Richmond, 6/1/64 and sent to Chimborazo Hospital the next day. Initials also given as "E. A." No other record. Not identified on postwar roster.

SAMUEL, _____: Only record is as Pvt. in Co. H, absent sick since 9/21 on 12/61 returns.

SANDERS, THOMAS W.: Conscript assigned 4/7/64 to Co. I. Present until reported absent sick on final 3/20/65 roll. Paroled 5/20/65 at Lousia C.H.

SANDY, SAMUEL: enl. 10/24/62 in Co. C. Present until shown detailed in brigade QM Dept. on 7-8/64 roll, and so detailed thru final ca. 3/30/65 roll. Paid as teamster in 1 and 2/65. May be the man of this name who d. 12/10/85, age 63, and is bur. in Early Cem., Rockingham Co.

SAUFLEY, JAMES M.: enl. 8/20/63 in Co. C. Previously in 52d Va. Inf. AWOL since 11/23 on 11-12/63 roll. POW 5/31/64 at Cold Harbor. Took the oath 5/29/65 at Elmira, resid. Waynesboro. May be the man of this name, 11/13/43-5/7/20, bur. Frieden's United Church of Christ east of Harrisonburg.

SAUFLEY, JOHN M.: enl. 11/64 in Co. C. Shown absent, POW, on ca. 3/30/65 final roll, the only roll with his name. POW 12/21/64 at Lacey's Springs. Transferred from Pt. Lookout for exchange 2/20/65. May be John M. Saufley, 12/15/44-2/8/96, bur. Massanutten Cross Keys Cem., Rockingham Co.

SAUNDERS, JOHN R.: enl. 4/1/62 in Co. I. In Chimborazo Hosp. No. 5, Richmond, with debility 5/24-6/28/64. Otherwise present on every roll thru final 3/20/65 roll.

SAUNDERS, WILLIAM PRESTON: b. 9/26/46 in Orange Co. enl. 3/1/64 in Co. I. Present on all rolls thru final 3/20/65 roll. m. Mollie E. Massey 1882. d. 2/21/21 in Orange Co.

SAUSSY, GEORGE NOWLAN: b. in Ga. Enl. 9/17/61 in (1st) Co. E, age 19. Previously in 1st (Olmsted's) Ga. Inf. POW 9/22/63 near Madison C.H. d. 2/25/65 at Elmira of variola, unmarried, resid. Savannah, Ga.

SAUSSY, ROBERT: enl. 9/17/61 in (1st) Co. E, age 21. Farmer. To Sgt. on 11/1/61 roll. To Lt. 2/11/63. Wded. near Quaker Rd., Dinwiddie Co., 10/27/64. Surrendered 5/23/65 at Augusta, Ga. Resid. Savannah, Ga. Worked for Central R.R. of Ga. and Ocean Steamship Co. of Savannah, Ga., postwar.

SAWYER, J.: Only record is of admission 5/6/64 as in Co. A to General Hosp. No. 9, Richmond, sent to Chimborazo Hosp. next day.

SCANLAND, LAWRENCE A.: enl. 2/13/63 in Co. K. Always present until AWOL on 1-2/65 final roll. POW 4/1/65 at Five Forks. Took the oath 6/19/65 at Pt. Lookout, resid. Fauquier Co. Shown also in various sources as Scantland, Scanlan.

SCHOOLEY, GEORGE S.: b. in Loudoun Co. enl. 7/18/61 in Co. K. Farmer. Sick since 7/25 on Nov. return and since 8/4 on 12/61 return. Discharged 2/17/62 for double inguinal hernia, being ruptured before entering army, age 22.

SCOTT, DAVID: enl. 4/22/61 in Co. G, age 21. Farmer. Horse shot and rendered unfit 6/1/61 in engagement at Fairfax C.H. d. 11/28/61 of typhoid fever at Warrenton (another source says Rappahannock Co.).

SCOTT, M. A.: Witnessed the pension application of J. E. Burkett 8/21/12 as formerly in Co. C. Probably identical to Michael Scott, shown on roster in Rockingham *Register* 5/31/61. No official record.

SCOTT, TURNER D.: enl. 4/24/61 in Co. H. Sheriff. To Lt. 7/1/61. Absent with leave on 9-10/61 roll. Otherwise present until dropped 4/20/62.

SCOTT, WILLIAM: b. 6/10/37. enl. 4/22/61 in Co. B. Farmer. To Cpl. on 9-10/62 roll. Present on all rolls thru 1-2/63 roll. No further record. d. 3/3/21, bur. Fredericksburg Confederate Cem.

SCOTT, WILLIAM D.: enl. 9/10/61 in Co. H. Present until he d. 2/4/62 near Haymarket, Prince William Co.

SCOTT, WILLIAM MERION: b. 1/29/34 at Port Republic. enl. 5/28/61 in Co. C. Butcher in Commissary Dept. since 10/22 on 9-10/61 roll. Teamster on 11-12/62 returns. Otherwise with company until detailed in brigade commissary on 7-8/64 roll thru final ca. 3/30/65 roll. d. 2/25/98, bur. Port Republic Cem.

SCROGGINS, JAMES M.: b. in Warren Co. enl. 3/1/63 in Co. B. Present on all rolls thru final 3/21/65 roll. Paroled 4/26/65 at Winchester, age 29, resid. Front Royal. Resid. near Rock Mills, claiming exposure during service, on 4/7/03. d. 3/8/21. Evidently identical to George M. Scroggins, wded. at Winchester 9/19/63 [sic] on postwar roster.

SEAMANS, WILEY T.: enl. 3/17/62 in Co. G. Detached pasturing horses on 7-8/63 roll. Absent sick on 7-10/64 rolls. Detailed in Danville hosp. on final 3/22/65 roll. d. suddenly ca. 6/1/81 at his sister's near Hyco. Wid. Nannie H., m. 1854.

SEATON, WILLIAM: enl. 7/24/61 in Co. A. Usually on extra duty as teamster in QM Dept. or sick 9/25 thru 12/31/61. On sick leave from 1/25/62 and reported sick from 2/62 until 1-2/63 roll when "recommended" to be dropped. Shown as deserter on 8/31/63 roll.

SELLERS, EMANUEL: Listed as in the company mustered in as Co. C in the 5/31/61 issue of Rockingham *Register*. No Confederate records.

SELLIS, J. W.: Admitted as in Co. G 11/29/63 to General Hosp. No. 9, Richmond, and sent to Chimborazo Hosp. next day. No other record, and doubtless an error, perhaps referring to William Lillis.

SENSENY, A. E.: On a list of POWs paroled 4/22/65 at Winchester as in Co. D. This is his only record, and surely is an error, as he is not on any of the several good postwar company rosters.

SETTLE, WILLIAM BROADDUS: enl. 3/1/62 in Co. B. On sick leave at 11-12/62 roll. Otherwise present until POW 7/21/63 at Chester Gap. Paroled 3/14/65 at Pt. Lookout. Still POW on final 3/21/65 roll. In Richmond hosp. with diarrhea 3/17/65, then 30 day furlough; in Charlottesville hosp. with same complaint 3/29-4/3/65. d. 7/12/12 in Culpeper Co. of Bright's disease, wid. Clarynd C. A., m. 1880. Postwar roster says age 18 on enl.

SETTLE, GEORGE W.: In Federal records as deserter from Co. B 10/17/64 who took the oath 10/18/64 at Bermuda Hundred, age 19. Released at Camp Hamilton prison 10/21/64, "went to Baltimore." No Confederate records, not on postwar roster.

SETTLE, ISAAC MORGAN: enl. 7/24/61 in Co. A. To Cpl. on 12/5/62 roll. After horses in Fauquier Co. on 12/62 return. Furloughed 8/29/63. Present on every muster roll thru final 3/27/65 roll. Paroled 4/21/65 at Winchester, age 22. d. 1907 at Brenham, Texas, wid. Sarah L. P., m. 1869.

SEWELL, HENRY C.: enl. 5/22/61 in Co. K. Farmer. Absent on sick furlough from 2/25/62 on 1-2/62 roll, but later shown AWOL thru 11-12/63 roll. Arrested as Rebel sympathizer 7/11/63 at his home about 2 miles above Falls Church, age 40, and various other times. Took the oath 1/28/65 at Pt. Lookout. Apparently identical to William H. Sewall, Co. K, on roll of veterans who met at Fairfax C.H. 6/20/84.

SHACKLEFORD, JAMES WILLIAM: b. 1835 in Fauquier Co. enl. 4/24/61 in Co. H as Cpl. Merchant. Pvt. on 5-6/62 roll. AWOL since 2/1/62, "deserted" on 2/28/63 roll, but back on 7-8/63 roll. To Cpl. 9/1/64. Otherwise present until absent sick since 3/1 on 3/22/65 roll. Paroled 4/22/65 at Winchester. Miller, farmer, merchandiser postwar. d. 11/12/16 at Remington, bur. community cem. there. Ca. 1898 veterans census says twice wded.

SHAFFER, FLAVIUS JOSEPH: enl. 3/18/62 in Co. H. Often sick or on horse leave. AWOL from 11/1 and marked as deserter on 11-12/62 roll, but back on 2/28/63 roll. In Chimborazo hosp. with scabies 5/19-5/29/64. Absent sick since 3/1 on final 3/22/65 roll. Paroled 4/25/65 at Winchester, age 22, resid. Fauquier Co., signs by mark, d. before 1903.

SHARP, JAMES: Paroled 4/21/65 at Winchester, as in Co. D, age 20, resid. near Berryville. No Confederate records. Not on postwar rosters.

SHAY, PATRICK: enl. 4/1/63 in Co. F. AWOL on 7-8/63 roll. Sent to Chimborazo hosp. No. 1, Richmond, with dysentery 10/63, and guard there ca. 2/1/64 thru 2/24/65 roll. POW 4/3/65 at Richmond hosp. Took the oath 6/15/65 at Newport News, signs by mark, resid. Rockbridge Co., and again 7/10/65 at Jackson hosp., Richmond. Over age 50. His service record includes a letter from a neighbor stating Shay's wife has run off with the Yanks to Ohio. Substitute, spelled Shea, on postwar roster.

SHEAS, GEORGE M.: enl. 3/1/64 in Co. B. Present on all rolls thru final 3/21/65 roll. Paroled 5/9/65 at Winchester, age 26, resid. Culpeper Co. Postwar roster spells name Sheads, d. before 5/07.

SHEARER, JOHN W.: In Federal records as POW 9/13/64 at White Post from Co. D. Took the oath 6/19/65 at Pt. Lookout, resid. Millwood, transportation furnished to Harpers Ferry. Also shown as Sherrall, Shirer. Not on postwar rosters.

SHELTON, JAMES D.: enl. 7/24/63 in Co. G. Detailed at pasture with disabled horses on 11-12/63 roll and on horse detail on 7-8/64 roll. Otherwise present thru 3/22/65 final roll. Admitted to Petersburg hosp. 4/1/65.

SHELTON, JAMES H.: enl. 4/1/62 in (2d) Co. E. d. 5/8/62.

SHEPARDSON, A.: enl. 10/10/64 in Co. C. Present on 9-10/64 roll, but AWOL on final ca. 3/30/65 roll.

SHEPHERD, CHAMP, JR.: enl. 3/22/63 (actually '64) in Co. D. Present until final 3/22/65 roll, when absent. Stated postwar that he enl. 4/64 and was paroled 4/15/65 at Berryville. Shoe drummer, age 62, resid. Winchester ca. 5/26/09.

SHEPHERD, GEORGE C.: b. 1842. enl. 5/4/61 in Co. D. Farmer. Absent sick 9-10/62 roll thru 11/62 return. Lost a month's pay by court-martial on 11-12/61 roll. Otherwise present until POW 2/22/64 at Berryville. Took the oath 6/16/65 at Ft. Delaware. d. 3/25/07, bur. Green Hill Cem., Berryville.

SHEPHERD, JOSEPH H.: b. 11/22/40 at Milldale, Clarke Co. enl. 4/20/61 in Co. D. Farmer. Courier for Gen. Jeb Stuart on 11/61 return. To Cpl. on 11-12/61 roll, on sick furlough since 12/8. To Pvt. on 5-6/62 roll. Courier for Gen. W. E. Jones on 11/62 return. Otherwise present until POW 2/22/64 at Berryville, age 24, "guerilla." Took the oath at Ft. Delaware 6/12/65. Alive in Richmond, 1900.

SHERMAN, JAMES W.: enl. 4/20/61 in Co. F as Cpl. To Pvt. 10/1/61 for 13 days AWOL. Present on 11-12/61 roll, but AWOL on rolls for 5-8/62. Postwar roster says procured Denis Thorne as substitute. May be identical to man of this name in Co. H.

SHERMAN, JAMES W.: enl. 8/1/62 in Co. H, but first shown on 9-10/62 rolls. Sick from 5/20/63. In Charlottesville hosp. with gonorrhea and fistula in ano 6/14-9/21/63, transferred to Lynchburg. Present on 7-8/64 roll, dated 12/30/64. Absent sick at hosp. since 2/1 on final 3/22/65 roll. Paroled 4/22/65 at Winchester, age 37, resid. Fairfax Co. May be the man of this name in Co. F.

SHIELDS, AUGUSTINE S.: enl. 8/19/61 in Co. G. Teamster in QM Dept. at various times 12/4/61-4/30/62. Present thru 5-6/62 roll. Shown enl. 12/6 on 11-12/63 roll and present thru final 3/22/65 roll.

SHIPP, HARVEY: enl. 3/5/62 in Co. C. Slightly wded. 4/29/63 at Fairmont. AWOL 8/20/63 on 7-8/63 roll. Deserter on 11-12/63 roll. Also on 9/63 clothing roll. Compare with H. J. Shipp.

SHIPP, H. J.: enl. 5/25/[63?] in Co. C. First shown on 7-8/63 roll, present. Next appearance on 11-12/63 roll, AWOL 12/29/63. On 9/63 clothing roll. Compare with Harvey Shipp.

SHORES, ALFRED W.: enl. 7/24/61 in C. A. Present on several rolls, including 11-12/61, on which he is shown sentenced to forfeit $8 pay. Absent sick since 10/10/62 thru 1-2/63 roll. AWOL since 7/1/63 on 8/31/63 roll. No further record.

SHORT, WILLIAM: Conscript assigned 2/25/64 to Co. F from Camp Lee, near Richmond. No record of his joining the regiment.

SHOWALTER, WILLIAM STUART: enl. 5/28/61 in Co. C as bugler. Made chief bugler of regiment 10/1/62. Present until discharged 12/10/62. d. 2/28/71 in Rockingham Co. Wid. Eliza Ann, m. 1851.

SHREVE, DANIEL TRUNDLE: b. 2/28/30 in Loudoun Co. On postwar roster of Co. K as Capt., "resigned in 6/61, and the company was reorganized." No Confederate records. d. 10/15/74, bur. St. Mary's Church, Barnesville, Md. Wid. Margaret Ellen Jones, m. 1852.

SHUMAKER, ABRAHAM: Conscript assigned 4/25/64 to Co. C. Detailed in brigade QM Dept. on all rolls thru final ca. 3/30/65 roll. In Richmond hosp. 4/26-4/27/64. Paid as blacksmith 1/65. d. 8/73, bur. Frieden's United Church of Christ, east of Harrisonburg. Wid. Margaret. Usually shown as "Shoemaker," but signature as above.

SHUMATE, _____: Only record is 12/62 return, which shows a man of this name in Co. H, sent to hosp. 12/17/62. Probably an error.

SHUMATE, CUMBERLAND GEORGE: enl. 7/21/61 in Co. D as Lt. Absent with leave on 1-2/63 roll. Wded. 6/9/63 at Brandy Station. Detailed to court 8/13/63, back on 8/31/63 roll. Wded. 6/11/64 at Trevillian's Station. KIA 7/20/64 at Berry's Ferry. Recommended by Gen. W. E. Jones for Col., 36th Va. Bn., 11/20/63: "of cool judgement in danger, well educated, of con—stant purpose and a rigid disciplinarian."

SHUMATE, EDWIN: enl. 7/21/61 in Co. D. On sick furlough 11-12/61 thru 9-10/62 rolls. Thirty day furlough 10/27/63 for preternatural mobility of hip joint from typhoid fever, resid. White Post. Not on rolls 11/62-6/64. Detailed 1/18/64 as clerk in QM Dept. at Florence, S.C., thru final 3/22/65 roll. Paroled 4/21/65 at Winchester, age 27. "Edward" on postwar rosters. A. R. Boteler wrote 9/4/62 "his character is irreproachable."

SHUMATE, GEORGE H.: enl. 4/18/61 in Co. D. d. of typhoid fever near Manassas (or at home) 12/13/61.

SHUMATE, JACOB L.: b. 1839. enl. 3/5/62 in Co. C. Absent sick 7/62 until POW 7/3/63 at Fairfield, Pa. Exchanged 10/30/64 from Pt. Lookout. At Richmond paroled POW camp ca. 10/31/64. Drew clothing as paroled POW 11/20/64. AWOL on final 3/30/65 roll. d. 1921, bur. Shumate-Vance Cem., Highland Co.

SHUMATE, THOMAS WILLIAM: b. 8/15/43. enl. 6/4/63 in Co. D. Wded. 6/9/63 at Brandy Station. On sick leave on 9-10/64 roll. Otherwise present until POW 2/17/65 in Warren Co., "Guerilla, not to be exchanged." Paroled 5/1/65 at Ft. McHenry. m. Eliza Burwell Smith, 1896. d. 3/2/27, bur. Green Hill Cem., Berryville.

SHUMATE, WILLIAM: enl. 1/61 in Co. C. AWOL on ca. 3/30/65 final roll, the only one with his name.

SIGLER, ANDREW JACKSON: b. 9/1/31. enl. 5/28/61 in Co. C. To Lt. 7/1/61. Reported POW 10/5/61 while on picket near Annandale, but no Federal records on this. Dropped 4/20/62. Later in 23d Va. Cav. d. 4/27/03 of "heart dropsey" at Tenth Legion, bur. Woodbine Cem., Harrisonburg. Wid. Malinda. Surname appears in various records as Zigler, Seigler.

SILVA, EMILIANO A.: b. 12/5/35 in Camden Co., Ga. enl. 9/17/61 in (1st) Co. E. Previously in 1st (Olmstead's) Ga. Inf. To Sgt. Maj. 8/62. Wded. 8/1/63 at Brandy Station. Paroled ca. 5/1/65 at Greensboro, N.C. Resid. Savannah, Ga. d. 3/22/07 at Confederate Soldiers' Home, Atlanta, Ga., bur. Savannah, Ga.

SIMMS, NOBLE T.: enl. 4/20/61 in Co. F. Sick near Pohick Church since 8/19 on 7-8/61 roll. Dishonorable discharged 10/1/61 by order of Secretary of War.

SIMMS, GEORGE: On postwar "original list" of Co. F.

SIMMS, ROBERT: on postwar "original list" of Co. F.

SIMMS, WILLIAM WALKER: enl. 3/1/62 in Co. B. Sick since 10/9 on 9-10/62 roll. In confinement on 11-12/62 roll. Detached looking for stolen horses 12/18/63. Wded. 6/29/64 at Yellow Tavern. Otherwise present until absent sick since 12/10/64 on final 3/21/65 roll. d. 5/23/05 in Ohio of paralysis. Wid. Sallie A.

SIMONS, CHARLES: enl. 4/24/61 in Co. H. Farmer. AWOL 6/9/61, "since in another company."

SIMPSON, FRANK A.: Conscript assigned 5/25/64 to Co. F, Farmer. Wded. 5/6/64 at Spotsylvania in right leg. In Richmond hosp. 5/9-5/16/64, Charlottesville hosp. 5/16-5/17/64, transferred to Lynchburg. Absent wded. thru final 2/24/65 roll.

SIMPSON, WILLIAM S.: enl. 3/18/62 in Co. D. Courier on 12/62 roll. Always present until POW 10/10/64 at Edinburg. Exchanged from Pt Lookout 2/13/65. Present on final 3/22/65 roll. Paroled 4/15/65 at Winchester, age 25. Took the oath 5/12/65 at Winchester, resid. Baltimore, Md.

SIMPSON, WILLIAM L: Conscript assigned 5/25/64 to Co. F. Present on 7-8/64 roll, but absent wded. at Louisa C.H. 6/10/64 on 9-10/64 roll. On horse detail on final 9-10/64 roll dated 2/24/65.

SINGLETON, A. J.: Only record is of parole 4/22/65 at Harpers Ferry as in Co. B, age 26. May be identical to James A.

SINGLETON, JAMES A.: enl. 3/1/64 in Co. B. Wded. 5/11/64 through left arm and into chest. Absent wded. on all rolls thru final 3/21/65 roll. In Richmond hosp. 5/12-6/8/64, then 60 day furlough, resid. Orange C.H. Paroled 5/19/65 at Harpers Ferry, age 24. May be identical to A. J.

SIPE, JACOB: enl. 11/25/62 in Co. C. Present only on 1-2/63 roll. Marked on 12/63 return as "by transfer Capt. Yancey 10th Va." 12/1/62, Madison C.H. Apparently identical to Jacob F. Sipe, Co. E, 10th Va. Inf., but that man is shown present on 10th Inf. rolls for 11/62-2/63. Jacob F. d. 1/5/65 at Elmira of varioloid.

154

SIPE, PATRICK H.: enl. 1/20/63 in Co. C. AWOL on 11-12/63 roll. Otherwise present thru 9-10/64 roll. Later in 23d Va. Cav.

SIPE, ROBERT A.: b. in Rockingham Co. enl. 11/25/62 in Co. C. Transferred from Co. E, 10th Va. Inf. Detailed at Gen. L. L. Lomax's HQ on 11-12/63 roll. Otherwise present on all rolls thru ca. 3/30/65 final roll. Paroled 4/9/65 at Appomattox, resid. Rockingham Co. Age 20 on 10/30/62 discharge. Probably identical to R. A. Sipe, 8/20/41-6/26/09, bur. Mt. Olivet Cem., Rt. 33 East, McGaheysville.

SISK, LEWIS: b. 5/6/29 in Fauquier Co. enl. 4/18/62 in Co. H. Farmer. AWOL since 6/8 on 5-6/62 roll. Discharged 8/18/62 for phthisis. d. 4/28/77, bur. Cool Spring Methodist Church Cem., Delaplane. Given name may be Louis.

SISSON, ABNER J.: enl. 5/4/61 in Co. I, age 30. Farmer. At home with rheumatism ca. 6/19/61. To Lt. 4/20/62. With squadrons ordered by Gen. T. J. Jackson on 11/62 return. Resigned 12/4/62 for "failing health & a wish to gratify my company and a total disqualification to do justice to myself or those under my charge." Arrested at home by Federals near Germanna Ford, Orange Co., ("age 42") and put in Old Capitol Prison 12/5/63. "Voted for ordinance and is a secessionist."

SISSON, CHAMBERS: enl. 6/1/64 in Co. I. POW 9/19/64 at Winchester. Paroled 3/15/65 at Pt. Lookout, but still shown absent as POW on final 3/20/65 roll.

SISSON, ELHANNON BENJAMIN: b. 5/22/45 in Orange Co. enl. 5/1/63 in Co. I. Present until in Richmond hosp. with gonorrhea 11/19-11/24/63 and with rubeola 4/20-5/24/64. Absent sick on final 3/20/65 roll. Paroled 5/15/65 at Louisa C.H., resid. there. d. 10/23/14, bur. Fairfax City Cem.

SISSON, WELFORD: enl. 4/1/62 in Co. I. Returned from desertion on 12/62 return. Tried by general court-martial at New Market for AWOL, sentence not read, on 1-2/63 roll. Present on all rolls thru final 3/20/65 roll.

SKIDMORE, BOYD: Federal records show him in Co. H, POW 8/15/63 at Thoroughfare Gap. Paroled 12/24/63 at Pt. Lookout. No Confederate records, not on postwar rosters.

SKINNER, JOHN P.: b. 1842. enl. 10/1/62 in Co. K. Wded. accidentally in right foot 10/11/63 near Brandy Station. In Richmond hosps. or on furlough 10/14/63-6/10/64. Wded. 9/9/64 at Winchester. Otherwise present until AWOL on final 1-2/65 roll. POW 3/13/65 at Fredericks Hall. Took the oath 6/19/65 at Pt. Lookout, resid. Loudoun Co. d. 1879, bur. Lewinsville Presbyterian Church Cem., Fairfax Co.

SLAGLE, GUSTAVUS: enl. 4/20/61 in Co. F. Present on 7-8/61 roll, "From exposure in service too rheumatic for active duty." Sent to hosp. at Richmond 10/17/61 and one month furlough on 11-12/61 roll. Reported AWOL from 1/1/62. No further record.

SLAUGHTER, EDWARD MERCER: b. 10/16/46 at "Clover Hill" near Woodville, Rappahannock Co. Att. VMI. enl. 9/1/64 in Co. B. On horse detail on 7-8/64 roll. KIA 11/12/64 at Newtown by bullet in brain the day after he had sought out Chaplain Davis to make a religious profession, bur. Slaughter Cem. (Clover Hill), Rappahannock Co. Brother of Thomas T. Known as "Mike."

SLAUGHTER, FRANCIS LONG: enl. 4/22/61 in Co. B, age 26. Farmer. To Cpl. on 1-2/62 roll. Horse KIA 5/23/62. Sent after deserters on 12/62 return. Sick since 10/10/64 on 9-10/64 roll. Otherwise always present until detailed in brigade commissary grazing cattle on final 3/21/65 roll. d. 1902. Wid. Sue Fitzhugh, m. 1872.

SLAUGHTER, JOHN PHILIP: b. 4/7/42 at Woodville, Rappahannock Co. enl. 4/22/61 in Co. B. Detailed in Culpeper hosp. dispensary on 10/61 return. POW 8/8/62, paroled 9/1/62 at Ft. Monroe. Present on 11-12/62 roll. Usually in Charlottesville hosp. with debility, dyspepsia, or as nurse 6/14/63-3/12/64. Absent sick since 1/1/65 on final 3/21/65 roll. d. 6/19/18, bur. Foster Cem., The Plains.

SLAUGHTER, PHILIP J.: enl. 4/22/61 in Co. B, age 19. Farmer. Transferred to "Medical Dept." 6/1/61. Sick since 9/10 on 10/61 return. On extra duty as hosp. steward since 6/20/62 on 5-6/62 roll. Detailed 12/9/63 to Charlottesville hosp. while unfit for field service. In Charlottesville hosp. with debility 5/18/64, furloughed next day. No further record. Postwar roster gives middle initial as "P.," and "discharged on account of ill health in 1861." Reportedly alive in 5/07.

SLAUGHTER, THOMAS TOWLES: b. at "Clover Hill" near Woodville, Rappahannock Co. enl. 3/1/62 in Co. B. Absent sick on 11/62 return. In Charlottesville hosp. with pneumonia 12/26/63-2/15/64. Otherwise present on all rolls thru final 3/21/65 roll. d. 3/8/34 in Washington, D.C., bur. All Saints Episcopal Chapel near Mitchells.

SLAYMAKER, AMOS B.: b. 6/20/35. enl. 6/20/61 in Co. K. Detailed for Commissary Dept. 11/20 on 11/61 return, and as clerk in same dept. 7th Brigade, since 12/1-1-2/62 roll, the last record of his service. d. 10/30/94, bur. Presbyterian Cem., Alexandria.

SMITH, CHARLES E.: b. 10/16/44. enl. 8/1/63 in Co. B. Previously in Co. B, 43d Bn. Va. Cav. Present thru final 3/21/65 roll. d. 3/14/22 in Rappahannock Co., bur. Culpeper Cem., Rte. 522. Wid. Mary C., m. 1879.

SMITH, CHARLES H.: b. 3/14/33. enl. 4/18/61 in Co. D as Sgt. Merchant and farmer. On special duty by order of Gen. Jeb Stuart 12/23-1/1/62. To Pvt. on 5-6/62 roll, "declined to re-enlist." On leave on 11-12/63 roll. In Clarke Co. for company clothing 1/1-1/15/64. POW 5/8/64 at Spotsylvania. Paroled 9/18/64 at Pt. Lookout. In Richmond hosp. with typhoid fever 9/23-10/1/64, then 40 day furlough. Otherwise present thru 3/22/65 roll. POW 4/1/65 at Dinwiddie C.H. Took the oath 5/29/65 at Pt. Lookout. Farmer and warehouse business postwar. m. Eliza Blackburn 1866. d. 12/20/04, bur. Green Hill Cem., Berryville.

SMITH, EDWARD: enl. 8/1/63 in Co. B. Present thru 9-10/64 roll. No further record. Not on postwar rosters.

SMITH, EDWARD A.: b. 8/24/31 in Md. enl. 3/8/62 in Co. K. POW 10/9/62 near Aldie. Exchanged 11/2/62 from Old Capitol Prison. Otherwise present until AWOL on final 1-2/65 roll. POW 4/5 at Five Forks. Took the oath 6/19/65 at Pt. Lookout, resid. Loudoun Co. m. Mary S. Burton 1866. Farmer in Broad Run Dist. in 1883.

SMITH, HENRY T.: enl. 12/17/62 in Co. G. Substitute for S. W. Younger. Present until KIA 7/3/63 at Fairfield, Pa.

SMITH, JAMES: enl. 2/1/63 in Co. B. Absent sick on 9-10/64 roll. Otherwise present thru final 3/21/65 roll. Postwar roster, as distinct from wartime records, shows two men of this name: 1) age 18 on enl. In 1863, badly wded. at Tom's Brook, unfit for service afterward, d. before 5/07; 2) age 17 on enl., badly wded. at Yellow Tavern, d. before 5/07.

SMITH, JOHN: enl. 9/17/61 in (1st) Co. E. "Reported in hospital, therefore not mustered" on 10/16/61 roll. Absent sick in Richmond hosp. 10/7 thru 11/61 return. Postwar roster says discharged 12/61 on account of physical disability, resid. Telfair Co. Middle initial maybe "V". Compare J. V. Smith.

SMITH, J. RICE: b. in Clarke Co. enl. 4/1/64 in Co. D. Present until AWOL on final 3/22/65 roll. Paroled 4/20/65 at Millwood, age 19. Moved to Georgia about 1890. President of the Georgia Chemical Works. Member of United Confederate Veterans Camp No. 435 of Augusta, Ga., d. 10/12/32.

SMITH, JOHN TYLER: b. in Telfair Co., Ga. enl. 9/17/61 in (1st) Co. E, age 21. Planter. Present until discharged 3/28/62 for congestive chills, unfit for duty since early 11/61. Postwar roster says subsequently KIA at Gettysburg in a Ga. Infantry regiment, resid. Tattnall Co. Known as J. Tyler Smith.

SMITH, J. V.: enl. 9/17/61 in (1st) Co. E. Postwar roster says detailed as clerk, regimental QM 5/63, resid. Savannah, Ga. First name may be John. Compare John Smith, (1st) Co. E.

SMITH, L. W.: Only record is a postwar roster of Co. A, which says "61 - 4 yrs. - Culpeper." No Confederate records, which are numerous for Co. A.

SMITH, MANSEL T.: enl. 5/27/61 in (2d) Co. E as Cpl. Age 25 on 2/16/62 roll. To Sgt. on 5-6/62 roll. To Pvt., detached guarding bridge on 11-12/62 roll. Transferred 2/6/63 to Co. G. On 20 day horse detail on 7-8/63 roll. Otherwise present until absent sick at Lynchburg hosp. on final 3/22/65 roll. Postwar roster says d. at home in Tennessee after war.

SMITH, MARTIN J.: On postwar "original list" of Co. F.

SMITH, TREADWELL, JR.: enl. 7/24/61 in Co. D. AWOL since 12/25 on 12/61 return. On sick furlough on 5-6/62 and 11-12/62 rolls. Horse KIA 9/13/63. To Cpl. on 11-12/63 roll. Otherwise present until absent on scout for Gen. Lee on final 3/22/65 roll. Postwar rosters say wded. at Trevillian's Station and at Brandy Station 6/9/63 and again in 1863, and KIA 4/2/65 at Five Forks.

SMITH, W. P.: An article published in 1915 shows him in Co. C, in Gen. Pegram Camp No. 1602 of United Confederate Veterans, Valley Head, W.Va., on a list of camp members who d. since 1906. Not in official records or postwar sources, but Co. C records are comparatively poor.

SMITH, WARREN C.: enl. 10/17/63 in Co. D. Absent with leave on 11-12/63 roll. Horse KIA 6/11/64 at Trevillian's Station. Otherwise present thru final 3/22/65 roll.

SMITH, WILLIAM B.: enl. 4/1/62 in (2d) Co. E. d. 5/5/62 near Liberty Mills, Orange Co., of typhoid fever. Wid. Nannie G., m. 1857.

SMITH, WILLIAM M.: b. in Fairfax Co. enl. 4/20/61 in Co. F. Sick at Culpeper since 10/18 on 12/61 return. AWOL on 5-6/62 roll. Discharged 7/26/62 on 7-8/62 roll. On horse furlough on 7-8/63 roll. To Cpl. on 7-8/64 roll, on detached service. Otherwise present until absent on cattle detail with Maj. Hawk on final 2/24/65 roll. Superintendent of alms house postwar. Resid. Alexandria 63 years on 2/9/14, age 84. d. 1/9/15, wid. Harriet S., m. 1852.

SMITH, WILLIAM N.: enl. 4/22/61 in Co. B, age 18. Clerk. Sick in Culpeper since 10/22 to 10/61 return, and since 2/4 on 1-2/62 roll. To Cpl. on 5-6/62 roll. On horse leave on 12/62 return. To Sgt. on 11-12/63 roll. Otherwise always present until absent in commissary dept. buying cattle on final 3/21/65 roll. Reportedly alive in 5/07, "captured a Union sword which is in Confederate Museum in Richmond."

SORRELL, ROBERT A.: b. in Spotsylvania Co. enl. 4/20/61 in Co. F. Reported discharged 7/30/62, but enl. again 9/1/62. Otherwise present until POW 7/17/63 at Snicker's Gap. Paroled 3/10/65 at Elmira. Laborer in Alexandria postwar, age 72 on 4/14/11. d. 3/28/14.

SOWERS, GEORGE H.: b. 7/4/35. enl. 4/25/61 in Co. D. Present on rolls thru 11-12/62, but absent by permission of Maj. Flournoy on 12/62 return. No further record. d. 2/13/19, bur. Rockland Community Cem., Warren Co.

SOWERS, JAMES O. S.: enl. 2/1/64 in Co. A. In Chimborazo Hosp. No. 1, Richmond, wded., admitted 6/1/64, then 60 day furlough. Present on all rolls thru final 3/27/65 roll. Paroled 4/21/65 at Winchester, age 20, resid. Fauquier Co. d. 3/15/03 at Leesburg. Postwar roster says wded. at Spotsylvania.

SOWERS, ROBERT LUDWELL: b. 1/6/47 in Clarke Co. Paroled 4/21/65 at Winchester, as in Co. A, resid. Fauquier. Farmer at Arcola, Loudoun Co., postwar. m. Harriet Eskridge. d. 12/14/25, bur. Leesburg Union Cem.

SOWERS, WILLIAM DANIEL: b. 6/19/44. enl. 10/1/61 in Co. A. Farmer. Previously in Co. I, 2d Va. Inf. On furlough since 2/9/60 on 1-2/62 roll. After horses in Fauquier on 12/62 return. POW 7/12/63 at Ashby's Gap. Paroled at Pt. Lookout 12/24/63. Otherwise present until ordered to hosp. 2/7/65 on final 3/27/65 roll. d. 4/8/78.

SPENCER, SAMUEL B.: enl. in Co. F, date unknown. First shown on 11-12/61 roll, present. To Orderly Sgt. 2/1/62. Transferred 6/23/62 to Co. B, 1st Md. Cav. Bn. Took the oath 6/12/65 at Pt. Lookout, resid. Washington, D.C.

SPICER, THOMAS: enl. 7/1/64 in Co. B. Absent wded. on 9-10/64 roll. Otherwise present thru final 3/21/65 roll. Postwar roster says age 17 on enl., wded. at Beverly in 1/65, alive in 5/07.

SPINKS, JOHN THOMAS: enl. 9/13/62 in Co. H. Farmer. POW 10/29/62 near Petersburg, (W.) Va., age 24, resid. Fauquier Co. Exchanged near Vicksburg, Miss., 12/2/62. Absent sick since 1/1/63 on 2/28/63 roll. Detailed as wagoner on 11-12/63 roll. In Richmond hosp. with herpes 7/17-8/17/64. Otherwise present until AWOL since 3/1/65 on final 3/22/65 roll. Paroled 4/18/65 at Edwards Ferry, Md., signs by mark. On ca. 1898 Fauquier Co. veterans census.

SPRUCE, GEORGE: b. 1837. enl. 5/27/61 in (2d) Co. E. Present on 2/16/62 roll. No further record. d. 1871, bur. Chatham Cem.

STARKE, WILLIAM BURWELL: b. 1842. enl. 4/22/61 in Co. B. Farmer. To Sgt. on 5-6/62 roll. Present until KIA 5/23/62 at Cedarville. Surname spelled Stark on Confederate and many postwar records.

STEBBINS, ALONZO E.: enl. 8/1/61 in (2d) Co. E. Age 27 on 2/16/62 roll. In Staunton hosp. since 10/27 on 10/31/62 roll with fistula in ano. In hosp. on 12/62 return. In Danville hosp. with debility 11/24/62-1/2/63. Otherwise present until he deserted 12/6/64 while on detail to get fresh horse.

STEPHENS, THOMAS C.: enl. 4/20/61 in Co. F as Sgt. Present until he got Alfred Mitchell as substitute 12/20/61. Spelled Stevens on postwar roster.

STEPHENS, THOMAS R.: enl. 1/9/62 in Co. G. On leave to get horse on 11-12/62 roll. $12 fine levied by court-martial 10/7/63 for petty larceny. In Richmond hosp. with tonsilitis 11/22-11/26/63. On horse detail on 7-8/64 roll. Otherwise usually present until AWOL on final 3/22/65 roll. Signs by mark on clothing rolls. Usually spelled Stevens in Confederate records, which may be correct.

STEPHENSON, DAVID: Only record is of parole as in Co. H at Winchester, 4/26/65, age 42, resid. Fauquier Co.

STEPHENSON, HENRY: b. 9/16/35. Att. Princeton College, N.J. enl. 8/14/61 in Co. D. Present, sentenced to forfeit one month's pay and allowances on 9-10/61 roll. On "special duty" by order of Col. C. W. Field on 11-12/61 roll. On sick furlough on 5-6/62 roll. Present on 9-10/62 roll, but absent as courier on 11-12/62 roll. No further record. m. Helen Murray Marbury. d. 2/17/04, bur. Mt. Hebron Cem., Winchester.

STEPHENSON, THOMAS E.: enl. 9/14/62 in Co. H. At home sick 10/20 thru 11/62 return. AWOL on 9-10/64 return. In Charlottesville hosp. with primary syphilis 12/30/64-2/23/65. Otherwise present until absent sick at hosp. since 1/1/65 on final 3/22/65 roll. Paroled 4/22/65 at Winchester, age 21, resid. Fauquier Co.

STEPTOE, ROBERT C.: enl. 8/14/61 in Co. D. Courier for Gen. W. E. Jones on 11-12/62 returns. Wded. at Trevillian's Station 6/11/64. POW 4/1/65 at Five Forks. Otherwise always present thru final 3/22/65 roll. Took the oath 6/19/65 at Pt. Lookout, resid. Jefferson Co., transportation furnished to Baltimore, Md.

STEWART, JOHN W.: Present on final 3/22/65 roll of Co. D (spelled Stuart). Paroled 4/22/65 at Winchester, age 18, resid. White Post (signed as Stewart). Not on postwar rosters.

STEWART, WILLIAM N.: enl. 10/7/61 in Co. A. Found guilty 1/14/62 of being AWOL 12/3-12/19/61, to forfeit $24 pay. POW 3/23/62 at Winchester (or Harpers Ferry 3/16/62). Exchanged ca. 8/5/62 from Ft. Delaware. Detailed in provost marshal's office or as detective on Va. Central R.R. 12/2/63 thru final 3/27/65 roll. In Richmond hosp. with diarrhea 8/28-9/1/64, then 35 day furlough. Postwar roster spells name Stuart.

STICKLER, _____: This name appears in Co. A on 11/62 return, "transferred to Capt. Grubb's Co., White's Battalion" in Oct. at Charles Town, but no other record of him has been found.

STIGALL, GRANVILLE H.: enl. 1/9/62 in Co. G. Farmer. Present until admitted 4/1/62 to Orange hosp., where he d. 5/22/62, age 28, leaving no wife or children. Father was James B. Stigall of Clover Depot, Halifax Co. Sometimes shown as Stegall.

STONE, JAMES CRISPIN: b. 2/8/32. enl. 4/1/62 in (2d) Co. E. Sick in camp on 5-6/62 roll. On detached service to get a horse 11/30/63. Wded. 8/21/64 near Berryville and sent to Staunton hosp., where he was on 9-10/64 roll. Absent sick on surgeon's certificate in Pittsylvania Co. on final 3/4/65 roll. m. Sarah Fannie Edwards 1855. d. 2/27/97.

STONE, JOHN BAILEY: enl. 3/15/62 in Co. H, and shown as Sgt. on 5-6/62 roll, the first with his name. Absent with leave on 2/28/63 roll. Otherwise present until KIA 6/9/63 at Brandy Station.

STONE, RICHARD: enl. 5/4/61 in Co. I. Present, returned from desertion 8/15/63 on 7-8/63 roll, his only record.

STONE, WILLIAM D.: enl. 5/27/61 in (2d) Co. E. Age 25 on 2/16/62 roll. To Lt. 4/20/62. With squadron ordered by Gen. T. J. Jackson on 11/62 return. Commanding company 7-8/64 roll thru final 3/4/65 roll. Ordered by Gen. J. Early to bring in absentees 2/5/65 and so absent on 2/28/65 report. Otherwise always present. Postwar roster says resid. Franklin Co.

STONE, WILLIAM JAMES: b. 12/13/36. enl. 5/4/61 in Co. I as Cpl. To Pvt., AWOL, on 5-6/62 roll. AWOL or deserter thru 1-2/63 roll. In Richmond hosp. with camp itch 11/28-12/14/63. On provost marshal duty on 7-10/64 rolls. Absent, detailed teamster on final 3/20/65 roll. d. 6/17/03 at Sparta, Mo., bur. Springfield, Mo., National Cem.

STRAYER, JOHN J.: Conscript assigned 1/29/64 to Co. C (another record says volunteered 5/29/64). Present on all rolls thru final 3/30/65 roll. Paroled 6/31/65 at Harrisonburg, age 19. Living at Port Republic 1/16/06.

STRINE, JOHN: Conscript assigned 6/18/64 to Co. C (roll says enl. 12/1/63). Detailed with brigade QM on all rolls, 11-12/63 thru final ca. 3/30/65 roll. Teamster on 1/65 pay roll.

STROTHER, DANIEL W.: enl. 4/24/61 in Co. H. Saddler. Generally AWOL 8/20/61 thru 1-2/62 roll. No further record.

STROTHER, ELZEY: enl. 3/18/62 in Co. H. Farmer. POW 6/2/62 in Hardy Co. and paroled, date unknown. Courier at Madison C.H. on 5-6/62 roll. POW 10/29/62 near Petersburg, (W.) Va. Exchanged near Vicksburg, Miss., 12/2/62. On horse leave on 12/62 return. POW 7/4/63 at South Mountain, Md. Paroled ca. 2/14/65 at Pt. Lookout. Present, paroled POW at Camp Lee near Richmond 2/18/65, but still shown absent as POW on final 3/22/65 roll. Paroled 4/25/65 at Winchester, age 22, resid. near Salem.

STROTHER, JAMES: enl. 8/4/63 in Co. K. His only record is 7-8/63 roll, where he is present, "received as a substitute for C. J. Coleman" on 8/1/63.

STROTHER, JAMES S.: enl. 4/24/61 in Co. H. Farmer. Present thru 11-12/61 roll. Absent on sick furlough since 2/5/62 on 1-2/62 roll. No further record.

STROTHER, JOHN W.: On a postwar roster of Co. A, "62 - 3 yrs. - Fauquier." The ca. 1898 Fauquier Co. veterans census has a man of this name in "Va. Cavalry." Probably identical to John Strother, 6/35 - 11/9/15, enl. 9/12/62 in Co. I, 12th Va. Cav., bur. Ivy Hill Cem., Upperville. No Confederate records in 6th Va. Cav.

STROTHER, WILLIAM G.: enl. 9/13/62 in Co. H. AWOL since 11/25 and marked deserter on 11-12/62 roll. Present under arrest on 2/28/63 roll. Thereafter present until AWOL on 9-10/64 roll. Reported by Richmond as deserter 3/1/65. Deserted 12/17/64 on final 3/22/65 roll. Paroled 4/22/65 at Winchester, age 21, resid. near Salem.

STUBBLEFIELD, WILLIAM CHAMP: enl. 2/1/63 in Co. I. Transferred from Co. A, 24th Bn. Va. Cav. On horse detail on 9-10/64 roll. Otherwise present on all rolls thru final 3/20/65 roll. To Lt. on parole 5/15/65 at Louisa C.H. Building contractor postwar. Resid. 1924-33 Atlanta, Ga., entered Confederate Soldiers' Home there 1929. d. 5/23/33 at the home, bur. Greenwood Cem., Atlanta.

STUBBS, JESSE H.: b. in Spotsylvania Co. enl. 5/4/61 in Co. I, age 20. Teamster from 11/29 on 12/61 return. At home sick on furlough from 1/29 on 1-2/62 roll. Generally detailed as wagoner in QM Dept. from 11-12/62 roll thru final 3/20/65 roll. m. Annie J. 1869. Miller, resid. Belmont, Spotsylvania Co. on 5/3/18. d. 1/11/19 of heart failure.

STUBBS, RICHARD: enl. 4/1/62 in Co. I. Present thru 5-6/62 roll. Detailed as teamster in commissary dept. 7/24/62. Furloughed 12/21/62. Detailed as miller with miller Jesse Stubbs in Spotsylvania Co. 11/14/63. d. 12/25/63 of disease at his father's home in Spotsylvania.

STUMP, JOSHUA: Conscript assigned 4/20/64 to regiment, no company specified, from Camp Lee, near Richmond. No record of his having reached the unit. May be the man of this name enl. 7/20/61 in Co. H, 136th Va. Militia and sick on all rolls thru 3/23/62.

SUDDUTH, ALBERT O.: b. 5/27/35 near Warrenton, Fauquier Co. enl. 4/24/61 in Co. H. Farmer. At home sick 9/8-10/15/61. Sent home sick 2/5/62 thru 5-6/62 roll. Absent sick on 7-8/63 roll. Otherwise present until POW 8/28/63 in Fauquier Co. Paroled 3/10/65 at Elmira. Still POW on final 3/22/65 roll. Paroled 5/7/65 at Winchester, resid. Fauquier Co. Farm hand postwar, resid. The Plains, claiming typhoid fever in service. d. 9/21/17, bur. Marshall Cem., Marshall.

SULLIVAN, JOHN A.: enl. 9/17/61 in (1st) Co. E. Detailed for service in Ordnance Dept. at Savannah, Ga., 8/13/64. Resid. Savannah, Ga.

SUTPHIN, JOHN ROBERT: enl. 3/1/62 in Co. B. Absent with leave on 9-10/64 roll. Otherwise present thru final 3/21/65 roll. Paroled 5/18/65 at Winchester, age 20, resid. Rappahannock Co. d. 5/25/14 of Bright's disease. Wid. Emma Shuler Sutphin, m. 1899. Shown as Robert Sutphin on C.S. records.

SWANN, PHILIP H.: enl. 4/25/61 in Co. D. Thirty day sick furlough from 12/17/61. To Cpl. on 9-10/62 roll. Generally sick from 12/14/62 until shown as scout for Gens. F. Lee and T. L. Rosser on 7-10/64 rolls. On horse detail on final 3/22/65 roll. Paroled 4/15/65 at Winchester, age 23, resid. Clarke Co.

SWART, JAMES H.: enl. 4/22/61 in Co. K as Sgt. Absent with leave since 2/17 on 1-2/62 roll, "since forwarded surgeon's certificate." Deserted 3/1 (or 10)/62.

SWARTZWELDER, LEONARD: On postwar rosters of Co. D.

SYMONS, JACOB N.: enl. 3/7/62 in Co. H. Present until AWOL 8/25/63. Under arrest in camp on 11-12/63 roll. Thereafter present thru final 3/22/65 roll. Paroled 4/22/65 at Winchester, age 22, resid. Fauquier Co.

SYMONS, JAMES W.: enl. 3/7/62 in Co. H. Present until he left on a scout 11/24/62 and was marked a deserter 12/12/62. Present again on 2/28/63 roll. POW 8/18/63 at Markham Station. d. 8/9/64 at Pt. Lookout. Sometimes shown as Simons.

TADLIER, W.: A man with something like this name of Co. G, was admitted 6/1/64 to General Hosp. No. 9, Richmond, and transferred next day to Chimborazo. Also shown as Tadlies. Almost certainly garbled, perhaps referred to William Saddler. No other records; not on postwar roster.

TALIAFERRO, CHARLES C., JR.: b. 1/26/42 at Martinsburg, (W.) Va.; moved to Orange Co. enl. 11/1/62 in Co. F as Cpl. Previously in 1st Co., Richmond Howitzers, and Co. H, 4th Va. Cav. On leave on 7-8/63 roll. To Sgt. on 7-8/64 roll. Paroled 5/17/65 at Winchester. Schoolteacher postwar in Greenville, Miss., Macon and Savannah, Ga. Returned 1892 to Orange; in House of Delegates. m. Miss Barclay 1881. Witnessed C. B. Hite pension application 12/11/26.

TALIAFERRO, ROBERT L.: att. Episcopal High School, Alexandria. enl. 11/1/62 in Co. F. Previously in Co. H, 4th Va. Cav. Horse leave from 12/13 on 12/62 return. On leave on 7-8/63 roll. Otherwise present until wded. and missing at Winchester 9/19/64. Postwar roster says "missing at Winchester, supposed to have been killed."

TALLEY, GEORGE W.: b. in Augusta Co. enl. 5/28/61 in Co. C. Carpenter. Discharged 1/3/62, age 23, for wound from a piece of shell received in a skirmish 7/16/61, resulting in spine injury. Unfit for service for 30 days before discharge. Resid. Port Republic.

TANNER, GEORGE WHITFIELD: enl. 5/1/63 in Co. I. Present on all rolls thru final 3/20/65 roll. d. 8/2/99 of pneumonia at his home near Parker's, Spotsylvania Co., age 58, bur. Tanner Cem., Spotsylvania. Wid. Sarah F., m. 1870.

TAPP, ELIJAH ADAMS: b. 1/23/20 in Culpeper. enl. 4/1/62 in Co. B. Farmer. Discharged 7/25/62 at Orange C.H., having served his 3 months enlistment. m. Mary Elizabeth Griffin 1846. d. 4/29/98, bur. family cem. in Amissville. Postwar roster says "over age, discharged."

TARPLEY, JOSEPH EDWARD: b. 10/21/26 at Whitmell, Pittsylvania Co. enl. 4/1/62 in (2d) Co. E. Present on 5-6/62 roll. No further record. d. 12/18/05 at Whitmell.

TAYLOR, ANDREW: On a postwar roster of Co. A, "discharged, over-age," as distinct from A. J. Taylor.

TAYLOR, ANDREW JACKSON: b. 1829 in Fairfax Co. enl. 7/24/61 in Co. A. On extra duty in QM Dept. as teamster since 9/25 on 10/61 return. On leave to get clothing on 11/62 return. No further record. Farmer in Fairfax Co. postwar, resid. Ash Grove 3/13/09. d. 1919, bur. Andrew Chapel Cem., Leesburg Pike at Trap Rd.

TAYLOR, JAMES W.: Only record is of parole as in Co. F 4/22/65 at Winchester, age 20, resid. Loudoun Co. Middle initial may be "M."

TAYLOR, JOHN: enl. 9/14/62 in Co. A. Present on rolls thru 11-12/63. Postwar roster says KIA at Cold Harbor.

TAYLOR, JOHN H.: enl. 3/10/62 in Co. G. Absent wded., POW and paroled on 9-10/62 roll (no Federal records on this). Thereafter always absent wded., and detailed on Richmond and Danville R.R. 1-2/63 roll thru final 3/22/65 roll.

TAYLOR, JOHN S.: enl. 5/1/61 in Co. F as Cpl. Present until detached 12/1/61 on extra duty in QM Dept. at Centerville. On detached duty thru 1-2/62 roll, then present again until discharged (no reason recorded) 7/20 (or 26)/62. d. 4/16/88 at Alexandria.

TAYLOR, MAHLON ROBERT: b. 1/3/44. enl. 10/5/62 in Co. K. Present until POW 6/9/63 at Brandy Station. Paroled 6/25/63 at Old Capitol Prison. Thereafter present until AWOL on final 1-2/65 roll. POW 4/1/65 at Five Forks. Took the oath 6/21/65 at Pt. Lookout, resid. Loudoun Co. Transportation furnished 6/22/65 to Washington, D.C. d. 10/11/27 in Prince William Co., wid. Mary H., m. 1887.

TAYLOR, WILLIAM: enl. 4/18/61 in Co. D. To Lt. 7/1/61. Present until dropped 4/20/62. Later Capt. and Major in subsistence dept. May be the man of this name, 6/30/27-12/4/91, bur. Grace. Episcopal Church, Berryville.

TEBBETTS, ROBERT B.: enl. 9/23/62 in Co. H. Present until AWOL since 8/25/63 on 7-8/63 roll, then present again until absent sick on 7-10/64 rolls. POW 1/14/65 in Fauquier Co. Took the oath 6/10/65 at Elmira, resid. Rectortown.

TERRETT, VEILLARD: On postwar "original list" of Co. F.

TERRILL, ROBERT M.: b. 12/22/38. enl. 5/4/61 in Co. I. Physician. Detached as hosp. steward at Culpeper hosp. dispensary thru 9/61 return. To Assistant Surgeon with Army of Potomac 10/3/61. To Surgeon with 9th Ga. Inf., George T. Anderson's brigade, 6/12/63. d. 2/5/70, bur. Graham Cem. on Rt. 20 west of Orange. Sgt. on postwar roster.

TERRY, BEN: Shown on a postwar roster of Co. G as enl. 1861. No Confederate record.

TERRY, JOSEPH COLEMAN: enl. 3/10/62 in Co. G. Twenty days horse leave from 12/18/62. Horse wded. in action and d. at Fairmont 5/4/63. In Richmond hosp. with fever 12/1-12/7/63. POW 5/12/64 at Yellow Tavern. Paroled 3/10/65 at Elmira and still POW on final 3/22/65 roll. d. 3/14/91 of "frostbite contracted in the army." Wid. Elizabeth F.

THOMAS, GEORGE A.: enl. 5/1/61 in Co. F as Sgt. POW 7/13/61 while scouting near Falls Church. Reportedly paroled 11/1/61 (no U.S. records on capture). After parole on duty in QM Dept. at Manassas. Not heard from since 5/1/62 on 7-8/62 roll. No further record.

THOMAS, J.: enl. 10/20/62 in Co. C. Present on 9-10/62 roll, his only record.

THOMPSON, CHARLES HENRY: b. 2/19/41. enl. 5/4/61 in Co. I. At home with measles on ca. 6/19/61 roll. On sick furlough since 12/28/61 on 1-2/62 roll. Otherwise present thru 11-12/63 roll and on 5/2/64 clothing roll. Descendants state he was KIA at Trevillian's Station.

THOMPSON, GEORGE W.: enl. 11/20/62 in Co. A. Present until POW 6/9/63 at Beverly Ford. Paroled 6/25/63 in Old Capitol Prison. Absent sick 8/2/63 until reported d. 8/64 on 7-8/64 roll. Mysteriously shown AWOL on 9-10/64 roll. Postwar sources say resid. Clarke Co., and "killed in Loudoun."

158

THOMPSON, GEORGE W.: enl. 8/19/61 in Co. G, age 22 on 9/10/61. On sick furlough 11/19/61 thru 1-2/62 roll. AWOL on 11/62-2/63 rolls. In Richmond and Danville hosps. with camp itch or scabies 4/20-7/20/64. Otherwise present thru final 3/22/65 roll.

THOMPSON, JAMES B.: b. in Orange Co. enl. 5/4/61 in Co. I. At home with measles on ca. 6/19/61 roll, age 26. To Cpl. on 5-6/62 roll. Horse KIA 10/9/64 at Rude's Hill, on horse detail on 9-10/64 roll. Otherwise present thru final 3/20/65 roll. Farmer and bricklayer postwar, resid. Tatum on 7/24/05.

THOMPSON, JIM: On a postwar roster of Co. G as enl. 1862. No Confederate records.

THOMPSON, JOHN: Member of Co. K, shown in Federal records as POW 11/22/63 in Loudoun Co. Paroled 9/18/64 at Pt. Lookout. In Chimborazo Hosp. No. 5, Richmond, 9/22-9/27/64 with acute diarrhea, then 45 day furlough. No further record; never shown on company rolls. Not on postwar rosters.

THOMPSON, JOHN GARNETT: b. 3/29/39. enl. 4/12/62 in Co. I, but first shown on 7-8/64 roll. Admitted to Charlottesville hosp. 7/3/63 and furloughed from there for 40 days 8/8/63. Present on 9-10/64 roll, but sick on final 3/20/65 roll. m. Ella Grey Bridwell postwar. Descendants say he never fully recovered from wd. in knee at Brandy Station in 6/63. Postwar roster says wded. at Brandy. d. 5/10/13, bur. Antioch Church, Mine Run.

THOMPSON, JOSEPH: b. 1838. enl. 5/26/61 in Co. K. Sick since 12/24 on 12/61 return. Otherwise present thru 6/30/62 roll, where Cpl. A receipt for pay shows service 5/1-10/25/62. No further record. d. 1917, bur. Oliver-Smith Cem. on Towlston Rd., Fairfax Co.

THOMPSON, LUTHER R.: enl. 1/15/63 in Co. I. In Petersburg hosp. with diarrhea 7/22-8/6/64, then transferred to S.C. hosp. Present on every roll thru final 3/20/65 roll.

THOMPSON, REUBEN L.: enl. 9/2/61 in Co. I. Sick since 12/27 on 12/61 return. To Cpl., absent on sick leave on 5-6/62 roll. To Sgt. of courier post for Gen. W. E. Jones 12/30/62 thru 1-2/63 roll. Furlough of indulgence 1/3/63 thru 11-12/63 roll. Horse KIA 9/1/64 in charge at Summit Pt., (W.) Va. Wded. and at hosp. on 9-10/64 roll. Absent sick since 12/21/64 on final 3/20/65 roll. "Died in 1864" on postwar roster.

THOMPSON, THOMAS SAMUEL: b. 7/19/46 in Halifax Co. enl. 4/1/64 in Co. G. Present thru final 3/22/65 roll. Resid. South Boston in 2/04; stated he was in North Carolina part of the war. d. 9/30/28 at Cluster Springs, bur. Rogers Chapel Baptist Church near Clover. One source gives middle name as Sanders.

THOMSON, ANDREW W.: enl. 8/19/61 in Co. G. Physician, age 33 on 9/10/61 roll. On sick furlough since 2/25/62 on 1-2/62 roll. Signs as acting Surgeon, 6th Va. Cav., at Camp Ashby 7/1/62. Detailed as hosp. steward until discharged by substituting John Lanton 12/17/62. Later Surgeon with 5th and 18th S.C. Vols., at Libby Prison, and for Federal POWs in Columbia, S.C. Postwar roster spells name Thompson (which may be correct) and says discharged, age limit.

THOMSON, DAVID MARSHAL: enl. 3/15/64 in Co. I. Admitted 6/1/64 to Richmond hosp. with wd. of left index finger. Absent, wded. 3/26/64, in hosp. on 7-8/64 roll. In Charlottesville hosp. with wd. of finger of left hand 9/6-9/13/64. In same hosp. with acute diarrhea 1/7-2/3/65. Present on final 3/20/65 roll. Paroled 5/20/65 at Louisa C.H.

THOMSON, JAMES HAMMER: b. 8/19/37. enl. 9/4/61 in Co. D. AWOL since 11/1 on 11/61 return. Courier for Gen. Jeb Stuart on 12/61 return thru 5-6/62 roll. Sentenced to lose 1 month's pay on 11-12/61 roll. Otherwise present utnil he got P. F. Topper as substitute 10/20/62. m. Virginia Baker. d. 1/26/08 at Baltimore, Md., age 71, bur. Mt. Olivet Cem., Frederick, Md.

THORN, DENIS W.: Shown on 5-6/62 roll of Co. A as KIA in skirmish at Strasburg. Postwar rosters spell name Thorne. Substitute for James W. Sherman, Co. F, transferred to Co. A.

THORN, JOHN W.: Record of events of Co. A for 5-6/62 has a Pvt. of this name KIA 6/1 near Strasburg.

THORNTON, CHARLES FRANKLIN: b. in Rappahannock Co. enl. 3/1/63 in Co. B. AWOL on 11-12/63 roll. Present on 7-8/64 roll (the only one where he is so shown). AWOL on 9-10/64 roll. On clothing rolls for 5/2 and 5/19/64. Paroled 6/7/65 at Winchester, age 23. Small farmer at Browntown postwar. d. 3/26/20 in Warren Co. Wid. Rosanah, m. 1877.

THORNTON, HOWARD GLENN: b. in Prince William Co. enl. 1/1/64 in Co. F. Farmer. Previously in Co. F, 4th Texas Inf. In Richmond hosp. with diarrhea 6/22-7/3/64, transferred to Huguenot Springs. In Charlottesville hosp. with diarrhea 8/9/64, then 60 days furlough. Present on company rolls thru 9-10/64. Absent sick on final 2/24/65 roll. Reported by Richmond as deserter 3/1/65. Paroled 4/26/65 at Winchester, age 22. Resid. Alexandria on 3/3/08, had been R.R. agent 25 years.

THORNTON, JOHN W.: b. in Rappahannock Co. enl. 6/1/62 in Co. B. Present until marked deserter on 11/62 return and 11-12/62 roll. Present again on 1-2/63 and 7-8/64 rolls, AWOL on 9-10/64 roll. No further record. Paroled 5/1/65 at Winchester, age 36. Resid. Washington on 6/17/08, stating he was home on furlough when Lee surrendered. One postwar roster has John Franklin Thornton, evidently a mistake.

THORNTON, MACARTA: enl. 4/1/62 in Co. I. In Richmond hosp. 5/29-5/30/64. To Sgt. on 7-8/64 roll. Sick at hosp. on 9-10/64 roll. Otherwise always present until wded. in thigh, penis, and scrotum and POW 12/21/64 at Lacey Springs. Paroled 2/16/65 at Ft. McHenry, age 24. In Richmond hosps. with thigh wd. 3/2-3/14/65, then 60 day furlough. Absent, POW, on final 3/20/65 roll.

THORNTON, WILLIAM H.: Appointed Lt. 4/20/62 in Co. F. On sick furlough on 7-8/63 roll. Otherwise present until POW 9/24/64 at Luray. Took the oath 5/30/65 at Ft. Delaware, resid. Orange Co.

THRIFT, CHARLES WILLIAM: b. in Loudoun Co. enl. 4/22/61 in Co. K as Orderly Sgt. To Lt. 4/20/62. Always present until KIA 8/23/62 at Fauquier White Sulphur Springs, when horribly mutilated by a shell. Often shown as William Thrift.

THRIFT, SANDERSON: enl. 7/15/61 in Co. K. Shown as present on 7-8/61 roll. No further record. Not on postwar rosters.

THROCKMORTON, JOHN ARISS: b. 3/3/15 at Meadow Farm, Loudoun Co. enl. 4/20/61 in Co. F. To Sgt. on 7-8/61 roll. To Lt. 8/19/61. To Capt. 4/20/62. Horse KIA 5/23/62 near Front Royal. Horse wded. 6/4/62 at Strasburg. Commanding regiment on 7-8/63 roll. Resigned 9/23/63, "The Department having seen fit to promote an outsider [Julien Harrison] to command my regiment." Still serving in regiment 11/25/63. Resignation accepted 12/16/63. Col. of Va. Militia pre-war. m. 1) Mary Barnes Tutt 1839, 2) Mary Crittenden. d. 5/28/91. His only son, Charles Beaujoilais Throckmorton, was a USA Regular Lt. and Capt. in the war.

TIMBERLAKE, THOMAS WILLIAM: b. 10/7/42. enl. 5/12/61 in Co. D. In Richmond hosp. 5/16-5/17/64. In Charlottesville hosp. with intermittent fever 6/12-7/29/64, including furlough. Present on all rolls until KIA 9/19/64 at Winchester. bur. Episcopal and Masonic Cem., Middleway, W.Va. Son of Richard and Frances.

TINDER, ALONZO: b. 1841 in Culpeper Co. enl. 11/9/61 in Co. I. Present until transferred 6/13/63 to Co. E, 9th Va. Cav. Tobacco dealer in Kentucky postwar, resid. there in 1915.

TINDER, AMOS E.: enl. 4/1/62 in Co. I. Always present until detailed on provost guard duty on rolls for 7-10/64. Present on final 3/20/65 roll.

TINDER, EDGAR A.: enl. 5/4/61 in Co. I, age 20. Ten day furlough from 2/20/63. In Richmond hosp. 6/10-6/11/64 with diarrhea. Detailed in hosp. on 7-10/64 roll. Otherwise present until detailed as courier on final 3/20/65 roll. Paroled 4/9/65 at Appomattox, resid. Orange Co.

TINDER, THOMAS ROBERTSON: enl. 4/1/62 in Co. I. Absent with leave on 11-12/63 roll. Horse KIA 10/19/64 at Cedar Creek, and on horse detail on 9-10/64 roll. Otherwise present thru 3/20/65 final roll. d. 10/20/65 of typhoid fever. m. 1851. Wid. Mrs. E. J. Swift, who remarried.

TINSLEY, HENRY EDWARDS: b. in Orange Co. enl. 8/24/64 in Co. I. Present until detailed on provost duty on 9-10/64 roll. Detailed as courier on final 3/20/65 roll. Wheelwright for 30 years postwar. Resid. Burr Hill, age 60 on 3/12/03. d. 3/24/08, bur. Tinsley Cem., Burr Hill. Wid. Amma G., m. 1874.

TINSLEY, P.: Only record is of parole 9/29/62 at Warrenton as in Co. A.

TINSON, JACOB K.: Shown as in Co. H on a list of men paroled 5/3/65 at Winchester. No other record. Compare Jacob K. Vinson.

TIPPETT, JOHN HENRY: enl. 7/15/61 in Co. K. Sick in camp on 1-2/62 roll. Deserted 3/7/62 on 6/30/62 roll. AWOL 5/1-9/6/62. POW 4/30/63 in Loudoun Co. Paroled 5/10/63 at Old Capitol Prison. Otherwise present until POW 7/15/64 at Elmira, resid. Leeburg. d. ca. 1878, m. Emily E. Havenner 1855.

TOLER, WASHINGTON NELSON: enl. 5/30/61 in Co. K. Sick in camp on 1-2/62 roll. AWOL on 6/30/62 roll, but excused by Gen. Jeb Stuart on 2/12/62 roll. Detailed as scout for Gen. Stuart thereafter until scout for Gen. Fitz Lee on 12/27/64 roll. Paroled 1/31/63 by Provost Marshal, Army of Potomac, but no record of POW. POW 2/21/63 in King George Co. Exchanged from Old Capitol Prison 3/29/63. AWOL since 10/21 on 9-10/64 roll. Present on final 1-2/65 roll. Paroled 5/10/65 at Conrad's Ferry, Md. Took the oath 5/17/65 at Headquarters, Defenses South of Potomac, resid. King George Co. Admitted 5/6/02 to Maryland Line Soldiers Home, Baltimore, Md., age 63, farmer. d. in Washington, D.C., bur. Alexandria. One source gives his dates as 1843-1893.

TOLLIVER, JOSEPH: Shown in Federal records as in Co. F, POW 8/14/64 at Berryville. Took the oath 7/7/65 at Elmira, resid. Winchester. No Confederate records.

TOPPER, PIUS FRANCIS: enl. 3/18/62 in Co. D. Accepted as substitute for James H. Thompson 10/20/62. Absent with leave, one month's pay deducted by sentence of court-martial on 11-12/63 roll. Otherwise always present until KIA 9/22/64 at Luray, bur. Green Hill Cem., Berryville. Unofficial sources state he was from Fairfield, Pa., and was wded. 6/9/63 at Brandy Station. Sometimes shown as F. P. Topper.

TORIAN, PAUL C.: b. in Halifax Co. enl. 3/17/62 in Co. G. Farmer. Discharged 5/19/62 for disease of heart, "has been in hospital 2 months and has done only one month's duty since he entered the army," age 20 (elsewhere 23). Afterward shown as absent sick until he appears mysteriously as "deserted" on 11/62 return.

TORIAN, RICHARD P.: enl. 1/24/62 in Co. G. Overseer. Absent guarding baggage on 9-12/62 rolls. On horse leave 1/25/63 thru 7-8/63 roll. Otherwise present on 11-12/63 roll thru final 3/22/65 roll.

TOTTEN, GEORGE M.: b. in Rappahannock Co. enl. 3/1/62 in Co. B. Carder. Wded. and horse KIA 5/23/62 at Cedarville. Sick on 11-12/62 returns. Under sentence of court-martial on 1-2/63 roll. POW (deserter) 7/23/63 at New Creek, (W.) Va., age 18. Took the oath 12/15/64 at Camp Chase, ordered to stay north of Ohio River. Carpenter, resid. Scrabble on 3/1/19. d. 8/30/21. "Deserted" on postwar roster.

TRENARY, BENJAMIN F.: b. 10/27/36. enl. 6/1/62 in Co. D. Wded. slightly 6/21/63 at Upperville. Horse KIA 9/13/63 near Brandy Station. Absent with leave on 11-12/63 roll. Detailed on provost guard at brigade HQ on 9-10/64 roll. Otherwise present thru final 3/22/65 roll. Paroled 4/24/65 at Winchester. d. 3/26/03, bur. Waterloo Crossroads, Clarke Co.

TRENARY, EDWARD S.: enl. 7/24/61 in Co. A. AWOL since 11/25 on 12/61 return. Absent sick from 3/20/62 and eventually dropped from rolls as permanently disabled. "Deserter" on 8/31/63 roll. Resid. Round Hill ca. 1900 claiming typhoid fever in 1862. d. 3/22/03, age 72. Wid. C. Lucy, m. 1856, who gave his name as Emanuel Singleton Trenary. Usually shown as "E. S."

TRENARY, THOMAS: Shown as a member of Co. A, "discharged," on postwar roster. No Confederate records.

TRIPLETT, GEORGE W.: On a postwar roster of Co. F. No Confederate records.

TRIPLETT, J. THOMAS: enl. 5/1/62 in Co. F. To Cpl. on 9-10/62 roll. Back to Pvt. on 11-12/63 roll. Present on every roll until AWOL on final 2/24/65 roll. Paroled 4/23/65 at Winchester, age 20, resid. Fairfax Co. Usually shown as Thomas Triplett. Postwar roster says wded. at Sharpsburg, Culpeper Co.

TRIPLETT, RICHARD C.: b. 1/10/41 at "Round Hill," Fairfax Co. enl. 4/20/62 in Co. F. To Lt. 7/1/61. Present until dropped at reorganization 4/20/62. Later in Mosby's 43d Bn. Va. Cav. Farmer postwar. Elected to House of Delegates from Fairfax 1891. On ca. 1898 Fairfax Co. veterans census. Bur. Presbyterian Cem., Alexandria.

TUCK, RICHARD FRANCIS: b. 1/17/41 in Halifax Co. Enl. 8/19/61 in Co. G. Farmer. Absent sick 3/14/62 until discharged 9/3/62 for paralysis, debility, and emaciation. enl. again 8/15/64. On horse detail on 9-10/65 roll. Paroled 4/25/65 at HQ 2d Div., 6th Corps. Farmer and merchandiser in Halifax Co. postwar, claiming measles, pneumonia, and typhoid fever during war. D. 7/28/19, bur. Tuck Cem., Halifax Co.

TUCKER, CREED IVERNON: Pvt. in Co. G on 5-6/62 roll, present. Co. clothing book has transferred. Received $50 bounty 3/11/62 for enl. in "18th Va. Regt." Middle initial sometimes shown as "J."

TUCKER, JAMES P.: enl. 3/22/62 in Co. G. Absent sick on 9-10/62 roll. Deserted 11/1/62. Confined in Castle Thunder, Richmond, on 7-8/64 roll, and absent in arrest at Petersburg on 9-10/64 roll. Often in Richmond hosps. with rheumatism or diarrhea 9/14-11/26/64, returned to Castle Thunder. Transferred 1/23/65 to F, 38th Va. Inf., "has never reported."

TURNER, ABSALOM: enl. 4/22/61 in Co. B, age 25. Farmer. Absent sick since 2/3 on 1-2/62 roll, and at hosp. on 11-12/62 roll. In Richmond hosp. 5/29-5/30/64. Otherwise present on all rolls until AWOL on final 3/21/65 roll. Reported by Richmond as deserter 3/1/65. Paroled 4/28/65 at Winchester, resid. Flint Hill. Reportedly d. before 5/07.

TURNER, GEORGE W.: enl. 10/28/63 in Co. D. Previously in 2d Va. Inf. In Charlottesville hosp. with morbi cutis 12/19/63, transferred to Staunton. Present on rolls for 7-10/64. Presence or absence not stated on final 3/22/65 roll. Paroled 4/19/65 at Winchester, age 27, resid. Winchester.

TURNER, HENRY WALKER: b. in Orange Co. enl. 3/5/62 in Co. C. Absent at "Mr. Bradford's" guarding cornfield on 7-8/63 roll. Thereafter present on all rolls thru final ca. 3/30/65 roll. Farmer at Mine Run, age 66, on 3/13/08. d. 6/16/19, bur. Turner-Almond Cem. on Rt. 608 west of Orange. Wid. Annie E., m. 1869.

TURNER, JOSEPH McLEOD: enl. 9/17/61 in (1st) Co. E as Sgt., age 22. To Lt. 1/18/63. KIA 11/8/63 at Stevensburg, Culpeper Co., "while acting with the most conspicuous gallantry as Aid-de-camp for Brig. Gen. P. M. B. Young." On Roll of Honor 12/10/64. Resid. Savannah, Ga.

TYNES, THOMAS JEFFERSON: b. 10/24/45 at Green Hill Ferry, Halifax Co. enl. 3/10/62 in Co. G. Teamster for the medical wagon on 11-12/63 roll. Generally present until transferred 7/15/64 to Wright's Battery, Va. Vols. (Heavy Art.). Moved to Maries Co., Mo., postwar. Later resid. Phelps Co., Mo., where he d. 10/20/17, bur. Goodall Cem., Arlington, Mo.

UNDRA, BYRON: Shown on 7-8/64 roll of Co. K as transferred in exchange for Pvt. G. V. Braden. No further record.

UPDIKE, BENJAMIN FRANKLIN: enl. 5/8/61 in Co. B, age 28. Farmer. Absent sick since 10/25 on 10/61 return and since 9/1/62 on 9-10/62 roll. Otherwise present until POW 1/12/64 in Rappahannock Co. Paroled 9/18/64 from Pt. Lookout. In Richmond hosp. with debility 9/23-9/27/64, then 60 day furlough. Absent sick since 12/1/64 on final 3/21/65 roll. May be Franklin Updike, 1836-1908, bur. Prospect Hill Cem., Front Royal.

UTZ, JOHN A.: enl. 2/16/63 in Co. B. Present on 1-2/64 roll, but thereafter shown AWOL until "deserted, dropped from the rolls" on final 3/21/65 roll. d. 12/6 (or 26)/16 in Rappahannock Co. Known as "Jack." Wid. Lucy M., m. 1867. After reading depositions and letters on Lucy Utz's pension claim, pension clerk John H. Johnson wrote "In view of all the circumstances, I am giving the applicant benefit of my doubt," and allowed the claim despite the notation of desertion.

VADEN, G. W.: Conscript assigned 4/7/64 to Co. C. In Danville hosp. with epilepsy 5/2-10/10/64, when returned to duty. No further record. Also shown as Vaiden.

VALENTINE, JOHN: enl. 5/25/63 in Co. C. Deserted "to the enemy" while on picket 8/26/63. Also shown as Valantine.

VAN CAMP, EUGENE BESTOR: b. 3/31/38 in Kentucky. Att. Georgetown (D.C.) Univ. enl. 4/20/61 in Co. F as Sgt. To Pvt., absent sick since 8/25/62 on 11/62 return. AWOL since 11/1/62 on 1-2/63 roll. Arrested 3/20/63 at Berlin, Md., "deserter" and "Rebel soldier," with a parole given at Baltimore. Accused by a Unionist 1/18/64 of trading cotton between Vicksburg, Miss., and Memphis, Tenn., and of being a spy (which may have been true). Son of Dr. Aaron Van Camp, a Confederate spy in Washington, D.C. Postwar roster says "deserted, captured & escaped to the enemy."

VANDEVENTER, ISAAC CLARKE: b. 4/11/44 in Loudoun Co. enl. 8/15/62 in Co. A. Farmer. Previously in 8th Va. Inf. Absent sick 5/28/63 until detailed to Engineer Dept. 2/23/64. In Petersburg hosp. with epilepsy 8/1-8/18/64. Discharged for epilepsy 8/18/64. Later with Mosby's 43d Bn. Va. Cav. Lived in West postwar, but returned to Va. d. 3/23/98, bur. Leesburg Union Cem. One source gives middle name as Cornelius.

VAN GIESEN, HENRY: enl. 9/17/61 in (1st) Co. E, age 25. Detailed as conductor on Central R.R. of Ga. on 3-4/64 roll. Resid. Savannah, Ga.

VANHORN, BURR W.: enl. 4/24/61 in Co. H. Carpenter. Sent home sick 8/14/61 and shown AWOL from 9/61. May be the man of this name who d. 3/21/83, age 56 years, 3 months, 12 days, and is bur. Marshall Cem.

VANHORN, ROBERT S.: enl. 5/8/61 in Co. B, age 24. Farmer. Discharged from Culpeper hosp. 8/12/61. Sick since 9/16 on 9-10/61 roll. POW 5/31/64 at Cold Harbor. Paroled 10/11/64 at Elmira. With detachment of paroled POWs at Camp Lee, near Richmond, ca. 10/31/64. Absent sick since 12/1/64 on final 3/21/65 roll. At 1920 Culpeper reunion.

VANSICKLER, JAMES CRAVEN: b. 4/8/41 in Loudoun Co. Federal records show him in Co. A, POW 12/11/63 at Snickersville (or Winchester). Took the oath at Ft. Delaware 6/21/65, resid. Loudoun Co. d. 9/26/12, bur. North Fork Regular Baptist Church Cem., North Fork. No Confederate records. Not on postwar roster.

VAUGHAN, EDGAR HOPSON: b. 5/6/43. enl. 8/19/61 in Co. G. Sick furlough since 2/16 on 1-2/62 roll. To Cpl. on 5-6/62 roll. To Sgt. on 11-12/63 roll. Twenty days horse leave from 12/16/63. In Richmond hosp. with camp itch 4/20-5/20/64. In Farmville hosp. with scabies 12/16/64-2/8/65. Otherwise present thru final 3/22/65 roll. Halifax Co. clerk of court 1879-93. Accidentally killed 9/22/93, bur. Oak Ridge Cem., South Boston.

VAUGHAN, JOHNSON: enl. 3/1/62 in Co. B. Sick since 9/10 on 10/61 return. Absent on furlough on 9-10/64 roll. Reported by Richmond as deserter 2/28/65. Otherwise always present thru final 3/21/65 roll. Postwar roster says age 35 on enl., d. before 5/07. Sometimes shown as Vaughn.

VEITCH, GEORGE WASHINGTON: b. 2/22/36. enl. 5/25/61 in Co. F. To Cpl. on 11-12/61 roll. To Lt. 4/20/62. Wded. 5/23/62 at Cedarville and POW 5/30/62 in hosp. at Front Royal. Exchanged 8/5/62 from Ft. Delaware. Sentenced by court-martial 1/30/64 to loss of rank and pay 3 months for drunkenness and conduct prejudicial to good order and military discipline. Otherwise present until POW 6/11/64 at Lousia C.H. Took the oath 6/16/65 at Ft. Delaware. Prominent Methodist layman postwar. d. 5/7/11, bur. Mt. Olivet Methodist Church Cem., Arlington. Brother of Richard A. Birch.

VEITCH, ISAAC A.: enl. 5/25/61 in Co. F. To Cpl. on 11-12/63 roll. Present on every roll until POW as Pvt. 5/12/64 at Spotsylvania. Took the oath 7/11/65 at Elmira, resid. Georgetown, D.C. Postwar roster says "wounded of [sic] Fairfax C.H."

VEITCH, RICHARD ALEXANDER: b. in Alexandria Co. (another sources says Fairfax Co.). enl. 8/1/62 in Co. F. Farmer. Found guilty by court-martial 1/30/64 of "Absenting himself from his command without authority, and remaining for the night," sentenced to six months hard labor, but remitted. Present until POW 2/22/64 at Snickersville ("carpenter"). Took the oath 6/15/65 at Ft. Delaware. Farmer and sheriff postwar, resid. Ballston 10/20/02, age 64. d. 2/18/07 in Washington, D.C. Wid. Martha, m. 1861. Brother of George W.

VINSON, JACOB K.: Paroled as in Co. H 5/3/65 at Winchester, age 19, resid. Fauquier Co. near Warrenton, signs by mark. No other record. Compare with Jacob K. Tinson.

von CZYINSKY, OSCAR: Federal records show someone of this or a similar name (Van Gysiseby, Van Grady) POW 9/24/64 at Luray as in Cos. A, G, or K, paroled at Pt. Lookout. Not in Confederate or postwar records, and may be a name used by Oscar von Unru.

von UNRU, OSCAR: b. in Prussia. Reported as enl. 1/1/61 in Co. K, but not shown on rolls until 9-10/64. Receipt signed 10/31/63 as Lt., Co. K. POW 9/19/64 at Luray, no record of parole. Horse KIA 9/24/64 (which may be correct date as POW). Lt. on detached service on 1/30/65 receipt. Present, detailed as drill master of 8th Va. Cav., on final 1-2/65 roll. Chaplain R. T. Davis wrote "He is a most gallant and efficient soldier, and an elegant swordsman." Previously in Polish revolution. Compare with Oscar von Czyinsky. Also shown as von Unruh, Undernee, Undru, Undrue.

WADDEL, WILLIAM W.: enl. 9/17/61 in (1st) Co. E, age 22. Admitted 12/29/61 to Moore Hosp. at General Hosp. No. 1, Danville, with remittent fever, sent to general hosp. at Front Royal. To Cpl. 12/1/63. Paroled 5/1/65 at Greensboro, N.C. Resid. Savannah, Ga.

WADDILL, EDWARD C.: b. 5/9/43. enl. 1/18/62 in Co. G. Present on every roll thru final 3/22/65 roll. d. 12/7/09, bur. Rogers Chapel Baptist Church, Highway 607, near Clover.

WADDLE, J. W.: Only record is of parole as in Co. F 4/21/65 at Winchester, age 22, resid. Fauquier Co., signs by mark. One James W. Waddle served in 4th Va. Cav. and Mosby's 43d Bn. Va. Cav. and may be identical.

WADE, CHARLES A. C.: b. in England. enl. 4/20/61 in Co. F. Sent to Richmond hosp. on sick furlough 6/21/61 and retained as clerk in Adjutant and Inspector General's Office until discharged on surgeon's certificate of disability 2/7/62. Later a clerk in the QM General's Office in Richmond. Member of Capt. S. F. Sutherland's Co., "Government Guard," composed of government clerks, on 7/2/62.

WADE, LUKE R.: Conscript assigned 3/14/64 to (2d) Co. E. Absent sick on all rolls thru final 3/4/65 roll. In Richmond and Farmville hosps. with debility or acute diarrhea 5/16-8/1/64. Co. rolls show him in Lynchburg hosp. Paroled 5/25/65 at Campbell C.H. Postwar roster says resid. Campbell Co.

WADE, NICHOLAS LAWSON: b. 1/28/24 in Person Co., N.C. Only record is 5-6/62 roll of Co. G, which states "discharged by substituting Everrette." Appointed commercial agent of Halifax Co. by Commissary General. d. 3/7/94, bur. Greenhill Cem., Danville. Postwar roster has Nick Wade.

WAESCHE, GEORGE W.: enl. 10/26/63 in Co. D, "transferred from Co. B, 12 Va. Cav." On detached service at brigade HQ on all rolls, as clerk for brigade QM on final 3/22/65 roll. Paid as clerk 1/1-1/31/64, and as courier 4/1-5/31/64.

WAGER, CHARLES H.: On 5-6/62 roll of Co. D as present. Discharged 1/20/64. No other Confederate records found; on some postwar roster.

WAGGERMAN, P. H.: enl. 7/1/61 in Co. K. Present on 7-8/61 roll. Detailed as courier to Col. Hunton 7/21 in 11/61 return. AWOL since 2/21/62 on 1-2/62 and 6/30/62 rolls. No further record. Not on postwar roster.

WALDEN, ZEPH TURNER: enl. 5/8/61 in Co. B, age 28. Farmer. Present until he left camp 2/8/62 and d. of disease in Rappahannock Co. 2/16/62.

WALDHAUER, DAVID: b. in S.C. Elected Lt. in (1st) Co. E 9/17/61. Age 29 on 10/16/61 roll. Sent to Ga. to recruit 2/19/62. To Capt. 12/2/62. Wded. 7/2/63 at Gettysburg, right arm amputated. Detailed as enrolling officer of 1st Dist. of Georgia 11/63. POW 12/1/64 at Stoney Creek. Took the oath 5/30/65 at Ft. Delaware. Resid. Savannah, Ga. Worked for Central R.R. of Ga. postwar.

WALKER, ADOLPHUS D.: b. 1836. enl. 9/26/61 in Co. H. Deserted 11/25/62 near Rectortown, returned 12/62, excused by Major C. E. Flournoy. AWOL since 2/20/63 on 2/28/63 roll. Present on 7-8/63 roll, then present until he deserted 3/22/64. No further record. d. 1913, bur. Marshall Cem.

WALKER, ARTHUR: enl. 9/26/61 in Co. H. Deserted 11/25/62 near Rectortown, returned 12/62, excused by Major C. E. Flournoy. POW 6/9/63 at Beverley Ford. Paroled 6/25/63 at Old Capitol Prison. POW 8/1/63 on 7-8/63 roll thru 11-12/63 rolls, but no Federal record of capture. No further record.

WALKER, JAMES C.: Conscript assigned 3/18/64 to Co. G. AWOL on 9-10/64 roll. Otherwise present thru final 3/22/65 roll.

WALKER, JOHN H.: enl. 8/19/61 in Co. G, age 19. On sick furlough over 3 months, no report, on 5-6/62 roll. AWOL on 11-12/62 roll. In Richmond hosp. with wd. on left cheek 2/9-2/25/64, then 35 day furlough. Absent wded. on 7-8/64 roll. Otherwise present until POW 9/19/64 at Winchester. Paroled 2/18/65 at Pt. Lookout. Absent with leave on final 3/22/65 roll.

WALKER, REUBEN KING: enl. 9/17/61 in (1st) Co. E, age 19. Admitted 12/22/61 to Danville hosp., sent to Charlottesville hosp. Paroled 5/1/65 at Greensboro, N.C. Resid. Darien, Ga.

WALKER, SAMUEL FRANCIS: enl. 10/1/62 in Co. H. Merchant. POW 10/29/62 near Petersburg, (W.) Va., age 23, resid. Fauquier Co. Exchanged 12/2/62 near Vicksburg, Miss., from Camp Chase. On horse furlough on 12/62 return. AWOL since 2/1/63 on 2/28/63 roll. AWOL since 8/1/63 on 7-8/63 roll. POW 10/15/63 on 11-12/63 roll, but no Federal records on this. Thereafter absent until shown as deserted 8/1/63 on final 3/22/65 roll.

WALKER, WILLIAM H.: enl. 5/4/61 in Co. I, age 38. To Lt. 7/1/61. At home sick since 1/20/62 on 1-2/62 roll. Dropped 4/20/62.

WALLACE, JAMES WILLIAM M.: On postwar roster of Co. D.

WALTER, HENRY: enl. 3/20/64 in Co. H. In Richmond hosp. with hemorrhoids 5/24-7/9/64, transferred to Lynchburg. Absent sick 10/1/64 thru final 3/22/65 roll. Paroled 4/25/65 at Winchester, age 24, resid. Fauquier Co.

WALTON, JAMES: Federal records show a man of this name in Co. K, POW 5/7/62 at Dog Town, exchanged 8/5/62 at Aiken's Ldg. from Ft. Delaware. No Confederate records. Not on postwar roster. A man claiming to be this person, b. 8/7/47 near Kinsale, Westmoreland Co., resid. Mississippi since 1886, and postwar a newspaperman, was pensioned by Miss. He gave his captain's name as "Burrell Cox." This pensioner d. 8/30/47 at East Miss. Insane Hospital, Meridian.

WARD, JOHN M.: Conscript assigned 5/26/64 to (2d) Co. E. Present thru final 3/4/65 roll. Also shown as Word.

WARE, CHARLES ALEXANDER: b. 4/26/41 in Clarke Co. enl. 4/25/61 in Co. D. Present until on sick furlough on 5-6/62 roll. Absent on detached service in hosps. 9-62-2/63 rolls. Assistant Surgeon with ambulance train between Winchester and Staunton 9/29-11/5/62 rolls. Signs as Asst. Surg., 18th Va. Cav., 2/1/64, and Asst. Surg., McClanahan's Battery, 12/3/64. Paroled 4/18/65 at Winchester as Acting Surgeon, Lomax's Cav. Division, age 25. M.D., St. Louis, Mo., 1875-90.

WARE, JAQUELIN SMITH: b. 2/7/46 at "Springfield," near Berryville, Clarke Co. enl. 8/1/63 in Co. D. On duty at Cavalry Corps or Division HQ as courier until present with company on 9-10/64 roll. AWOL on final 3/22/65 roll. Paroled 5/1/65 at Summit Pt., resid. Clarke Co. Farmer postwar. m. Helen Glasswell Grinnan 1900. d. 11/28/19 at Berryville.

WARFIELD, _____: Shown on 11/62 return as in Co. C, absent paroled. No other record. May refer to Warfield Lee.

WARING, JOSEPH FREDERICK: b. 1832. enl. 9/17/61 in (1st) Co. E as Capt. Planter on Skidaway Island, Ga. Wded. 12/4/61. To Lt. Col. 12/2/62. Paroled at Greensboro, N.C., as Col. General Forwarding Agent of Central R.R. of Ga. postwar. d. 10/5/76.

WARREN, JOSEPH: enl. 7/1/62 in (2d) Co. E. Present on 7-8/63 roll. Absent on detail to get clothing for company from 12/30/63 on 11-12/63 roll. No further record.

WASHBURN, JOSEPH, JR.: enl. 9/17/61 in (1st) Co. E. Age 28 on 10/16/61 roll. To Cpl. on 11/1/61 roll. Wded. slightly at Williamsburg 5/5/62. To Sgt. in 7/62. Transferred to Chatham (Ga.) Art. in exchange for W. J. Grubb in 8/63. Resid. Savannah, Ga.

WASHINGTON, GEORGE: On postwar "original list" of Co. F.

WATSON, FLETCHER BANGS: b. 11/27/41 in Chatham. Grad. Trinity College, N.C. enl. 8/19/61 in Co. G. On sick furlough 9/14/61 thru 5-6/62 roll. To Cpl. on 9-10/64 roll. To Sgt. 11/7/62. In Richmond hosp. with fever 10/3-10/30/63. Sick in hosp. on 11-12/63 roll. Otherwise present until wded. 5/11/64 at Yellow Tavern in right shoulder, sent to Richmond and Danville hosps. Present on final 3/22/65 roll. POW 4/1/65 at Five Forks. Took the oath 6/22/65 at Pt. Lookout. Lawyer, editor, farmer, and superintendent of schools in Pittsylvania Co. postwar. m. Pattie Booker Tredway 1870. d. 10/26/17, bur. Chatham Cem. "His loyalty and devotion to the education of the youth of his native county were boundless."

WATSON, JAMES EPHRAIM: b. 11/1537 at Lebanon, (W.) Va. enl. 7/14/61 in Co. D. To Commissary Sgt. 5/2/62. In Charlottesville hosp. with fever 8/29-10/21/63, and with typhoid fever 11/23-12/30/63. WIA 10/9/64. Otherwise present thru final 3/22/65 roll. Paroled 4/20/65 at Winchester, resid. near Smithfield. d. 1914 at Charles Town, W. Va., bur. Episcopal and Masonic Cem., Middleway. Brother of John.

WATSON, JOHN J.: b. 1/9/38. enl. 7/14/61 in Co. D. Absent sick 8/20/62 thru 1-2/63 roll, and on 11-12/63 roll. On duty at enrolling office in Harrisonburg on 7-10/64 rolls. WIA 9/19/64 at Winchester. Absent, detailed for light duty in brigade commissary dept. on final 3/22/65 roll. Transportation ordered from Washington, D.C., to N.Y. City 4/24/65. Paroled 5/31/65 at Harrisonburg. Farmer at Uvilla, W.Va., postwar. d. 9/28/14, bur. Edge Hill Cem., Charles Town, W.Va. Brother of James E.

WATSON, THOMAS SYLVESTER: b. 1839. Enl. 7/14/61 in Co. D. Absent on sick furlough on 5-12/62 rolls. Absent with leave on 11-12/63 roll. Otherwise present until absent wded. and at hosp. on 7-8/64 roll thru final 3/22/65 roll. Paroled 4/25/65 at Winchester, resid. Jefferson Co. Farmer near Middleway, W.Va., postwar. D. 1920, bur. Episcopal and Masonic Cem., Middleway. Postwar roster says wded. 6/11/64 and 10/9/64.

WATSON, WALTER M.: enl. 4/1/62 in Co. I. Present on all rolls thru final 3/20/65 roll. d. 3/21/12 in Orange Co. Wid. Elizabeth R., m. 1860.

WATSON, WILBUR FISKE: b. 1839 in Pittsylvania Co. enl. 5/27/61 in (2d) Co. E. Lawyer. Present only on 7-8/61 roll. Discharged on surgeon's certificate of disability 8/24/61 (or 62). d. 1863, bur. Chatham Cem.

WAUGH, CHARLES STUART: b. 10/22/23. enl. 5/4/61 in Co. I. Discharged 8/10/61 "by order of Gov. Letcher." Shown as present on 5-6/62 roll, but no further record. d. 12/30/08 at Orange, bur. Waugh Cem. on Brush Mountain northeast of Orange.

WAY, JOSEPH L.: enl. 9/17/61 in (1st) Co. E. Age 35 on 10/16/61 roll. Paroled 5/1/65 at Greensboro, N.C. Resid. Liberty Co., Ga.

WEAVER, F. H.: enl. 5/28/61 in Co. C. In Richmond hosp. 3/18-4/23/62. Absent with leave on 11-12/63 roll. Otherwise present on all rolls thru final ca. 3/30/65 roll.

WEAVER, HORACE: enl. 3/16/62 in Co. H. Deserted 11/25/62, excused 12/3/62 by Major C. E. Flournoy. Paroled 3/28/63 by Federals, but no record as POW. POW 3/31/63 near Brentsville. Paroled from Old Capitol 4/17/63. Courier to Gen. Jeb Stuart on 7-12/63 rolls. Paid as scout 4/25-10/30/63. AWOL on 12/30/64 roll. Deserted 12/1/64 on 3/22/65 final roll. Paroled 5/26/65 at Winchester, age 38, resid. Fauquier Co.

WEAVER, JOSEPH GUSTAVUS: b. in Rappahannock Co. enl. 1/1/63 in Co. B. Carpenter. Deserted 11/28/63. POW 12/6/63 at Culpeper C.H. Wrote from Pt. Lookout 8/8/64 "I am a Union man and always was," and 9/10/64 "my principal is north, my home is in Boon Co. Ky. I wish to Remain north." enl. 10/12/64 in Co. D, 4th U.S. Vol. Inf. To Cpl. 11/1/64. Deserted 5/8/65 at Cincinnati, Ohio. Resid. Boston, Culpeper Co., and Scrabble postwar. No records were found in Washington, D.C., and he was pensioned by Va. d. 1937, age 97, bur. Old Joe Weaver Cem., Boston.

WEAVER, MASON A.: enl. 5/23/62 in Co. H, evidently while AWOL from 17th Va. Inf. Clerk. Federal records show him POW 5/23 (or 25)/62 at Warrenton, paroled 6/10/63 at Old Capitol Prison. Sent to Harrisonburg hosp. 6/28 on 5-6/62 roll. Left on scout 11/24 on 11/62 return. Otherwise present until 12/62 return has him transferred 12/1/62 to 17th Va. Inf., but no record he went to that unit. POW 8/18/63 at Markham Station as in 6th Va. Cav., held at Pt. Lookout, but no record of parole.

WEAVER, ROBERT F.: enl. 5/28/61 in Co. C as Lt. Dropped 4/20/62. Later Lt. in Co. B, 23rd Va. Cav. Paroled 5/20/65 at Staunton, age 24.

WEAVER, ROBERT L.: Federal records show this man in Co. H, POW 8/18/63 at Markham, paroled 3/10/65 at Elmira. No Confederate records. Not on postwar rosters.

WEAVER, VIRGIL: enl. 3/16/62 in Co. H. Physician. Discharged 12/16/61 from Co. B, 8th Va. Inf., for bleeding from lungs, age 22. Absent sick on 5-6/62 roll. Courier to Gen. Jeb Stuart on 7-8/63 roll. Commended for bravery near Catlett's Station 10/13/63. To Lt. on 11-12/63 roll, on leave since 12/26/63. Strongly recommended by Gen. Jeb Stuart 2/6/64 "from personal observation of many instances of 'valor & skill'." Gen. R. E. Lee wrote 2/8/64 "he has shown boldness, skill & intelligence" as scout in enemy lines. To Capt. 2/19/64 for valor and skill. d. 5/12/64, bur. Confederate Cem., Spotsylvania. Postwar rosters say KIA 5/7/64 at Todd's Tavern.

WEAVER, WILLIAM: enl. 11/20/64 in Co. B. Reported as deserter by Richmond 2/28/65, to be found in Fauquier Co. Present on final 3/21/65 roll. May be William S. Weaver, d. 1/8/94, age 73, bur. Orlean Cem.

WEAVER, WILLIAM T.: enl. 10/1/62 in Co. H. Absent sick on 2/28/63 roll. Otherwise present until POW 8/2 (or 8)/63 at Flint Hill. Paroled 12/24/63 at Pt. Lookout. On Confederate clothing roll as paroled and exchanged POW 1/3/64. Elizabeth Weaver filed a claim as his widow 9/14/64.

WEBB, HORACE: enl. 4/1/62 in Co. I. Present on 5-6/62 roll. Paid 9/13/63 for service 5/1-7/20/63. No further record.

WEBSTER, GEORGE W.: enl. 3/14/62 in Co. F. Plasterer. On sick furlough at Dogtown on 5-6/62 roll. Otherwise present until POW 2/20/64 at Upperville, age 26, apparently b. in Philadelphia, Pa. Resid. Fairfax Co. Took the oath 6/7/65 at Ft. Delaware.

WELCH, LUTHER M.: b. 10/13/29. enl. 4/19/63 in Co. H. AWOL since 8/27/63 on 7-8/63 roll. Present on 11-12/63 roll. No further record. d. 1893, bur. Marshall Cem.

WELCH, WILLIAM RANDALL: b. 5/10/31 in Fauquier Co. enl. 4/24/61 in Co. H as Sgt. Carpenter. On furlough 2/9-3/13/62. To Lt. on 5-6/62 roll. To Capt. on 2/28/63 roll. Present until his resignation was accepted 12/14/63. Gen. L. L. Lomax wrote "The company and service will be much benefitted in my opinion by an immediate acceptance . . . He is not suited for an officer." Resid. Marshall postwar. d. 10/7/15, bur. Marshall Cem.

WELLS, GEORGE WILLIAM: Conscript assigned 2/15/64 to Co. F. Wded. 9/19/64 at Winchester and sent to Lynchburg hosp. Thereafter absent wded. thru final 2/24/65 roll. Paroled 4/14 (or 15)/65 at Lynchburg.

WEST, HENRY E.: Pseudonym of Conrad Badenhop, q.v.

WHEAT, FRANK W.: enl. 7/24/61 in Co. D. To Sgt. 10/18/61. On sick furlough on 5-6/62 roll. Otherwise present until AOWL on final 3/22/65 roll. Paroled 5/20/65 at Charlottesville as Lt.

WHEAT, JOSEPH N.: b. 1/8/44 in Berryville (another source says Albemarle Co.) enl. 8/1/63 in Co. D. Present until POW 9/19/64 at Winchester. Paroled 3/15/65 at Pt. Lookout. Absent, POW, on final 3/22/65 roll. Carpenter in Albemarle Co. postwar, claiming wd. at Winchester. d. 8/31/31 at Lee Camp Soldiers' Home, Richmond, after amputation of right leg, bur. Hollywood Cem., Richmond.

WHEELER, _____: Shown as deserting 12/16/62 from Co. A at camp near Harrisonburg on 11-12/62 roll and as AWOL on 12/62 return.

WHEELER, RICHARD HENRY: enl. 4/20/61 in Co. F. To Sgt. on 1-2/62 roll. Present until discharged 7/26/62.

WHIPPLE, ANDREW B.: enl. 7/29/61 in Co. C. Present until he deserted 9/20/62 at Paris. Substitute for William W. Hedrick.

WHITE, ADIN C.: b. in Loudoun Co. enl. 4/22/61 in Co. K as Cpl. Farmer. Present until he d. 4/16/62 near Brandy Station of typhoid pneumonia, age 22. Single, leaving no wife or children, he was survived by his father Richard.

WHITE, CHARLES: enl. 7/1/62 in (2d) Co. E. In Charlottesville hosp. 11/25/62 with debility. Present on all rolls thru final 3/4/65 roll. In Chimborazo Hosp. No. 5, Richmond, 3/28/65 with frostbitten feet. Paroled 5/6/65 at Greensboro, N.C. Took the oath 5/20/65 at Greensboro.

WHITE, JAMES H.: enl. 6/23/61 in Co. I as Sgt., age 36. Absent sick on several rolls. To Lt. 4/20/62. Resigned 10/8/62, "feeling myself incompetent to do justice to the men as their capt. or 1st Lieutenant." Resignation approved by Gen. R. E. Lee 10/21/62, but White signs as Capt. commanding Co. I 10/26/62, and 1st Lt. commanding company 2/18/63. Postwar roster says resid. near Ruckersville, resigned Fall 1862. "In our first valley campaign fell in love with a girl about Lacey Springs, and he pretty soon got out."

WHITE, JAMES LOVELACE: b. 2/14/43 in Halifax Co. Transferred to Co. G from Co. H, 14th Va. Inf. in exchange for William Coleman and first shown on Co. G roll for 9-10/64. Student. Present thru final 3/22/65 roll. Salesman postwar, resid. Roanoke 1922. d. 2/22/29.

WHITE, JOHN RICHARD, JR.: b. 3/23/42 at "Locust Thicket," Loudoun Co. enl. 8/1/62 in Co. D. Present until wded. 10/9/62, then absent wded. thru final 3/22/65 roll. Paroled 4/20/65, no place shown. m. Margaretta Holmes McGuire. d. 12/31/17 at Lee Camp Soldiers' Home, Richmond, bur. Green Hill Cem., Berryville. Postwar sources say wded. at Luray, also in 8th Va. Inf.

WHITE, NASON: enl. 4/1/62 in (2d) Co. E. d. 5 or/6/20)/61. Survived by Mary C. White of Pittsylvania Co., his mother.

WHITEHEAD, JOHN RICHARD: b. 8/7/44 near Berger's Store, Pittsylvania Co. Att. Emory and Henry College. enl. 3/6/62 in Co. G as Cpl. Student. To Sgt. 9/23/62. POW 6/9/63 at Beverly Ford. Paroled 6/25/63 from Old Capitol Prison. On horse detail on 7-8/63 and 9-10/64 rolls. In Richmond hosps. 5/6-5/7/64; 5/20-5/26/64 with wd. of right side, then 60 days furlough. Otherwise present thru final 3/22/65 roll. Postwar farmer, merchant, sheriff, and treasurer of Pittsylvania Co. m. Sallie Hunt Graves 6/22/64. d. 6/4 (or 13)/02 in Chatham.

WHITEHEAD, JOSEPH A.: enl. 7/1/64 in Co. G. Present thru final 3/22/65 roll. Postwar roster says resid. Pittsylvania Co.

WHITEHEAD, WILLIAM JOSEPH: b. 7/6/46 in Pittsylvania Co. Paroled 6/6/65 at Franklin C.H. as in Co. G. Previously in 24th Va. Cav. and 8th (Dearing's) Confederate Cav. d. 10/23/27 at Beaver Park, Colorado.

WHITING, CARLISLE F.: enl. 3/1/62 in Co. D. Previously wded. 7/21/61 at 1st Manassas. Absent with leave on 5-6/62 roll. Thereafter always present until 9-10/64 roll, when absent on scout for Gen. T. L. Rosser. Postwar roster says KIA 12/64 on scout at Luray.

WHITING, CLARENCE C.: b. in Va. enl. 3/1/62 in Co. A. Detached on special duty or as courier for Gen. Jeb Stuart on all rolls. Commended by Stuart for "signal zeal and intelligence" at Williamsburg 5/5/62. POW 5/31/62 at Fair Oaks. Exchanged 8/5/62 from Ft. Delaware, age 18. Transferred 12/1/62 to Co. G, 7th Va. Cav.

WHITLOCK, MARTIN T.: enl. 2/10/64 in Co. C. Present thru final 3/22/65 roll. Shown as AWOL from Co. G on final 3/22/65 roll. Paroled 4/24/65 at Maynard House, near Richmond, as in (2d) Co. E, resid. Culpeper Co.

WHITMORE, JOHN S.: b. in Rockingham Co. enl. 5/25/63 in Co. C. Previously in 10th Va. Inf. Present until 7-8 and 9-10/64 rolls, when AWOL. No further record until paroled 5/2/65 at Harrisonburg, age 25, resid. Augusta Co. d. Summit, Augusta Co., 9/16/12.

WHITT, JOHN: enl. 8/19/61 in Co. G. Age 36 on 9/10/61 roll. Present on all rolls thru 5-6/62 roll. Co. clothing book has discharged 8/19/62.

WHITT, THOMAS: enl. 8/19/61 in Co. G. Age 33 on 9/10/61 roll. Present consistently thru final 3/22/65 roll. Age 70, resid. Danville on 5/12/00.

WHITTINGTON, ROBERT W.: enl. 7/25/61 in Co. D. Previously in Co. A, 122d Va. Militia. Blacksmith on 10/61 roll. AWOL from 11/7/61. Advertised as deserter 1/31/61. No further record. On ca. 1898 Fauquier Co. veterans census, age 67.

WHITWORTH, THOMAS C.: b. 9/2/44. enl. 8/19/61 in Co. G. Present until discharged 8/19/62. Farmer postwar. Resid. Columbia, S.C., from ca. 1879. Applied to Home for Confederate Veterans at Columbia 5/25/25. Wife Mary E.

WIGGINTON, BENJAMIN: enl. 4/22/61 in Co. B as Sgt., age 29. Farmer. To Lt. 7/26/61. Horse KIA 5/23/62 at Cedarville. On 10 days furlough on 1-2/63 roll. Absent sick since 8/15 on 11-12/63 roll. POW 1/12/64 in Rappahannock Co. Took the oath 5/31/65 at Ft. Delaware, resid. Rappahannock Co.

WIGGINTON, JAMES D.: b. 12/15/40. enl. 5/15/61 in Co. D. Farmer. AWOL since 12/25 on 11-12/61 roll, sentenced to lose $24 pay. Thereafter always present until POW 3/20/64 in Clarke Co. Paroled 2/25/65 at Camp Chase. In Richmond hosp. with debility 3/8-3/9/65, then 30 day furlough. Paroled 4/20/65 at Winchester. Physician postwar, resid. Jefferson Co. all his life. d. 2/11/08 at Summit Pt., bur. Episcopal and Masonic Cem., Middleway, W.Va.

WIGGLESWORTH, CLAIBORNE: enl. 5/4/61 in Co. I, age 33. Sick at home with measles on ca. 6/19/61 roll. Present until wded. in thigh 6/9/63 at Brandy Station. Absent wded. until detailed in QM Dept. at Gordonsville on 7-10/64 rolls. Absent sick on final 3/20/65 roll.

WILEY, CORNELIUS: enl. 9/28/62 in Co. A. Present thru 1-2/63 roll. Postwar sources say d. in hosp. at Orkney Springs, resid. Clarke Co.

WILEY, RICHARD H.: b. in Loudoun Co. enl. 4/22/61 in Co. K. Present until he d. 6/12/62.

WILKINSON, W. S.: On a postwar roster of Co. C. No Confederate records.

WILLIAMS, B. F.: Appears on a 6/61 return as in (1st) Co. E, left by his company in hosp. sick 6/27 at Camp of Instruction at Ashland. No other record. Not on postwar roster.

WILLIAMS, CHARLES: enl. 5/27/61 in (2d) Co. E. Age 29 on 2/16/62 roll. Detached at Gordonsville guarding baggage on 12/62 return. Reported POW 11/7/63 at Brandy Station, but this appears to be wrong. Otherwise present until POW 2/1/64 at Robinson River, and thereafter POW thru final 3/4/65 roll. Took the oath 6/21/65 at Ft. Delaware.

WILLIAMS, F. L.: Shown as in Co. H on 11/61 return, absent since 9/1 working as wheelwright. No other record. Not on postwar rosters.

WILLIAMS, FRANCIS M.: enl. 5/27/61 in (2d) Co. E. Absent POW, "not enlisted" on 2/16/62 roll; reported exchanged in 10/62, but no Federal records on capture. Guarding bridge at Mt. Crawford on 12/62 return. Thereafter present thru final 3/4/65 roll. Known as "Frank."

WILLIAMS, J. F.: Only record is of parole 4/18/65 at Edwards Ferry as in Co. K, age 22.

WILLIAMS, JOHN W.: enl. 3/8/62 in Co. K. Wded. 9/22/62 at Paris. POW wded. 10/1/62 at Point of Rocks, confined at Ft. McHenry, Md. Back in C.S. lines by 1/20/63, no record of parole. Detailed with disabled horses on 7-8/63 roll. Thereafter present until AWOL on final 1-2/65 roll. Paid as teamster 4/30, 10/30/63.

WILLIAMS, LEROY EUSTACE: b. 1839 in Clarke Co. Att. U.Va. enl. 8/15/61 in Co. D. Law student. Horse KIA 6/1/62 near Strasburg. In Charlottesville hosp. with fever 12/6/63-2/5/64. Found guilty of AWOL 3/7/64, to forfeit 6 months pay and be reprimanded. Wded. through left lung and hand at Trevillian's Station 6/11/64, thereafter absent wded. thru final 3/22/65 roll. Retired to Invalid Corps ca. 12/7/64. Paroled 5/1/65 at Summit Pt. Real estate dealer at Louisville, Ky., postwar. d. 4/13 at Anchorage, Ky.

WILLIAMS, THOMAS EDWIN: b. in Va. enl. 6/4/61 in Co. D. Discharged 12/4/61 by promotion to Assistant Surgeon. To Surg. 2nd N.C. Cav. 11/3/64. Paroled 5/1/65 at Summit Pt., age 28.

WILLIAMS, THOMAS H.: enl. 9/17/61 in (1st) Co. E. Age 18 on 10/16/61 roll. Deserted, remaining in Svannah, Ga., on its evacuation 12/21/64. Resid. Savannah, Ga.

WILLIAMS, WILLIAM D.: enl. 11/8/61 in Co. G. Present until absent on sick furlough since 2/18/62 on 1-2/62 roll. d. 3/7/62.

WILLIAMS, WILLIAM T.: enl. 4/1/62 in (2d) Co. E. d. 5/7/62 at General Hosp. No. 2, Lynchburg, of rubeola, bur. at Lynchburg.

WILLINGHAM, A.: Only record is 5-6/62 roll of Co. D, which shows him AWOL. Not on postwar rosters.

WILLINGHAM, JOHN THOMAS: enl. 10/25/63 in Co. A. Previously in Co. A, 39th Bn. Va. Cav. AWOL since 10/25/63 on 7-8/64 roll. Present on 9-10/64 roll. AWOL since 1/18/65 on final 3/27/65 roll. Resid. Clarke Co. in 1870.

WILLIS, ACHILLE MURAT: enl. 4/22/61 in Co. B as Orderly Sgt., age 33. Farmer. Discharged 6/20/61 to accept appointment as Lt. in Co. K, 49th Va. Inf. Later Capt. in 7th and 12th Va. Cav. Regts.

WILLIS, ALBERT G.: enl. 3/1/63 in Co. B. Present on all rolls thru final 3/21/65 roll. Reported by Richmond as deserter 2/28/65. Postwar roster says age 30 on enl., reportedly d. before 5/07.

WILLIS, EUGENE H.: enl. 9/15/63 in Co. I. Transferred from Co. A, 15th Va. Inf. Horse KIA 6/29/64 near Reams Station. Courier for Gen. L. L. Lomax on 7-10/64 rolls. Present on final 3/20/65 roll. Reportedly alive in 7/09.

WILLIS, JAMES A.: enl. 8/15/64 in Co. I. Horse KIA 9/19/64 at Winchester. Present on all rolls thru 3/20/65 final roll.

WILLIS, MARION GORDON: b. 4/7/46 in Orange Co. enl. 8/15/64 in Co. I. Absent wded. on 9-10/64 roll. In Charlottesville hosp. with gelatio 1/24-2/26/65. Absent sick on final 3/20/65 roll. m. Lucy Taylor Gordon 1866. Resid. Fredericksburg from 1873. Merchant, city council member, mayor of Fredericksburg postwar. d. 2/10/30 in Fredericksburg, bur. City Cem., Fredericksburg.

WILLIS, NATHANIEL HITE: b. 3/25/42 at Rock Hall. enl. 6/11/61 in Co. D. Two weeks sick furlough from 11/24/61. To Cpl. on 9-10/62 roll. Horse KIA 7/3/63. To Sgt. on 11-12/63 roll. In Charlottesville hosp. with morbi cutis 12/24/63-1/30/64. Wded. 6/10/64 at Trevillian's Station and absent wded. thru 10/31/64 roll. Present on final 3/22/65 roll. POW 4/2/65 at Dinwiddie C.H. Took the oath 6/22/65 at Pt. Lookout. d. 10/26/14 at Charles Town, W.Va., bur. Zion Episcopal Church there.

WILLIS, WILLIAM BYRD: b. 3/23/36. enl. 10/1/62 in Co. I. Courier for Gen. Jeb Stuart since 12/24 on 11-12/62 roll, and for Gen. W. E. Jones on 1-2/63 roll. To Lt. on 7-8/63 roll. Signs as commanding both Cos. I and F on 9-10/64 rolls. Present on final 3/20/65 roll of Co. I. Resid. Hyattsville, Md., in 1907. d. 8/18/13, bur. Graham Cem. west of Orange.

WILLIS, WILLIAM F.: b. in Rappahannock Co. enl. 11/15/63 in Co. C. Present until AWOL on 9-10/64 roll. Paroled 6/14/65 at Winchester, age 37, resid. Rappahannock Co. Farmer postwar, resid. near Sandy on 4/29/03. On a postwar roster of Co. B.

WILMARTH, JOHN J.: enl. 7/24/61 in Co. A. Clerk. On furlough since 2/9/62 on 1-2/62 roll. Regimental orderly on 8/13/63 roll. Bearer of dispatches 1/23-2/3/64. Wded. 5/31/64 in right leg, in Richmond hosp. 6/1-6/22/64, then 40 day furlough. POW 9/24 (or 26)/64 at Luray. Exchanged 2/10/65 from Pt. Lookout. Absent with leave on final 3/27/65 roll, "having been exchanged & not yet notified." Paroled 5/8/65 at Winchester, age 24, resid. Loudoun Co. Postwar roster gives Jack Wilmouth.

WILMER, GEORGE THORNTON: b. 5/8/19 at Alexandria. Grad. Va. Theological Sem. 1843, William and Mary, D.D. 1860. enl. 8/19/61 in Co. G. Episcopal clergyman. Detailed as Commissary Sgt. 9/19-10/27/61. Appointed regimental chaplain 10/18/62, but "not yet joined" on all rolls. Professor at William and Mary 1869-76, and Univ. of the South 1876-87.

WILSON, ANDREW: In U.S. records as POW 5/6/64 in Franklin Co., Pa., no company shown, deserter from 1st N.Y. Vet. Vol. Cav. Held at Ft. Delaware, transferred 6/17/64 to Washington, D.C. No further record, not found on rolls of 1st N.Y. Vet. Cav. No Confederate records.

165

WILSON, ENOCH CROSBY: b. 6/10/33. enl. 7/24/61 in Co. A. To forfeit $12 pay by order of regimental court on 7-8/61 roll. AWOL since 12/23 on 12/61 return. To forfeit $24 pay by order of general court-martial on 1-2/62 roll. Accidentally wded. in arm 8/28/63. AWOL since 11/1/63 on 11-12/63 roll. Otherwise present until POW 5/12/64 at Yellow Tavern. Took the oath 6/21/65 at Elmira, resid. Harpers Ferry. d. 12/16/95, bur. Harmony Methodist Church, Hamilton.

WILSON, JOHN W.: Shown on U.S. records as conscripted 6/4/64 at Richmond in Co. C, POW 7/18 (or 20)/64 in Fauquier Co. (or Frederick, Md.). Asked to take the oath 9/15/64, age 17, "he objects to being exchanged as it was against his wishes that he entered the Rebel service." Paroled 3/10/65 at Elmira for exchange. No Confederate records.

WILSON, WILLIAM C.: enl. 6/30/62 in Co. B as substitute for John Butler. Absent sick in hosp. on 11-12/62 roll. Otherwise present thru 1-2/63 roll. POW 4/14/64 in Rappahannock Co. Received 6/17/64 at Ft. Delaware, no record of release found. Resid. Castleton, age 57, on 3/24/03. d. 2/7/23. Postwar roster says enl. 3/64, "taken prisoner and detained till close of war."

WIMSATT, JOHN SAMUEL: In U.S. records as POW 8/5/63 at Thoroughfare Gap from Co. H. Paroled 12/24/63 at Pt. Lookout. Also appears as Winstead, Wimsett. No Confederate records in 6th Va. Cav. Apparently identical to J. Samuel Wimsatt, 39th Bn. Va. Cav.

WINES, JAMES W.: enl. 1/28/63 in Co. H. Horse KIA 6/9/63 near Brandy Station. Present on 2/28/63 and 11-12/63 rolls and on clothing rolls for 5/2 and 5/19/64. Otherwise absent sick thru 9-10/64 roll. Postwar roster says KIA at Lacey's Springs, 12/64.

WINES, WILLIAM HENRY: enl. 4/24/61 in Co. H. Wagoner. AWOL since 6/12 on 6/30/61 roll. Sent home again 10/22 and AWOL 11/1/61 thru 12/61 return. Guarding baggage at Manassas on 1-2/62 roll. Deserter since 11/25/62 on 2/28/63 roll. AWOL since 8/25/63 on 7-8/63 roll. Present on 11/63-8/64 rolls, but AWOL on 9-10/64 roll. Reported by Richmond as deserter 3/1/65. Deserted 12/17/64 on final 3/22/65 roll. d. 1/1/01, bur. odd Fellows' Cem., Clarksburg, W.Va.

WOMACK, CHARLES ALEXANDER: b. 1843. enl. 11/9/63 in (2d) Co. E. In Richmond hosp. with acute diarrhea 8/9-8/18/64, then 35 day furlough. Horse KIA 10/19/64 at Belle Grove. Twenty-two day horse detail from 10/27/64. Sick in Richmond hosp. on 3/4/65 final roll. POW 4/3/65 at Jackson Hosp., Richmond. Took the oath at Newport News 7/1/65, resid. Pittsylvania Co. d. 1928, bur. Womack Cem., Pittsylvania Co.

WOMACK, JAMES A.: b. in Pittsylvania Co. enl. 5/27/61 in (2d) Co. E. To Cpl. 7/23/61. Age 26 on 2/16/62 roll. To Sgt. on 5-6/62 roll. Present on all rolls until KIA 5/30/64 at Cold Harbor and bur. where he fell.

WOOD, DRURY B.: enl. 3/17/63 in Co. G. Previously Lt., Co. F, 53d Va. Inf. On 20 days leave from 12/16/63. POW 5/12/64 at Yellow Tavern. Took the oath at Elmira 6/14/65, resid. Danville. Inexplicably shown absent with leave on final 3/22/65 roll.

WOOD, J. M.: Conscript assigned to regiment 5/26/64. No company shown. No further record. May be identical to James Madison Wood.

WOOD, JAMES MADISON: b. 8/17/40. enl. 4/22/61 in Co. B. Farmer. Wded. and horse "lost" 5/23/62 at Cedarville. Absent wded. until present on 1-2/63 roll. On detached service at bridge near Mt. Crawford 3/20-3/31/63. Otherwise present until detailed buying cattle on final 3/21/65 roll. Paroled 5/10/65 at Winchester. Farmer, on Rappahannock Board of Supervisors postwar, resid. Oak Hill. m. Anna Eliza Bragg. d. 7/4/24, bur. Sperryville Cem.

WOOD, WILLIAM S.: enl. 5/4/61 in Co. I. Age 26 on ca. 6/19/61 roll. Absent with leave 11/18-12/15/61. Otherwise present thru 1-2/62 roll. May be the man of this name, b. in Fauquier Co., who enl. 10/25/64 in Co. C, Mosby's 43d Bn. Va. Cav., age 29, paroled 5/18/65 at Winchester, resid. Rappahannock Co.

WOODING, HARRY: Shown as in Co. C, resid. Danville on postwar roster. May refer to Thomas H. Wooding, (2d) Co. E.

WOODING, THOMAS H.: enl. 5/27/61 in (2d) Co. E. Age 23 on 2/16/62 roll. To Cpl., absent wded. in foot on 5-6/62 roll. In Richmond hosp. with chronic diarrhea 10/21-10/28/63, then transferred to Danville. To Sgt. on 9-10/64 roll. Otherwise present thru final 3/4/65 roll.

WOODVILLE, EDMOND STEVENSON: b. 6/30/31. enl. 4/1/62 in Co. I. Absent with sick leave on 5-6/62 roll. Returned from desertion on 12/62 return. In Richmond hosp. with catarrh 11/28/63-1/26/64. Otherwise present thru final 3/20/65 roll. Resid. near Indiantown postwar. d. 8/23/01, bur. Locust Grove. Wid. Julia Adlaide, m. 1888. Some postwar sources give first name as Edwin, and middle as Steven or Stephenson, d. 1904.

WOODVILLE, GEORGE CAMACK: enl. 3/15/64 in Co. I. Present thru final 3/20/65 roll. Postwar roster says wded. 1864 in Valley. d. 7/1/23 at Lignum, wid. Lucy L., m. 1879.

WOODWARD, JAMES R.: enl. 9/24/62 in Co. H. Reported POW 10/15/62 near Salem, paroled, and not yet returned on 12/62 return, but no U.S. records on this. Present again on 2/28/63 roll and thereafter thru final 3/22/65 roll. POW 4/1/65 at Five Forks. Took the oath 6/21/65 at Pt. Lookout, resid. Fauquier Co.

WOODY, WILEY: b. in Pittsylvania Co. enl. 7/1/63 in (2d) Co. E. Farmer. POW 9/14/63 near Culpeper. Paroled 3/14/65 at Elmira. In Richmond hosp. with debility 3/19-3/25/65, then 60 day furlough. Age 58 on 3/9/04. d. 3/5/20, wid. Sallie E., m. 1867.

WOOLENHAM, _____: Shown on a postwar roster of Co. A as deserted. May be identical to John T. Willingham.

WOOLF, HENRY CLAY: enl. 3/8/62 in Co. K. AWOL on 6/30/62 roll. AWOL sick on 7-8/63 roll. Otherwise present until wded. 5/7/64 at Spotsylvania and d. in field hosp. the following night. Sometimes shown as Wolfe.

WOOLF, SAMUEL A.: b. 2/14/33. enl. 6/20/63 in Co. K. AWOL since 10/18/64 on 9-10/64 roll. Otherwise present. AWOL on final 1-2/65 roll. Paroled 4/24/65 at Winchester. On ca. 1898 Fauquier Co. veterans census. d. 1/14/10, bur. Sharon Cem., Middleburg.

WOOLFOLK, JOHN W.: b. in Orange Co. enl. 5/4/61 in Co. I as Sgt., age 29. Farmer. Sick at home on ca. 6/19/61 roll. Discharged 2/13/62 for valvular disease of heart, "unable to bear any excitement." To Pvt. on 5-6/62 roll, enl. 4/1/62. To Lt. 12/4/62. Fifteen days sick furlough from 1/29/63. Sick in camp on 7-8/63 roll. Wded. 8/21/64 in neck and thereafter absent wded. In Charlottesville hosp. with hemorrhoids 10/4-10/5/64, transferred to Gordonsville. Absent at hosp. since 2/1 on final 3/20/65 roll. "Little" John Woolfolk, twice wded., on postwar roster.

WOOTON, O. R.: enl. 3/28/62 in Co. G as Cpl. Present until discharged 12/16/62 by substituting John Concedine. Postwar roster shows John Wooten, discharged for ill health.

WORSHAM, PATRICK: b. in Pittsylvania Co. enl. 8/19/61 in Co. G, age 32. Clerk. Present until discharged 1/18/62 for enlargement of the heads of the bones forming the knee joint, age 20 [sic].

WORSHAM, RICHARD E.: enl. 8/19/61 in Co. G. To Cpl. 1/15/62. On detached service on 5-6/62 roll. To Sgt. on 7-8/64 roll. In Richmond hosp. wded. in right arm 7/3/64, d. there of chronic diarrhea 9/15/64.

WRENN, ALBERT W.: enl. 5/25/61 in Co. F. Present, sick near camp on 7-8/61 roll. Present until POW 8/3/64 at Burke Station. Paroled 3/14/65 at Elmira. POW 5/7/65 at Fairfax C.H. and paroled there same day, age 24, signs by mark.

WRENN, CHARLES B.: enl. 5/25/61 in Co. F. Present until discharged 7/26/62.

WRENN, JAMES W.: enl. 10/1/61 in Co. F. Present until discharged 7/30/62 as Cpl. enl. again 9/1/62 as Sgt. Sick at hosp. on 7-8/64 roll. Present on 9-10/64 roll, but presence or absence not stated on final 2/24/65 roll. d. 3/21/65 of pneumonia at Lynchburg hosp., bur. City Cem., Lynchburg.

WRENN, MARSHALL: Shown on a 1909 roster of Co. I.

WRENN, WILLIAM H.: b. 1842. enl. 5/25/61 in Co. F. Present until detailed and sent back with horses on 7-8/63 roll. Thereafter present thru final 2/24/65 roll. Paroled 5/6/65 at Fairfax C.H., age 22, signs by mark. Postwar roster says wded. at Cold Harbor. Resid. Merryfield, Fairfax Co., 12/22/02, claiming wd. from grapeshot at Deep Creek in retreat from Richmond. d. 1929, bur. "The Mount" Cem., Fairfax Co.

WRIGHT, DANIEL J.: enl. 3/1/63 in Co. C. Absent sick on 7-8/64 roll. Otherwise present thru final ca. 3/30/65 roll. Paroled 5/30/65 at Harrisonburg, age 26. Witnessed pension application of Margaret Shumaker (Shoemaker) 6/15/00.

WRIGHT, EDWIN J.: enl. 3/15/62 in Co. I. Farmer. Sent to Culpeper hosp. sick 8/26/63 on 7-8/63 roll. To Sgt. 12/16/63. Wded. in flesh of left leg 5/7/64, age 19. In Richmond hosp. wded. 5/9-5/29/64, then 60 day furlough. Absent wded. on 9-10/64 roll. AWOL on final 3/20/65 roll.

WRIGHT, GEORGE WASHINGTON: b. 11/1/30 in Orange Co. enl. 4/1/62 in Co. I as Sgt. Absent on leave, wded., on 11-12/62 roll. Otherwise present until detailed 7/20/63 as Commissioner of Revenue of Orange Co., Pvt. Thereafter absent detailed as revenue commissioner until discharged 1/22/64 for service in that office. d. 1/12/95 in Orange Co.

WRIGHT, ISAAC H.: b. 1849 in Rockingham Co. enl. 1/65 in Co. C. Previously in 3d (Chrisman's) Bn., Va. Reserves, and Co. B, 7th Bn. Va. Reserves. In Richmond hosp. 2/5/65, then 15 days furlough. Paroled 5/30/65 at Harrisonburg, "age 18." Carriagemaker postwar in Rockingham Co. and Parkersburg, on Parkersburg city council. Wife Sarah A., m. 1873. Resid. Parkersburg 1898.

WRIGHT, JOEL S.: enl. 3/1/63 in Co. C. Farmer. Present until wded. in breast 5/6/64. In Richmond hosp. 5/9-5/23/64, transferred to Staunton, age 21. Absent wded. until AWOL on final ca. 3/30/65 roll.

WRIGHT, WILLIAM H.: enl. 2/10/63 in Co. B. Absent sick on 7-10/64 rolls. AWOL since 3/8/65 on final 3/21/65 roll. Postwar roster says age 35 on enl. d. 7/12/14 at home in Rappahannock Co. Wid. Lydia A., m. 1850.

WRIGHT, W. S.: b. 1/20/47. Only record is a Richmond hosp. register which has him in Co. C, in hosp. 2/5/65, then 15 day furlough. d. 6/30/89, bur. Prospect Hill Cem., Front Royal.

WYANT, J. R.: enl. 2/10/64 in Co. C. POW 5/31/64 at Cold Harbor. Held at Pt. Lookout, but no record of parole found. In Richmond hosp. as paroled POW 3/6-3/7/65. Absent, POW, on final ca. 3/30/65 roll. Also shown as Wint.

WYNCOOP, G. ALEX: enl. 4/22/61 in Co. K. Thirty day furlough from 2/11/62. AWOL on 6/30/62 roll. Otherwise present until shown as deserting 9/8/63 near Culpeper C.H. on 11-12/63 roll. Shown as deserted on 5/21/63 clothing roll.

WYNKOOP, GEORGE WASHINGTON: b. 6/26/35 in Loudoun Co. enl. 10/10/62 in Co. K. Sick since 12/24 on 12/61 return. Otherwise present until severely wded. 6/21/63 near Upperville, and thereafter absent wded. until shown AWOL on final 1-2/65 roll. Paroled 4/24/65 at Harpers Ferry, "age 28," signs by mark. d. 8/28/99, bur. Green Hill Cem., Berryville.

WYNKOOP, JAMES: enl. 10/10/62 in Co. K. Deserted about 11/25/62. May be identical to James M., 1/18/44-3/25/11, bur. Lakeview Cem., Hamilton. m. Virginia A. Miller 1874.

WYNKOOP, RICHARD A.: enl. 10/1/62 in Co. K. Wded. accidentally 11/29/62, and reported again for duty 2/12/63. Thereafter present until deserted 10/18/63 near Bristow Station. Shown as deserted on 5/21/63 clothing roll. May be identical to Richard, 1838-3/27/65 (this man was a single farmer when he d. of consumption).

YANCEY, ALEXANDER J.: Conscript assigned 4/25/64 to Co. C. Wded. 5/31/64. Admitted 6/9/64 to Chimborazo Hosp. No. 1, Richmond, then 60 day furlough. Shown absent, wded., on rolls until detailed in brigade commissary dept. on final ca. 3/30/65 roll.

YANCEY, CHARLES ALBERT: b. 2/19/39 in Rockingham Co. Att. U.Va. enl. 5/1/62 in Co. C. Previously Lt., Co. F, 146th Va. Mil. To Sgt. 10/1/62. Present on every roll thru final 3/30/65 roll. Lawyer in Harrisonburg postwar. m. Julia P. Morrison 1867. d. 11/14/80, bur. Woodbine Cem., Harrisonburg. Brother of Capt. Edward S.

YANCEY, EDWARD SMITH: enl. 5/28/61 in Co. C. To Capt. 7/1/61. Recommended to be dropped from rolls 2/4/63 "for prolonged absence from duty without leave." This order was revoked 5/18/63, his resignation having been accepted to take effect 9/1/62. Capt. Yancey explained in a letter of 4/19/63 that he tendered his resignation for ill health in 5/62, that he was relieved from command in June, and did not return to the regiment until 9/1/62, when he was told his resignation was accepted. d. 8/13/85, age 50, bur. Mt. Olivet Cem., McGaheysville. Brother of Charles A.

YATES, ROBERT H.: Shown as enl. 4/1/61 in Co. B, but appears only on 5-6/62 roll, where he is stated to be discharged. Discharged 6/18/62.

YATES, SAMUEL H.: enl. 4/22/61 in Co. B, age 20. Farmer. On furlough on 1-2/62 roll. Otherwise present until KIA 5/23/62 at Cedarville. Postwar roster gives middle initial as "R."

YOUNG, JOHN A.: enl. 1/15/63 in Co. I. Absent sick at hosp. since 11/20/63 on 11-12/63 roll. Otherwise always present thru final 3/20/65 roll.

YOUNG, JOHN R.: enl. 5/4/61 in Co. I, age 46. Present until shown AWOL on 5-6/62 roll, and AWOL, over 45, on 11-12/62 roll. No further record.

YOUNG, SAMUEL W.: enl. 9/12/62 in Co. A. POW 6/9/63 at Beverly Ford. Paroled 6/25/63 at Old Capitol Prison. In Charlottesville hosp. with scabies 1/29-2/4/65. Otherwise always present thru 3/27/65 final roll. Paroled 5/8/65 at Winchester, age 21, resid. Loudoun Co. Drew a pension in Pulaski Co., Ark., in 1915. d. 11/27/18, wid. Sarah Jane.

YOUNG, WILLIAM: Shown on a postwar roster of Co. I. No Confederate records.

YOUNGER, S. W.: enl. 3/10/62 in Co. G. Present until discharged 12/17/62 by substituting Henry T. Smith. Probably identical to Samuel W. Younger, a wool buyer for the QM Dept. in Richmond.

ZOMBRO, JOHN L.: enl. 10/1/62 in Co. F. Present until shown AWOL on 7-8 and 9-10/64 rolls. No further record.

ZULAVSKY, SIGISMUND: b. at Godova, Hungary. enl. 5/15/61 in Co. D. Photographer. Reputedly was earlier a Major in Austrian army. Sentenced to lose $24 on 11-12/61 roll. Otherwise present until discharged 4/25/62 for chronic bronchitis, "his general health and strength is such as to render him unable to discharge his duties as a soldier." Later a Lt. commanding a rocket battery in the Army of Tennessee. Offered on 12/27/64 to raise a company of cavalry in south Alabama. "Count F. Zoulaski" on postwar roster.

BIBLIOGRAPHY
Manuscripts
Adjutant and Inspector General's Office, C.S.A. Inspection Reports and Related Records Received by the Inspection Branch in the Confederate A & IGO Office. National Archives microfilm publication M935.
Applications for Admission, R. E. Lee Camp Soldiers Home. Virginia State Library and Archives.
Biographical File. Enoch Pratt Library, Baltimore.
Alfred Ball Carter Letters: Minor Family Papers. Virginia Historical Society.
Case Files of Investigations by Levi C. Turner and Lafayette C. Baker, 1861-66. National Archives microfilm publication M797.
Case files. Record Group 123, Records of the U.S. Court of Claims. National Archives (Suitland, Md.)
Company A, 6th Virginia Cavalry, Postwar Roll. Photocopy provided by Harold E. Howard, Lynchburg.
Company B, 6th Virginia Cavalry, List of Killed and Wounded at Cedarville or Nineveh, May 23, 1862, Ms. #20181. Virginia State Library and Archives.
Company B, 6th Virginia Cavalry, Muster Roll. In possession of the author.
Company D, 6th Virginia Cavalry, Ordnance Return and Appraisement of Horses, 1864-65, Chapter VIII, Volume 242, Record Group 109, War Department Collection of Confederate Records. National Archives.
Company D, 6th Virginia Cavalry, "Roll of the Clarke Cavalry" (postwar). Clarke County Courthouse, Berryville.
Company G, 6th Virginia Cavalry, Account Books for Clothing and Arms. 2 Vols. Collection of Lewis Leigh, Jr., Fairfax.
Compiled Service Records of the Officers and Men Belonging to the 6th Virginia Cavalry. Part of National Archives microfilm publication M324.
Compiled Service Records of Various Confederate Units. National Archives microfilm publications.
Compiled Service Records of Confederate Generals, Staff Officers, and Non-regimental Enlisted Men. National Archives microfilm publication M331.
Confederate Horse Claims, Entry 863, Record Group 92, Records of the Office of the Quartermaster General. National Archives.
Confederate Papers Relating to Citizens and Business Firms. National Archives microfilm publication M346.

Court-Martial Case Files, Selected, Record Group 153, Records of the Judge Advocate General's Office. National Archives.

George W. Davis Account Book, 1898: Tipped-in Clipping, "Roll of Company H, 6th Regiment Va. Cavalry, commanded by W. R. Welch." Virginia Historical Society.

Reverend Richard T. Davis Letters: Davis-Preston-Saunders Collection (#4951). Manuscripts Department, Alderman Library, University of Virginia.

Death Certificates. Department of Human Services, District of Columbia.

John C. Donohoe Diary, Microfilm Duplicate Copies at Virginia State Library and Archives and Virginia Room, Fairfax City Regional Library, Fairfax.

John C. Donohoe Letters. Typescripts in possession of Mrs. Mary Walton, Livingston, Alexandria.

Fairfax County Cemetery Inscriptions: Transcriptions. Virginia Room, Fairfax City Regional Library, Fairfax.

Thomas H. Foster Prison Diary. In possession of James R. Mejdrich, Wheaton, Ill.

S. Bassett French Biographical Sketches. Virginia State Library and Archives.

Funeral Expense Rolls of Confederate Pensioners, Department of Accounts, Comptroller's Office. Virginia State Library and Archives.

Georgetown University Alumni Records, Special Collections, University Archives. Georgetown University, D. C.

Daniel A. Grimsley Letters. Virginia State Library and Archives.

Joseph Jackson Halsey Commissary Receipts: Thomas Jonathan Jackson Papers. Perkins Library, Duke University.

Joseph Jackson Halsey Letters: Morton-Halsey Papers (#3995). Manuscripts Department, Alderman Library, University of Virginia.

Headstone Application Files, Record Group 92, Records of the Office of the Quartermaster General. National Archives (Suitland, Md.).

Fitzhugh Lee, Report of the Operations of His Cavalry Division, A.N.V., from May 4th, 1864, to September 19th, 1864 (December 20, 1866). Eleanor S. Brockenbrough Library, Museum of the Confederacy.

Letters Received by the Confederate Adjutant and Inspector General, 1861-65. National Archives microfilm publication M474.

Letters Received by the Confederate Secretary of War, 1861-65. National Archives microfilm publication M437.

Lists of Union Soldiers Paroled by the 6th Virginia Cavalry, 1862, Entry 107, Item #926, Record Group 249, Records of the Office of the Commissary General of Prisoners. National Archives.

Jonathan Taylor Mann Letters. Owned by William Mann, Fredericksburg.

Manuscript File, Entry 183, Record Group 109, War Department Collection of Confederate Records. National Archives.

Matriculation Books, University of Virginia. Manuscripts Department, Alderman Library, University of Virginia.

Herod T. Miley Letters: Thomas Miley Papers. Perkins Library, Duke University.

Mount Olivet Cemetery Records, Georgetown, D.C.

"Muster Rolls of Clarke County, 1861-1865" (1914). Clarke County Courthouse, Berryville.

S. D. Myers, List of Civil War Veterans Collected by, 1939. Rockingham County Courthouse, Harrisonburg.

Hugh and Washington Nelson Letters, Lewis Leigh, Jr., Collection, Book 2, #24-26. United States Army Military History Institute, Carlisle Barracks, Pa.

Silas C. K. Nicholas Prison Diary. In possession of William A. Turner, Clinton, Md.

Orders and Circulars Issued by the Army of the Potomac and the Army and Department of Northern Virginia, C.S.A., 1861-1865. National Archives microfilm publication M921.

Pardon Petitions and Related Papers Submitted in Response to President Andrew Johnson's Amnesty Proclamation of May 29, 1865 ("Amnesty Papers"). National Archives microfilm publication M1003.

Passport Applications, Record Group 59, General Records of the Department of State. National Archives.

Pension Applications under the Virginia Acts of 1888, 1900, and 1902. Virginia State Library and Archives.

Pension Files, Selected: Texas State Archives, Austin; Tennesseee State Library and Archives, Nashville; South Carolina Department of Archives and History, Columbia; Georgia State Archives, Atlanta; Kentucky Department for Libraries and Archives, Frankfort; Archives Division, Oklahoma Department of Libraries, Oklahoma City; Office of the Adjutant General, Missouri National Guard, Jefferson City.

Pension Files for Union Veterans Previously in the 6th Virginia Cavalry, Selected, Record Group 15, Records of the Veterans Administration. National Archives.

Population and Slave Schedules of the Eighth Census of the United States, 1860, Selected. National Archives.

Post Returns, Posts in Virginia: Ashland, Entry 65, Record Group 109, War Department Collection of Confederate Records. National Archives.

Rockingham County Enrolling books. Virginia Historical Society.

Roll of Honour[sic], Confederate Memorial Literary Society, Volume 136 (1913). Eleanor S. Brockenbrough Library, Museum of the Confederacy.

Roster of Ex-Confederate Soldiers and Sailors, Act of Jan. 25, 1898. Record Room, Fauquier County Courthouse, Warrenton.

George W. E. Row Letter to Nannie E. Row, January 29, 1865. Typescript in possession of Robert K. Krick, Fredericksburg.

Samuel Burks Rucker, Sr., "Recollections of My War Record During the Confederacy." Jones Memorial Library, Lynchburg.

Cordelia G. Sansone, "Muster Roll of Ex-Confederate Soldiers and Sailors of Fairfax County, Virginia, in the War in Defense of Virginia, 1861-1865." Typescript in Virginia Room, Fairfax City Regional Library, from original in Fairfax County Courthouse.

Sixth Virginia Cavalry File, Department of Military Affairs Records. Virginia State Library and Archives.

Sixth Virginia Cavalry Regimental Returns, Filed with Muster Rolls, Record Group 109, War Department Collection of Confederate Records. National Archives.

Tabular Statement of the Organization and Present Condition of the Cavalry Division, A.N.V., Commanded by Maj. Gen. J. E. B. Stuart, May 23, 1863, Entry 65, Record Group 109, War Department Collection of Confederate Records. National Archives.

Elijah Tapp Discharge Paper, 1862. In possession of Maddox G. Tapp, Front Royal.

Unfiled Slips and Papers Belonging in Confederate Compiled Service Records. National Archives microfilm publication M347.

Union Provost Marshal's File of Papers Relating to Individual Civilians. National Archives microfilm publication M345.

United Daughters of the Confederacy, Genealogical and Related Information from Descendants of Members of the 6th Virginia Cavalry. In possession of Harold E. Howard, Lynchburg.

United Daughters of the Confederacy, Black Horse Chapter, U.D.C. Remembers; A Collection of Historic Memorabilia Concerning the War Between the States Related by the Members of the Black Horse Chapter, Warrenton, Sara Criswell, historian. Photocopy of typescript in possession of Robert K. Krick, Fredericksburg.

United Daughters of the Confederacy, Rawley Martin Chapter, The Book of Remembrance. Pittsylvania County Courthouse, Chatham.

United Daughters of the Confederacy, Rawley Martin Chapter, List of Veterans attending dinner, Sept. 30, 1916; Register of attendees at yearly UDC meeting, Sept. 30, 1909-1912, Sept. 27, 1913. Pittsylvania County Courthouse, Chatham.

United Daughters of the Confederacy, Rawley Martin Chapter, Muster Roll of ... Pittsylvania County, Va., in the War in Defense of Virginia, 1861-1865. Pittsylvania County Courthouse, Chatham.

Vaughan, E. H. Letter to Robert F. Farley, July 21, 1888. In possession of Andrew A. Farley, Jr., Danville.

Virginia Military Institute alumni records.

Newspapers and Periodicals (various Issues)

Alexandria *Gazette*
Baltimore *Sun*
Berryville *Clarke Courier*
Charles Town *Spirit of Jefferson*
Confederate Veteran
Fredericksburg *Star*
Georgia Historical Quarterly
Leesburg *Loudoun Times*
Leesburg *Mirror*
Leesburg *Washingtonian*
Proceedings of the Clarke County Historical Association
Richmond *Enquirer*
Richmond *Sentinel*
Richmond *Times-Dispatch*
Southern Historical Society Papers
Virginia Magazine of History and Biography
William and Mary Quarterly
Winchester *Evening Star*

Published Primary Sources

Baird, Nancy Chappelear, ed. *Journals of Amanda Virginia Edmonds: Lass of the Mosby Confederacy, 1859-1867.* Stephens City, 1984.

Duncan, Alexander McC. *Roll of Officers and Members of the Georgia Hussars....* [Savannah, 1907].

Grimsley, Maj. Daniel A. *Battles in Culpeper County, Virginia, 1861-1865, and other articles by...* Culpeper, 1900.

Hopkins, Luther W. *From Bull Run to Appomattox: A Boy's View.* Baltimore, [1908, 1911, 1915].

Johnson, Robert Underwood, and Clarence Clough Buel, eds. *Battles and Leaders of the Civil War.* 4 volumes. New York, 1888.

McClellan, Henry B. *The Life and Campaigns of Major-General J.E.B. Stuart, Commander of the Cavalry of the Army of Northern Virginia.* Richmond, 1885.

McDonald, Archie P., ed., *Make Me a Map of the Valley: The Civil War Journal of Stonewall Jackson's Topographer Jedediah Hotchkiss.* Dallas, 1973.

McDonald, Capt. William N. *A History of the Laurel Brigade, Originally the Ashby Cavalry of the Army of Northern Virginia and Chew's Battery.* Bushrod C. Washington, ed. Baltimore, 1907.

Marshall, Fielding Lewis. *Recollections and Reflections of Fielding Lewis Marshall, A Virginian of the Old School.* Maria Newton Marshall, comp. Orange, 1911.

Moore, Ammishadai, Jr. "The Clarke Cavalry," in Thomas D. Gold, *History of Clarke County, Virginia, and its connection with the War Between the States.* Berryville, 1914.

Moore, Frank. *The Rebellion Record: A Diary of American Events* . . . . 11 volumes. New York, 1864-1869.

"Muster Roll of Captain Edward B. Powell Company, 2 Regiment, 6th Brigade, 2 Division, Virginia Militia to August 31st, 1861." *The Historical Society of Fairfax County.* Volume 13, 1973-1975.

Myers, Frank M. *The Comanches: A History of White's Battalion, Virginia Cavalry.* Baltimore, 1871.

Neese, George M. *Three Years in the Confederate Horse Artillery.* Lee A. Wallace, Jr., ed. Dayton, 1983.

Opie, John N. *A Rebel Cavalryman With Lee Stuart and Jackson.* Chicago, 1899.

Ramey, Emily G., and John K. Gott, eds. *The Years of Anguish: Fauquier County, Virginia, 1861-1865.* Warrenton, 1965.

Richardson, James D., ed. *A Compilation of the Messages and Papers of the Confederacy, Including the Diplomatic Correspondence, 1861-1865.* 2 volumes. Nashville, 1906.

Summers, Festus P., ed. *A Borderland Confederate: The Civil War Letters and Diaries of William L. Wilson.* Pittsburgh, 1962.

Swank, Col. Walbrook D., ed., *Confederate Letters and Diaries,* 1861-1865 (Chapter II, Part A: "Letters and Diary of a Confederate Prisoner of War, William W. Downer, Private, Company I, 6th Virginia Cavalry"). Charlottesville, 1988.

United States War Department. *War of the Rebellion: A Compilation of the Official Records of the Union and Confederate Armies.* 128 volumes. Washington, 1880-1901.

Other Sources

Baird, Nancy Chappelear. *Fauquier County, Virginia, Tombstone Inscriptions.* n.p., 1970.

Bee Line Chapter, National Society Daughters of the American Revolution. *Tombstone Inscriptions, Jefferson County, West Virginia.* Marceline, Mo., 1981.

Benedict, G. G. *Vermont in the Civil War: A History of the Part Taken by the Vermont Soldiers and Sailors in the War for the Union, 1861-5.* 2 volumes. Burlington, 1888.

Biographical Directory of the American Congress, 1774-1971 . . . . Washington, 1971.

Boatner, Mark Mayo, III. *The Civil War Dictionary.* New York, 1959.

Brock, R. A. *Virginia and Virginians.* Richmond, 1888.

Brown, Alexander. *The Cabells and their kin.* . . . Richmond, 1939.

Brown, Stuart E. *Annals of Clarke County, Virginia.* Berryville, 1983.

Bruce, Philip A. *History of Virginia.* 6 volumes. Chicago, 1924.

Calfee, Berkeley Gilkeson. *Confederate History of Culpeper County.* Culpeper, 1948.

Calkins, Christopher M. *Thirty-six Hours Before Appomattox: April 6 and 7, 1865.* n.p., 1980.

Coddington, Edwin B. *The Gettysburg Campaign: A Study in Command.* New York, 1968.

Consolidated Index of Claims Reported by the Commissioners of Claims to the House of Representatives from 1871-1880. Washington, 1892.

Cullum, George W. *Biographical Register of the Officers and Graduates of the U.S. Military Academy at West Point, N.Y.* . . . . 3 volumes. Boston, 1891.

Divine, John E. *8th Virginia Infantry.* Lynchburg, 1983.

⸺. *35th Virginia Cavalry Battalion.* Lynchburg, 1985.

Duvall, Porter, ed. *Men, Places, & Things.* Danville, 1891.

Evans, Clement A., ed. *Confederate Military History.* 12 volumes (expanded editions). Atlanta, 1899.

Fleming, James Anderson, and Nancy Chappelear Baird. *Fauquier County, Virginia, Tombstone Inscriptions, Supplement.* Stephens City, 1984.

Franklin County Historical Society, comp. *Cemetery Records of Franklin County, Virginia.* Baltimore, 1986.

Freedom Hill Chapter, National Society Daughters of the American Revolution. *Orange County, Virginia, Cemeteries.* McLean, 1979.

Freeman, Douglas Southall. *Lee's Lieutenants: A Study in Command.* 3 volumes. New York, 1942-1944.

Frye, Dennis E. *2nd Virginia Infantry.* Lynchburg, 1984.

⸺. *12th Virginia Cavalry.* Lynchburg, 1988.

Garber, Virginia Armistead. *The Armistead Family, 1635-1910.* Richmond, 1910.

General Register of the Members of the Phi Kappa Sigma Fraternity, 1850-1930. Philadelphia, 1930.

Gold, Thomas D. *History of Clarke County, Virginia.* . . . Berryville, 1914.

Gordon, Armistead C. *The Gordons in Virginia, with Notes on Gordons of Scotland and Ireland.* Hackensack, 1918.

Gott, John K. *A History of Marshall (formerly Salem), Fauquier County. Va.* [Middletown, 1959].

Green, Raleigh Travers, comp. *Genealogical and Historical Notes on Culpeper County, Virginia.* . . . Culpeper, 1900.

Hale, Laura Virginia. *Four Valiant Years in the Lower Shenandoah Valley, 1861-1865.* Strasburg, 1968.

Hardesty's Historical and Geographical Encyclopedia. New York, Richmond (etc.), 1883-1885.

Hardy, Stella P. *Colonial Families of the Southern States.* New York, 1911.

Hartzler, Daniel D. *Marylanders in the Confederacy.* Silver Spring, 1986.
Hayden, Horace E. *Virginia Genealogies.* Baltimore, 1959.
Heitman, Francis B. *Historical Register and Dictionary of the United States Army.* . . . 2 volumes. Washington, 1903.
Hinkins, Virginia. *Stonewall's Courier: The Story of Charles Randolph and General Jackson.* New York, 1959.
Hoar, Jay S. *The South's Last Boys in Gray: An Epic Prose Elegy.* Bowling Green, Ohio, 1986.
Ingmire, Frances T. *Arkansas Confederate Veterans and Widows Pension Applications.* St. Louis, 1985.
Irvine, Dallas. et al. *Military Operations of the Civil War: A Guide-Index to the Official Records of the Union and Confederate Armies, 1861-1865.* Washington, 1968-1972.
Jewell, A. M. "Death Records of Loudoun County." 1853-1866 [unpublished].
_____. "Tombstone Inscriptions, Loudoun County Cemeteries." [Unpublished].
Johnson, Allen, and Dumas Malone, eds. *Dictionary of American Biography.* 11 volumes. New York, 1936.
Johnson, Elisabith B., and C. E. Johnson, Jr. *Rappahannock County, Virginia: A History.* Orange, 1981.
Johnson, John Lipscomb. *The University Memorial.* Baltimore, 1871.
Kinney, John M., comp., revised by Peggy Oakley. *Index to Applications for Texas Confederate Pensions.* Austin, 1977.
Klein, Margaret C. *Tombstone Inscriptions of Orange County, Virginia.* Baltimore, 1979.
Krick, Robert K. *Lee's Colonels: A Biographical Register of the Field Officers of the Army of Northern Virginia.* Dayton, 1984.
_____. " '. . . The Cause of All My Disasters': Jubal A. Early and the Undisciplined Valley Cavalry" [unpublished typescript, *ca. 1989].*
Lang, Wendall. "Time-Lapse." *Civil War Times Illustrated,* October 1985.
Lee, Howard B. *The Burning Springs and Other Tales of the Little Kanawha.* Morgantown, 1968.
Mann, Flora P. *History of Telfair County.* Macon, Ga., 1949.
Massanutton Chapter, National Society Daughters of the American Revolution. "Cemeteries East of U.S. Highway #11, Rockingham Co., Va., Church and Family Cemeteries." 1965-1971.
Mather, Otis M. *Six Generations of LaRues and Allied Families.* . . . Hodgenville, Ky., 1921.
Matter, William D. *If It Takes All Summer: The Battle of Spotsylvania.* Chapel Hill, 1988.
Mickle, William E. *Well Known Confederate Veterans.* New Orleans, 1907.
Nuckolls, Bertha. Sally Stetson Tongren, ed. *The First Virginia Nuckolls and Kindred.* Boston, n.d.

Orange County Civil War Centennial Committee. *Civil War Centennial, Orange Court House, 1861-1865.* Orange, 1965.

Pecquet du Bellet, Louise. *Some Prominent Virginia Families.* 4 volumes. Lynchburg, 1907.

Powell, William H. *Powell's Records of Living Officers of the United States Army.* Philadelphia, 1890.

Rawley Martin Chapter, Virginia Division, United Daughters of the Confederacy. *War Recollections of the Confederate Veterans of Pittsylvania County, Virginia, 1861-1865.* [n.p., ca. 1961].

Read, Alice. *The Reads and their Relatives.* Cincinnati, 1930.

Richey, Homer. *Memorial History of the John Bowie Strange Camp, United Confederate Veterans. . . .* Charlottesville, 1920.

Ruby, James S., ed. *Blue and Gray: Georgetown University and the Civil War.* Washington, 1961.

Schele de Vere, Maximilian. *Students of the University of Virginia.* Baltimore, 1878.

Scott, W. W. *A History of Orange County, Virginia. . . .* Richmond, 1907.

Schevchuk, Paul M. " 'Cut to Pieces': The Cavalry Fight at Fairfield, Pennsylvania, July 3d, 1863." [unpublished typescript, February 1985].

Simpson, Craig M. *A Good Southerner: The Life of Henry A. Wise of Virginia.* Chapel Hill, 1985.

Tyler, Lyon G. *Encyclopedia of Virginia Biography.* 5 volumes. New York, 1915.

Waldrep, George Calvin, III. *Halifax County Cemeteries.* Greenville, S.C., 1985.

Walker, Charles D. *Memorial, Virginia Military Institute.* Philadelphia, 1875.

Wallace, Lee A., Jr. *A Guide to Virginia Military Organizations, 1861-1865.* Lynchburg, 1986.

Warner, Ezra J. *Generals in Blue: Lives of the Union Commanders.* Baton Rouge, 1964.

_____. *Generals in Gray: Lives of the Confederate Commanders.* Baton Rouge, 1959.

Wayland, John W. *A History of Rockingham County, Virginia.* Dayton, 1912.

_____. *Men of Mark. . . of Harrisonburg and Rockingham County, Virginia.* Staunton, 1943.

Wert, Jeffry D. *From Winchester to Cedar Creek: The Shenandoah Campaign of 1864.* Carlisle, 1987.

Whitehorne, Joseph W. *A Self-Guided Tour: The Battle of Cedar Creek.* Strasburg, 1987.

Williamson, James J. *Mosby's Rangers.* New York, 1896.

Wise, Barton H. *The Life of Henry A. Wise, 1806-1876.* New York, 1899.